Preface

I wrote the first edition of this book some four years ago on the back of ten years of experience in discrimination law. The first seven of those were with the Commission for Racial Equality and thereafter with a City law firm.

Since writing the first edition I have joined Dibb Lupton Broomhead to head up employment law and this second edition would not have been possible without the input and effort of Paul Ball, a member of our employment law team at Dibb Lupton Broomhead, now the largest such team in the United Kingdom.

Since the first edition was published there have been a startling number of significant developments in the field. The most important of these has to be the removal of the limit of the damages that can be awarded in a discrimination case. In the case of *Ministry of Defence v Cannock [1994] IRLR 509* Mrs Cannock received a record £200,000 (ironically, although the decision by the Employment Appeal Tribunal in her case led to a general reduction in the level of awards in the cases taken by servicewomen forced to leave the armed forces on grounds of pregnancy, Mrs Cannock actually had her award increased by the EAT). Other significant developments have been the power of tribunals to withhold the name of parties in sexual misconduct cases and, of course, the passing through Parliament of the *Disability Discrimination Act*. During this time there has also been a steady increase in the level of utilisation of the various discrimination law statutes.

In writing a book such as this there is an inevitable debt to that which has gone before, such as David Pannick's *Sex Discrimination Law*, LAG's *Sex and Race Discrimination in Employment, Sex Discrimination and Equal Pay* by John Whitmore and Colin Bournes, and also the Equal Opportunities Review, which always provides swift and authoritative comment on developments in this area of the law. This book is aimed to be a companion to *Tolley's Employment Handbook*.

Paul Ball and I would both like to record our appreciation to Alan Radford for his patient and painstaking editing and also to Kamaljit Pawar for his assistance with background research, particularly in relation to the Education chapter.

Paul Ball has asked me to express his appreciation to everyone who put up with him whilst he was working on the book, particularly Felicity.

I would like to dedicate this second edition to my children, Ryan and Ella. Will legislation still need to be as it is now when they start their employment careers?

Paul Nicholls

Regional Managing Partner,
Dibb Lupton Broomhead,
Carlton House,
18 Albert Square,
Manchester M2 5PE

Contents

Contents

Table of Statutes

Table of Statutes

Table of Statutes

x

Table of EC Legislative Material

Table of Statutory Instruments

Table of Cases

Table of Cases

Table of Cases

Table of Cases

Abbreviations and References

General

ACAS	=	Advisory, Conciliation and Arbitration Service
CBI	=	Confederation of British Industry
CRE	=	Commission for Racial Equality
DoE	=	Department of Employment
DSS	=	Department of Social Security
EAT	=	Employment Appeal Tribunal
ECJ	=	European Court of Justice
EEC	=	European Economic Community
EOC	=	Equal Opportunities Commission
GOQ	=	genuine occupational qualification
LIFO	=	'last in, first out'
NDN	=	non-discrimination notice
Sch	=	Schedule
SI	=	statutory instrument
SMP	=	statutory maternity pay
SR & O	=	Statutory Rules and Orders (superseded by statutory instruments)

Statutes

DDA	=	Disability Discrimination Act 1995
DPA	=	Disabled Persons (Employment) Act 1944
EPCA	=	Employment Protection (Consolidation) Act 1978
EqPA	=	Equal Pay Act 1970
LGA	=	Local Government Act 1988
RRA	=	Race Relations Act 1976
SDA	=	Sex Discrimination Act 1975
SDA 1986	=	Sex Discrimination Act 1986
TURERA	=	Trade Union Reform and Employment Rights Act 1993

Law Reports and other references

All ER	=	All England Law Reports
EOR	=	Equal Opportunities Review
ICR	=	Industrial Cases Reports
IRLR	=	Industrial Relations Law Reports
IRLB	=	Industrial Relations Law Bulletin
WLR	=	Weekly Law Reports

1   Introduction

1.1   The aim of this book is to provide the personnel manager, employment law practitioner, welfare adviser, trade unionist and individual with a ready guide to enable them to obtain swift answers to the practical day-to-day problems in the employment field that arise out of the application of the *Sex Discrimination Act 1975*, the *Race Relations Act 1976*, the *Disability Discrimination Act 1995* and related legislation. For this reason the book has been arranged around general topic heads and it is hoped that this will facilitate its use. There is a brief introductory overview to set the chapters in context.

1.2   **PREVENTING DISCRIMINATION IN EMPLOYMENT**

Nowadays the corporate ethos of every company or corporation of any standing is not to discriminate, but it remains a fact that there are, and always will be, individuals who hold prejudicial attitudes towards ethnic minorities and/or women. In these circumstances there always will be discrimination. This can be made much less likely if the company has a well thought out and well implemented equal opportunity policy. If discrimination is a disciplinary matter and can lead to dismissal, the prejudiced employee is going to be much less likely to exercise those prejudices in the course of his employment. Equal opportunities are simply about good employment practice and will have beneficial side effects generally in the managerial process and in providing management information.

1.3   **THE DISABILITY DISCRIMINATION ACT 1995**

The *Disability Discrimination Act 1995* is now on the statute book but does not come into full force until January 1997. In the meantime the provisions of the *Disabled Persons (Employment) Act 1944* are applicable. Regulations relating to the new Act, and a Code of Practice, are to be published early in 1996. The *Disability Discrimination Act 1995* is potentially the most significant item of employment legislation for 30 years. Employers would be well advised to prepare for its advent now, not just in respect of employment practices, but also services to customers.

1.4   **DISCRIMINATION CASES**

The cost of bringing or defending a claim is often disproportionate to the damages or compensation that can be awarded. Because costs are not normally awarded against the losing party in the industrial tribunal, it is frequently unrealistic for an individual to pursue a claim without the assistance of one of the statutory bodies or his or her trade union. Discrimination cases tend to last a lot longer than ordinary claims in the industrial tribunal, are emotionally charged, and the nature of the cross-examination of witnesses is more akin to that of a criminal court than in the industrial tribunal or in civil cases generally. Judgments in race and sex discrimination claims are frequently peppered with the word 'guilty' which is, of course, appropriate to the criminal jurisdiction and not to civil matters.

Anyone who has been involved in a discrimination claim either as the applicant or indeed as the individual accused, or a member of management of the company accused, will know that such proceedings are highly stressful to all concerned, and take up an enormous amount of managerial and administrative time.

The burden of proof in a complaint of racial discrimination is always on the applicant. However, an applicant may be assisted in circumstances where it is proper for an industrial tribunal to draw the inference that the discrimination alleged has in fact taken place. Statistics show that only about 20% of such claims are likely to succeed if they get as far as being heard by the industrial tribunal (although success rates for applicants are rising slowly). Most claims do not get that far and are settled one way or another, or withdrawn, beforehand. Since the first edition of this book was published, the limits on damages for discrimination claims have been removed. Challenging a 'glass ceiling' is suddenly economically worth considering for the individual involved. When damages were limited at £11,000, it was rarely worth pursuing the claim.

It still takes a considerable amount of courage and persistence to take a claim to the industrial tribunal and studies done by the Equal Opportunities Commission indicate that individuals are rarely satisfied with the process of the law. There are occasions in every area of the law where an individual will 'try it on' but in the author's experience that is rare in the field of discrimination. A more frequent occurrence is that individuals perceive that they have been discriminated against on grounds of race or sex in circumstances where the discrimination has, in fact, been motivated by other reasons. Either these reasons have not been disclosed to the individual at the appropriate time, or else he or she has been given spurious reasons for the decision made which ultimately increase that person's suspicion and certainty that discrimination has, in fact, been on grounds of race or sex.

1.5 DISCRIMINATION LEGISLATION

Position at common law

Discrimination legislation is a contemporary phenomenon. Prior to the Second World War, with few exceptions, discrimination of any kind was lawful and the nearest the law came to any kind of protective legislation related to limitations on the employment of women and children arising out of early Victorian excesses. That is not to say that there were not problems, and the earliest discrimination case was one brought at common law by a black cricketer (*Constantine v Imperial London Hotels Limited [1944] 2 All ER 171*).

Mr Constantine (later Sir Learie Constantine) was a famous cricketer who was refused accommodation by an hotel, contrary to its common law duty. The refusal was racially motivated. Mr Constantine was described by the judge as 'a man of high character and attainment, a British subject from the West Indies, and, although he was a man of colour, no ground existed on which the defendants were entitled to refuse to receive and lodge him'. He was awarded nominal damages of five guineas. The judgment (and tone of the passage quoted above) must have been as offensive as the refusal itself. It took time but the legislation has come a long way since then.

1.6 Disabled Persons (Employment) Act 1944

The first real anti-discrimination legislation related to the disabled. In 1944, a *Disabled Persons (Employment) Act* was passed which required all employers to have in their employment a quota of disabled people. The impetus for this legislation arose from concern at the large number of wounded ex-servicemen in the labour market and the need to require employers to employ them notwithstanding any disabilities they may have suffered as a result of their war injuries. This Act remains in force until January 1997 when it will be superseded by the controversial *Disability Discrimination Act 1995*. This latter Act is broadly modelled on the *RRA* and *SDA*, with clear influences from the *Disabilities Act* of the USA. It is likely to have dramatic impact. Government planning is reported to revolve around estimates of 3,000 claims annually lasting an average of five days each!

1.7   **Race Relations Acts 1965 and 1968**

The first *Race Relations Act* was introduced in 1965. In the late 1950s, the government of the day had actively encouraged New Commonwealth citizens to emigrate to the United Kingdom in order to deal with the chronic shortage of unskilled and semi-skilled labour. Without such an influx into the labour market, the National Health Service and transport systems of the country would probably have completely broken down from manpower shortages. However, problems arose almost immediately and the New Commonwealth citizens were met with overt discrimination of every kind and in every facet of their lives. The *1965 Act* dealt only with discrimination in public places and was a very limited piece of legislation. In 1968 a further Act was introduced which covered employment and housing and widened the general scope of legislation considerably from the *1965 Act*. It did not provide any direct access for individuals to the courts to complain about discrimination but created the Race Relations Board to whom complaints about discrimination could be made and whose investigation officers would consider such complaints. If agreement could not be reached, the Board could take enforcement proceedings.

1.8   **Existing domestic legislation**

It was only in 1970 that any protection was accorded to women with the *Equal Pay Act* of that year. Prior to this there was no prohibition on discrimination against women and separate remuneration tables for men and women were commonplace, negotiated, of course, by the male dominated trade union movement. The *Equal Pay Act* had a five-year introduction period to coincide with the introduction of the *Sex Discrimination Act 1975 (SDA)*. The following year, in 1976, a further *Race Relations Act (RRA)* was introduced. Despite the fact that the *RRA* occupied many hours of parliamentary time, its wording is in all material factors identical to that of the *SDA* (and was intended to be so).

The *Disability Discrimination Act 1995* is a significant development in discrimination legislation. For the first time, discrimination against a person on grounds of their disability is unlawful. The practical impact of this Act cannot yet be assessed, as many of its provisions will come into effect through Regulations in the near future.

1.9   **Influence of the EEC**

Both the *SDA* and the *RRA* owed a great deal to the influence of the USA and of European law, particularly the effect of the direct application of *Article 119* of the Treaty of Rome (equal treatment) and the various Directives emanating from Europe. The European influence really relates only to the *SDA* although it was administratively and legislatively convenient to ensure that in the United

Kingdom, the two Acts were fundamentally the same. The EEC Treaty provides no specific protection in respect of race except insofar as it prohibits any discrimination within EEC countries against other EEC nationals. There is not the same history of protection against race discrimination in the greater part of Europe as there is in the United Kingdom. On the whole, the protection against discrimination on grounds of race in Europe is inadequate and compares unfavourably with the United Kingdom.

In regard to equal treatment of women, the United Kingdom, broadly speaking, trails the rest of the EEC and, as a result of this, the European influence continues to bear heavily on the law in this area, both in the development of case law and in requiring further amendments to the *SDA* (most notably the *SDA 1986*). Every aspect of the employment relationship has been affected, often at great potential cost to employers and benefit to employees, and most recently in respect of the equalisation of retirement ages and pension provision.

1.10   THE CURRENT POSITION

There is no limit on the amount of compensation that tribunals can award in sex and race discrimination cases (and also in disability discrimination cases). A tribunal award may also include an element for 'injury to feelings' but this generally ranges only from between £500 to £5,000.

Nonetheless, there is a general consensus within the country that discrimination on grounds of race, sex or disability is odious and unacceptable. Industrial tribunal cases involving either sex discrimination or race discrimination tend to attract a considerable amount of publicity. Local newspapers always cover such stories in some detail and even relatively modest claims against large corporations still attract national publicity. Claims of both race and sex discrimination against the police have held the news headlines, particularly when a race relations claim by an Asian policeman was upheld. Claims of sexual harassment also give rise to considerable tabloid interest of a less than attractive kind. Certain tabloid journalists relish the prospect of the salacious details of the particular harassment involved. Tribunals now have the power to make restricted reporting orders, which can protect the identity of the individuals involved. However, the details of such cases can still be published.

The *RRA*, the *SDA* and the *Disability Discrimination Act 1995* provide for the industrial tribunal to hear discrimination claims arising out of the employment relationship. All other claims are heard by designated county courts. Although the legislation provides protection against race and sex discrimination in housing, education and the provision of every kind of service, it is in the employment field that the legislation is most utilised. Currently, claims to the industrial tribunal are running at between 1,300–2,000 claims each year for both race and sex discrimination and the statistics of the Commission for Racial Equality and the Equal Opportunities Commission, who have the power to assist such claims, indicate that many more people take preliminary steps towards making a claim in the industrial tribunal without a claim actually being made.

1.11   ABOUT THIS BOOK

The book is arranged in sections under convenient headings, although to avoid repetition it is not practicable to arrange the book as a complete dictionary and so a comprehensive index is provided. A limited knowledge of the framework of the institutions is assumed within each section, but such knowledge can be acquired by cross-referencing within the book, as well as by reading the legislative overview provided later in this chapter.

The *Race Relations Act 1976* and the *Sex Discrimination Act 1975* are dealt with in the book as being identical and without, except where it is expressly appropriate, distinguishing between the two pieces of legislation. Whilst the underlying motivation for discrimination against women and against ethnic minorities may, or may not, be very different, the legislative framework is virtually identical. Disability and other forms of discrimination are also dealt with in this book. It may well be that in the not too distant future there will be one body of law and one Commission to look after it in respect of all types of discrimination, be it age, disability, race or sex, as is the case in Canada. In many ways this would seem much the most sensible way of dealing with this area of the law.

The book contains guidance and (at the end of Chapter 53) a checklist for anyone involved in taking a case to an industrial tribunal, and another checklist for anyone involved in defending a case in a tribunal. There is also a checklist to help employers to deal with the new maternity provisions (at the end of Chapter 44). Outline guidance in relation to the formulation of an equal opportunity policy is also provided. In the discrimination field, prevention is much better than cure and a sensible and well thought out equal opportunity policy, which is properly implemented, will ensure that a company is far less likely to be faced with a claim and, should it be faced with one, much better equipped to deal with it and to avoid unfair liability for unauthorised discriminatory acts by individual employees.

The law as stated in this book is up to date to 30 September 1995. No developments since that date have been included. In particular, Regulations and the Code of Practice relating to the *Disability Discrimination Act 1995* have yet to be published. It is an area of the law where consensus has proved difficult and a degree of tension still exists between the approach of the European Court of Justice and that of the domestic courts in England and Wales, as well as between the approach of the Employment Appeal Tribunal and that of the Court of Appeal. In these circumstances, there can be sudden radical changes as to the application of the law and anyone using this book would be well advised to examine the most recent editions of the Equal Opportunities Review which monitors such developments with great precision.

The cases that have been cited are, almost without exception, from the Employment Appeal Tribunal and above. Industrial tribunal decisions can be cited to other tribunals but are not in any way binding upon them. Tribunal decisions are frequently useful in illustrating a point. I have largely avoided using them in this fashion to avoid confusion and to avoid creating the impression that a particular matter is settled law when it has not been subjected to the scrutiny of an appellate jurisdiction.

1.12   LEGISLATIVE OVERVIEW

This handbook deals basically with five statutes:

—   *Sex Discrimination Act 1975* (as amended by the *SDA 1986*);

—   *Race Relations Act 1976*;

—   *Equal Pay Act 1970*;

—   *Employment Protection (Consolidation) Act 1978* (as amended);

—   *Disability Discrimination Act 1995*.

The *Disability Discrimination Act* is different from the *Race Relations Act* and the *Sex Discrimination Act* and is dealt with discretely and separately in DISABILITY (18).

The *Employment Protection (Consolidation) Act 1978 (EPCA)* (which is dealt with in outline in Chapter 26) was introduced to provide individuals with protection from dismissal from their jobs without reasonable cause and, together with related employment protection legislation, to provide such protection against victimisation for trade union activities, the right to maternity leave, the right to an employment contract and other such matters. In some cases (such as maternity leave) the legislation is directly within the scope of this handbook but by and large the *Employment Protection (Consolidation) Act* overlaps with the *Race Relations Act* and the *Sex Discrimination Act* and individuals will frequently have a choice of forum in which to bring their claim.

A dismissal motivated by reasons of race or sex will inevitably be unfair and contrary to the *Employment Protection (Consolidation) Act 1978, s 54*, subject to the individual qualifying for protection by that Act. All individuals are entitled to a written contract of employment within two months of commencing employment (unless they are working for one month or less) with a company. After two years' continuous employment, they are entitled not to be dismissed unfairly, i.e. without good reason and without proper procedures having been followed. If they have been unfairly dismissed, they may take a claim to the industrial tribunal, which may recommend that they be given their jobs back (although the employer can decline to accept this recommendation) or they can be compensated up to a certain statutory maximum. This is dealt with in detail in DISMISSAL (21).

There is no express protection from discrimination on grounds of sexual orientation but the *Employment Protection (Consolidation) Act* provisions relating to unfair dismissal do provide a little protection to individuals who are homosexuals. This is dealt with in SEXUAL ORIENTATION (51).

As has already been mentioned, the *Race Relations Act* and the *Sex Discrimination Act* are almost the same in respect of all material provisions. There are three forms of discrimination that are made unlawful by the two Acts. These are dealt with in separate chapters but in outline they are as follows.

(1)   *Direct discrimination* (see DIRECT DISCRIMINATION (17))

Direct discrimination consists of treating somebody on the grounds of race or sex less favourably than one would otherwise.

(2)   *Indirect discrimination* (see INDIRECT DISCRIMINATION (36))

Indirect discrimination occurs where one applies a consistent criterion to everybody but it has an adverse impact on a particular group of individuals because of their ethnic origin or sex. An obvious example is a minimum height requirement which might statistically have an adverse impact on certain racial groups and, of course, would also have an impact on women. Indirect discrimination is permissible if it can be justified on objective grounds for reasons other than race or sex.

(3)   *Victimisation* (see VICTIMISATION (54))

In common parlance, victimisation includes discrimination generally, but as far as the legislation is concerned, it has a specialised meaning. It relates to circumstances where an individual is treated less favourably than somebody else would be because he has made a complaint of discrimination that would come within the Act, should there be evidence which proves discrimination.

The *Sex Discrimination Act* prohibits discrimination against men and women except in limited special circumstances (see GENUINE OCCUPATIONAL QUALIFICATION (33)) and also prohibits discrimination against people on the grounds that they are married (but not that they are single, although in certain circumstances such a criterion might be indirectly discriminatory). (See MARITAL STATUS (38).)

The *Race Relations Act* prohibits discrimination on 'racial grounds'. This term includes ethnic or national origins, citizenship, place of birth and also acquired ethnicity (see RACIAL GROUP, RACIAL GROUNDS, NATIONAL AND ETHNIC ORIGIN (48)).

The *Disability Discrimination Act 1995* prohibits discrimination against disabled persons on the grounds of their disability. It is expressed in different terms from the *RRA* or *SDA*, and is dealt with separately in this book. Until January 1997 the *Disabled Persons (Employment) Act 1944* remains in force – it is dealt with in the second part of DISABILITY (18).

Almost every element of the employment contract is covered by the *RRA* and *SDA*, including recruitment, terms and conditions, and dismissal (see EMPLOYMENT (24) and DISMISSAL (21)). There is no minimum period of employment before an applicant can make a complaint of racial or sexual discrimination, unlike the two-year qualifying period for an unfair dismissal claim (although this qualifying period has itself been held to be indirectly discriminatory in *R v Secretary of State for Employment, Ex parte Seymour-Smith and Perez [1995] IRLR 464*). He or she can make a complaint in the industrial tribunal but this must be made within three months of the alleged discrimination taking place (see TRIBUNALS (53)).

The burden of proof in a discrimination claim is always on the individual to show that he or she has suffered discrimination (see BURDEN OF PROOF (6)). In making a claim the complainant is able to take advantage of the provision of the discovery of documents as well as the fact that tribunals can now order answers to interrogatories (see DISCOVERY, INTERROGATORIES AND FURTHER PARTICULARS (19)) and also to issue a questionnaire prior to taking action, to try to identify the material facts (see QUESTIONNAIRE PROCEDURE (47)).

Whilst individuals have the right to make complaints to the industrial tribunal about particular acts of discrimination, the legislation has also created three enforcement bodies, the Equal Opportunities Commission (EOC), the Commission for Racial Equality (CRE) and the National Disability Council (NDC). The EOC and CRE, as well as being able to assist those individuals with their complaints in the industrial tribunal, also have wider investigative powers (see INVESTIGATIONS (37)).

It is not just employers who are covered by legislation but also trade unions (see TRADE UNIONS AND EMPLOYERS' ORGANISATIONS (52)). Any type of employer is within the scope of the Act including voluntary bodies, partnerships and single individuals. Contract workers are also covered by the legislation (see CONTRACT WORKERS (14)).

There are some special circumstances in which it is lawful to discriminate but these are very limited (see POSITIVE DISCRIMINATION (43) and GENUINE OCCUPATIONAL QUALIFICATION (33)).

2   Advertising

2.1   ADVERTISEMENTS

Prior to the introduction of the *RRA* and the *SDA* it was not unusual to see discriminatory signs outside factories saying such things as 'no blacks' or 'no Irish'. It was similarly lawful to place such advertisements in newspapers for positions, although this was less frequent. As a matter of course, however, jobs used to specify 'bar*man*' or 'sales*man*' or '*man* required' and the jobs being offered were intended to be limited to men only. The *RRA* and *SDA* outlawed both the underlying practice of discriminating on grounds of race or sex and also the advertising of such a practice or the advertising of positions on such a restrictive basis.

2.2   THE FUNDAMENTAL RULE

The basic rule is that it is unlawful to advertise a position in a manner which restricts those who could apply or who can be appointed by virtue of race or by sex. [*RRA s 29; SDA s 38*]. If such an advertisement is published then both the advertiser and the publisher are liable (see 2.15 below). Only the Commission for Racial Equality or the Equal Opportunities Commission, as appropriate, may prosecute and the penalties are weak (see 2.14 below) but an individual who would otherwise apply for a position but for a discriminatory advertisement will be able to make a claim in the industrial tribunal in respect of discriminatory arrangements for the position [*RRA s 4(1)(a); SDA s 6(1)(a)*] (see 2.18 below).

2.3   DISCRIMINATORY ADVERTISEMENTS

The *RRA* and the *SDA* have different provisions about advertising. In both cases it is unlawful to publish any advertisement that suggests an intention to discriminate (on grounds of race or sex respectively). [*RRA s 29; SDA s 38*]. In the *RRA*, such advertisements are always unlawful except in the case of a limited number of designated exceptions, whereas under the *SDA* it is enough to show that the discriminatory 'act' advertised is not, in fact, technically unlawful. [*Sec 38(2)*]. The exceptions fall broadly within three categories:

(*a*)   where race or sex is a GENUINE OCCUPATIONAL QUALIFICATION (33);

(*b*)   where there is under-representation of ethnic minorities or women in a particular grade, or type of job, an advertisement may be designed specifically to attract applications from the 'class' under-represented;

(*c*)   advertising certain limited training opportunities.

2.4   EXCEPTIONS

The circumstances in which it is permissible to advertise a post in a discriminatory manner are slightly different where the sex of the individual is involved from those where the race of the individual is involved. It is therefore helpful to divide the exceptions into the following categories for the purpose of analysis:

(*a*)   where the exception applies on grounds of either race or sex;

(*b*)   where the exception applies only to circumstances in which racial origins are concerned; and (*c*)   where the exception applies only to circumstances in which the sex of the individual is pertinent.

2.5   Exceptions common to race and sex

It is permissible to advertise a post in a discriminatory manner in the following circumstances.

(*a*)   For jobs where race or sex is a 'genuine occupational qualification' (GOQ). The criteria are dealt with in GENUINE OCCUPATIONAL QUALIFICATION (33). [*RRA ss 5, 10, 29(2)(a); SDA ss 7, 38(2)*].

(*b*)   Under statutory authority (i.e. defence contract work where UK citizenship is required). [*RRA ss 29(2)(a), 41; SDA ss 38(2), 51*].

(*c*)   For advertising positions or training *within the company*. The employer must have identified that, within the past twelve months, there were no individuals of a particular racial group, or sex, doing a particular job or type of job at the workplace, or the proportion of that racial group, or sex, doing that job or type of job was small in comparison to members of that racial group, or sex, at the workplace or within the local recruitment area. [*RRA s 38; SDA s 48*]. This provision justifies discriminatory advertising for a post but it does not permit an employer to discriminate in respect of the actual appointment itself. For example, if a white employee applied for a post that the management had decided to encourage a black employee to fill (there being no, or very few, black persons in that type of post relative to the workforce as a whole or to the make-up of the local community), and the white employee was actually the best qualified for the post, that person must be appointed. The availability of the training can be limited to a particular racial group.

(*d*)   For advertising job or training opportunities *outside the workplace* to groups defined by race or sex. The employer must have identified that, within the past twelve months, there were no individuals, or proportionately few, of a particular racial group, or sex, doing a job or type of job in Great Britain as a whole, or that area of the country. Again, this provision justifies discriminatory advertising for a post, but it does not permit an employer to discriminate in respect of the actual appointment itself. For example, if a man applied for a post that the management had decided to encourage a woman to fill (there being no, or very few, women in that type of post relative to the workforce in Great Britain or in that particular area within Great Britain), and the man was actually the best qualified for the post, he must be appointed. The training must be expressly to qualify individuals for work in which their racial group, or sex, is under-represented, and can be limited to that group. [*RRA ss 29(2)(a), 37(1)(2); SDA ss 38, 47(1)(2)*].

2.6   Exceptions applicable to race only

It is permissible to advertise a post in a discriminatory manner in the following circumstances.

(*a*)   Where the position advertised is designed to provide training skills to a non-UK resident for use outside the UK (for instance, UK clinical experience for non-UK doctors). [*RRA ss 6, 29(2)(a)*].

2.7 Advertising

(*b*)   Where the advertisement relates to employment outside the UK, and the class of persons required for such employment is defined other than by reference to colour, race, or ethnic or national origins. [*RRA s 29(3)*].

(*c*)   Where advertising facilities or services are being advertised which are designed to meet the special needs of a particular racial group in regard to their education, training or welfare provided for by virtue of *RRA Part VI*. [*RRA ss 29(2)(a), 35-39, 41*]. This is dealt with in detail in POSITIVE DISCRIMINATION (43).

2.7   Exceptions applicable to sex only

It is permissible to advertise a post in a discriminatory manner in respect of sex:

(*a*)   where the post is advertised with a condition or requirement that proportionately fewer members of one sex can comply with, but which can be justified irrespective of sex – for example, a position where heavy lifting is required [*SDA ss 1(1)(b), 38(2)*]; and

(*b*)   where the employment is for religious purposes, and the employment is limited to one sex for doctrinal reasons. [*SDA ss 19, 38(2)*].

2.8   TERMINOLOGY

Inherently sexist terminology such as salesman, waitress, postman etc. is unlawful unless the advertisement makes explicit that the post is open to both sexes. [*SDA s 38(3)*].

2.9   INDIRECT DISCRIMINATION AND ADVERTISING

Race discrimination

The Commission for Racial Equality (CRE) Code of Practice sets out advice on advertising at paragraph 1.6 of the Code and draws particular attention to three possible indirectly discriminatory forms of advertising and suggests how they can be avoided:

(*a*)   by not confining advertisements to journals or publications which would exclude or disproportionately reduce the number of applicants from a particular racial group;

(*b*)   by not prescribing requirements such as length of residence or experience in the UK; and

(*c*)   when prescribing qualifications, by making clear that fully comparable overseas qualifications are acceptable.

(As to the meaning of indirect discrimination, see *RRA s 1(1)* and *SDA s 1(1)*, and INDIRECT DISCRIMINATION (36).)

All three of these suggestions are advisory. A strict 'O' level qualification was deemed acceptable as a criterion by a particular tribunal (*Raval v DHSS [1985] ICR 685*), but that case was decided on the law prior to the implementation of the Code and, unless an employer had given proper consideration to the equal opportunity implications of the selection criteria, it is unlikely that a tribunal would find such a criterion justified in the light of the Code of Practice. Indirectly discriminatory criteria are not unlawful if they can be justified on non-racial grounds.

There are other potentially indirectly discriminatory criteria in an advertisement. Examples include imposing a geographical criterion (for example, specifying that the individual must live within two miles of the workplace, or will not be considered if they have a particular post code) (*Hussein v Saints Complete House Furnishers [1979] IRLR 337*). Such a criterion will only be *prima facie* discriminatory if it can be shown that it has a disproportionate impact on a particular racial group. If it does have such an impact the employer must be able to satisfy a tribunal as to justification, otherwise the advertisement will be unlawful. The CRE has taken proceedings in relation to such advertisements in the Birmingham area.

2.10 Sex discrimination

The Equal Opportunities Commission (EOC) Code of Practice also sets out advice on advertising, at paragraph 19. Broadly, it recommends that:

(*a*)   job advertising should be carried out in such a way as to encourage applications from suitable candidates of either sex (in terms of both the wording of the advertisements and in the publications in which they are placed);

(*b*)   advertising material should be reviewed to ensure that it avoids stereotyping men and women; and

(*c*)   where vacancies are filled by promotion or transfer, they should be published to all eligible employees in such a way that they do not restrict applications from either sex.

Advertisements that impose restraint on family commitments, or that require supervisory experience and impose an age criterion, or set a single height requirement or require extensive overtime are all *prima facie* indirectly discriminatory on the grounds of sex. Such advertisements are, however, only unlawful if the employer is unable to justify the requirement on non-sexual grounds on a reasonable basis to the satisfaction of an industrial tribunal.

2.11 TRADE UNIONS

Trade unions may advertise training opportunities, targeted to train people in specific racial groups, or of one or other sex, to enable them to hold posts, on the same basis as employers may do so in respect of internal advertising (see 2.5 (*c*) above), that is, where they have identified that there has been an under-representation in the particular union position during the previous twelve months. [*SDA s 48(2); RRA s 38(3)(4)*]. Trade unions can also advertise for members on a discriminatory basis to encourage members of a particular racial group or sex to join, where there has been under-representation of that racial group, or sex, within the union during the previous twelve months. [*SDA s 48(3); RRA s 38(5)*]. They may also advertise reserved positions defined by sex (*note that this does not apply to race*) for elected, or non-elected, union positions. [*SDA s 49*].

2.12 THE MEANING OF 'PUBLISH'

A scruffy note in a shop window comes within the scope of the Acts as much as a box spread in, for example, the *Guardian*. Internal memoranda notifying internal vacancies also constitute publishing. The definition of publish has been dealt with extensively by the courts in relation to libel.

2.13 Advertising

2.13 WORD-OF-MOUTH RECRUITMENT

Word-of-mouth recruitment could never be directly discriminatory (unless adopted with an express discriminatory purpose, for example to ensure that there is no need to consider any black Africans). However, such recruitment will frequently constitute indirect discrimination against ethnic minorities and, possibly, against women. Both the EOC and CRE Codes of Practice advise against word-of-mouth recruitment (EOC, para 19(c); CRE, para 1.10).

Word-of-mouth recruitment almost inevitably preserves the pre-existing workforce profile, in that recruitment is through the social network of the existing workforce which will be likely to be ethnocentric and, if women are under-represented, likely to preserve that under-representation. The problem is likely to have a greater impact, however, with regard to ethnic minorities as the social context of an existing all-white workforce will be likely to exclude ethnic minorities from consideration. The practice will have an adverse impact with regard to women only as a result of the male workforce exercising their own prejudice regarding the recruitment of women, there being no inherent social network bar that will operate as in the case of ethnic minorities. The CRE conducted an investigation in 1982 into word-of-mouth recruitment at Massey Ferguson and made a finding that there was a discriminatory practice, but did not issue a non-discrimination notice. So far as the author is aware, there has been no tribunal application involving a complaint of indirect discrimination arising out of word-of-mouth recruitment. This is perhaps surprising, given that so many local authorities in particular operate the practice, usually at the request of the relevant trade union. Internal advertisement of promotional vacancies has the same effect, but the cost and internal morale arguments are likely to find favour with a tribunal as justification for such a practice. Both Codes urge that vacancies should be widely advertised.

2.14 PENALTIES

Proceedings for enforcement can only be taken by the respective Commissions within six months of the offending advertisement. Proceedings are in the industrial tribunal for employment-related advertisements; in the county court otherwise. [SDA s 72; RRA s 63].

The penalties available are so minimal that one could almost suspect that the relevant clause got mislaid during drafting. At first instance, the tribunal or county court can only declare that a contravention has occurred. [SDA s 72(2)(a); RRA s 63(2)(a)]. Surprisingly there are no powers to fine. Once a tribunal order is final (i.e. not open to, or subject to, appeal) the Commission may apply to a county court for an injunction to restrain a person from publishing further advertisements. [SDA s 72(4); RRA s 63(4)]. In county court proceedings, the application for an injunction can be made at the same time as for the declaration. Once an injunction has been obtained, contravention would lead to proceedings for contempt of court.

2.15 WHO MAY BE PROSECUTED?

Proceedings can be brought against the advertiser or publisher or both. [SDA s 38(1); RRA s 29(1)]. As a matter of practice, in the past the CRE and EOC have been more likely to proceed against the advertiser than the publisher. The publisher can escape liability if he has relied upon a statement made by the advertiser that the publication would be lawful [SDA s 38(4); RRA s 29(4)], as long as it was reasonable for him to rely on such a statement. This is a difficult test but, particularly with national newspapers, a certain level of knowledge and expertise about the *RRA* and the *SDA* will be assumed by an industrial tribunal.

2.16 DEFENCES

As mentioned above, the publisher of an advertisement can rely on a credible statement made by the advertiser that the advertisement would not be unlawful. [*SDA s 38(4); RRA s 29(4)*]. Anyone who makes such a statement to a publisher knowing it to be (or reckless as to whether it is) false or misleading is liable to a fine of up to £5,000 (level 5 on the standard scale). [*SDA s 38(5); RRA s 29(5)*].

2.17 EXERCISE OF PROSECUTING POWER BY THE COMMISSIONS

In practice both the CRE and EOC have been reluctant to exercise their powers to litigate in this area and there have been few prosecutions despite a considerable number of complaints received each year about advertisements, usually in respect of 'positive action' advertisements. In the past, assurances as to future conduct have satisfied the CRE and EOC. The Employment Appeal Tribunal (EAT) has advised that employers should obtain advice from the CRE and EOC about advertisements that take advantage of exceptions to the legislation (*London Borough of Lambeth v Commission for Racial Equality* [*1990*] *IRLR 231*). Both the CRE and EOC have a team of individuals dealing with such enquiries.

2.18 INDIVIDUAL RIGHT OF ACTION

Whilst only the CRE or EOC can prosecute in respect of the advertisement itself, any individual with an interest in the position may take individual proceedings in an industrial tribunal alleging discrimination in respect of the arrangements for making the appointment [*RRA s 4(1)(a); SDA s 6(1)(a)*] (see *Tottenham Green Under-Fives' Centre v Marshall* [*1989*] *ICR 214*) and be awarded damages for loss of opportunity and injury to feelings. [*RRA s 57(4); SDA s 66(4)*]. The publisher would also be vulnerable to such proceedings on the grounds of having aided and abetted the discriminator. [*RRA s 33; SDA s 42*].

2.19 DISABILITY

The provisions of the *Disability Discrimination Act 1995* relating to discriminatory job advertisements are different from the provisions of the *SDA* and *RRA*, and are dealt with separately (see DISABILITY (18)).

3 Age Discrimination

There is no express legislation prohibiting discrimination on grounds of age. As a general rule age limits (positive or negative) are, therefore, usually lawful. However, the Labour Party has recently committed itself to introducing legislation prohibiting discrimination on the grounds of age.

3.1 AGE DISCRIMINATION AS UNLAWFUL INDIRECT DISCRIMINATION

Age discrimination may be unlawful where an age limit can be shown to have an adverse proportional impact on grounds of either sex or race and cannot be shown to be otherwise justifiable. In *Price v Civil Service Commission [1978] ICR 27*, the Civil Service required all job applicants to be under 28. The EAT held that this was discriminatory to women because of a tendency to leave the job market to raise a family and then return. Justification is dealt with separately (see INDIRECT DISCRIMINATION (36)). Age discrimination used to be indirectly racially discriminatory on occasion because of immigration patterns (see *Perera v Civil Service Commission [1983] ICR 428*). This is unlikely to have application today. Employers should satisfy themselves, however, that a redundancy action related to age does not have a disproportionate impact on any particular racial group.

In *Jones v University of Manchester [1993] IRLR 218*, the Court of Appeal held that a job advertisement stating that the university was looking to appoint somebody aged between 27 and 35 was a 'requirement' within the meaning of *SDA s 1(1)(b)(i)*, and therefore was indirectly discriminatory. However, the university was able to justify the age requirement objectively without reference to the sex of applicants.

3.2 AGE DISCRIMINATION IN OTHER COUNTRIES

In other countries, age discrimination is *per se* unlawful (e.g. Canada and New Zealand). A House of Commons Select Committee has rejected the suggestion that similar legislation should be enacted in the UK, although there is growing political pressure for such legislation as the 'baby boom' generation gets older.

3.3 RETIREMENT AGE

It is unlawful to specify separate retirement ages for men and women [*Sex Discrimination Act 1986, s 2, amending SDA s 6(4)*]. Employment may continue beyond 60, or 65, subject to the provisions of the individual employment contract. In July 1995 the *Pensions Act* received the Royal Assent. A key provision of this is the equalisation of the state pension ages for men and women at 65. This provision will have effect from the year 2020, although the provisions will be phased in over the previous decade.

Some employers will allow employees to work beyond the normal retirement age. If this is a contractual right, it must be equally available to all employees, regardless of sex. Employers could leave the matter as a discretion depending on the individual circumstances (needs of the business or the individual's personal circumstances) but any such exercise should be monitored very carefully as to outcome. If it transpired that discretion was being operated disproportionately in favour of male employees, then they would be vulnerable to an application under the *SDA* by a female member of staff not permitted to work beyond the normal retirement age.

Employees over the normal retirement age cannot bring any claim under the *EPCA* [*EPCA s 64(1)(b)*]. There is no such restriction in respect of the *RRA* or *SDA*.

Different treatment of men and women over the age of 60 will be unlawful even where the motivation is to deal with apparent inconsistencies created by the fact that women are entitled to a state pension at the age of 60 whereas men are not. This is illustrated in the case of *James v Eastleigh Borough Council [1990] ICR 554*). The Council operated a special discount for pensioners in respect of admission to its swimming pools and related it to the pensionable age of 60 for women and 65 for men. Mr James made a complaint of sex discrimination. It was accepted that the council's motivation was not related to sex but nonetheless, because the fundamental determinant of who received cheap admission to the swimming pools was that of sex, the complaint would be upheld.

In *Bullock v Alice Ottley School [1992] IRLR 564*. The school had different retirement ages, of 60 for administrative and domestic staff, and of 65 for maintenance and ground staff. All of the maintenance and ground staff were male, and the vast majority of the administrative and domestic staff were female. Mrs Bullock made a complaint of sex discrimination when she was dismissed at the age of 61. The tribunal dismissed her complaint, but on appeal the EAT held that she had been unlawfully discriminated against. Ward J (President of the EAT) suggested that retirement ages must be the same throughout the employer's undertaking. However, the Court of Appeal held that there was no evidence of direct or indirect discrimination. Giving the leading judgment, Neill LJ said:

> 'For my part I can see nothing in section 5(3) or in any other provision in the 1975 Act [i.e. *the Sex Discrimination Act*] which prevents an employer having a variety of retiring ages for different jobs, *provided* that in the system which he uses there is no direct or indirect discrimination based on gender. In the case of alleged direct discrimination the question is: would a man in the same job have been treated differently?'

There was no evidence of direct discrimination in this case. It was open for the employer to have different retirement ages for groups of employees as there was a genuine material factor in the decision, i.e. the difficulty in recruiting trained gardeners and maintenance staff. In relation to indirect discrimination, the reason for the higher retirement ages for men and women was objectively justified on grounds unrelated to sex (namely the difficulty in recruiting skilled maintenance staff).

4   AIDS

AIDS is a disease that creates considerable fear and misunderstanding in the workplace, usually entirely misplaced. Employers can find themselves faced with pressure from the workforce to discriminate against HIV-positive individuals, or acting in anticipation of such pressure.

4.1   NO SPECIFIC LEGISLATION

There is no specific legislation protecting individuals suffering from AIDS, but such individuals enjoy the benefits of the *EPCA* to the same degree as any other. In addition, individuals at a 'progressive stage' of the HIV virus will be protected by the provisions of the *Disability Discrimination Act 1995*, from January 1997. They are entitled not to be unfairly dismissed. [*EPCA s 54*].

A study published by the National Aids Trust in 1993 (*HIV and AIDS in the workplace – an examination of cases of discrimination*) showed that only six unfair dismissal cases involving AIDS or HIV had actually reached the tribunal hearing stage out of over 2,000 legal enquiries. The study also showed that a major stumbling block for employees seeking redress is the two years' service requirement for unfair dismissal claims. In the recent Court of Appeal decision is *R v Secretary of State for Employment, Ex parte Seymour-Smith and Perez* [*1995*] *IRLR 464* it was held that the two-year qualifying period indirectly discriminated against women. At the time of going to press the Government was believed to be appealing against the decision.

There is nothing to prevent an employer from failing to employ any individual with AIDS. In July 1992, the National Aids Trust launched a Charter, *Companies Act!*, encouraging employers to introduce non-discriminatory practices in relation to employees and potential employees with HIV and AIDS. The signatories to the Charter include Marks & Spencer, Midland Bank, National Westminster Bank, Sainsbury's and IBM.

4.2   DISMISSAL

It is not appropriate to apply the disciplinary code to AIDS sufferers, although it may be appropriate to terminate the employment relationship on grounds of ill-health. Also, in limited circumstances, an industrial tribunal may accept that the dismissal was for 'some other substantial reason' if, say, health and safety considerations applied or there was an outright refusal of other work colleagues to work with the individual. These circumstances would apply to only a very limited number of high risk occupations. There is usually no reason why an HIV-positive individual should not work absolutely normally. If his sickness record becomes a problem then such an individual can be treated in the same way as any other individual would be and, subject to doctors' reports on likely recovery for a return to work and to consultation with the employee, dismissed on grounds of ill-health.

Should an individual, dismissed for health and safety reasons or peer group pressure, complain of unfair dismissal, it is a matter of fact for the tribunal as to whether, in all the circumstances, that dismissal was fair. Employers are likely to be vulnerable in respect of AIDS-related dismissals as this is an area where there is no set expectation as to whether such dismissals are reasonable or otherwise.

4.3 APPOINTMENT

There is no protection from discrimination in the appointment or promotion process for an AIDS sufferer or HIV-positive individual, or indeed for an individual suffering from any other illness.

4.4 GUIDANCE

The Department of Employment has published a booklet on the subject, PL 893, available from the Department of Employment (ID6), Caxton House, Tothill Street, London SW1H 9NF. Many employers' handbooks specify how many days of sickness will be tolerated before termination of employment is considered. An employer taking steps prior to expiration of such a specified time period should be able to show that the illness was such that there was no chance of recovery and that the contract was inevitably going to be impossible for the employee to fulfil.

5   Appeals

5.1   Appeals from an industrial tribunal are to the Employment Appeal Tribunal (EAT). EAT procedure is governed by the Employment Appeal Tribunal Rules 1993 (*SI 1993 No 2854*) (*the 'EAT Rules'*). Appeals from the county court are to the Court of Appeal (see 5.17 below).

5.2   INDIVIDUAL COMPLAINT

A party may appeal only against a decision of an industrial tribunal on a point of law and not against findings of fact properly arrived at by the tribunal. If the tribunal has failed to take into account evidence that it should have considered, or taken into account evidence which it should not have considered, then that is an error of law. If a decision is such that no reasonable tribunal could have arrived at that conclusion on the evidence before it, then that is also an error of law. If a tribunal has made a finding that it simply did not believe one or other party then that is not appealable. Subject to its having directed itself correctly, drawing or failing to draw an inference of discrimination is a matter of fact for the tribunal, as is determining justification in an indirect discrimination application. An appeal will not be permitted on the basis of new evidence if that evidence was available at the time of the original hearing (*Wileman v Minilec Engineering Ltd* [*1988*] *ICR 318*), nor will an appeal be permitted that raises new grounds not put before the tribunal.

5.3   AGAINST A NON-DISCRIMINATION NOTICE

A non-discrimination notice (NDN) is issued by either the CRE or EOC. Any appeal against an NDN must be lodged at the industrial tribunal (except where the acts to which the requirement relates are outside the jurisdiction of the industrial tribunal, in which case the appeal is to the county court). [*SDA s 68; RRA s 59*]. The appeal is against the requirement of the NDN, either on the grounds that the requirement is unreasonable or based on an incorrect finding of fact. In essence, this enables the tribunal to review the entire investigation. The appeal must be lodged within six weeks of the NDN having been served. Further appeal lies thereafter from the tribunal to the EAT on a point of law. If it is alleged that the CRE or EOC (as the case may be) has exceeded its powers, appeal is by way of application for judicial review in the High Court.

5.4   AGAINST A FINDING THAT A DISCRIMINATORY ADVERTISEMENT HAS BEEN PUBLISHED

(See ADVERTISING (2).) Appeal is to the EAT in the normal way. The same applies to an appeal against a finding that pressure to discriminate has been applied, or that instructions to discriminate have been given.

5.5   TIME LIMIT

An appeal must be lodged with the Registrar at the Employment Appeal Tribunal, Audit House, 58 Victoria Embankment, London EC4Y 0DS within 42 days of the date on which the tribunal's (written) decision was sent to the appellant, except with leave of the EAT. An appeal out of time must include an explanation for the delay. Time limits are usually strictly adhered to (*Duke v Prospect Training Services Ltd [1988] ICR 521*).

5.6   MANNER OF APPEAL

The appeal must be in the prescribed form, which is available from the EAT. The appeal does not need to be on the form supplied by the EAT but must be set out in the prescribed manner. It must set out the names of the appellant, the respondent and their representatives, the grounds for the appeal and the particulars of the grounds of appeal, and must be accompanied by a copy of the tribunal judgment from which the appeal is being made.

5.7   SPECIAL PROCEDURE, PRELIMINARY HEARING

The EAT issued a practice direction in 1985 (*[1985] ICR 684*) to deal with appeals which it appears to the Registrar are based on a challenge to the findings of fact by a tribunal. There will then be a preliminary hearing at which only the appellant appears and has to satisfy the EAT that the appeal is one that should properly be heard. If the appellant does not do so, the appeal is dismissed; if he does, the appeal will be listed for full hearing.

5.8   INTERLOCUTORY MATTERS

An appeal may be made to the EAT against any decision of an industrial tribunal on a point of law, including a decision to grant, or refuse to grant, an order of discovery or of further particulars.

5.9   PROCEDURE

The parties are under a duty to furnish the EAT with the documents that were before the industrial tribunal, and such other documentation as may be admissible. The Chairman's notes of evidence are not now usually supplied automatically but either party may apply to the Registrar for an order for their supply. Such a request should provide reasons (for example, that the tribunal ignored express oral evidence put before it, consideration of which contention would require the Chairman's notes of evidence). The documentation should be provided to the EAT at the earliest opportunity. The EAT compiles a bundle and supplies both sides with an index. The listing date is agreed with the parties.

5.10   RESTRICTED REPORTING ORDERS

In any case involving allegations of sexual harassment or other sexual misconduct, under *EAT Rules, Rule 23* the tribunal may of its own initiative, or on the application of either party, make a restricted reporting order. However, such an order will not be given unless each party has had an opportunity to make oral representation on this point.

A restricted reporting order, specifying the person who is not to be identified, will remain in force until the tribunal has 'promulgated' its decision (i.e. the date that the tribunal's decision is sent to the parties).

Where a restricted reporting order is in force, a notice of this fact will be placed on the list displayed at the tribunal, and also on the door of the tribunal.

5.11 Appeals

5.11 THE HEARING

The appeal is one of legal argument. A High Court judge sits with two lay assessors from a panel of experienced industrial tribunal lay members. The appellant puts his case, the respondent replies and then the appellant has the last word unless there is a cross-appeal in which case the respondent will have the last word on the cross-appeal.

5.12 POWERS OF THE EAT

The EAT has all the powers of an industrial tribunal [*EPCA 12 Sch 21(1)*] and may make any order that the industrial tribunal could have made, and may substitute its own order for that of the tribunal. Frequently, however, the matter will be remitted to the same, or a differently constituted tribunal for rehearing or reconsideration of a material point where there has been a misdirection.

5.13 DELAY

The EAT usually only has available the President of the EAT to sit as a judge and, as a result, there is a considerable backlog of cases, and a delay of a year before the appeal is heard is common. Parties may request an expedited hearing in relation to interlocutory appeals but delays are still substantial.

5.14 INTEREST ON AWARDS

Under the *Industrial Tribunals (Interest) Order 1990 (SI 1990 No 479)* interest accrues on a tribunal award if it remains unpaid 42 days after the date on which the tribunal's decision is sent to the parties. Interest accrues at the rate specified in the *Judgments Act 1838 s 17*, currently 8% (see REMEDIES (49)).

5.15 COSTS

Costs are not normally awarded against the losing party in the EAT. Costs will only be awarded, on a similar basis as in the industrial tribunal, if the proceedings have been unnecessary, improper or vexatious or unreasonably conducted or delayed (*EAT Rules, Rule 34*).

5.16 LEGAL AID

Legal aid is available to an applicant in the EAT subject to the normal legal aid criteria of merit and financial ability.

5.17 FURTHER APPEAL

An appeal from a decision of the EAT is to the Court of Appeal with leave from the EAT or from the Court of Appeal. An appeal from a decision of a county court is to the Court of Appeal; in certain circumstances, leave to appeal is required. The time limit for registering an appeal is four weeks from the date on which the judgment or order being appealed against was sealed or drawn up, or otherwise with leave (which is only given in exceptional circumstances). Thereafter further appeal lies with the House of Lords with leave of the Court of Appeal or House of Lords. Very few cases are able to proceed to the House of Lords. Costs will normally be awarded to the successful party in the Court of Appeal and above.

5.18 **EUROPEAN COURT OF JUSTICE**

Article 177 enables a matter turning on the application of European Community law to be referred to the European Court of Justice either at the initiative of the court hearing the matter or on the application of a party to the proceedings. An industrial tribunal and the appellate courts must give effect to European Community law.

5.19 **SUMMARY OF TIME LIMITS**

The main time limits in relation to proceedings in discrimination cases are summarised below.

Proceedings	*Time limit*
Application to industrial tribunal	Complaint must be made within 3 months of act of discrimination complained of
Application to county court (other than under *RRA* or *SDA*)	Action must be commenced within 6 years of date on which cause of action arose
Application to county court under *RRA* or *SDA* (normally applicable to non-employment cases only)	Action must be commenced within 6 months of the date on which the act to which it relates was done (but where the assistance of the CRE or EOC is sought, the time limit is extended to 8 months)
Review of industrial tribunal decision	Application for review must be made within 14 days of publication of decision
Appeal to Employment Appeal Tribunal	Appeal must be lodged within 42 days of the sending of the industrial tribunal's written decision to the appellant
Appeal to Court of Appeal from EAT or county court	Appeal must be lodged within 4 weeks of the date on which the order of the EAT or county court was sealed or drawn up
Appeal to House of Lords from Court of Appeal	Where leave of the House of Lords to appeal is sought (i.e. the Court of Appeal has refused leave), a petition together with a copy of the order complained of must be lodged with the House within 1 month of the making of the order
Referral to the European Court of Justice	No time limits as such; see 5.18 above for circumstances in which referral takes place

6 Burden of Proof

6.1 BURDEN IS WITH APPLICANT

It is for the individual to satisfy the tribunal that his dismissal, or other cause of action (failure to appoint, promote etc.), has been on grounds of race, sex, or marital status.

6.2 NATURE OF BURDEN

An individual must show in essence that he would have been given the job applied for, or a promotion, pay rise or whatever, but for his race or sex. This is not an easy matter as discrimination is peculiarly a matter within the knowledge of the alleged discriminator. Because of this particular difficulty with race and sex discrimination cases, industrial tribunals have developed an approach which, if the applicant establishes a *prima facie* case, requires the alleged discriminator to satisfy the tribunal with an 'innocent explanation'. If he fails to do this then the tribunal will normally draw an inference of discrimination.

6.3 THE PRIMA FACIE CASE

To establish a *prima facie* case, the applicant must show that his treatment is commensurate with having been discriminated against on racial (see RACIAL GROUNDS (48)), or sexual, or marital status grounds (see MARITAL STATUS (38)). The applicant must be of a different race (or sex) and there must have been differential treatment. At its most simple, if a woman has not been promoted and a man has, then she will show a *prima facie* case. The employer will then be called upon to provide the 'innocent explanation' (for example, better qualifications on the part of the man). (See *Qureshi v London Borough of Newham [1991] IRLR 264*).

6.4 THE INNOCENT EXPLANATION

If objective criteria such as qualifications, length of service, appraisal reports or the like are employed, then consideration of the 'innocent explanation' is straightforward enough. Difficulties arise when amorphous subjective criteria have been operated which could, in fact, act as a cloak for discrimination (*Baker v Cornwall County Council [1990] IRLR 194*), criteria such as 'leadership potential', ability to fit in, and long term potential. These are frequently legitimate criteria but when using them, the employer would be well advised to ensure that interviewing staff have received equal opportunity training and are able to provide a cogent defence of their selection. The burden of proof remains with the applicant but the degree of evidential satisfaction that an employer will be called upon to furnish will relate directly to the strength of the *prima facie* case. This in turn will relate to obvious objective criteria, that is, the strength on paper of the various candidates.

6.5 THE INFERENCE

The tribunal will not just accept at face value the explanations given to it but will 'look behind' those explanations to see whether, in fact, sex or race discrimination has taken place (*Owen & Briggs v James [1982] ICR 618*). If the tribunal is not satisfied with the explanation proffered by the employer, then it will normally draw an inference of unlawful racial or sexual discrimination. In *King v The Great Britain-China Centre [1991] IRLR 513*, the Court of Appeal gave guidelines in relation to the burden of proof which, although not formally reversing the burden of proof, recognised that it involves the balancing of factors for and against the finding of unlawful discrimination. In this case the applicant (who was Chinese but educated in Britain) satisfied the criteria for the post of Deputy Director of the centre in that she had experience of life in China and was fluent in Chinese. However, she was not short-listed for interview; in fact all of the applicants who were short-listed for interview were white, and the successful applicant was an English graduate in Chinese. The tribunal upheld her claim of unlawful racial discrimination on the grounds that the respondents had failed to demonstrate that the applicant had not been treated unfavourably, or that the unfavourable treatment was not because of her race. On appeal to the EAT, the respondents were successful on the grounds that the industrial tribunal had approached the case on the basis that there was a formal burden of proof on them. The applicant appealed to the Court of Appeal which overruled the decision of the EAT. It held that, as the respondents had not given a satisfactory explanation for their actions, the tribunal was entitled to draw an inference that the discrimination was racially based. This did not involve a formal burden of proof on the respondents. In relation to the burden of proof, however, the Court of Appeal (leading judgment given by Neill LJ) set out the following guidelines:

(*a*)   It is for the applicants to make out the case of discrimination. If they are unable to prove their case on the balance of probabilities, they will fail;

(*b*)   However, it is unusual to find direct evidence of discrimination, as few employers will be prepared to admit this, and in some cases discrimination will not be ill-intentioned but merely based on an assumption that the applicant would not have 'fitted in';

(*c*)   Therefore, the outcome of the case will usually depend on what inferences it is proper to draw from the primary facts before the tribunal—these may include inferences drawn from the replies to the statutory questionnaires;

(d)   There will be cases where the non-selection is clearly not on discriminatory grounds, but a finding of different treatment and a finding of difference in race or sex will often point to the possibility of unlawful discrimination. In these circumstances, a tribunal is able to look to the respondents for an explanation. If no explanation or an unsatisfactory explanation is provided, the tribunal is entitled to draw the inference that the discrimination was on grounds of race or sex. However, this is not a matter of law, rather it is of 'common sense';

(*e*)   The concept of a shifting evidential burden of proof is unhelpful. At the conclusion of evidence, the tribunal should make findings as to the primary facts in issue and draw all such inferences from those facts that it considers proper. The conclusion should then be reached on the balance of probabilities, bearing in mind the difficulties that applicants face in proving unlawful discrimination, and the fact that they have the formal burden of proof.

Before any explanation is required from the respondents, therefore, the applicant must establish that he/she has a case to answer by showing (i) that he/she has been treated differently, and (ii) that there is a difference on the grounds of race or sex, which suggest the possibility of unlawful discrimination. If the respondents fail to provide a satisfactory explanation for the difference in treatment, then the tribunal is able to infer that the reason for the difference for the treatment is on grounds relating to race or sex, and can therefore find that unlawful discrimination has taken place. The inference will be made as a matter of 'common sense', but is not to be made as a matter of law.

The Court of Appeal held in *Barclays Bank plc v Kapur and others (No 2) [1995] IRLR 87* that the respondents had shown that the reasons for the difference in treatment were not on grounds of race, as white employees in the same situation as the applicants would have been treated in exactly the same way.

6.6   EFFECT OF BURDEN OF PROOF

The approach developed by the courts results in a requirement on employers not simply to assert an explanation but also, to a degree, to satisfy the tribunal with that explanation. Whilst this requirement does not place a formal legal burden of proof on the employer, in approaching equal opportunities employers would be well advised to act on the assumption that, in essence, it does have this effect and to devise their policies accordingly. The level of satisfaction required will depend on the strength of the applicant's case. Employers who have trained the relevant staff and who follow clear, consistent criteria in recruitment, promotion and discipline will be better placed to refute any allegations of unlawful discriminatory conduct.

6.7   EVIDENCE THAT MAY BE TAKEN INTO ACCOUNT

The strict rules of evidence do not apply in the industrial tribunal, and tribunals have discretion in the conduct of applications before them (*Industrial Tribunals (Constitution and Rules of Procedure) Regulations 1993 (SI 1993 No 2687), Rule 9*). This means that tribunals can admit second-hand (hearsay – 'I heard x say to y') evidence at their discretion which may be of importance in a discrimination case (discriminators rarely admit their discriminatory attitude to the 'victim' but may be overheard talking to a third party). The questionnaire exchange is admissible and may be taken into account by the tribunal to the extent of drawing an inference that the unlawful discrimination took place (see QUESTIONNAIRE PROCEDURE (47)). The CRE or EOC (as appropriate) Code of Practice is admissible and may be taken into account by the tribunal. An employer may call evidence as to the existence and operation of an equal opportunity policy and of previous 'good conduct' in equal opportunity. The applicant may call evidence to rebut such good conduct evidence and also statistical evidence of the respondent's previous conduct in appointments or promotions (or whatever) at the relevant grade (*WMPTE v Singh [1988] ICR 614*). Previous and subsequent conduct by the respondent is also admissible, subject to relevance and reasonableness (*Chattopadhyay v Headmaster of Holloway School [1982] ICR 132*).

6.8   WHEN THE BURDEN IS ON THE EMPLOYER

The burden of proof is on the employer in the following instances.

(*a*)   In showing justification in regard to an indirect discrimination claim. In *Ojutiku and Oburoni v Manpower Services Commission [1982] IRLR 418*, the Court of Appeal considered in some detail what is meant by 'justification'. It was held that the term 'applies a lower standard than the term "necessary"' and that the party applying the discriminatory condition must 'prove it to be justifiable in all the circumstances on balancing its discriminatory effect against the discriminator's need for it. But that need is what is reasonably needed by the party who applies the condition'. The decision in *Ojutiku* was subsequently reviewed by the Court of Appeal in *Hampson v Dept of Education and Science [1989] ICR 179*. (See INDIRECT DISCRIMINATION (36).)

(b)   In showing that he took 'reasonable steps' to prevent the act of discrimination complained of and thereby avoid vicarious liability (*Enterprise Glass Co Ltd v Miles [1990] IRLIB 412*).

(c)   In showing that an exemption from the main provisions of the Act applies, for instance, that the matter comes within the 'genuine occupational qualification' (GOQ) exception (*London Borough of Lambeth v Commission for Racial Equality [1990] IRLR 231 (CA)*).

7   Child Care Provision

7.1   BACKGROUND

Complex bureaucracy actively discourages the growth of workplace nurseries. The demographic consequences of an increasing need to persuade skilled women workers to return to employment at the earliest opportunity are likely to lead to tax concessions and standardisation of regulations affecting child care provision. For the present, the rather unsatisfactory current situation is set out below.

7.2   ON-SITE CRÈCHE/NURSERY

The *Children Act 1989* (which replaced almost identical provisions in the *Nurseries and Child-Minders Regulation Act 1948*) empowers and requires each local authority to set regulations in respect of workplace nurseries (for children up to eight) and crèches (and child minders). Each local authority has its own requirements and regulations setting minimum staffing levels and facilities. These are usually rigorous and demanding. There is, at present, no nationwide norm; although the Secretary of State has the power to issue guidelines in the form of regulations, he has not yet done so. Any employer considering operating a crèche should contact the local district council to identify relevant local regulations. The local authority will specify staffing levels (1:6 in Brent, 1:3 in Westminster), minimum facilities and other similar matters. It is also necessary to obtain planning consent where change of use of an existing building or construction of new premises is concerned. The environmental health department has to be consulted as to the fire regulations. An employer should also ensure that its public liability insurance cover extends to the nursery and its occupants.

7.3   VOUCHER SCHEMES

For many staff, particularly those who commute long distances, an on-site nursery is not a solution. There are a number of schemes whereby employers provide subsidised child care. One such scheme is run by Mercer-Fraser in association with the National Childminding Association. Vouchers are purchased by the employer, given to relevant staff and can be used to employ child minders who are members of NCMA. Luncheon Vouchers run a similar scheme but do not require the child minder to be accredited by NCMA.

Potentially these schemes could be indirectly discriminatory against men. If they are exclusively available to female staff, this would be indirectly discriminatory. *SDA s 2(2)* exempts from the provisions of the *SDA* special treatment afforded to women in connection with childbirth, but although they are the product of the event, it would be stretching the natural meaning of the exemption to suggest that this encompasses provision for toddlers. Other criteria are also likely to be potentially indirectly discriminatory. A provision that provides vouchers or additional payment to single-parent families would indirectly discriminate against men because fewer men are in that situation. It would, however, be an exceptional tribunal that did not find the 'labour market' justification acceptable. (Note that a provision for payment to female single-parent staff only would be unlawful as direct discrimination.) If the benefit is not limited to single-parent households, then any criterion that is designed to direct the benefit to women rather than men, and is thereby *prima facie* indirectly discriminatory, may be more difficult to justify.

Employers would be well advised to consider the criteria to be employed with care. To establish a claim of indirect discrimination, an individual has to show that he has been subjected to some absolute criterion or condition. Employers would, therefore, be well advised to incorporate an overriding discretion into any child-care benefit criteria. Criteria that related to marital status would be unlawful by virtue of *SDA s 3*.

7.4   TAXATION

Provision of a workplace nursery is not a taxable benefit [*Finance Act 1990, s 21*], nor is the provision of a nursery pooled between specific employers. All other child-care provisions (vouchers, child-minding subsidy etc.) are taxable at value.

7.5   TEMPORARY PROVISION

An employer who wants to run a crèche for less than six days a year does not need local authority consent. [*Children Act 1989, 9 Sch 5*]. This enables employers to provide crèche and nursery facilities at an office function, Christmas party or outing. Insurance cover should still be confirmed.

8   Codes of Practice

8.1   POWER TO ISSUE CODES

Both the CRE and EOC have issued codes of practice, giving guidance on good employment practice. In 1991, the European Commission issued a Recommendation and Code of Practice in relation to sexual harassment (*Commission Recommendation on the protection of the dignity of women and men at work; A Code of Practice on measures to combat sexual harassment*). The Commission for Racial Equality obtained Parliamentary approval for their Code of Practice on Race Relations first and this came into force on 1 April 1984 by virtue of *SI 1983 No 1081*. The Equal Opportunities Commission Code of Practice came into effect a year later on 30 April 1985 by virtue of *SI 1985 No 387*. Parliament had the choice of approving or rejecting the codes; it was not empowered to amend them. The CRE Code is reproduced in Appendix 1.

The CRE are seeking to amend the Code of Practice on Race Relations, and published a consultative document in 1994. A draft Code of Practice was issued in 1994. The differences between the first and the revised Code of Practice are discussed in 8.11 below.

8.2   LEGAL STATUS

These codes are not legally binding but will be admissible in any tribunal proceedings under the relevant Act and are to be 'taken into account' by any industrial tribunal considering any application under the relevant Act. [*RRA s 47(10); SDA s 56A(10)*].

8.3   CONTENT

Both codes of practice aspire to provide statements of good employment practice. They provide detailed advice on compliance with the legislation and good practice beyond compliance. They provide advice to employers on the implementation of permissible positive action initiatives. The content and organisation of the codes are slightly different.

8.4   CRE CODE

The Race Relations Code is divided into four sections and sets out separately the responsibilities of employers, employees, trade unions and employment agencies. The most controversial recommendation is that employers should monitor the ethnic origin of their workforce (paras 1.33-1.43).

8.5   EOC CODE

The Sex Discrimination Code is divided into two sections, Part 1 'The role of good employment practices in eliminating sex and marriage discrimination' and Part 2 'The role of good employment practices in promoting equality of opportunity'. The EOC Code also recommends monitoring (paras 37-40), contains more detailed provisions with respect to disciplinary provisions (para

32) and gives detailed advice about appropriate circumstances that justify a 'genuine occupational qualification' (paras 15-17), but otherwise is not as clearly or as helpfully set out as the earlier CRE Code.

8.6   **EUROPEAN COMMISSION RECOMMENDATION**

The Recommendation of the European Commission defined 'harassment' for the first time as:

> 'conduct of a sexual nature, or other conduct based on sex affecting the dignity of women and men at work, including conduct of superiors and colleagues, is unacceptable if:
>
> (a)   such conduct is unwanted, unreasonable and offensive to the recipient;
>
> (b)   a person's rejection of or submission to such conduct on the part of employers or workers (including superiors or colleagues) is used explicitly or implicitly as a basis for a decision which affects that person's access to vocational training, access to employment, continued employment, ·promotion, salary or other employment decisions; and/or
>
> (c)   such conduct creates an intimidating, hostile or humiliting work environment for the recipient;
>
> and . . . such conduct may, in certain circumstances, be contrary to the principle of equal treatment within the meaning of [the Equal Treatment Directive]'.

This Code is not binding, but has been used by a number of industrial tribunals in harassment cases. The Code states that the essential characteristic of sexual harassment is that it is *unwanted* by the recipient. (See HARASSMENT (34)).

8.7   **APPLICATION OF CODE TO SMALL EMPLOYERS**

The codes of practice are general advisory statements and some of the recommendations are not appropriate for small employers. Both codes expressly state that the application of the code must relate to the size of the employer (EOC Code, para 3; CRE Code, Introduction, para 2.2). As a result, whilst small firms are required to comply with the relevant legislation, any tribunal considering the application of the code will bear in mind the size of the undertaking in question.

8.8   **POSITIVE ACTION**

The scope for positive discrimination is very limited. Both codes give advice on permissible positive action (CRE Code, paras 1.44-1.45; EOC Code, paras 41-43). (See POSITIVE DISCRIMINATION (43).)

8.9   **EQUAL OPPORTUNITY POLICY**

The CRE Code expressly recommends the adoption of an equal opportunity policy (para 1.4) with responsibility for its implementation given to a member of senior management. They recommend that the policy should be negotiated with the trade unions where appropriate and made known to all staff and, if possible, to all job applicants. If an employer has an equal opportunity policy implemented in the light of the recommendations of the code then in any proceedings under the Act this will be a matter that will be taken into account by the industrial tribunal. The EOC Code is not explicit in recommending an equal opportunity policy but contains a series of recommendations that amount to such advice.

It would be unwise for an employer to effect a policy that only dealt with race or disability, or only dealt with sex and marital status, as this could be used to imply adverse inferences in any application under the legislation not covered by the policy. There is no requirement for a policy for the consideration of disabled employees but an equal opportunity policy normally covers disability as well. There is nothing to prohibit employers from having a policy on sexual orientation, age, political persuasion etc. Any employer with an equal opportunity policy that predates the code should review it in the light of the recommendations set out in the code. However, an equal opportunity policy does not have to implement every recommendation of the codes of practice.

8.10   IMPLEMENTATION

The codes set out recommendations and a framework. Each employer should consider his own needs and resources carefully. An over-ambitious equal opportunity policy is worse than none at all. If the employer's own policy is not implemented, it will be an embarrassment in any proceedings and could well result in an adverse finding in a particular case. The codes set out recommendations that go beyond the basic provisions of either Act and are designed to facilitate achievement of the legislative goals. An employer who can show that he has reviewed work practices in the light of the codes, and who has an equal opportunity policy which attempts to ensure compliance with the codes, will frequently be able to satisfy a tribunal that he should not be liable for unauthorised acts of discrimination by individual employees by virtue of *RRA s 32(2)* or *SDA s 41(2)*. An employer who has not taken such steps is increasingly unlikely to be able to satisfy an industrial tribunal in that regard.

8.11   REVISED CRE CODE OF PRACTICE

A revised CRE Code of Practice was issued in 1994, and the consultation period ended on 30 November 1994. The revised Code is yet to be laid before Parliament. There were a number of reasons for the Code being revised, including two studies in 1993, by the General, Municipal and Boilermakers' Union (*Divided by Degrees*), and the Labour Force Survey. Both of these surveys showed that ethnic minorities were twice as likely to be unemployed as white people. Further reasons for the revision of the Code were the large-scale privatisation of public utilities, the increasing use of compulsory competitive tendering in areas of public service, as well as a growing awareness of equality of opportunity in the employment context.

The main differences between the first Code of Practice and the revised Code are as follows:

(a) Part 1 – Responsibilities of employer
There are extended footnote references in this section, notably to the Department of Employment's Ten Point Plan (which is a guide to employers for achieving equality of opportunity in employment). The revised Code

recommends the introduction of Annual Action Plans, which involve the setting of achievable equality targets, the introduction of race-relations training, and regular monitoring of the Annual Action Plans and Equal Opportunity Policy. The revised Code also gives detailed advice on the use and content of standard application forms.

The revised Code contains advice for employers in a dismissal/redundancy situation, including alternatives to a policy of 'last in, first out' (which can be indirectly discriminatory).

The revised Code also gives guidance on the introduction and use of employee appraisals, as well as the use of race-related training as part of an equal opportunity policy. It recommends the use of equal opportunity clauses in all third party contracts. Where the undertaking concerned is a public authority, there is a limit on the number and content of questions that can be asked (see CONTRACT COMPLIANCE (13)).

(b) Part 2 – Responsibilities of employees and trade unions
The revised Code contains more detailed guidance regarding the liability of individual employees and trade unions for acts of discrimination in the employment context, including personal liability, and responsibility for payment of any compensation awarded. The Code recommends making discriminatory conduct by employees a disciplinary offence, both for the employer and for the trade union of which the employee is a member. The Code also recommends that unions should introduce structural changes to encourage ethnic minority participation and representation.

(c) Part 3 – Responsibilities of employment agencies
Employment agencies have the responsibilities outlined in Part 1 of the Code, in their role as employers, and also have responsibilities under the Code in their role as job suppliers. The revised Code is stated to apply also to careers services and other referral agencies. The most notable addition to this Part of the Code is the recommendation that employment agencies report to the CRE all incidences of discriminatory instructions; this recommendation comes as a response to a formal investigation by the CRE into a company and two employment agencies in Bradford (see COMMISSION FOR RACIAL EQUALITY (9)).

(d) Part 5 – TECs, LECs and providers of vocational/employment training
This is a totally new section of the CRE Code. It points out that these bodies are under a dual obligation: (i) as employers, and (ii) in ensuring equality of opportunity as regards access to training.

8.12   CRE STANDARDS FOR RACIAL EQUALITY

The CRE Code of Practice relates only to the employment context. In 1995, the CRE issued two standards: *Racial Equality Means Business* (a standard for employers), and *Racial Equality Means Quality* (a standard for local government).

The standards do not have any legal status and so are not admissible in tribunal proceedings under the *RRA*. However, the standards are intended to provide a link between good employment practice as laid down in the Code of Practice, and other business strategies, such as responding to the interests of the communities in which those businesses operate.

8.13   Codes of Practice

The standards provide a checklist for organisations in developing racial equality programmes, including the implementation of an action plan and making a public commitment to a practice of equality, continual review of procedures, training and education, and obtaining and analysing ethnic origin data. The standards also have a measurement section, to help organisations assess what has been done and what challenges remain. This includes selection, policy and planning, and racial equality training.

8.13   In May 1995 the EOC published a draft Code of Practice on Equal Pay. The purpose of this Code is to assist employers in eliminating the consistent pay gap between male and female employees. The Code recommends that employers should use an equal pay policy, and undertake a pay review. If there is any pay inequality found following such pay review, the code recommends that action should be taken to redress this. To ensure that the system of equal pay is maintained, the Code recommends a system of monitoring of salaries.

As with the other codes of practice, this Code will not be legally binding. It will however be admissable in any tribunal proceedings under both the *SDA* and the *EqPA*.

9   Commission for Racial Equality

9.1   HISTORY

The Commission for Racial Equality (CRE) was established by the *Race Relations Act 1976* and was formed by the merger of the old Race Relations Board and Community Relations Commission. It is funded through the Home Office from the public purse at an annual cost of approximately £15 million.

9.2   DUTIES

It has a dual role reflected in its statutory duties:

(*a*)   to work towards the elimination of discrimination;

(*b*)   to promote equality of opportunity, and good relations, between persons of different racial groups; and

(*c*)   to keep the operation of the *RRA* under review.

[*Sec 43(1)*].

There are those who consider that this dichotomy of role inhibits the function of the CRE. It has both the 'carrot' role with its promotion work and a duty to wield the 'stick' by way of enforcement proceedings against transgressors.

9.3   POWERS

The CRE's powers can conveniently be divided into five distinct categories:

(i)   assisting individuals with complaints to the industrial tribunal or county court;

(ii)   conducting formal investigations;

(iii)   promoting good equal opportunity practice and racial equality;

(iv)   providing grant aid to local organisations promoting racial equality; and

(v)   conducting or sponsoring research into matters of concern to race relations.

9.4   ORGANISATION

The CRE underwent a restructuring in 1994, and as a result more of its duties are carried out by the regional offices. Each of the regional offices has its own structure. However, London remains the largest office and it is divided into three divisions:

1.   Equality Assurance Division:

(i)   local government and related services;

(ii)   private sector employment, urban policy and training;

(iii)   health and public sector employment;

(iv)   criminal justice, immigration, racial violence and the uniformed services; and

(v)   formal investigations.

2.   Corporate Standards Division:

    (i)   personnel;

    (ii)   finance/planning;

    (iii) information systems/technology;

    (iv)   audits/scrutiny;

    (v)   performance review; and

    (vi)   corporate training.

3.   Law Enforcement Division:

    (i)   complaints;

    (ii)   complainant aid;

    (iii) CRE litigation; and

    (iv)   legal advice.

9.5   ASSISTING COMPLAINANTS

Of most frequent concern to individuals and employers alike is the power of the CRE to assist individuals in taking cases to the industrial tribunal. The organisation of this function within the CRE and EOC is different. The EOC organises this work on a 'type' basis whereas the CRE has a 'Complaints Department' within the Legal Division which is organised on a regional basis and deals with all applications for assistance in the tribunal or county court.

This latter power is provided by *RRA s 66* and enables the CRE to assist individuals in taking proceedings pursuant to the Act if:

(*a*)   the case raises a question of principle;

(*b*)   taking into account the complexity of the case, the relative position of the individual and the employer, or any other matter, it would be unreasonable to expect the individual to proceed unassisted; or

(*c*)   there is any other special consideration.

This provides a wide discretion. The decision as to whether or not to provide assistance is made by a committee of Commissioners (the Complaints Committee). This committee sits monthly and considers reports compiled by officers based in small regional teams in the CRE's Complaints Department (complaints officers). More than 1,000 applications are received annually. The complaints officers will usually assist an individual in drawing up an *RRA s 65* questionnaire (see QUESTIONNAIRE PROCEDURE (47)) and in drafting the application to the industrial tribunal. The reply to the questionnaire is utilised by the CRE to consider the merits of an application for assistance. It can frequently take several months for the CRE to reach a decision on assistance.

9.6   FORM OF ASSISTANCE GIVEN

The CRE has a wide discretion as to the form of assistance given to a complainant. It may be limited to assistance with conciliation or legal representation at the industrial tribunal. The CRE may allocate a case that it is supporting to its small in-house legal team, or a solicitor from an approved panel may be instructed, or occasionally one of the CRE's complaints officers will handle the case. Pending a final decision on representation, the CRE's complaints staff will usually assist an applicant with tribunal correspondence and the like.

9.7   CONDUCTING FORMAL INVESTIGATIONS

The CRE is empowered by *RRA s 48* to conduct formal investigations. Such an investigation may be in relation to any matter pertaining to their general powers which, as already mentioned, are:

(*a*)   to work towards the elimination of discrimination;

(*b*)   to promote equality of opportunity and good race relations; and

(*c*)   to keep the working of the *RRA* under review.

The CRE nominates one or more of its Commissioners and, subject to approval by the Secretary of State, may appoint additional Commissioners to conduct the investigation [*RRA s 48(2)(3)*], but the actual investigation itself is conducted by CRE staff answerable to the appointed Commissioner(s). The formal investigation will usually be conducted by one of the CRE's regional offices (if the matter is a regional one). If the formal investigation involves work throughout Great Britain, or it is a general investigation, then the investigation will be carried out by the Equality Assurance Division in the London office. (See INVESTIGATIONS (37).)

9.8   Types of investigation

There are two types of investigation:

(*a*)   a named persons investigation, and

(*b*)   a general investigation.

As the term implies, a named persons investigation is directed expressly at a company or persons who the CRE has reason to believe have been operating a discriminatory practice, whereas a general investigation is more by way of a research project into, say, employment practices in a particular industry. The powers and procedures to be followed in a formal investigation are dealt with in detail at INVESTIGATIONS (37).

9.9   OTHER ENFORCEMENT POWERS

Only the CRE has the power to take proceedings in respect of alleged discriminatory advertisements [*RRA s 29*], or instructions or pressure to discriminate [*RRA ss 30, 31*], by virtue of *RRA ss 58* and *63*. It may proceed either by way of an application to the industrial tribunal for a declaration that the discrimination complained of took place (and subsequently to the county court for an injunction if it considers that there will be a repeat offence) [*RRA s 63*] or by the issuance of a non-discrimination notice subsequent to or in the course of, a formal investigation. [*RRA s 58*]. To date, the CRE has not issued any non-discrimination notices in respect of alleged discriminatory advertisements or pressure or instructions to discriminate, but has commenced proceedings in the tribunal not infrequently. (See ADVERTISING (2) and PRESSURE TO DISCRIMINATE (45).)

9.10 Commission for Racial Equality

A non-discrimination notice was issued against Salford Van Hire Co Ltd in 1993 for offering more generous hire terms for cars to white than to Afro-Caribbean or Asian customers. At the end of 1994, there were seven non-discrimination notices in force.

Formal investigations have also been carried out against Britannia Products Ltd, and two employment agencies, Brook Street and Network Recruitment Agency in Bradford. Non-discrimination notices were issued against Britannia Products Ltd and Network Recruitment Agency.

9.10 PROMOTIONAL WORK

The CRE also provides an advisory service to employers and trade unions in relation to equal opportunity practice.

9.11 CODE OF PRACTICE

As part of its promotional duties the CRE has produced a code of practice [*RRA s 47*] (see CODES OF PRACTICE (8)) which sets out advice to employers, trade unions, employment agencies and individuals on complying with the law and good equal opportunity employment practice. The CRE may review its code, subject to Parliamentary approval. [*RRA s 47(9)*].

9.12 GRANT AID

The CRE has responsibility for funding bodies connected with the promotion of racial equality and good race relations. There is an internal department which deals with this function. For this purpose, the CRE funds a network of Councils for Racial Equality across the country. These are usually to be found in urban areas where there is a high proportion of ethnic minorities and are described in 9.16 below. The CRE also funds ethnic minority self-help groups, arts projects and independent local initiatives.

9.13 RESEARCH

The CRE has an internal research department and also funds external research into topics related to racial equality. The CRE is also under a duty to keep the *RRA* under review and produced a consultation document and subsequent recommendations in 1988. A number of changes in the *RRA* and its operation were proposed including the setting up of a specialist discrimination tribunal and modifications to the formal investigation procedure. The CRE completed its second review of the *RRA* in 1992. A number of further changes in the *RRA* were proposed, including wider enforcement powers for the CRE, the introduction of compulsory ethnic monitoring, and the introduction of specialist tribunals to deal with instances of discrimination. These proposals were rejected by the Government in July 1994. However, the Government accepted the concept of legally binding undertakings from employers that they will change procedures which disadvantage a particular group. The CRE has also, in the past, been willing to answer legal enquiries from third parties, such as employers and trade unions, subject to these not being from an employer relating to a matter for which an application for assistance to the CRE by an individual has been made.

9.14 **OFFICES**

The head office is Elliot House, 10/12 Allington Street, London SW1E 5EH (Tel: (0171) 828 7022). It is close to Victoria Station. There are also five regional offices. The addresses of these are:

BIRMINGHAM
Alpha Tower
11th Floor
Suffolk Street
Queensway
Birmingham
B1 1TT
Tel: (0121) 632 4544

LEEDS
Yorkshire Bank Chambers
1st Floor
Infirmary Street
Leeds
LS1 2JT
Tel: (0113) 2434413/4

SCOTLAND
Hanover House
41/51 Hanover Street
Edinburgh
EH2 2PJ
Tel: (0131) 226 5186

LEICESTER
Haymarket House
4th Floor
Haymarket Shopping Centre
Leicester
LE1 3YG
Tel: (0116) 2517852

MANCHESTER
Maybrook House
5th Floor
40 Blackfriars Street
Manchester
M3 2EG
Tel: (0161) 831 7782/8

9.15 **STAFFING**

The CRE employs approximately 230 staff nationwide; most of these are based at the London office.

9.16 **COUNCILS FOR RACIAL EQUALITY**

There is also a network of Councils for Racial Equality. These are usually part funded by the CRE but are not under their direct control. Each is a separate legal entity, usually an unincorporated association. They have no legal powers but frequently employ a member of their staff to help individuals with complaints of discrimination in the industrial tribunal and to develop equal opportunity policies with local employers. Councils for Racial Equality are frequently able to assist employers with lists of interpreters and with cultural and general equal opportunity advice. As with any locally-based organisation, the quality of the service they provide varies considerably.

9.17 **OTHER RACE RELATIONS ADVISERS**

The Department of Employment has a team of race relations advisers. These operate completely independently from the CRE and see their role as exclusively advising employers on equal opportunities and on avoiding problems. The service is confidential. ACAS also has a small team of equal opportunity advisers, also confidential.

9.18   Commission for Racial Equality

9.18   OTHER RACE RELATIONS BODIES

There are a large number of 'self-help' and 'civil rights' type organisations in existence. Some of these are funded in part by the CRE and some are not. The CRE keeps an informal list of such organisations; better known examples are Black Rights UK, West Indian Standing Conference, Bangladesh Welfare Association, and Northern Complainant Aid Fund. These bodies have no formal powers.

10   Comparator

10.1   The *Equal Pay Act 1970 (EqPA)*, the *SDA* and *RRA* involve an individual complaining of discrimination by making comparisons with real or theoretical comparators. (See also EQUAL PAY (29)).

10.2   EQUAL PAY COMPARATOR

The comparable man

To establish an equal pay claim, a woman has to show that a man is employed, at a higher rate of pay than she is receiving, in doing similar work or work of equal value.

10.3   Must be a real man

The *EqPA* does not permit comparison with a theoretical male employee in the way that the *SDA* and *RRA* do. To establish a complaint, the woman must establish a real job holder or job holders. There is nothing to prevent her from casting her net beyond a single comparator (*Hayward v Cammell Laird Shipbuilders Ltd [1988] IRLR 257*).

10.4   Previous job holder

A woman can compare herself with a man who previously did her job (Treaty of Rome (EC Treaty), *Article 119; Macarthys Ltd v Smith [1980] IRLR 210*).

10.5   Comparator must be in the same employment

EqPA s 1(6) provides that the comparable male must be employed by the same employer or any associated employer at the same establishment or at establishments of the employer or associated employer in Great Britain (including that one) for which there are common terms and conditions of employment generally or for the relevant class of employees. The terms need not be identical, but can include staff on the same terms at different grades (*Leverton v Clwyd County Council [1989] ICR 33*).

In *British Coal v Smith; North Yorkshire County Council v Ratcliffe [1994] IRLR 342*, the Court of Appeal held that the comparable male can be employed at a different establishment of the same employer, but must be on *exactly the same terms* (except for pay) as male employees at the applicant's establishment. It is not necessary that the terms and conditions of employment of female employees at both establishments are 'common' or the same.

10.6   Associated employer

The definition of associated employer is that used in employment protection legislation generally. An employer is an associated employer if that employer is controlled by the other employer or if both employers are controlled by the same third party. A woman is, therefore, able to compare herself with a man doing like work or work of equal value at another site of the same employer or part of that group of employers, if it is part of the same group of companies or in the control of the same company.

10.7 Comparator

10.7 Contractors

A contractor will not be an associated employer and so cannot provide the comparator, or, more importantly, will prevent an individual comparing herself with a man employed by the contracting company (*Macarthys Ltd v Smith [1980] IRLR 210*).

10.8 COMPARATOR IN *RRA* AND *SDA* CASES

Direct discrimination

To show direct discrimination, a woman has to show that she has received less favourable treatment compared with that shown to a man, or that which would have been shown. [*SDA s 1(1)(a)*]. The same is true for an *RRA* application. The comparison has to be relevant. If a woman complains of failure to have the opportunity to be promoted she has to show that she was denied an opportunity to apply where men were not (any woman not denied the opportunity would be fatal to a direct discrimination claim).

10.9 Theoretical comparator

If, for example, male and female employees are being considered for promotion, and no appointment is made at all, an unsuccessful woman can compare herself with a fictional man with her experience, qualifications and circumstances. It will not matter that some men failed to achieve promotion in the course of the same selection, although the woman will have to show that, *prima facie*, the men failed to be promoted on legitimate grounds and that if one of them possessed her experience and qualifications, he would have been appointed. In an *RRA* case the individual may compare himself with a theoretical person with his experience, qualifications and circumstances but of a different, favoured, racial group.

10.10 Indirect discrimination

In considering a complaint of indirect discrimination, the selection of the comparator group is of importance. (See INDIRECT DISCRIMINATION (36).) In an indirect discrimination case a theoretical male group, or group of different ethnic origin, is still permissible but may present problems to the applicant who has to show disproportionate impact. A straightforward example of a theoretical comparator group in an indirect discrimination case would be provided in a case where an experience and age bar prevented a woman from being shortlisted and there were no male applicants, as a result of which no appointment was made. It would be easy to establish the theoretical group of males who would be able to satisfy such conditions.

In *Jones v University of Manchester [1993] IRLR 218*, the university advertised a post stating that it was looking to appoint somebody aged between 27 and 35. The applicant challenged this on the grounds that it was a requirement which indirectly discriminated against female mature students (i.e. who had obtained their first degree on or after their 25th birthday). An industrial tribunal upheld her complaint of sex discrimination on the grounds that the relevant pool for comparison was graduates who had obtained their degrees as mature students. Within this group the proportion of women who could comply with the age requirement was found to be considerably smaller than the proportion of men who could comply. The EAT allowed the university's appeal on the basis that this pool was too limited. The vacancy was open not only to mature students but to all graduates. It was not possible for the applicant to further subdivide the comparison pool. The Court of Appeal dismissed the applicant's appeal. The relevant pool of comparison was all candidates who satisfied the requirements for the job except for the age limit at the source of the applicant's complaint, and a further subdivision (i.e. mature students) was not permissible.

11 Conciliation

11.1 ACAS

The most usual method of conciliation is through the Advisory, Conciliation and Arbitration Service. There is also an additional method not involving ACAS, where the individual is represented by a solicitor.

11.2 DESCRIPTION OF SERVICES AND SCOPE OF ACAS

The Advisory, Conciliation and Arbitration Service (ACAS) was set up in 1975, by virtue of the *Employment Protection Act 1975 (EPA)*, as an independent conciliation service. It is a body of the State and its powers and functions are set out in the *EPA* and other legislation. It is funded through the Department of Employment but is otherwise independent of the Government. ACAS has a number of functions in resolving trade disputes, ranging from national bargaining disputes and strikes to individual problems. It is divided into two separate departments; one covers trade disputes, the other individual conciliations.

ACAS has advisory officers who specialise in equal opportunities and who would probably take a role in the conciliation of any trade dispute which turns on an equal opportunity issue. Individual conciliation is dealt with by teams of conciliation officers divided on a territorial basis. Each officer has his own case-load with regard to which he is largely autonomous. There is no specialisation in discrimination cases within the individual conciliation function of conciliation officers and, as a result, officers are primarily used to dealing with unfair dismissal claims, redundancy and so forth. Discrimination claims make up only 10% of their work (ACAS annual report 1994).

In the past there has been some reluctance on the part of ACAS officers to become involved in discrimination claims and this is borne out by the conciliation rates: a conciliation rate of 59% as against 67% for unfair dismissal (clearance rates in all cases, including those where proceedings have not yet started – ACAS annual report 1994). More sensitivity is required to obtain a result. The compromise of 'principle' is involved on both sides. Both the *RRA* and *SDA* impose upon ACAS (through one of its conciliation officers) the duty to attempt to promote a settlement if both parties request the service to do so, before or after tribunal proceedings have been commenced, or the ACAS officer can attempt to conciliate on his own initiative if he considers that there is a reasonable prospect of settling. The settlement can be financial or for re-instatement or perhaps simply for a promise of fair treatment in the future. The service is provided free of charge. [*RRA s 55; SDA s 64; Employment Protection (Consolidation) Act 1978 (EPCA) ss 133, 134*].

11.3 APPROACHING ACAS

After commencement of tribunal proceedings

If tribunal proceedings have been started by an individual, an ACAS officer should contact the parties. However, sometimes this fails to happen, or one or other side wants to deal with the matter swiftly. If proceedings in the tribunal have been started and either side wishes to involve ACAS, that party should telephone the regional ACAS office and ask for the duty officer (see 11.10

below). If the agreement has already been arrived at, the ACAS officer will record the details and will contact the parties to finalise matters within a day or two. If agreement has yet to be arrived at, the ACAS officer will ask the employer what he is willing to offer (or the employee what he is willing to accept) and then contact the other party.

11.4   Prior to commencement of tribunal proceedings

ACAS has recently changed its practice in matters where proceedings have not yet actually been started. It is now reluctant to become involved if an agreement has already been arrived at by the parties. *RRA s 55(2)* and *SDA s 64(2)* impose a duty on the conciliation officer to act where a complaint could be made, but before it actually has been, at the request of either party. The conciliation officer is charged with endeavouring to promote a settlement of the complaint without the matter going to a tribunal. Employers are wisely reluctant to resolve matters without ACAS involvement as they need to be sure there is no question of a referral to the tribunal. ACAS would seem to be *'ultra vires'* if it declines to act in circumstances where an agreed settlement of a potential complaint required its involvement to enable it to be finalised. The matter has yet to be put to the test. It is regrettable that ACAS is now reluctant to provide the sort of swift service that used to be provided in such agreed situations in the past. The procedure is now that either party (preferably the individual rather than the employer) should contact a 'notification officer' at the regional ACAS office (see 11.10). It is probable that ACAS will still respond to genuine urgent deadlines and meetings can be held at its offices at short notice.

Where an employee is unrepresented ACAS is, however, rightly reluctant to conclude agreements that exclude an individual's right to pursue a claim at the industrial tribunal prior to proceedings having been commenced. It is likely to want the wording of any agreement to be specific to the matter being settled and to be satisfied that both parties are fully aware of their respective rights and the implications of concluding an agreement.

11.5   HOW CONCILIATION WORKS

All tribunals send a copy of the originating application and notice of appearance to ACAS, and it can help the ACAS officer in his job if he gets all additional documents from the parties.

On receipt of the tribunal documents, the ACAS officer will usually get in touch with both sides. He will usually have salary and other benefit details from the tribunal documentation, but if it is a situation where the employment is continuing, he will wish to be appraised of the salary difference in a promotion complaint or the like. The officer's primary concern will be to find out whether the parties are willing to settle. There is no reason why either party should not get in touch with the officer directly. ACAS has an excellent clerical back-up team to take messages for officers, who frequently work from home.

11.6   CONFIDENTIALITY OF ACAS DISCUSSIONS

Conversations with ACAS are privileged and information provided cannot be referred to in the industrial tribunal, except with the express consent of the individual who gave that information. [*RRA s 55(4); SDA s 64(4)*]. The ACAS officer will repeat what is said to him to the other side unless asked for specific assurances not to do so (which he may sometimes decline to give). This can be a useful way of communicating a position to the other side without having to talk to them directly, but it needs to be kept in mind when talking to ACAS.

11.7   ENFORCEABILITY OF AGREEMENTS

In common law any agreement to compromise proceedings between the parties for which there has been proper consideration (that is, a payment or a promise to do, or not to do, something) will be binding and settle the claim. It is not, however, possible to contract out of statutory employment rights except through an ACAS agreement. It is only possible to contract out of statutory rights through ACAS, unless the agreement is made with the individual represented by a solicitor, is in writing, and complies with various other criteria (see below).

11.8   SCOPE OF AGREEMENT

An ACAS agreement can specify matters outside the jurisdiction of the tribunal (for instance, agreement to implement an equal opportunity policy). Those elements outside the express statutory jurisdiction of ACAS will have the same status as any other contractual agreement between parties and will be enforceable. If either party fails to comply with an ACAS agreement, conciliation agreement or a tribunal order, enforcement is through the county court.

11.9   ACAS AGREEMENTS BINDING

Once agreement has been arrived at using ACAS, it is final and cannot be reopened. The oral agreement of both parties to the ACAS officer is sufficient to conclude the process (*Gilbert v Kembridge Fibres [1984] ICR 188*). This is then confirmed on a form ACAS call the 'COT 3'. Such an agreement would only be set aside if the ACAS officer had acted in bad faith (*Slack v Greenham (Plant Hire) Ltd [1983] ICR 617*). Surprisingly, there is no requirement on the ACAS officer to apprise either side of the relevant statutory provisions, although as a matter of course he would usually do so.

Once a settlement is agreed through ACAS, the tribunal is notified, although as a matter of courtesy (particularly if a hearing date is imminent) the parties should also write to the tribunal informing it that agreement has been reached. After the COT 3 form has been signed, the tribunal formally records that the matter has been settled. In discrimination cases it can be important that the terms of the agreement remain confidential to the parties; equally, on occasion, one or both parties may be particularly anxious that the settlement is on the public record. Tribunal practice tends to vary and some publish the settlement schedule whilst others do not. If the terms of the agreement are (agreed) to be confidential, they should be set out on a separate schedule, the ACAS COT 3 recording: 'The parties having settled on terms agreed'. A party wishing a settlement to be public can ask the tribunal to set out the terms in full (so long as there is no confidentiality term) and can ask the ACAS officer to try to ensure that this happens. The terms of the settlement can be publicised unless there is an express agreement to the contrary.

As mentioned above, *RRA* or *SDA* proceedings do not actually have to be commenced for ACAS to be used to secure a binding agreement or for there to be a binding compromise agreement. A potential discrimination claim can also be resolved by agreement through ACAS. [*RRA s 55(2); SDA s 64(2)*]. The wording of such an agreement has to be precise as it will be restrictively construed. A tribunal (let alone ACAS at the time of the agreement) is going to be reluctant to prevent an individual from pursuing a claim beyond contemplation at the material time, although it may be theoretically possible to contract to do so.

11.10 CONTACTING ACAS

ACAS headquarters are at 27 Wilton Street, London SW1X 7AZ. Tel: 0171-210 3613. However, for enquiries, leaflets etc. a person should contact his or her regional office, as listed below.

Regional offices

Northern Region
Westgate House, Westgate Road, Newcastle-upon-Tyne NE1 1TJ
Tel: 0191-261 2191

Cumbria	Tyne and Wear	Cleveland
Northumberland	Durham	

Yorkshire and Humberside Region
Commerce House, St Albans Place, Leeds LS2 8HH
Tel: (0113) 2431371

North Yorkshire	South Yorkshire	Humberside
West Yorkshire		

London Region
Clifton House, 83-117 Euston Road, London NW1 2RB
Tel: 0171-388 5100

South East Region
Westminster House, 125 Fleet Road, Fleet, Hants GU13 8PD
Tel: (01252) 811868

Cambridgeshire	Hertfordshire	Hampshire
Norfolk	Essex	(except Ringwood)
Suffolk	Berkshire	Isle of Wight
Oxfordshire	Surrey	East Sussex
Buckinghamshire	Kent	West Sussex
Bedfordshire		

South West Region
Regent House, 27a Regent Street, Clifton, Bristol BS8 4HR
Tel: (0117) 974 4066

Gloucestershire	Cornwall	Dorset
Avon	Devon	Ringwood
Wiltshire	Somerset	

Midlands Region
Leonard House, 319 Bradford Street, Birmingham B5 6ET
Tel: (0121) 666 7576

Northamptonshire (except Corby)	Staffordshire (except Burton-on-Trent)	Hereford & Worcester
Shropshire	West Midlands	Warwickshire

11.11   Conciliation

Nottingham Office: Anderson House, Clinton Avenue, Nottingham NG5 1AW
Tel: (0115) 9693355

Derbyshire (except	Leicestershire	Lincolnshire
High Peak District)	Corby	Burton-on-Trent
Nottinghamshire		

North West Region
Boulton House, 17-21 Chorlton Street, Manchester M1 3HY
Tel: (0161) 228 3222

Lancashire	High Peak District	Greater Manchester
Cheshire	of Derbyshire	

Merseyside Office: Cressington House, 249 St Mary's Road, Garston, Liverpool
L19 0NF
Tel: (0151) 427 8881

Scotland
Franborough House, 123-157 Bothwell Street, Glasgow G2 7JR
Tel: (0141) 204 2677

Wales
3 Purbeck House, Lambourne Crescent, Llanishen, Cardiff CF4 5GJ
Tel: (01222) 761126

11.11 NON-ACAS CONCILIATION

Both the CRE and EOC have the power to assist in achieving settlements of tribunal proceedings or prospective proceedings [*SDA s 75(2)(b); RRA s 66(2)(b)*] but, oddly, settlements procured solely through their offices do not exclude the tribunal's jurisdiction and an ACAS COT 3 is still required. The CRE are understood to be seeking the power to conciliate.

The parties can negotiate a settlement between themselves without involving ACAS, or by private arbitration, but such a settlement will only prevent the individual from having his claim heard by the tribunal if the agreement complies with *section 39 TURERA 1993* (see 11.12 below).

A tribunal will take note of a settlement arrived at outside ACAS when considering a remedy, and the pursuit of a claim in the face of a reasonable settlement is a matter which a tribunal could take into account in considering whether or not to take the unusual step of awarding costs.

11.12 Under the *Trade Union Reform and Employment Rights Act 1993 (TURERA 1993), s 39*, it is possible for an agreement to be reached between parties in an industrial tribunal case without ACAS involvement. This is known as a compromise agreement, and serves to bind the parties so long as:

(*a*)   it is in writing;

(*b*)   it relates to the employee's particular complaint;

(*c*)   the employee has obtained independent legal advice from a qualified lawyer (solicitor or barrister) as to the terms and effect of the proposed agreement;

(*d*)   the adviser has a policy of insurance covering the risk of a claim by the employee in respect of loss arising from the advice;

(*e*)   the agreement identifies the employee's adviser; and

(*f*)   the agreement states that the conditions regulating such agreements under the relevant statute are satisfied.

As with COT 3 agreements, compromise agreements can also exclude an employee's rights to bring proceedings for matters not originally pursued in the industrial tribunal (such as equal pay, sex discrimination, wrongful dismissal).

Such agreements will be binding even before tribunal proceedings have commenced, so long as the above conditions are satisfied. As regards the 'policy of insurance' requirement for compromise agreements, there has been considerable debate as to whether this includes the protection given by the Solicitors' Indemnity Fund (SIF). The SIF is not, technically, a policy of insurance, and this raised doubts as to the binding nature of compromise agreements concluded after the individual had received advice from a solicitor. The Law Society obtained leading counsel's opinion, and also wrote to the Secretary of State for Employment requesting that the legislation be amended. The Secretary of State declined to introduce an amendment to the legislation but confirmed that the Government's intention had been that the SIF would be covered by the phrase 'policy of insurance'.

Although it is still possible that a tribunal could decide this point differently, the response from the Secretary of State is likely to be persuasive should this point ever be disputed.

11.13 NEGOTIATIONS

It is not possible to provide instructions on negotiations in a book like this. Suffice it to say that ACAS officers are used to any number of 'absolutely final' offers! It does help them in their job if one or other party provides a reasoned starting figure. In terms of resolving disputes, ACAS officers are amoral; their job is to secure a settlement and, if they have a reasoned proposal, they are more likely to work at securing agreement to it.

11.14 'WITHOUT PREJUDICE' CORRESPONDENCE

To avoid correspondence that deals with attempts to settle being referred to at the tribunal (where it might be seen to imply an admission of liability), the words 'without prejudice' should be set out boldly at the head of the letter. Such correspondence is not admissible by virtue of the ordinary rules of evidence. A tribunal will admit correspondence that is not properly 'without prejudice', so it is important to separate correspondence that is making an offer to settle litigation or potential litigation from that dealing with other matters, such as disputes of fact between the parties. This is perhaps best achieved by writing two separate letters, one 'without prejudice' dealing with settlement and one 'on the record' dealing with the facts.

12 Constructive Dismissal

12.1 DEFINITION

An employee can terminate his contract of employment if his employer is in 'repudiatory breach' which means, in essence, that the employer is in breach of a fundamental term of the contract (*Western Excavating (ECC) Ltd v Sharp [1978] ICR 221*).

Where an employee resigns (for example in a moment of anger), this may still amount to constructive dismissal – even where the employee's words or actions make it clear that he/she has resigned. An employer is under a duty to investigate the circumstances of the resignation to see if anything comes to light which casts doubt on the otherwise clear intention of the employee. The failure to do this could allow an industrial tribunal to disentitle an employer from relying on an employee's resignation, and result in a finding of unfair dismissal, as in *Kwik-Fit (GB) Ltd v Lineham [1992] ICR 183*.

12.2 DISCRIMINATION

If an employee is subjected to a work environment in which he is discriminated against or subjected to racial or sexual harassment to the extent that he can tolerate it no longer, he will have a claim for constructive dismissal (as well as for race or sex discrimination).

The fundamental breach is either of the obligation to provide a safe place of work or of the general requirement of trust and confidence to sustain an employment contract.

An employee who 'puts up' with a breach can be held to waive the breach and is not able to rely upon it if he attempts to do so some time after the event. An employee would not, for instance, be likely to sustain a claim for constructive dismissal in respect of a single incident of racial abuse after, say, a month's delay. A less serious repetition, or another incident of abuse that was not racial, could entitle the employee to treat matters as cumulative and rely on the original breach (see *Lewis v Motorworld Garages Ltd [1986] ICR 157* for a general approach to constructive dismissal, and *Bracebridge Engineering Ltd v Darby [1990] IRLR 3 (EAT)*).

12.3 APPROACH OF TRIBUNAL

As is always the case where a judgment of fact is required, much will depend on the assessment of those particular facts by the particular tribunal hearing the matter. A situation where, for example, a single unrepeated incident of harassment by a supervisor leads an employee to leave after some months, for fear (even if without foundation) of a repetition of the harassment, is unlikely to convince a tribunal that constructive dismissal has occurred, but it might do so. Such an example illustrates how difficult it is to give definitive advice when it is entirely a matter of judgment of fact for the particular tribunal (see *De Souza v Automobile Association [1986] ICR 514*, and HARASSMENT (34)).

12.4 EMPLOYEE RESPONSE

It is not a prerequisite for proving constructive dismissal that the employee leave without notice but, by virtue of the fact that there must have been a fundamental breach by the employer, it is likely. An employee might give notice of termination, setting out the discrimination complained of, and look to the employer to investigate and put matters right during the notice period. There remains doubt as to whether it is possible to 'cure' a fundamental breach, but if the employee accepts the continuation of the contract, he would have no claim in relation to dismissal. It is certainly not possible to 'cure' an act of discrimination. It has either happened or it has not. The subsequent conduct of the employer might well be a factor in assessing damages and would also be relevant in considering whether the employer should be held liable for unauthorised acts by another employee. [*RRA s 32; SDA s 41*].

12.5   GRIEVANCE PROCEDURE

The availability of a grievance procedure (particularly if clearly linked to an equal opportunity policy) will be something that the tribunal will look at. An employer could argue that there was no fundamental breach if an individual responsible for discriminatory conduct was acting 'on a frolic of his own' and, pursuant to the employment contract, the employer had an effective equal opportunity policy which provided (i) for that individual to be disciplined for such conduct, and (ii) for the availability of an accessible grievance procedure through which the employee could channel his complaint. In such circumstances the employer would be able to show that he had taken reasonable steps to prevent the discrimination taking place and would not be liable pursuant to the discrimination legislation (so long as the policy could be shown to be 'alive' and not just so many 'fine words').

The breach will, however, have taken place before the grievance procedure would be appropriate, and so failure to use the procedure is unlikely to prove fatal to an individual's claim. The first stage of many grievance procedures requires the individual to raise his complaint with his direct supervisor. In cases of harassment this is likely to be the harasser. It is therefore advisable for employers to allow for this first stage to be omitted in cases where discrimination of any kind is alleged.

12.6   CAUSE OF LEAVING

To be able to sustain a claim of unfair dismissal or wrongful dismissal, the employee must show that he has left because of the breach. For example, a female member of staff may have suffered sexual harassment from her senior officer but put up with it. She then obtains a higher paid appointment with a competitor and leaves. Whilst the reason she started seeking the position may have been the harassment, the reason she left was the offer of higher paid employment. She would, of course, still be able to claim for injury to feelings pursuant to the *SDA* in relation to the harassment.

Walking off the job is an extreme measure for an employee to take and full of risk. The burden of proof is upon the employee to show that he was 'dismissed' and he is, almost by definition, likely to have financial difficulties and will not have received notice pay.

12.7   WHAT AN EMPLOYER SHOULD DO

On occasion, an employee will give no indication to his employer of any underlying problem at the time of leaving, and will leave without specifying a reason. For this reason it is good practice to have a 'leaver's debriefing form' or an 'exit interview'. This is a practice adopted by many employers and can provide useful data to flesh out and explain staff turnover figures. Ideally, a meeting should be held and reasons for leaving probed, but otherwise a standard form can be used. This is particularly useful where an employee has either phoned or written, ending his employment without notice. The failure of the employee to respond to such a form at all, or a response which fails to set out the adverse circumstances later alleged, will (subject to the other information available and procedures generally adopted) provide the basis for a 'reasonably practical steps' defence to any discrimination claim and will be taken into account by a tribunal assessing the real reason for the termination of the employment.

If an employee sets out an allegation of harassment in the letter of resignation, it is advisable to hold an immediate preliminary investigation to establish whether disciplinary action needs to be taken, or whether some other procedure is genuinely effective. The employee should be informed in writing that this step is being taken. The employee should certainly be invited to withdraw his resignation, invited to use the grievance procedure and asked to co-operate in providing information for the preliminary investigation.

If this is a case of a 'rogue' employee 'trying it on', then there should be a disciplinary history on which the employer can rely in subsequently terminating the employment in the normal way. If, after a thorough investigation, it is concluded that there is no foundation to the allegations *and* that those allegations were malicious and not made in good faith, then after a proper disciplinary hearing, it would not be unfair, or constitute victimisation pursuant to the *RRA* or *SDA*, to dismiss the employee. Those disciplinary proceedings must, however, examine the question of motivation. It will be victimisation of an employee to dismiss him in effect for having made a complaint of discrimination in good faith. This can provide difficulties.

Employees can make apparently ludicrous allegations which are unsupportable by the facts, but make them in good faith from a complete misreading of those facts. For example, in one tribunal case (*D'Ettore v Trust House Forte, unreported*), an employee alleged that he was being discriminated against on racial grounds in respect of his pay because of his race. There was no substance in the suggestion and this employee had tended to be 'awkward' in other ways. This was the last straw and he was dismissed, this being recorded on his personnel file as 'dismissed for accusing his manager of discrimination'. The tribunal decided that the accusation had been made by the employee in good faith and that he had been victimised. He won his case.

The nature of the allegations will determine whether or not it is appropriate for the employee to return to work. If serious allegations of sexual harassment have been made, the alleged perpetrator should, in any event, have been suspended pending the investigation and possible disciplinary action. If that suspension has taken place, it would be appropriate to ask the individual making the allegations to return to work; in other circumstances it may be more appropriate to invite him to remain at home on full pay. If possible, such steps should be agreed.

Once the facts are established, if appropriate, a disciplinary hearing should be convened in respect of the discriminator, and the individual's grievance hearing should also be convened. If the grievance is upheld, normally all an employer is going to be able to offer the aggrieved employee is vindication.

Depending on the particular facts, upholding a grievance may also involve a conclusion that the individual has suffered discrimination, which conclusion could be taken into account in the tribunal (and lead to a requirement of admissions in that forum if proceedings are subsequently brought). It may be, however, that the grievance will reveal a failure to follow procedures or obey instructions that, whilst not relating to discrimination, warrant upholding the grievance and taking disciplinary action in respect of the perpetrator.

If the grievance is not upheld, this may not satisfy the individual, but the employer will be well placed to resist any tribunal application. The investigation process and the resultant 'messages' which that process conveys to staff may, however, satisfy the individual.

12.8 PAYMENT OF COMPENSATION

Payment of compensation can be made without the involvement of ACAS as long as a compromise agreement satisfying the conditions laid out in *TURERA 1993, s 39* is reached (see CONCILIATION (11)).

13   Contract Compliance

13.1   BACKGROUND

In the late 1970s, there was a growing practice among local authorities to do business with only those companies who satisfied them that they complied with their particular standards of equal opportunity policy. One of the problems with this was that each local authority had its own particular requirements, and, more importantly, its own particular forms to complete and bureaucratic procedures to go through. In response to this situation, and perhaps for political reasons of its own, the Government made contract compliance (by local authorities, health authorities and other statutory bodies) largely unlawful. [*Local Government Act 1988 (LGA)*].

13.2   CONTRACT COMPLIANCE GENERALLY UNLAWFUL

Except for the valid questions set out in 13.3 below, contract compliance is now unlawful and local authorities and similar statutory bodies are no longer permitted to take into account 'non-commercial matters' in awarding contracts, drawing up lists of contractors etc. and a company will be able to apply for judicial review to set aside any such action by a local authority as unlawful.

13.3   VALID QUESTIONS PURSUANT TO *LGA*

Such bodies are, however, able to ask limited questions in respect of health and safety compliance, backgrounds of individual staff where child care or similar matters are involved and a limited number of questions in regard to equal opportunity and race relations. The authority is expressly limited in the questions that can be asked and cannot ask further questions about, for example, proportions of ethnic minority staff. The following questions may be asked of a contractor or potential contractor for inclusion on an approved list [*LGA s 18(5); DoE circular 8/88*]:

'1.   Is it your policy as an employer to comply with your statutory obligations under the *Race Relations Act 1976* and accordingly, your practice not to treat one group of people less favourably than others because of their colour, race, nationality or ethnic origin in relation to decisions to recruit, train or promote employees?

2.   In the last three years, has any finding of unlawful racial discrimination been made against your organisation by any court or industrial tribunal?

3.   In the last three years, has your organisation been the subject of formal investigation by the Commission for Racial Equality on grounds of alleged unlawful discrimination?

If the answer to question 2 is in the affirmative or, in relation to question 3, the Commission made a finding adverse to your organisation:

4.   What steps did you take in consequence of that finding?

5.   Is your policy on race relations set out

   (*a*)   in instructions to those concerned with recruitment, training and promotion;

(*b*)   in documents available to employees, recognised trade unions or other representative groups of employees;

(*c*)   in recruitment advertisements or other literature?

6.   Do you observe as far as possible the Commission for Racial Equality's Code of Practice for Employment, as approved by Parliament in 1983, which gives practical guidance to employers and others on the elimination of racial discrimination and the promotion of equality of opportunity in employment, including the steps that can be taken to encourage members of the ethnic minorities to apply for jobs or take up training opportunities?

Description of evidence

In relation to question 5: examples of the instructions, documents, recruitment advertisements or other literature.'

13.4   APPLICATION OF *LGA*

The *LGA* applies to a limited number of public bodies. [*LGA 2 Sch*]. It includes all local authorities, police authorities, education committees and the like. It does not extend to government departments.

13.5   CONSEQUENCE

A local authority, or other relevant statutory body, can decline to contract with a company not satisfying the authority or body in respect of its answers to these questions (subject to the overriding requirement for the authority or body to behave administratively fairly). This is obviously a serious consequence of the company losing an industrial tribunal case pursuant to the *RRA*. The authority is required to give the contractor a reason for refusal to include him on an approved list or for taking similar action. [*LGA s 20*].

13.6   QUESTIONS RELATING TO *SDA* UNLAWFUL

Surprisingly, the Equal Opportunities Commission did not press for the inclusion of similar provisions relating to sex discrimination, as the CRE did for race discrimination, during the passage of the *LGA*. As a result no provision was made. Islington London Borough Council framed a requirement after the enactment of the *LGA* obliging employers to observe the minimum standards required by the *SDA*, and to provide information and documentation to enable the Council to satisfy itself that they were doing so. The Divisional Court found the provision to be unlawful and granted an application for judicial review by the Building Employers Federation (*R v London Borough of Islington, ex parte Building Employers Federation, [1989] IRLR 382*). It may be that the EOC will lobby for an amendment to the Act to put equal opportunities regarding sex on an equal footing with those regarding race. There does not seem to be any logical reason why this should not be the case.

13.7   ETHICAL INVESTMENT BY NON-SPECIFIED BODIES

There is no statutory prohibition on non-specified bodies from operating some form of 'contract compliance' so long as they do not act *ultra vires* by so doing. Certain 'ethical' investment funds set out to satisfy themselves that companies in

13.7   Contract Compliance

which investors' funds are allocated are equal opportunity employers. There is no obligation to answer questionnaires associated with these funds; the only consequence is that such funds will not invest in companies that do not satisfy them that the relevant criteria are met by answering the questions. Equally any 'consumer' company, charity or association could specify that it will not purchase services or goods from any company not satisfying certain equal opportunity criteria, so long as such action did not contravene other objects and duties (for instance, so long as such a policy cannot be shown to be a drain on charitable funds).

14   Contract Workers

14.1   DEFINITION

A contract worker is defined as an individual doing any work for another, a 'principal', where he is not employed by the principal himself but is working for someone else who has a contract with the principal to carry out that work. The provision logically extends through subcontractors.

14.2   SCOPE

For the purposes of both the *Race Relations Act 1976* and the *Sex Discrimination Act 1975*, contract workers have substantially the same protection against the individual contracting their work as if they were directly employed. They are protected in the normal way from unlawful treatment by their direct employer. [*RRA s 7; SDA s 9*].

It is unlawful for the principal to discriminate against a contract worker:

(*a*)   in the terms on which he allows him to do the work, or

(*b*)   by not allowing him to continue with the work, or

(*c*)   in the way he affords him access to any benefits or facilities or services, or deliberately refusing or omitting to afford access, or

(*d*)   by subjecting him to any other detriment.

14.3   DIRECT DISCRIMINATION

A female or ethnic minority contract worker is protected by these provisions from being singled out on racial or sexual grounds by the principal. For instance, where an individual in a contract team is singled out for, say, disciplinary action at the behest of the principal, the consideration of the case will be as if the principal and the employer were both employing the individual. A deliberate policy to employ women or ethnic minority individuals only by way of subcontract status would be unlawful.

In the case of *BP Chemicals Limited v Gillick and Roevin Management Services Limited* [*1995*] *IRLR 128*, the EAT held that a contract worker was entitled to bring proceedings under *SDA s 9* when she had not been permitted to return to work after maternity leave, where she worked as a project account assistant for BP, and was paid by an employment agency, Roevin Management Services Limited.

14.4   INDIRECT DISCRIMINATION

It is possible that the provisions referred to above also permit comparison with directly employed staff, thereby making an employer vulnerable to claims of indirect discrimination in relation to differential terms for contract workers compared with direct staff. The *Equal Pay Act 1970* expressly requires comparison with persons in the same employment [*EqPA 1970, s 1(2)*] but the *SDA* and *RRA* are silent on this point. The matter at issue would be the appropriate pool for consideration (to compare subcontract staff with other

14.5   Contract Workers

subcontract staff or to compare them with directly employed staff). If the individual was able to satisfy the tribunal that comparison with directly employed staff was legitimate, then the next issue would be whether it was justified on economic grounds (see INDIRECT DISCRIMINATION (36)). The problem is particularly cogent in respect of subcontract cleaning and similar work where it may be that a predominance of female staff are employed with an element of dictation in the terms of employment by the principal, where those terms are considerably less favourable than those of directly employed staff. Employers would, therefore, be well advised to avoid dictating the detail of wages and similar terms upon which subcontractor staff are employed.

14.5   PRESSURE TO DISCRIMINATE

Any instruction or pressure by a principal on a subcontractor to discriminate against one of his staff is unlawful. (See PRESSURE TO DISCRIMINATE (45).)

14.6   Liability of principal

If an employee can show that a principal pressurised his employer into discriminating against him, or was knowingly involved in discriminating against him, the principal will also be liable for the discrimination by the employer. [*RRA ss 32, 33; SDA ss 41, 42*].

15   Contracts of Employment

15.1   DISCRIMINATORY TERMS

It is unlawful to offer discriminatory terms of employment on grounds of either race [*RRA s 4(2)*] or sex [*SDA s 6(2)*], or to pay women less than men for similar or equal value work. [*EqPA s 1(1)*].

15.2   ORDINARY LAW

TURERA 1993 introduced new requirements in relation to employees' rights to receive a statement of the main terms and conditions of their employment as follows:

All employees (save those who are employed for less than one month) are entitled to a written statement of the terms and conditions of their employment within two calendar months of the commencement of their employment. Certain particulars must all be contained in one document, known as the 'principal statement', and these particulars are:

(*a*)   the names of the parties;

(*b*)   the date the employee's employment began;

(*c*)   the date the employee's period of continuous employment began;

(*d*)   the scale or rate of remuneration or the method of calculating it;

(*e*)   the intervals at which remuneration is paid;

(*f*)   the terms and conditions relating to the hours of work;

(*g*)   the terms and conditions relating to holidays, including holiday pay;

(*h*)   the employees's job title and/or a brief description of his work; and

(*i*)   the employee's place of work, or an indication of the places where the employer may reasonably expect the employee to work.

Certain other particulars must also be given to an employee, but these need not be in the 'principal statement'. They include: the period for which the employment is expected to continue (if it is not permanent), or the date it is to end; any collective agreements which affect the terms and conditions of employment; details of the grievance and disciplinary procedure; details of any pension (and particulars of that pension); and also whether the employee is likely to be required to work outside the UK for more than one month (if so, details of this).

Under the new provisions, there is only limited scope for employers to make reference to terms and conditions contained in other documents, such as details relating to sickness and sick pay, pension schemes, statutory notice periods, notice periods in collective agreements, and details of disciplinary procedures.

15.3   RIGHT TO A CONTRACT

All employees, save those who are employed for less than one month, are entitled to a statement of the main terms and conditions of employment within two months of the start of their employment. This will effectively constitute the employees' contract of employment. The contract will eliminate areas of doubt that would otherwise have to be determined upon the basis of a finding of custom and practice.

15.4   TERMS OF CONTRACT

The contract of employment is not limited to these 'required' matters and should also refer to all other material terms governing the employment relationship, for instance the right to search employees, confidentiality etc., and to the employer's equal opportunity policy. There is no requirement for all terms to be written. Some are generally implied (the employee's duty of fidelity, for example) and others may be determined by custom and practice.

In the case of *Meade-Hill v The British Council [1995] IRLR 478*, the Court of Appeal held that the inclusion of a mobility clause in a contract of employment can constitute indirect discrimination, and is unenforceable unless it can be objectively justified. Mrs Meade-Hill was a Grade G employee of the British Council. When she was promoted to Grade G, her contract of employment was varied with her agreement to incorporate a mobility clause. The British Council was considering moving its head office from London to Manchester, and indicated that it might be necessary to invoke the mobility clause. Mrs Meade-Hill's husband was based in London and earned considerably more than she did, and she claimed it would be very difficult for him to earn an equivalent income if the mobility clause was invoked and he was required to move with her. In the event, The British Council did not invoke the mobility clause against Mrs Meade-Hill, however, by this stage she had commenced county court proceedings for a declaration under *SDA s 77(2)* that the mobility clause was unenforceable as it was indirectly discriminatory.

Mrs Meade-Hill argued that the mobility clause was to her detriment because she was a secondary wage earner. She argued that a greater proportion of women were the secondary wage earners in a family unit and unable to comply with such a clause. The employers argued that they had not applied a requirement to Mrs Meade-Hill because she had not actually been required to re-locate. If at some point in the future she was required to relocate, then at this stage it should be determined whether she was able to comply with the clause.

The Court of Appeal rejected the employer's arguments. Mrs Meade-Hill was complaining about the requirement that she must work wherever her employer requested, and as a married woman and secondary wage earner she was not able to comply with this requirement. Under *SDA s 77(5)*, employees are able to obtain removal or modification of discriminatory terms of employment, without having to wait until that term is enforced against them. Therefore, the mobility clause in Mrs Meade-Hill's contract was a matter of general application from the moment that she signed the contract, and it was sufficient for her to be able to show that the clause could potentially operate as a requirement with which she was unable to comply.

This decision does not prevent employers using contractual mobility clauses, however, employees are now able to have such a clause struck out on the grounds that it is indirectly discriminatory. An employer must be able to show that a mobility clause is objectively justified on grounds not related to the employee's sex. This can be achieved by redrafting mobility clauses to confirm that where the employee is not practically able to comply with an employer's use. of the mobility clause, then the clause will not be invoked, or by stating that the personal circumstances of each employee will be taken into account by the employer determining whether to invoke such a mobility clause.

15.5 TERMS VARIED BY STATUTE

There are a number of instances where statutory provisions override, or imply terms into, an employment contract, for example statutory minimum notice. Two such instances, which relate to equal opportunity and discrimination respectively, are dealt with below.

15.6 Equality clauses

Every employment contract is deemed to include an 'equality clause', if such a clause is not already set out, giving women equal pay with men for like work, equivalent work and work of equal value. This 'statutory' clause extends to benefits as well as pay. Because it is deemed to have altered the contract from its inception, this is a far-reaching provision. [*EqPA s 1(1)*]. This is dealt with in full in EQUAL PAY (29).

15.7 Void and unenforceable terms under RRA and SDA

(*a*)   Any contractual clause purporting to exclude, or limit, the ambit of the *RRA, SDA* or *EqPA* (except any contract made with the assistance of an ACAS officer for the purpose of settling a complaint) is unenforceable by any person in whose favour the clause would operate. [*RRA s 72(3); SDA s 77(3)*].

(*b*)   Any contractual clause –

　　(i)   the inclusion of which renders the making of the contract unlawful by virtue of the *RRA* or *SDA*; or

　　(ii)   which is included to further an act or omission rendered unlawful by the *RRA* or *SDA*; or

　　(iii)   which provides for an act or omission so rendered unlawful,

is void. [*RRA s 72(1); SDA s 77(1)*]. Thus, a term in a contract for a club 'bouncer' requiring him to permit only ten black people into the club on any one night would be void.

(*c*)   However, (*b*) above does not apply to a contractual clause the inclusion of which constitutes, or is in furtherance of, or provides for, unlawful discrimination against a party to the contract (e.g. a term in a female employee's contract limiting access to the works' sports facilities to men), but any such clause is unenforceable against that party. [*RRA s 72(2); SDA s 77(2)*].

15.8 ENFORCEMENT

A purported term of the contract which is void will simply not be part of the contract at all. A contractual term which is unenforceable against a party to it will usually remain part of the contract. However, in respect of a contract to which 15.7(*c*) above applies, any individual 'interested' in such a contract may apply to the county court for an order removing or modifying any term which

15.8   Contracts of Employment

constitutes, is in furtherance of, or provides for unlawful discrimination. There are safeguards to ensure that before any such order is made, all persons affected are given notice of the application and have the opportunity to make representations to the court. [*RRA s 72(4); SDA s 77(4)*].

Alternatively, in appropriate circumstances, an individual might commence proceedings under the *RRA, SDA* or *EqPA* on the basis of an individual complaint.

16 Courts

16.1 MAIN FORUM

The primary forum for the resolution of employment-related discrimination claims is the industrial tribunal. [*RRA s 54; SDA s 63; Disability Discrimination Act, s 8*].

16.2 THE INDUSTRIAL TRIBUNAL

The industrial tribunal deals with the following.

1. Equal pay claims.

2. Racial discrimination and sex discrimination claims relating to:

   (*a*) appointment (including complaints about appointment procedures and arrangements);

   (*b*) the employment contract in every aspect, its terms and conditions including pay and benefits;

   (*c*) complaints by contract workers;

   (*d*) complaints against trade unions in respect of terms of membership benefits etc.;

   (*e*) complaints against qualifying bodies;

   (*f*) complaints against employment agencies;

   (*g*) complaints against partnerships about the granting of partnership, the terms etc.;

   (*h*) appeals against non-discrimination notices that relate to employment matters; and

   (*i*) counterclaims by employers arising out of the employment contract (but only where the employee has brought proceedings in the tribunal for breach of contract).

3. Claims under the *Disability Discrimination Act* relating to:

   (*a*) appointment;

   (*b*) the employment contract.

Industrial tribunals now also have jurisdiction to deal with claims arising from breaches of contract, under the *Industrial Tribunals Extension of Jurisdiction (England and Wales) Order 1994 (SI 1994 No 1623)* (there are similar regulations in respect of Scotland). This jurisdiction is limited to damages for breach of an employment contract or other connected contracts and sums due in pursuance of such a contract, up to a maximum of £25,000.

(See TRIBUNALS (53).)

16.3 THE COUNTY COURT

The county court deals with all claims brought within the scope of the *RRA*, *SDA* and *Disability Discrimination Act* not within the jurisdiction of the tribunal. *[RRA s 57; SDA s 66; DDA s 22]*. The general rule is that the industrial tribunal deals with discrimination in all matters connected with the employment relationship and the county court deals with discrimination in other fields, for example service provision, education and housing. The county court also has the power to remove or vary a clause in a contract which furthers unlawful discrimination. *[RRA s 72(5); SDA s 77(5); DDA s 23]*. (See CONTRACTS OF EMPLOYMENT (15).) Proceedings under either Act can only be commenced in a *designated* county court. *[RRA s 57; SDA s 66]*.

The time limit for commencing proceedings in the county court is six months from the date of the act complained of. *[RRA s 68; SDA s 76]*.

16.4 EMPLOYMENT APPEAL TRIBUNAL

The Employment Appeal Tribunal deals with all appeals from industrial tribunal decisions. It has the same powers as the industrial tribunal. It may make any order that the industrial tribunal could have made, and may substitute its own order for that of the tribunal. (See APPEALS (5).)

16.5 COURT OF APPEAL

The Court of Appeal hears appeals from decisions of the EAT. Leave to appeal must be obtained either from the EAT or, if that is refused, from the Court of Appeal itself. There is a short time limit of 28 days from the date of judgment for registering an appeal to the Court of Appeal.

16.6 HOUSE OF LORDS

A further appeal from the Court of Appeal lies to the House of Lords (in exceptional cases it is possible to 'leapfrog' the Court of Appeal and go straight to the House of Lords from the EAT). Leave to appeal to the House of Lords must be obtained from the Court of Appeal or from the House of Lords itself.

16.7 EUROPEAN COURT OF JUSTICE

A matter can be referred to the European Court of Justice (ECJ) at any stage if a court (including a tribunal) considers that there is a matter raising a question of the application of the EC Treaty or an EC Directive. The ECJ is also in effect the final appeal court and has superior jurisdiction to the House of Lords.

16.8 PRECEDENT

An industrial tribunal decision does not bind any other tribunal on a point of law. Such a decision may be cited, however, and taken into account by another tribunal. Legal authorities are known as 'precedents' or 'authority'. Tribunals are bound by precedents from the EAT, Court of Appeal, House of Lords and ECJ. The EAT is bound by precedent from the Court of Appeal, the Court of Appeal by the House of Lords and so on. Sometimes a decision of the EAT may still contain findings of law that are good authority even though the case was ultimately determined by the House of Lords, as the appeal may have raised more than one point of law, only one of which was appealed beyond the EAT. The point of law not appealed remains good authority.

Almost all decisions of any consequence affecting discrimination are reported in the Industrial Relations Law Reports (IRLR), The Equal Opportunity Review

(EOR) or the Industrial Cases Reports (ICR). These are published monthly and then compiled into annual volumes. The reference is by the year, the report and the page number. For example, the case of *Owen & Briggs v James* was decided in the Court of Appeal in 1982 and before that in the EAT in 1981. It was reported in both sets of reports. In the Court of Appeal the references are *[1982] ICR 618* (page 618 of the 1982 volume of ICR), *[1982] IRLR 502* and in the EAT *[1981] ICR 377*, *[1981] IRLR 133*. In this particular case, the Court of Appeal merely affirmed the decision of the EAT and the important judgment is that of the EAT.

Cases may also be reported in the mainstream law reports such as the All England Reports (All ER or AER) or Weekly Law Reports (WLR), but any such decision will almost certainly have been reported in the specialist industrial reports. The CRE has produced a set of reports but these are largely summaries. Some unreported cases are mentioned in journals and it is possible to obtain the transcripts of unreported cases from the computer retrieval system LEXIS which is run by the legal publishers Butterworths.

As a last point on the subject, bear in mind that tribunals are wary of having too much law argued before them and they prefer to look at the facts, which is the function for which they are best suited.

17   Direct Discrimination

17.1   INTRODUCTION

Direct discrimination is the most straightforward type of discrimination. It is discrimination as commonly understood where a person is treated differently by reason of his race, sex or marital status. There is a mistaken belief that it is necessary to show an unlawful 'motive' for an action to constitute direct discrimination. It is possible to discriminate on racial and sexual grounds even if that is not the motivation for the treatment. The important fact is what, subjectively, is the reason for the treatment and if this relates to the sex or race of the individual, then it will be directly discriminatory (*James v Eastleigh Borough Council [1990] ICR 554*). (See also INDIRECT DISCRIMINATION (36).)

17.2   REASON FOR TREATMENT

In fact, it is the reason for the treatment that matters rather than the motive. This distinction is illustrated by the House of Lords in *James v Eastleigh Borough Council [1990] ICR 554*. The local authority set different age limits for men and women for concessionary rates at the swimming pool and other local amenities. It was established that their motive for doing this was not related to sex but to providing subsidies to meet perceived needs. It was administratively convenient to relate this to statutory pensionable age. The House of Lords concluded, however, (by a majority) that the reason for the treatment was the sex of the applicant and that he therefore had a legitimate claim. (See also *R v Birmingham City Council, ex parte EOC [1989] IRLR 173*.)

17.3   FEAR OF PREJUDICE IN OTHERS

It will also constitute direct discrimination if an action is caused by fear of prejudice in others, for instance declining to appoint an individual for fear of racially motivated unrest (*R v CRE, ex parte Westminster City Council [1985] ICR 827*) or dismissal of an individual because of a refusal to accept discriminatory instructions (*Zarczynska v Levy [1979] ICR 184*).

Motive may be relevant in that it will usually be a guide to the reason for any particular treatment.

17.4   SUBCONSCIOUS DISCRIMINATION

The courts have also recognised the concept of subconscious direct discrimination (*West Midlands Passenger Transport Executive v Singh [1988] ICR 614; British Gas v Sharma [1991] IRLR 101*). It is possible for an individual to exercise subconscious prejudices because of his upbringing and perceptions without his being aware of the fact. It is for this reason that training in interview techniques and the effect of stereotypes is so important. There is a significant difference between a situation where an individual has discriminated directly on grounds of racial or sexual malice and one where the individual has been unaware of stereotyping assumptions that he is making which lead him to discriminate. The latter is capable of cure by appropriate training; the former only by fear of penalty. Such assumptions might include discounting employment experience in other countries, or making assumptions about racial or sexual characteristics – perhaps assuming that a woman would not be assertive, for example.

17.5 OTHER MOTIVES

Sex or race need only be part of the reason for the relevant treatment; so long as it is a substantial part, the complaint will succeed. The fact that other, legitimate, motivations or reasons may have also contributed to the treatment complained of is not a bar to a finding of direct discrimination (*Owen & Briggs v James [1982] ICR 618*).

17.6 BURDEN OF PROOF

In the area of burden of proof for direct discrimination, following the Court of Appeal decision in *King v Great Britain–China Centre [1991] IRLR 513* the burden of proof has altered (although not shifted) in that once the individual complaining of discrimination has established the *prima facie* case, then a tribunal is entitled to look to the employer for an explanation for the alleged discriminatory acts. If no explanation is forthcoming, or an unsatisfactory explanation is provided, then the tribunal is entitled to infer that the discrimination did in fact take place. Therefore, the burden of proof has not been reversed – rather, it involves a balancing of factors for and against the finding of unlawful discrimination. (See BURDEN OF PROOF (6).)

17.7 GENERAL

The Sex Discrimination and Equal Pay (Remedies) Regulations 1993 (SI 1993 No 2798) removed the upper limit on an industrial tribunal's powers to award compensation in sex discrimination cases. These regulations were a direct result of the ECJ decision in *Marshall v Southampton and South West Hampshire Area Health Authority (No 2) [1993] IRLR 445*. An industrial tribunal is now entitled to include interest on an award of compensation, which runs from the mid-point date between the beginning of the discriminatory act complained of and the hearing date.

18 Disability

18.1 THE LAW

Before 1995, there was no specific prohibition against discrimination in respect of disabled persons, with the exception of the *Disabled Persons (Employment) Act 1944*, which required all employers with more than 20 employees to keep a quota of registered disabled people and ensure that at least 3% of their employees were registered disabled. In addition, disabled employees (like all employees) were protected under the *EPCA* against unfair dismissal so long as they had the requisite period of service. In 1993 the House of Lords passed the Civil Rights (Disabled Persons) Bill, however, Government pressure resulted in this failing to be passed by the House of Commons – the principal Government objection being the cost of implementing the proposal (estimated at £17.5 billion).

18.2 THE NEW LEGISLATION – UNCERTAINTY

In the Budget of November 1994, the Government announced that it would introduce legislation to protect disabled people against discrimination in the workplace. Mr William Hague, then the Minister for the Disabled, stated that the existing quota system would be abolished. The Disability Discrimination Bill was issued in January 1995, and this chapter is written as though the terms of this Bill have become law. The Bill had passed through Parliament's committee stages at the time of writing, and was expected to receive its third (and final) reading in the House of Lords on 24 October 1995, after Parliament reconvened following the summer recess. It is anticipated that the Bill will receive the Royal Assent before the end of 1995.

The Bill contains many new concepts. It is drafted so as to leave many of the provisions to be implemented by a series of Regulations, which are yet to be published. This chapter can do no more than set out the structure of the legislation. What is clear is that the Bill is a major advancement for equal opportunities issues, and it is a clear indication of the importance of equal opportunities on the political and social agenda. However, for employers, service providers, trade organisations, and persons responsible for dealing with interests in property, the provisions of the Bill are likely to require considerable adjustment and prior planning. It is almost inevitable that judicial clarification of many aspects of the new legislation will be required.

18.3 DEFINITION OF 'DISABLED'

Section 1(1) of the *Disability Discrimination Act* states that a person has a disability 'if he has a physical or mental impairment which has a substantial and long-term adverse effect on his ability to carry out normal day-to-day activities'. This includes progressive conditions, such as multiple sclerosis and cancer, where the condition is expected to have a substantial effect on the person's ability to carry out day-to-day activities in the future. However, people who have a recurring condition, i.e. which affects the person only briefly but which is nevertheless debilitating, such as severe hay fever, will not come under the *Act*.

People who were registered under the *1944 Act* will automatically come under the ambit of the *1995 Act*, so there will be no loss of rights that they previously held.

In relation to employment, goods, facilities and services the definition of disability includes people who have had a history of disability but may have recovered.

In *Schedule 1* of the *Disability Discrimination Act*, 'mental impairment' is deemed to include an impairment resulting from a mental illness but only if it is a clinically recognised illness. A 'long-term effect' must last or be reasonably expected to last for at least 12 months. Severe disfigurements, such as loss of limbs are also covered by the Act.

An individual does not lose his or her rights under the Act just because the condition is being controlled by medication. For example, an epileptic whose condition is being controlled by a course of medication will be covered by the Act. An exception is people who have problems with eyesight but circumvent this by the use of spectacles and lenses.

An impairment is taken to affect normal day-to-day activity if it affects one (or more) of the following:

(*a*)   mobility;

(*b*)   manual dexterity;

(*c*)   physical co-ordination;

(*d*)   continence;

(*e*)   ability to lift, carry or otherwise move everyday objects;

(*f*)   speech, hearing or eyesight;

(*g*)   memory or ability to learn or understand; or

(*h*)   perception of the risk of physical danger.

18.4   SCOPE OF THE DISABILITY DISCRIMINATION ACT

Section 4 of the *Disability Discrimination Act* makes discrimination against disabled people unlawful as regards employees and job applicants. This includes discrimination in the terms of employment offered to disabled persons, promotion opportunities, and dismissal or any other detriment.

'Discrimination' for the purposes of the *Disability Discrimination Act* is less favourable treatment which relates to the disabled person's disability, which the employer is unable to show is justified. This is different from the *SDA* and *RRA* in that discrimination against disabled persons is not sub-divided into direct or indirect discrimination – there is only one type: treatment which is less favourable than that which would be given to people without such a disability.

If a person imposes a condition or requirement which has the effect of excluding a disabled person, then this will fall into the definition of 'discrimination'. If the employer is unable to justify his actions under *section 5* of the *Act* (see below), then the disabled person will be able to seek compensation for discrimination contrary to the *Act*.

18.5   JUSTIFICATION – SECTION 5

An employer can show that discriminatory treatment of a disabled person is justified if and only if the reason for the treatment of the disabled person is both 'material' and 'substantial' to the circumstances of the case. Regulations have yet to be put into effect which will expand on what constitutes material and substantial.

18.6 Disability

This definition is different from the definition of justification in the *SDA* or *RRA*. Under these *Acts* justification can be on any objective grounds so long as they are not related to sex or race.

18.6 DUTY OF EMPLOYER TO MAKE ADJUSTMENTS

Where the disabled person is at a disadvantage compared to people who are not disabled, *section 6* of the *Disability Discrimination Act* obliges employers to take reasonable steps to prevent arrangements or features at the workplace having such an effect. This section relates to the employer's arrangements for the selection of potential employees, as well as to any terms, conditions or arrangements relating to promotion, transfer, training or any other benefit by the employer.

This *section* applies to employees, applicants and potential applicants for employment who are disabled persons.

Examples of reasonable adjustment are given in *section 6(3)*:

(*a*)   making adjustments to premises;

(*b*)   allocating some of the disabled person's duties to another person;

(*c*)   transferring the disabled person to fill another vacancy;

(*d*)   altering work hours;

(*e*)   assigning him to a different place of work;

(*f*)   allowing the person to be absent during work hours for rehabilitation, assessment or treatment;

(*g*)   giving him, or arranging for him to be given training;

(*h*)   acquiring or modifying equipment;

(*i*)   modifying instructions or reference manuals;

(*j*)   modifying procedures for testing or assessment;

(*k*)   providing a reader or interpreter;

(*l*)   providing supervision.

The *Act* states that the nature of the considerations which should be taken into account in determining whether or not it is reasonable for an employer to take any of the above steps include:

(i)   the extent to which taking the step would prevent the effect in question;

(ii)   the extent to which it is practicable for the employer to take the step;

(iii) the financial and other costs that would be involved in taking the step and the extent to which taking it would disrupt any of the employer's activities;

(iv)   the extent of the employers financial and other resources;

(v)   the availability to the employer of financial or other assistance in taking the step.

Where the employer fails to comply with any duty in relation to a disabled person imposed by *section 6*, *section 4* contains a presumption that less favourable treatment has taken place. It is possible for the employer to justify his failure to comply with a duty on the grounds that even if he had made the necessary adjustment, then he would still be justified in treating the disabled person less favourably than he would have treated someone without such a disability.

18.7   SMALL BUSINESS EXEMPTION

The employment discrimination-related provisions of the *Disability Discrimination Act* do not apply to employers with fewer than 20 employees (*section 7*). This provision has caused much controversy in light of the fact that small employers employ more than a third of the total workforce.

The reasoning behind this provision is that the costs to each employer of making such adjustments would be disproportionate in comparison with the number of employees involved.

The number can be altered (downwards) by application to the Secretary of State. Therefore, no employer with more than 20 employees can ever escape the duty to make reasonable adjustments.

The problem with exempting such employers is that they will continue to move in and out of the jurisdiction of the *Act* depending on the number of employees at any one time. It is as yet unclear whether employees of associated offices are to be included in the number of employees, or whether employees of the same employer, but working at different places of work, will be included. However, these matters should be clarified in Regulations that will bring most of the *Act* into force, and in any areas of doubt a tribunal will almost certainly decide in favour of the individual.

Whilst 'employer' is not defined, this *section 7* is an exemption and will, therefore, be construed tightly. In the absence of any provision regarding different establishments of the same employer, this exemption should be taken to relate to the total number of employees in the UK (full-time or part-time), although this section may be subject to further clarification.

18.8   DISABLED PERSONS' REMEDIES

The *Disability Discrimination Act* makes provision for a disabled person to present an application to an industrial tribunal on the grounds that he has been discriminated against. The burden of proof lies with the individual and, therefore, the *Disability Discrimination Act* is the same as the *SDA* and *RRA* in this respect (see BURDEN OF PROOF (6).)

Where the claim is well-founded, the tribunal has the power to make a declaration as to the disabled person's rights, and order the employer to pay compensation. The tribunal is also empowered to make a recommendation that the employer take action to reduce the adverse effect on the disabled person of the matter which is complained of.

Under *section 8(4)* any compensation that a tribunal may award can include compensation for injury to feelings, as with race and sex discrimination. It is not clear whether the amount of compensation awardable by a tribunal will be subject to any limit – this, however, seems unlikely.

There is also provision for interest on such awards in line with ordinary tribunal awards (see REMEDIES (49)), and also that agreements complying with the requirements set down in *section 39* of *TURERA 1993* will be binding (see CONCILIATION (11).)

18.9 Disability

18.9 DISCRIMINATORY JOB ADVERTISEMENTS

Under the *Disability Discrimination Act* there is a presumption that an employer's reason for refusing to offer employment to a disabled person is on the grounds of disability (*section 11*), where:

(*a*)   the employer advertised the vacancy (before or after the disabled person applied for it);

(*b*)   the advertisement indicated or is understood to have indicated that any application for the vacancy would be determined to any extent by reference to the successful applicant not having any disability or category of disability which includes the disabled person's disability, or because of the employer's reluctance to have to make any adjustments required by *section 6*;

(*c*)   the employer has refused to offer the disabled person the employment.

Problems with this part of the *Act* have been highlighted. For a person to bring a claim in respect of discriminatory advertising, he will have had to have applied for and been rejected for employment, and he must also show that the advertisement indicated (or was understood to have indicated) that the successful applicant would not be suffering from a disability or category of disability which the individual suffered from. This will be difficult to sustain, unless employers word advertisements for vacancies that suggest such an intention.

There is no equivalent provision in the *SDA* or *RRA* (i.e. that the person bringing the complaint must have actually applied for and been refused the advertised position) (see ADVERTISING (2)).

18.10 DISCRIMINATION IN RELATION TO CONTRACT WORKERS

Liability under the *Act* extends to principals (i.e. those for whom contract workers perform the work on behalf of a third party) for any discrimination against disabled persons [*DDA s 12*]:

(*a*)   in the terms on which he is allowed to work;

(*b*)   by not allowing him to do or continue to do it;

(*c*)   by refusing him benefits or omitting access to them;

(*d*)   by subjecting him to any other detriment.

18.11 TRADE ORGANISATION

Section 13 of the *Act* makes it unlawful to discriminate against applicants or members in relation to:

(*a*)   the acceptance of a disabled person's membership to an organisation; or

(*b*)   to be discriminatory in the terms granted; or

(*c*)   to deprive a disabled person of benefits; or

(*d*)   vary the membership or any other detriment.

A trade organisation is defined as an organisation of workers or employees or any other organisation whose members carry on a particular profession or trade for the purposes of which the organisation exists (e.g. a trade union or an employer's forum).

Again, such an organisation discriminates against a disabled person if that person is treated less favourably than someone who does not have the disability and the treatment cannot be shown to be justified. Such organisations are under a duty to make reasonable adjustments in the same way as employers.

18.12 DISCRIMINATION IN THE PROVISION OF GOODS, FACILITIES AND SERVICES

Section 16 of the *Disability Discrimination Act* prohibits discrimination against disabled people as regards the provision of services, which includes access to public places, hotel accommodation, facilities for banking, insurance, loans, credit or grants, facilities for entertainment, recreation or refreshment and access to means of communication and to information services. In addition, facilities provided by employment agencies and the services of other professions are also covered under this provision.

Discriminatory actions prohibited by *section 17* of the *Act* are also stated as 'less favourable treatment', on the grounds of the person's disability, than would be given to people without that disability. The service provider will be treated as unlawfully discriminating against the disabled person unless he or she is able to justify the conduct, on the same grounds as discrimination in employment, and also on other grounds:

(*a*)   by allowing the disabled person access to such goods, there would be danger to the health and safety of any person;

(*b*)   that the disabled person is incapable of entering into an enforceable agreement or giving an informed consent;

(*c*)   where the provision of services is refused, because the provider would otherwise be unable to provide the service to members of the public;

(*d*)   where the services are provided on different terms than to other members of the public, because the different treatment is necessary to enable the service to be provided to the disabled person and to members of the public; and

(*e*)   that the provider of services is allowed to charge a disabled person more for providing a service where the extra amount reflects the extra cost in providing the service.

Section 18 of the *Disability Discrimination Act* imposes a duty on the provider of the services to take all reasonable steps in order to change the policy or procedure so that it no longer affects the disabled person unless a deviation from the duty can be justified by the above criteria. In respect of physical features, such as steps at an entrance to a building, this will include the duty to either remove or alter them so that they do not affect disabled persons, or provide an alternative method of entry so that it is of use to disabled persons, e.g. providing a ramp. If an auxillary aid could ensure or help a disabled person to make use of a service, for example the provision of information on audio tape, then it would be the duty of the service provider to provide the aid so far as it would be reasonable to do so.

The provider of services is not required to take steps which would cost more than the 'prescribed maximum'. The Government estimates that the prescribed maximum will be approximately 5% to 10% of the rateable value of the premises in question.

18.13 Disability

By *section 19* of the *Act*, it is unlawful for a person who has the power to dispose of premises to do so in such a way that discriminates against a disabled person. This includes:

(*a*)   the terms on which premises are offered to a disabled person;

(*b*)   by refusing to dispose of the property to a disabled person; or

(*c*)   the treatment of the disabled person in relation to any list of persons in need of premises of that description.

In relation to a person who manages a premises it is unlawful to discriminate against a disabled person by refusing benefits, facilities, or by evicting the person or by subjecting him to any other detriment, or by imposing less favourable terms upon him as regards access to such benefits, etc. Similarly, if a person's consent or licence is required to dispose of any premises, then it is unlawful to refuse to give it for reasons relating to the disability of the disabled person.

All the above is subject to an exemption in *section 20* of the *Act* for small dwellings (see below). However a person who has an estate or interest in the premises and wholly occupies them (e.g. a homeowner) is free to discriminate unless in order to dispose of the premises an estate agent or an advertisement is used.

Discrimination is allowed under *section 20* of the *1995 Act* by the relevant occupier (i.e. the person with the power to dispose of premises or whose licence or consent is required to dispose of the premises) if:

(*a*)   he shares residence with other people in the same premises;

(*b*)   he shares accommodation in the premises with people who are not members of his household;

(*c*)   the shared accommodation is not storage accommodation or a means of access; and

(*d*)   the premises are small premises.

'Small premises' are defined as:

(i)   those where only the relevant occupier and his household reside in the accommodation occupied by him;

(ii)   in addition to the accommodation occupied by the relevant occupier, there is room on the premises for at least one other household on a separate tenancy or agreement;

(iii)   there are normally no more than two such other households.

In addition, small premises includes those where no more than six other people could reside in addition to the relevant occupier and his household.

Again, discrimination is defined as treating someone less favourably than someone who does not have that disability unless justified where justification bears much the same meaning as for services.

18.14 Enforcement

A disabled person who has been discriminated against by a provider of services will have the right to claim breach of a statutory tort in the county court, subject to the usual time limits.

18.15 VICTIMISATION

The *Disability Discrimination Act* also protects disabled persons from victimisation for commencing proceedings in a tribunal (or under other provisions of the Bill), or any person who has given evidence in such proceedings on behalf of the disabled person. This provision mirrors the *SDA* and *RRA* exactly, and so a disabled person who alleges victimisation will be able to rely on existing precedents under the *SDA* and *RRA* (see VICTIMISATION (54)).

18.16 NATIONAL DISABILITY COUNCIL

The *Disability Discrimination Act* establishes the National Disability Council (NDC) which has the duty to advise the Government as to the elimination of discrimination against disabled persons, and measures likely to reduce such discrimination.

Despite arguments that the Council would be ineffective without them, the *Act* does not give the NDC any investigatory powers (unlike the CRE and EOC). The NDC has power to prepare proposals for a code of practice dealing with discrimination against disabled persons. In reality it will only be an advisory body.

18.17 QUESTIONNAIRE PROCEDURE

The *Disability Discrimination Act* provides for a questionnaire similar to the *RRA* and *SDA* questionnaire to be formulated, to assist disabled persons who think they have been discriminated against to determine whether proceedings should be brought (see QUESTIONNAIRE PROCEDURE (47)).

*   *   *

The legal position until the 1995 Act becomes law

The provisions of the *Disabled Persons (Employment) Act 1944* apply until 31 December 1996 only. Thereafter, the provisions of the *Disability Discrimination Act 1995* will apply.

18.18 THE LAW

There is no specific prohibition against discrimination in respect of disabled persons, but there is statutory provision in relation to the employment of disabled people dating from 1944. The *Disabled Persons (Employment) Act 1944 (DPA)* imposes an obligation on all employers of 20 or more people to employ a quota of registered disabled people. The *Employment Protection (Consolidation) Act 1978*, as amended, also protects all employees (including disabled employees) from being unfairly dismissed subject to a qualifying period of 2 years' continuous employment. Such an employee may be dismissed only for a justifiable reason, but note that ill-health may constitute such a reason where the employee can no longer fulfil his duties (see 18.25 below).

18.19 DEFINITION OF 'DISABLED'

DPA s 1(1) defines a disabled person as someone 'substantially handicapped in obtaining or keeping employment' or work on his own account because of 'injury, disease, or congenital deformity' (mental as well as physical – *Sec 1(2)*) for which they would otherwise be qualified or suited.

18.20 Disability

18.20 REGISTER OF DISABLED PERSONS

DPA s 6, together with the *Disabled Persons (Registration) Regulations 1945 (SR & O 1945 No 938), Regs 8-10*, provide for a register of disabled persons to be maintained. This is kept by the Department of Employment, and the entry shows that the person is both disabled within the definition of the Act and also capable of employment. The quota requirements of the *DPA* relate to the employment of registered disabled employees.

18.21 OBLIGATION UPON EMPLOYERS

Every employer with more than 20 employees is required to employ at least 3% registered disabled employees ('the quota'). [*DPA ss 9, 10; Disabled Persons (Standard Percentage) Order 1946 (SR & O 1946 No 1258)*]. Effectively, therefore, an employer with between 20 and 34 staff must employ one registered disabled person; with between 34 and 67 staff, two registered disabled persons; and three registered disabled persons for every 100 thereafter.

18.22 FILLING VACANCIES

An employer is prohibited from filling a vacancy with any person other than a registered disabled person if, after filling the post, less than the 3% quota of registered disabled persons are employed.

18.23 REDUCED QUOTA PERMIT

An employer may apply to the Secretary of State for Employment for a reduced quota on the grounds that the 3% quota is too great in his particular circumstances. [*DPA s 11*]. The Secretary of State will refer the application to the local District Advisory Committee. These committees are charged with advising the Secretary of State on matters relating to the employment of disabled people and can be contacted through the Department of Employment.

18.24 DISMISSING DISABLED STAFF

An employer should not dismiss a registered disabled person employed by him 'unless he has a reasonable cause for doing so' if, after the dismissal, the number of registered disabled persons employed would fall below the quota. [*DPA s 9(5)*]. 'Good cause' would include disciplinary matters. This provision protects disabled staff during redundancy selection and disabled staff should not be made redundant if this would breach the 3% threshold.

18.25 DISMISSAL ON GROUNDS OF ILL-HEALTH

If an employer takes the view that an employee can no longer fulfil his duties because of his disability, he is then entitled to dismiss that employee subject to proper procedures being followed. The first step should be to arrange for the employee to see the company doctor, or alternatively to obtain the employee's consent for the company to obtain an assessment from its own doctor. In either case, the employee's consent is required for the medical report to be released to the company. [*Access to Medical Reports Act 1988*]. If the report indicates that the employee is not fit to do the job for which he is employed, the employer should discuss the implication of the report with the employee. The employer should then look for alternative work for the employee within the company; dismissal of the employee on notice will be appropriate only if there is none available.

18.26 DESIGNATED EMPLOYMENT

Certain types of employment can be designated as especially suitable for disabled persons and, except with a permit from the Secretary of State, only disabled persons can be employed in such a job. Only attendants of electrically operated lifts and car parks have been so designated as yet. [*DPA s 12(1); SR & O 1946 No 1257*].

18.27 RECORDS

Employers are obliged to monitor the number of disabled persons in their employment and keep full records of all matters which may be relevant for showing compliance with the Act. [*DPA s 14*].

18.28 ANNUAL REPORT

Companies employing more than 250 staff are also obliged to set out their policies in regard to the employment of the disabled in their directors' report. [*Companies Act 1985, 7 Sch 9*].

18.29 PENALTIES

The penalties are draconian. Failure to appoint a disabled person, or dismissing a disabled person without good cause when the number of disabled persons employed would fall below the quota, is a criminal offence carrying a level 3 fine (up to £1,000) or three months' imprisonment (or, for a company, a level 5 fine, i.e. up to £5,000); other contraventions carry a lesser fine. Proceedings are by summary trial in the magistrates' court. [*DPA ss 9(6), 19(3)*]. No proceedings may be brought, however, without the consent of the Secretary of State, or an officer designated by him. Such proceedings must be within twelve months of the alleged contravention, or within three months of the contravention coming to the notice of the Secretary of State (whichever is later) and, in most instances he must consult the District Advisory Committee before commencing such proceedings.

18.30 LIABILITY OF DIRECTORS

Where a corporate body is guilty of an offence, each and every director will be deemed guilty unless he proves that the offence was committed without his knowledge and that he had used all due diligence to prevent the commission of the offence.

18.31 IMPLEMENTATION

There can be few company directors not liable to imprisonment for three months under this statute! It is perhaps an example of where the draconian nature of the penalty has undermined the effectiveness of the legislation. As mentioned above, no proceedings can be taken without leave of the Secretary of State and then after a cumbersome consultation process.

18.32   Disability

The Department of Employment has produced a comprehensive code of practice on the employment of disabled persons. It covers:

(*a*)   setting up a policy on disabilities within a company;

(*b*)   the law relating to employment of individuals with disabilities;

(*c*)   the characteristics of people with disabilities and what this means for employers;

(*d*)   an examination of typical concerns of employers;

(*e*)   good recruitment practice;

(*f*)   options to consider for disabled employees;

(*g*)   the role of employees and trade unions; and

(*h*)   a directory of sources of financial and other practical help available to assist in the employment of individuals with disabilities.

19   Discovery, Interrogatories and Further Particulars

19.1   BACKGROUND

The courts have long recognised 'the particular difficulties' for an applicant in proving discrimination, 'even when it has taken place'. Usually, all the material information will be in the possession of the employer.

19.2   BASIC PRINCIPLES

The *Industrial Tribunals (Constitution and Rules of Procedure) Regulations 1993 (SI 1993 No 2687)* (the '*IT Regs*') empower an industrial tribunal to 'grant . . . such discovery or inspection (including the taking of copies) . . . as might be granted by a county court'. [*IT Regs, Rule 4(1)(b)*]. Parties to proceedings should disclose all documents in their possession if an order of general discovery is made, but may specify those documents that they object to producing by reason of privilege or otherwise. A party can only be obliged to disclose those documents that are relevant, that is, necessary for fairly disposing of the proceedings, either by establishing positive evidence of discrimination or rebutting contentions in defence, or for saving costs. (A document need not be disclosed where it is privileged, that is, part of an exchange of letters trying to settle the dispute and marked 'without prejudice', or letters between the party and his own solicitors.) There is no obligation to disclose documents if an order is not made, but if voluntary discovery is given, any document which reasonably relates to a disclosed document should also be disclosed (*Birds Eye Walls Ltd v Harrison [1985] ICR 279*). Tribunals now have the power to order discovery and inspection of documents of their own motion.

19.3   NORMAL PROCEDURE

As a matter of practice in the industrial tribunal, it is unusual for a general order of discovery by exchange of lists to be made. More usually, the party requiring specific documentation will first request that from the other side, and only if that request is declined will an order be sought. An order may be given by a tribunal without a hearing, but the party having to disclose the documents (or a party refused disclosure) may seek an interlocutory hearing to deal with the issue at which argument may be advanced. It is unlikely that such a hearing would need to hear evidence. On occasion the tribunal will examine the documentation itself to see whether or not it is relevant and disclosable (*Science Research Council v Nassé [1979] ICR 921*). Strictly, 'discovery' is the process of requiring a list of documents in existence, either relating to the issue or generally. Inspection is the appropriate order for requiring a party to produce a document either by allowing the other party reasonable access to look at it and copy it himself, or more usually by sending photocopies of the relevant material.

19.4   CONFIDENTIAL DOCUMENTS

The House of Lords has determined that confidentiality is not a reason for refusing to make an order for the disclosure of documents (*Science Research Council v Nassé [1979] ICR 921*). This issue most often occurs when an individual wishes to have discovery of the application forms of the other candidates to a post. Since *Nassé*, the tribunals have usually been willing to make this order, but if, however, an employer considers that the confidentiality outweighs the probative value to the applicant, or that the other application forms are not relevant, he can ask the tribunal to examine the documents to consider whether they are really relevant. Confidential details such as names etc. may also be blocked out, but where the applicant is legally represented, it may be simpler to obtain undertakings as to confidentiality from the applicant's representative.

As with discovery in the county court, in certain circumstances it may be possible for a party to avoid disclosure of certain documents if those documents are protected from disclosure by 'public interest immunity'. In the EAT case of *Commissioner of Police of the Metropolis v Locker* [1993] IRLR 319, the Police Commissioner sought to be protected from disclosure of certain documentation made in the course of Mrs Locker's use of the grievance procedure. However, the EAT held that the police discrimination grievance procedure was different from the police disciplinary and complaints procedure (where statements have been held to be subject to public interest immunity), because the grievance procedure is a purely internal system designed to promote non-discriminatory practices and to secure remedies for victims of any discriminatory practices that are found.

19.5   STATISTICAL DATA

The Court of Appeal has determined that statistical data is relevant in considering a complaint of unlawful discrimination and, if such data is kept, will order its disclosure (*West Midlands Passenger Transport Executive v Singh* [1988] ICR 614), so long as it is relevant to the complaint under consideration. By way of example, if an individual complains of a refusal to promote on racial grounds, the tribunal would order disclosure of the statistics of promotion by ethnic origin at that level over a reasonable preceding period, but would not order disclosure of general recruitment statistics. The tribunal cannot order disclosure of statistical data not yet compiled, but will be willing to order disclosure of primary material from which such statistical information may be gleaned (*Carrington v Helix Lighting Ltd* [1990] ICR 125).

19.6   THE QUESTIONNAIRE

If the applicant requests statistical data in the questionnaire, a failure to provide it without good reason could lead to an adverse inference being drawn by the tribunal (*Carrington v Helix Lighting Ltd* [1990] ICR 125).

19.7   OPPRESSIVE REQUEST

If an order of discovery were to cause an unreasonable increase in the length and cost of the hearing or if it would put an employer to considerable cost and inconvenience, no order will be made (*West Midlands Passenger Transport Executive v Singh* [1988] ICR 614).

19.8   PREVIOUS INCIDENTS AND SUBSEQUENT EVENTS

So long as an individual can show that it is relevant, he will be permitted discovery of documentation relating to previous events, or matters subsequent to the application to the tribunal (*Selvarajan v ILEA* [1980] IRLR 313; *Chattopadhyay v Headmaster of Holloway School* [1982] ICR 132).

19.9 PROCEDURE

The party requiring discovery or, more usually, inspection of particular documents should write to the other side setting out the request. As a matter of practice, a 'county court' type request for a general exchange of lists of documents is unusual (there is no reason why it should be). It is usual to set out the particular documents required and the reasons for requiring them. If the other party refuses to respond to the request, or to comply with it in whole or part, then an application for the order should be made to the tribunal. The tribunal may grant or refuse the order without a hearing, but the aggrieved party has a right to a hearing on the matter, either to set aside the tribunal order or against the refusal to make the order. Evidence will rarely be heard, but may be. A full tribunal hears such an application and the hearing is public. Either party may appeal to the EAT on a point of law against a decision of the tribunal on discovery or inspection.

19.10 FAILURE TO COMPLY WITH DISCOVERY ORDER

If a party fails to comply with an order for disclosure of documents, then the tribunal has the power to strike out their Originating Application or Notice of Appearance (as the case may be). In *National Grid Company v Virdee* [*1992*] *IRLR 555*, NGC failed to comply with an order for discovery, this failure becoming apparent during the course of the tribunal hearing. There was no indication that NGC's actions were deliberate, and as soon as the omission came to light, NGC's representatives made arrangements for disclosure of the documents. Mr Virdee's legal representative then sought an adjournment so that the documentation could be considered, and subsequently requested an order that NGC's Notice of Appearance (or relevant part thereof) be struck out. The tribunal granted this order. On appeal to the EAT, the tribunal's decision was reversed, because a punitive order to strike out was inappropriate in the circumstances. The EAT held that in exercising its discretion as to whether or not a pleading should be struck out, a tribunal should be aware that this should only be done in the most serious cases, e.g. where any judgment ultimately obtained without the disclosure of the relevant documentation can no longer be considered to be a fair judgment. The circumstances did not exist in this case.

19.11 SUMMARY

Discovery of documentation is enormously important to the applicant in a discrimination case. Frequently he will not be privy to the details of, say, the successful candidates for the position which he has failed to obtain, without discovery of the application forms. The courts have recognised this reality and tribunals are generally inclined to grant discovery of such material without a hearing, as it has become established practice to do so.

19.12 INTERROGATORIES

The power for tribunals to order interrogatories is a new power granted by *IT Regs, Rule 4(3)*. On the application of either party or of its own initiative the tribunal can require a party to provide written answers to any questions, if the answer will clarify any relevant issues and the proceedings would be assisted by the answer being available before the full hearing. Any order as to interrogatories will be in written form, and will specify a time limit within which the written answers must be furnished. The tribunal has power to extend this time limit [*Rule 15(1)*].

19.13 Discovery, Interrogatories and Further Particulars

The party required to comply with an order for interrogatories may apply to set aside the order, or to have it varied [*Rule 4(5)*]. If the party fails to comply with the interrogatories order, the tribunal has power to strike out the Originating Application or Notice of Appearance (whichever is relevant).

Once the answers to interrogatories have been provided, the tribunal will take the answer into account in the same way as any other evidence.

19.13 FURTHER AND BETTER PARTICULARS

Under *IT Regs, Rule 4(1)(a)*, an industrial tribunal has the power to order a party to provide 'further particulars of the grounds on which that party relies and of any facts and contentions' relevant to the proceedings. The tribunal can make such an order of its own motion, or following an application by either party. However, it is more usual for further and better particulars to be provided following a written request.

Where a party's Originating Application or Notice of Appearance contains only basic assertions or denials, further particulars are appropriate for ensuring that the issues in dispute will be more clearly defined.

Further and better particulars have the same weight as all statements made in an Originating Application or Notice of Appearance, and in effect are added to the Originating Application or Notice of Appearance (as the case may be).

20   Discrimination

20.1   DEFINITION

The *Race Relations Act 1976* and the *Sex Discrimination Act 1975* both provide an identical statutory definition of unlawful discrimination, of which there are three forms:

(*a*)   direct discrimination;

(*b*)   indirect discrimination; and

(*c*)   victimisation.

Sex discrimination is, of course, on grounds of sex or marital status, but race discrimination is discrimination on the basis of colour, race or ethnic origin (see RACIAL GROUNDS (48)).

There are separate chapters on DIRECT DISCRIMINATION (17), DISABILITY DISCRIMINATION (18), INDIRECT DISCRIMINATION (36), MARITAL STATUS (38), and VICTIMISATION (54), and therefore these concepts are not dealt with here. This chapter outlines other forms of discrimination, with references where appropriate to other chapters where these are dealt with in greater detail.

20.2   OTHER FORMS OF DISCRIMINATION

Religion

Except in Northern Ireland, which is outside the scope of this book, there is no prohibition of religious discrimination (although in certain circumstances, particular requirements will constitute indirect racial discrimination because of the actual adherence of a much higher proportion of one racial group, as opposed to another, to a particular religious belief with specific customs and prohibitions (*Mandla v Dowell Lee* [*1983*] *ICR 385*)).

20.3   Age

There is no prohibition of age discrimination but, again, in certain circumstances, an age bar may indirectly discriminate on grounds of race (*Perera v Civil Service Commission* [*1983*] *ICR 428*) or sex (*Price v Civil Service Commission* [*1978*] *ICR 27*). (See AGE DISCRIMINATION (3).)

20.4   Sexual orientation

There is nothing unlawful about discriminating against an individual on the grounds of his sexual orientation, unless the individual could show that this discrimination was sex-specific (that is, that the prejudice operates against gay men rather than lesbian women or vice versa). In respect of appointment, promotion and treatment short of constructive dismissal, an individual is unprotected by statute from adverse treatment. However, if a homosexual is dismissed because of his homosexuality, then he is afforded protection by the *Employment Protection (Consolidation) Act 1978 (as amended)*, but only in so far as every individual is protected from capricious dismissal. Such an individual is entitled not to be dismissed except on grounds which render the dismissal fair, and with the operation of proper procedures. He would be entitled to compensation and, if appropriate, a reinstatement or re-engagement order (and further compensation if this were not complied with). An individual is also entitled to a safe system of work and employers should be wary of unfettered harassment of an employee by work colleagues because of his sexual orientation, which may lead to a constructive dismissal claim. (See SEXUAL ORIENTATION (51).)

20.5 Political persuasion

It is not unlawful to discriminate for or against an individual because of his political persuasion, unless such discrimination is indirectly discriminatory. Discrimination against membership of expressly foreign political parties would indirectly discriminate on grounds of race and needs to be justified on non-racial grounds.

20.6 Trade union membership

In limited circumstances, it is unlawful to discriminate against an individual on the grounds of trade union membership or non-membership. [*EPCA, as amended*]. This subject is outside the scope of this book (see *Tolley's Employment Handbook*). The burden of proof on an individual who claims that he has been refused employment on the grounds of his membership or non-membership of a trade union is the same as in an application under the *RRA* or *SDA*. (See BURDEN OF PROOF (6).)

20.7 General

Unless the discrimination constitutes indirect discrimination contrary to the *RRA* or *SDA*, an employer may be as capricious as he pleases. An employer should bear in mind that, in the case of a claim of indirect discrimination, he must satisfy the tribunal as to his explanation, and if such an explanation does not have any logical basis, the tribunal may not accept it.

20.8 NORTHERN IRELAND

Neither the *SDA* nor the *RRA* has effect in Northern Ireland. However, the *Sex Discrimination (Northern Ireland) Order 1976 (SI 1976 No 244)*, which does have effect, is practically identical to the *SDA*. Therefore, discrimination on the grounds of sex is prohibited to the same extent as in Great Britain.

Surprisingly, there is no equivalent to the *RRA* in Northern Ireland, so this is the only part of the United Kingdom where it is lawful to discriminate against an individual on the grounds of race, nationality, ethnic or national origin. The Government launched a consultative document in December 1992 entitled *Race Relations in Northern Ireland*, but this made no commitment to extend race relations legislation to Northern Ireland. The consultation period ended in March 1993, and in May 1995 the Government confirmed that legislation would be introduced to prohibit discrimination on the grounds of race in Northern Ireland. No legislation had been introduced at the time of writing.

Political and religious discrimination is prohibited in Northern Ireland by the *Fair Employment (Northern Ireland) Act 1976*. There is a body which deals with political and religious discrimination, the Fair Employment Commission, whose address is:

Andras House
Great Victoria Street
Belfast
BT2 7BB

Tel: (01232) 240020

21   Dismissal

21.1   SCOPE

It is unlawful to dismiss an employee by reason of his race or sex. [*RRA s 4(2)(c); SDA s 6(2)(b)*].

21.2   NO QUALIFYING PERIOD

An employee is protected from being dismissed on racial or sexual grounds from the moment he commences employment. Unlike ordinary unfair dismissal, there is no qualifying period of service (2 years' continuous service). However, the Court of Appeal held in *R v The Secretary of State for Employment Ex parte Seymour-Smith and Perez* [*1995*] *IRLR 464*, that the 2 years' service requirement was itself indirectly discriminatory against female employees, as they were more likely to take career breaks and because of this more likely to move to new employers, and, therefore, unable to claim unfair dismissal until they had acquired 2 years' service with each employer.

The Government is believed to be appealing against this decision. Whilst the position is still unclear, employers would be well advised to treat all employees as if they have the right to claim unfair dismissal, irrespective of the length of service, and particularly those employees with more than 12 months' service. This is because, although this decision only affects public-sector employees and does not have general application, it is possible that the Government could introduce legislation extending the scope of this decision and with retrospective effect.

In any event, in an equal opportunities environment, consistency of treatment of all employees irrespective of their length of service, is desirable to avoid the possibility of any difference in treatment being tainted with discrimination on the grounds of sex.

Whilst the Court of Appeal in *Seymour-Smith and Perez* held that the qualifying periods were indirectly discriminatory against women, this decision also means that male employees with less than 2 years' service will be able to claim unfair dismissal. If this was not the case, then a male employee dismissed when he had less than 2 years' service would be able to claim he had been directly discriminated against on the grounds of his sex.

21.3   TIME LIMIT

An employee must, however, make a claim within three months of the alleged discriminatory dismissal [*RRA s 68; SDA s 76*] except where a tribunal considers it just and equitable to entertain a late claim. [*RRA s 68(6); SDA s 76(5)*]. Where an employee has been dismissed, the relevant date of dismissal is the actual date on which the dismissal took effect, not the date on which the notice of dismissal was given (*Lupetti v Wrens Old House Ltd* [*1984*] *ICR 348*).

The EAT held in *Biggs v Somerset County Council* [*1995*] *IRLR 452*, that retrospective claims by former part-time employees were subject to the usual three-month time limit. It is not known at the time of writing whether this decision will be appealed; but in any event, further retrospective claims are likely. (See PART-TIME EMPLOYEES (40).)

21.4 OVERLAP WITH EMPLOYMENT PROTECTION (CONSOLIDATION) ACT

There is nothing to prevent an employee with the relevant service from making simultaneous claims under the *EPCA* and either the *RRA* or the *SDA* (or, indeed, all three). The damages overlap and the tribunal will only compensate actual loss once, but the *Employment Protection (Consolidation) Act 1978* provides, in addition, a basic award, although it does not compensate injury to feelings. The discrimination legislation does not provide a basic award but damages will be awarded for injury to feelings.

21.5 BURDEN OF PROOF

It is for the individual to satisfy the tribunal that his dismissal has been on grounds of race or sex. If the employer can show that contractual disciplinary procedures were applied, then the individual may not even be able to show a *prima facie* case unless he or she can point to an instance where a white person or a man was more favourably treated. Where, however, an individual is able to show that a comparator was given a different disciplinary penalty arising out of the same or similar facts, or accorded a different procedure, then the employer will be called upon to satisfy the tribunal with an innocent explanation of those facts (*Chattopadhyay v Headmaster of Holloway School [1982] ICR 132*). It is extremely difficult for employees to prove dismissal on racial grounds. Employers are, however, best advised to ensure that the disciplinary procedure is properly implemented in all instances of dismissal, and it is desirable to have some system that monitors the outcome of disciplinary hearings to ensure that there is no discriminatory trait. (See BURDEN OF PROOF (6).)

Guidelines were laid down by Neill LJ in *King v The Great Britain–China Centre [1991] IRLR 513* (see BURDEN OF PROOF (6)).

21.6 DISMISSAL AND RACIAL DISCRIMINATION

Code of practice

The CRE Code of Practice recommends that:

(*a*)   staff responsible for dismissing other staff should be instructed not to discriminate on racial grounds (para 1.17);

(*b*)   in applying disciplinary procedures, consideration should be given to the effect on the individual of:

  (i)   racial abuse or provocation,

  (ii)   communication and comprehension difficulties,

  (iii)   differences in cultural background or behaviour (para 1.23).

Employers with large numbers of ethnic minority staff, or with any staff with language difficulties, should consider ensuring that disciplinary rules and safety commands are available in translation.

21.7 Interpreter

Where a member of staff speaks little or no English, he may be able to substantiate a claim under both the *RRA* and *EPCA* if steps are not taken to provide interpretation and to ensure that the procedure and allegations are understood. Usually, a colleague will be able to assist in this but otherwise local Councils for Racial Equality (whose addresses may be obtained from the Commission for Racial Equality – see 9.14 COMMISSION FOR RACIAL EQUALITY) will be able to provide a list of interpreters.

21.8 Redundancy

The Race Relations Code of Practice recommends that redundancy criteria should be examined to ensure that they are not unlawfully discriminatory (para 1.17). This relates to indirect discrimination, as the days in the late 1950s when trade unions were known to negotiate expressly racist redundancy policies are no more. Frequently, employers adopt a 'last in, first out' policy (LIFO). An analysis of staff records may indicate that such a policy is indirectly discriminatory. With an end to large-scale immigration this is less likely than it was in the past, but a company that has implemented an equal opportunity policy in the recent past may find that the impact of that policy on recruitment has been a greater proportion of new recruits than of long-serving employees being of ethnic minority origin. Discriminatory employment patterns do repeat themselves and there may be an adverse proportion of ethnic minority staff with short service because of previous redundancy exercises by LIFO. Employers should also be cautious about a 'last in, first out' policy if it involves selecting part-timers first, because this will probably be indirectly sexually discriminatory (see *Clarke and Powell v Eley (IMI Kynoch) Ltd [1982] IRLR 131*).

21.9 Justification

A LIFO redundancy policy that resulted in a disproportionate impact on ethnic minority staff is not indirectly discriminatory and in contravention of the *RRA* if it can be otherwise 'justified'. [*RRA s 1(1)(b)(ii)*]. The Race Relations Code of Practice does not address the question of justification. For any employer, there are strong arguments that a long-standing LIFO policy negotiated by a trade union is justifiable on grounds of economics (likely to be a strong argument where a company's financial situation has already forced redundancies) or industrial relations. If an employer used a redundancy selection policy which related to the race of the employees, because of threatened union action if such a policy was not used, then the redundancy would be unfair and discriminatory. Justification is, however, a matter for each individual tribunal and two tribunals addressing the same question could quite easily come to different conclusions (*Raval v DHSS [1985] ICR 685*), but it is likely that an employer could justify LIFO.

21.10 REFUSAL TO ACCEPT DISCRIMINATORY INSTRUCTIONS

It is contrary to the *SDA* or the *RRA* (as appropriate) to dismiss an employee for refusing to accept discriminatory instructions – for example, that the employee should refuse to serve white customers (*Zarczynska v Levy [1979] ICR 184*).

21.11 DISMISSAL AND SEX DISCRIMINATION

Code of practice

The EOC Code recommends that care should be taken to ensure that an employee who has made a complaint of unlawful discrimination should not be victimised by being dismissed (or disciplined) (para 31(a)). Paragraph 32 provides as follows:

(*a*)   care should be taken that members of one sex are not disciplined or dismissed for conduct that would be overlooked in the other;

(*b*)   conditions of access to voluntary redundancy benefit should be irrespective of sex;

(*c*)   where there is a general downgrading or short-time working, the arrangements should not unlawfully discriminate against one sex;

(*d*)   all reasonable steps should be taken to prevent sexual harassment or other unfavourable treatment on grounds of sex.

21.12 Redundancy

The EOC Code advises that redundancy procedures affecting predominantly one sex should be reviewed to remove adverse effects which could not be justified (para 32(b)). A policy that involved selecting women for redundancy first would be directly discriminatory and unlawful. Other redundancy policies might, however, constitute indirect discrimination. A rule that part-time workers should be the first to go will indirectly discriminate and is unlikely to be justifiable (*Bilka-Kaufhaus GmbH v Weber von Hartz [1986] IRLR 317; Briggs v North Eastern Education Library Board [1990] IRLR 181*). If, under an agreement, certain sections of the workforce where women predominated (say the canteen) would be the first to be laid off, that agreement would be *prima facie* indirectly discriminatory, but might be justifiable on economic grounds.

21.13 APPEALS

Most disciplinary procedures include a right to appeal. Indeed, a finding of unfair dismissal may result from a denial of the right to appeal, as in *West Midlands Co-operative Society v Tipton [1987] IRLR 112*. An appeal can either be a review of the original decision, or a complete re-hearing. Any new information that has come to light since the original decision should be considered at the appeal. The employee should be informed of the outcome of the appeal, and the decision should be confirmed in writing.

An employee is not protected from discrimination during the appeal process, if this takes place after the date of dismissal – *Post Office v Adekaye [1995] IRLR 297*. This is because neither the *SDA* nor the *RRA* protects ex-employees. In this case, the employee brought proceedings alleging that she had been discriminated against during her appeal against dismissal. The employee had initially complained of less favourable treatment than her white comparator employee before her dismissal, however, she sought to rely on discrimination during the appeal hearing as she had missed the time limit for claiming in respect of the actual dismissal. The EAT commented that it was unsatisfactory that discrimination at her appeal hearing following her dismissal was not covered by the *SDA* or the *RRA*, and thought that Parliament would have intended both Acts to cover such discrimination if this had been considered at the time the Acts were passed. However, the wording of both Acts was clear, and the employee was not protected.

21.14 CONSTRUCTIVE DISMISSAL

As a general principle, an employee can terminate his contract of employment if his employer is in 'repudiatory breach' which means, in essence, that the employer is in breach of a fundamental term of the contract (*Western Excavating (ECC) Ltd v Sharp [1978] ICR 221*).

Applying this principle to discrimination cases, where an employee is subjected to a work environment in which he is discriminated against or subjected to racial or sexual harassment to such an extent that he can tolerate it no longer and leaves the employment, he will be entitled to claim for constructive dismissal (as well as for race or sex discrimination).

The 'repudiatory breach' in such a case is either of the obligation to provide a safe place of work or of the general requirement of trust and confidence to sustain an employment contract.

(See CONSTRUCTIVE DISMISSAL (12).)

22   Dress Requirements

22.1   SEX DISCRIMINATION

It is not a matter of sex discrimination to require women to wear skirts as part of a uniform, or to forbid men to wear jewellery. A uniform regulation will only be discriminatory if it is applied only to members of one sex in a particular grade. It could be sex discrimination to require waitresses to wear a uniform, or conform to certain standards of dress, but not make the same requirement of men. In a case involving a bookshop, female staff were required to wear skirts where no dress requirement was placed on the men. The EAT held that there was no less favourable treatment of the women, because there was no comparable requirement that could be put on men (*Schmidt v Austicks Bookshop Ltd [1978] ICR 85*).

22.2   RACE DISCRIMINATION

It may be a matter of *indirect racial discrimination* to impose certain dress regulations on ethnic minorities. A uniform requirement involving the wearing of a skirt of less than full length may be indirectly discriminatory against any ethnic minority in which the Muslim religion is dominant. Those individuals 'cannot comply' with a skirt requirement because of cultural taboos. It is unlikely, in normal shop assistant or waitress situations, that any such requirement would be considered otherwise 'justifiable'. It is straightforward to ask a uniform designer to produce a suitable alternative in consultation with the individual concerned.

22.3   CAN EXCEPTIONS TO THE DRESS CODE BE LIMITED?

There is a fear on the part of some employers that once an exception has been made to the dress code, then all staff must be allowed to wear trousers if they wish. If the employer does not wish to allow a general exception, then a dress code that allows exemption only on grounds of religious belief or other exceptional circumstances is permissible. Discrimination on religious grounds is not, of itself, unlawful. Such a code would have a disproportionate impact on white women but how would it be detrimental to them? Such a requirement would not prevent the woman from working, as a strict skirt requirement would for Muslim women. If the policy does allow for exceptions (perhaps for an individual with an unsightly scar on her leg), then the requirement would not be absolute. To constitute indirect discrimination a condition or requirement must be absolute (*Meer v London Borough of Tower Hamlets [1988] IRLR 399*).

22.4   ENFORCEMENT OF THE DRESS CODE

Enforcement of the dress code should be through the giving of normal disciplinary warnings, but a failure to obey a reasonable instruction from management can amount to gross misconduct. If there is no existing dress code (whether express or implied), and the employer wishes to introduce one, there may be difficulties since this constitutes a variation of the employment contract (in which case, the necessary steps required to achieve this should be followed). In fact, most employers have an implied dress code, it being custom and practice for staff to dress presentably.

22.5 Dress Requirements

In *Stoke-on-Trent Community Transport v Cresswell* (unreported), the EAT upheld the tribunal's decision that a female employee's dismissal for wearing trousers was unlawful sex discrimination contrary to the *SDA*. This was because male employees were not subject to any rules or disciplinary sections in respect of their dress.

A number of recent cases have held that different dress requirements are not discriminatory:

Burrett v West Birmingham Health Authority [1994] IRLR 7: Ms Burrett was employed as a staff nurse in the casualty department, where female nurses were required to wear a cap (which was not supplied as a matter of hygiene, and which served no other practical purpose); male nurses were not required to wear this hat. The industrial tribunal dismissed her claim that she had been unlawfully discriminated against on the grounds that, although male and female nurses uniforms differed, male nurses would have been disciplined in the same way as she had been if they had refused to wear the male nurse uniform. The EAT dismissed Ms Burrett's appeal. It helped that the requirement to wear a cap was not 'less favourable treatment' within *SDA s 1(1)(a)*. The fact that she felt it demeaning was not a relevant factor, as it is for the tribunal to decide whether there has been less favourable treatment.

In a number of recent cases, male employees have sought to rely on the provisions of the *SDA* in relation to their employers' dress requirements. In *Blaik v The Post Office [1994] IRLR 280*, male employees were required to wear a tie as part of their uniform, whereas female employees only had to wear a blouse or a shirt. Mr Blaik was dismissed for consistent refusal to wear a tie. He said his refusal was due to the fact that female employees were not under a similar requirement. His complaint was dismissed by both the industrial tribunal and the EAT because the requirement was not regarded as so serious as to amount to a 'detriment' under *SDA s 1(1)(b)*. He also brought a complaint under the *Equal Treatment Directive* on the grounds that male and female employees must be guaranteed the same working conditions without discrimination on grounds of sex. However, the EAT dismissed his claim as there was sufficient remedy under domestic law, and there was not sufficient disparity between the provisions of the *SDA* and the *Equal Treatment Directive* to suggest that it might be necessary for individuals to rely directly upon the European legislation.

James v Bank of England (unreported): The Bank of England's dress code required all staff to 'present a neat and businesslike appearance avoiding extremes of dress', i.e. male employees were expected to wear a suit, whereas female employees were 'persuaded' that certain items (jeans, short skirts or dresses, T-shirts etc.) were not businesslike. Mr James felt that the mandatory requirement for men to wear a suit, whilst women were given a wider choice of dress, amounted to unlawful sex discrimination. The industrial tribunal held that there had not been direct discrimination and concluded that the Bank's dress code was enforced without distinction between men and women, and it was no more expensive for male employees to meet the suited requirement than it was for female employees to meet a generally required standard. The EAT dismissed Mr James's appeal. It was irrelevant that the dress code was expressed in a positive way for men, but in a negative way for women, and it was also irrelevant that female employees were only to be 'persuaded' about what dress was appropriate. As long as the dress code was interpreted equally strictly in respect of male and female employees, then there was no discrimination.

Dress appearance requirements may also be discriminatory in a non-employment context. For example, in *McConomy v Croft Inns Ltd [1992] IRLR 561*, the Northern Ireland High Court held that it was unlawfully discriminatory for a public house to bar a man for wearing earrings. The defendants argued that men wearing earrings was regarded as being outside the minimum standard of dress as required in the admissions policy for the bar in question. However, the Northern Ireland High Court held that the reason for Mr McConomy's treatment was his sex; a woman wearing earrings would not have been treated in the same way as he was.

In the recent case of *Gatehouse v Stretton Leisure Ltd* (unreported), an industrial tribunal upheld the applicant's complaint that she had been unlawfully discriminated against on the grounds of her sex after she was warned that if she did not alter her hairstyle, she would have to look for a new job. By contrast, in *Lloyd v Computer Associates* (unreported), an industrial tribunal held that a male employee who was dismissed for refusing to have his hair cut was not discriminated against on the grounds of his sex.

The EAT in *Smith v Safeway plc [1995] IRLR 132* upheld the applicant's complaint that his dismissal – on the grounds that the length of his hair contravened the employer's rules of appearance for male staff – was unlawful sex discrimination. However, the EAT was divided between the lay members and Pill J. The two lay members of the EAT had no difficulty in finding that the applicant had been subjected to less favourable treatment, and unlike other dress restrictions, a restriction on length of hair had a continuing effect outside working hours. There was clearly a detriment to the employee which the employers had not objectively justified. However, Pill J dissented on the grounds that the requirement reasonably related to current perceptions of conventional appearance for men and women, and did not involve treating one sex less favourably than the other.

This decision suggested that tribunals would be more likely to take account of the changes in society's attitude as regards appropriate standards of dress at work for men and women. However, subsequent decisions have reverted to type, as in *Maycock v Waitrose Ltd* (unreported).

22.6 EXAMPLES OF RACE DISCRIMINATION

Indirect racial discrimination through dress codes was found in *Malik v Bertram Personnel Group Ltd* (unreported). Ms Malik (a Muslim) was offered a job as a trainee recruitment consultant, but when she indicated that she wished to wear trousers for religious reasons (contrary to the company policy that women staff should wear skirts), the company withdrew the offer of employment. An industrial tribunal upheld her complaint of racial discrimination and held that the company's policy of allowing women to wear trousers on religious grounds was not genuine, the true situation being that the company was anxious to maintain a policy that women employees did not wear trousers. This view was supported by the fact that the company had made no attempt to ascertain the genuineness of Ms Malik's reason for wanting to wear trousers. The policy was discriminatory in its effect because a higher proportion of Muslim women would not be able to comply with it, compared with the proportion of non-Muslim women who could not comply.

23   Education

23.1   ADMISSION TO EDUCATION

The *SDA* and *RDA* both contain prohibitions as regards discrimination in relation to education, access to education and various other related areas. [*SDA Pt III; RRA Pt III*].

It is unlawful to discriminate against a person on the grounds of sex or race in the admission of pupils to an educational establishment. [*SDA s 22; RRA s 17*]. Discrimination bears the same meaning as that used for employment-related discrimination.

In both cases, discrimination is unlawful in relation to:

(*a*)   the terms on which admission to the establishment is made; or

(*b*)   the refusal or deliberate omission to accept an application for admission.

Admission criteria will be indirectly discriminatory if the exclusion of a greater proportion of pupils from certain racial groups or persons of one sex cannot be objectively justified.

23.2   Discriminatory Examples

Dress requirements
Dress requirements relating to school uniforms that result in the rejection of a pupil may be discriminatory. In a case involving a school in Birmingham, a Sikh boy was refused admission on the grounds that he had to follow the dress code by removing his turban and cutting his hair. The House of Lords ruled that this was race discrimination contrary to the *RRA*. (*Mandla v Dowell Lee [1983] IRLR 209*). This was a requirement which a considerably smaller proportion of members of the boy's racial group, i.e. Sikhs, could not comply. There was no objective justification for the requirement (see RACIAL GROUP, RACIAL GROUNDS, NATIONAL AND ETHNIC ORIGIN (48)).

Dress requirements for girls in schools can also be discriminatory, such as where muslim girls refused to remove 'hajibs' (veils) or who would not change from their 'shalwar-kameez' (trouser suits). Where expulsion has been the result, it has been found to constitute indirect discrimination. Indeed, the fact that they are required to wear a uniform at all may be sufficient to constitute a 'detriment' for the purpose of the *RRA* (see INDIRECT DISCRIMINATION (36)).

Dress codes of any kind which would mean that individuals could not comply due to racial or cultural reasons will usually be indirectly discriminatory unless they can be objectively justified.

Schools can impose different uniform requirements upon girls and boys, because dress requirements in schools are matters at the discretion of school heads and governors. [*Education (No 2) Act 1986, s 16*]. Yet schools are still duty bound to observe the provisions of the *SDA*, and uniform requirements in relation to both sexes must be imposed equally (see DRESS REQUIREMENTS (22)).

Catchment areas
The use of these is allowed in determining admission to an overly subscribed school. However, they may be indirectly discriminatory if they unjustifiably

exclude a particular group. In *R v Bradford MBC Ex parte Sikander Ali, The Times 21 October 1993*, there was no discrimination when the council decided to allocate places to an oversubscribed school by allowing only a specific catchment area which excluded an area that was predominantly Asian. This was because a greater proportion of non-white children had also not received places either.

Academic Standards
The requirement of an academic attainment in excess of a particular knowledge level may also be indirectly discriminatory if it excludes a higher proportion of a particular sex or racial group and would have to be justified.

23.3   EDUCATION AND DISABILITY DISCRIMINATION

Unlike race and sex, there are no express provisions as such which relate to the discrimination against disabled people in education. The law is based on the idea that disabled persons have the right to be educated, not on the idea that they have the right to be totally free from discrimination in education. Hence educational establishments are under a duty to provide facilities for education and access to those facilities for disabled people. For example, there is a general duty on all providers of premises to ensure means of access to the building/premises/parking facilities and sanitary facilities so far as is reasonable and practical to do so. The type of premises that this deals with include universities, schools, and training colleges. [*Chronically Ill and Disabled Persons Act 1970, s 8*].

The main provisions relating to the education of disabled persons are contained in *Part II* of the *Education Act 1993*. See paragraphs 23.14 and 23.15.

The *Disability Discrimination Act 1995* introduced additional requirements as regards the provision of education to disabled persons. See paragraphs 23.16 and 23.17.

23.4   PUPILS AT AN EDUCATIONAL ESTABLISHMENT

Where the person is a pupil of the establishment it is unlawful to discriminate:

(*a*)   in the way that the person is afforded access to any benefits, facilities or services or by deliberately refusing access to them; or

(*b*)   by excluding the person from the establishment or subjecting that person to any other detriment.

[*SDA s 22; RRA s 17*].

23.5   Discriminatory Examples

Assessment techniques
The use of assessment techniques of pupils which exclude one sex or ethnic group or, if pupils are tested on the basis of some culturally biased system for example, one that presumes some uniformity in linguistic or religious attributes will be indirectly discriminatory unless the requirement can be objectively justified.

Work Placements
The failure to send pupils on certain work placements on the grounds of race or sex (*CRE v Fearn and British Electrical Repairs (BER)*), or not providing the

appropriate careers advice to pupils on these grounds or persuading them to go into a particular career, will be indirectly discriminatory. If pupils of a certain race or sex are denied access (without an objectively justified reason) to a work placement or shadowing programme, then a cause of action may lie against both the school and the employer.

Curriculum
A benefit that should be available to all pupils is access to the school curriculum. Historically, boys have achieved higher grades than girls in subjects such as the sciences, which was due to boys taking predominantly science subjects and girls taking subjects in the arts. The National Curriculum is directed at removing sex discrimination, and all schools (single sex and co-educational) are required to provide a common core of key subjects for all pupils. However, it is not unlawful to have single sex classes in a co-educational school provided that both sexes are given access to the same benefits and opportunities.

Awarding of Grants
It is unlawful to discriminate in the way that grants are awarded. However, an exception exists where the discrimination is authorised by statute. For example, a requirement that all grants be given to those who live in this country adversely affects overseas students, but is authorised by statute. Similarly, charging overseas students higher fees is allowed by statute. However, a private school or college cannot do this as they have no statutory authorisation.

A further exception is in the case of a charitable instrument award. Where there is a provision that restricts the award to persons of a particular racial or ethnic origin, the instrument is read as though there is no such restriction. [*RRA s 34(1)*].

On the other hand, however, there are no specific prohibitions against an instrument which restricts the beneficiaries to a particular nationality.

Charitable trusts which are created with the purpose of conferring benefits on persons of one sex only are exempt from the provisions of the *SDA*. [*SDA s 43*]. However, trusts created for the purposes of, or in connection with, an educational establishment which restrict the benefit that it provides to one sex, may have the restriction modified or removed. This is achieved by way of an application to the trustees (or responsible body of the trust) by the Secretary of State. The Secretary of State has the power to order the removal or modification of the discriminatory restriction if he is satisfied that this will be 'conducive to the advancement of education without sex discrimination'. [*SDA s 78(2)*].

If the trust is created by way of a will or a gift, no such order can be made until 25 years after the gift or bequest has taken effect, unless the donor or testator or his personal representatives have consented in writing to the application being made [*s 78(3)*]. The Secretary of State will require that the applicant publish a notice, which contains the particulars of the order proposed and stating that representations may be made to him within a specified period of time (being a minimum period of one month). The notice must be published in a manner prescribed by the Secretary of State. The publishing costs of doing so are borne by the trust.

Suspension and Expulsion Criteria
To expel or suspend someone from an educational establishment solely on the grounds of their race or sex constitutes direct discrimination.

CRE research into discrimination in education found that black pupils in secondary schools were, earlier in their schooling, four times more likely to be expelled for less serious acts and after shorter periods than their white counterparts, and were less likely to be re-admitted. *(Birmingham LEA & Schools: Referral and suspension of pupils CRE, 1985.)*

Exclusion or suspension criteria within which a higher proportion of pupils of one sex or a particular racial group fall constitutes indirect discrimination unless it can be justified on objective grounds.

Accommodation ancillary to education
In relation to student accommodation, a university, school or college cannot discriminate. This extends to say halls of residence, residential colleges etc. Private landlords may discriminate in certain limited cases but an educational establishment cannot help such persons to do so.

23.6 EDUCATIONAL ESTABLISHMENTS

Both *Acts* apply to the 'responsible bodies' (such as a Local Education Authority ('LEA') or a board of governors) of all educational establishments. These include:

(*a*)   Those maintained by a Local Education Authority;

(*b*)   Independent schools that are not special schools;

(*c*)   Special schools not maintained by a Local Education Authority;

(*d*)   Grant maintained schools;

(*e*)   Universities; and

(*f*)   City Tech Colleges.

[SDA s 22 and RRA s 17].

23.7 LOCAL EDUCATION AUTHORITY

LEAs are bound by the obligation not to discriminate under the *SDA*, the *RRA* and also when performing any of their functions under the *Education Acts 1944–81*, e.g. the provision of school meals or transport services.

An example is *R v Birmingham City Council Ex parte Equal Opportunities Commission [1989] IRLR 173*, where the House of Lords held that the LEA operated a discriminatory policy of allocating places, because less places were given to girls than boys. The LEA had discriminated in the performance of its obligations under *Education Act 1944, s 8*.

An LEA's responsibilities in performing its statutory obligations are limited in that the wishes of the parents are paramount. For example, if parents wish their child to be transferred to a school with a smaller proportion of ethnic minority pupils, an LEA is not required to investigate the subjective nature of this wish *(R v Cleveland County Council Ex parte CRE, The Times 25 August 1992)*.

Under *Education Act 1980, s 6* parents can express a preference for the school that they wish their children to attend. In this case, the Secretary of State decided that the LEA's actions in acceding to a parent's wish to have her child transferred to a school which had a smaller proportion of ethnic minority pupils was not discriminatory. The CRE argued that if all parents were allowed to move their children from one school to another based on the racial make up of a school then the effect would be segregation, and sought judicial review of the Secretary of State's decision. The CRE was unsuccessful and so it would appear that LEAs are able to discriminate if this is in accordance with the wishes of the parents within the catchment area.

23.8 SPECIAL NEEDS OF RACIAL GROUPS

RRA s 35, deals with the special needs of persons from other racial groups (e.g. the requirement for extra English lessons). It is not unlawful to afford persons of a particular racial group access to facilities or services to meet the special needs of that group with regard to their education, training, welfare or any ancillary benefits, e.g. the provision of after-school lessons or learning books which have a double translation.

It is not unlawful to give someone (who is not ordinarily resident in Great Britain) secondary training when that person is not likely to remain in Great Britain after the training. For example, it is lawful to provide foreign students who are studying for a period at a higher education establishment, with a supplementary course in English.

23.9 SINGLE SEX SCHOOLS

There is an exception in *SDA s 26* in relation to single sex schools. Discrimination on the grounds of sex (but not race) regarding the terms on which admission to an educational establishment is allowed, as is the refusal or deliberate omission to accept an application for admission to an educational establishment.

However, a requirement of equal access remains, and girls must have the same chance of attending such a school as boys (and vice versa). In addition, the responsible bodies of single sex schools should offer facilities which are no less favourable than those at other schools. So for example, the choice of subjects should be the same, so as not to limit access of girls to the sciences.

This provision also applies to schools that are for all intents and purposes single sex except that there are certain pupils of the opposite sex present whose admission is exceptional or whose numbers are comparatively small, and whose admission is confined to a particular course of instruction or teaching class. [*SDA s 26*].

If a school is single sex (or would be if it were not for a comparatively small number of pupils of the opposite sex) and has a mixture of boarders and non-boarders and only a single sex is allowed to board, then it is not unlawful to discriminate in relation to the admission of a single sex or in relation to the boarding facilities provided.

There is a similar exception in respect of teachers and other staff in single sex schools. In *SDA s 7(2)(c), (d)* and *(e)*, there is a limited GOQ in relation to single sex boarding schools, where teachers also lodge at the premises. In these limited circumstances, the school is entitled to appoint as a teacher (or someone in a position involving direct contact with the pupils) someone of the same sex as the pupils. However, this GOQ will apply in very limited circumstances and advice should always be taken if circumstances similar to these ever arise.

23.10 CONVERSION TO A CO-EDUCATIONAL ESTABLISHMENT

By *SDA s 27*, if a single sex school decides to convert to a co-educational establishment, it can obtain a transitional exemption order which will allow it to discriminate by refusing entry to certain individuals specified in the exemption order, for the duration of the transitional period.

However, by *SDA s 27(4)*, exemption is given only in relation to the refusal or deliberate omission to admit pupils to the school; discrimination in relation to other parts of the Act (e.g. in relation to employees of the school) remains unlawful.

An exemption order in relation to public educational establishments is obtained from the Secretary of State and in relation to private educational establishments, from the EOC. In this case the EOC will have regard to the nature of the premises at which the establishment is based, the accommodation, the facilities available and the financial resources of the responsible body.

23.11 PHYSICAL TRAINING/SPORTS

There is also an exemption in relation to physical education which is a further or higher education course under the *Education Reform Act 1988*.

However, in schools the *SDA* operates and it is unlawful to offer certain traditional sports or activities only to girls or boys depending on their sex. Therefore, both sexes must have equal access to sports and other extra curricular activities and this may be by way of single sex or mixed classes.

23.12 BRINGING A CLAIM FOR DISCRIMINATION IN EDUCATION

Very few claims have been brought under *Part III* of either the *SDA* or the *RRA*. This may be due to a number of factors, e.g. because children are involved, and because of the longer time scales involved (see below).

A claim for race or sex discrimination in relation to education is presented to a county court. The claim is for a breach of statutory duty. [*RRA s 57; SDA s 66*]. The damages available are the same as those in the High Court and may include damages for injury to feelings (see REMEDIES (49)).

Any claim for discrimination (contrary to the *SDA* or *RRA*) in State education (but not universities) can only be instituted once notice of the claim has been given to the Secretary of State and either the Secretary of State has satisfied the claimant that no further time is required to consider the matter, or two months have elapsed since the claimant notified the Secretary of State. [*RRA s 57(5); SDA s 66(5)*]. However, none of these requirements apply to any counterclaim made by the educational body complained against.

23.13 Time Limits in which to bring a claim

By *RRA s 68; SDA s 76*, a claim must be instituted within six months of the act complained of. If the claim relates to a state education establishment which is not a university, this time limit is extended by a further two months upon notice being given to the Secretary of State.

If the claim relates to private or university education, then the period remains six months extendable by a further three months in race discrimination cases if assistance is requested from the CRE (see below).

23.14 Education

If the claim is for racial discrimination, and an application for assistance has been made to the CRE within this period of six months, the time limit is automatically extended by a further two months in order for the appropriate investigations to be carried out [*RRA s 68(3)*]. If the CRE writes to the applicant confirming that the application for assistance is being considered, the time limit is automatically extended by a further month. [*RRA s 66(4)*]. Such a letter will usually be sent to the applicant as a matter of course. There are no equivalent provisions in the *SDA*.

As with any claim for sex or race discrimination, the county court has the power to consider any complaint which is out of time if in all the circumstances of the case it is considered just and equitable to do so.

23.14 EDUCATION AND DISABILITY

The main provisions relating to the education of disabled people in primary, secondary and further education comes in the form of *Part II* of the *Education Act 1993* which has largely supplanted the *Education Act 1981*. Disabled people are referred to as having a 'Special Education Need' – a learning difficulty that prevents a child from making use of educational facilities which other children of the same age could use.

Codes of practice are issued by the Secretary of State in relation to the education of people with special needs, which all LEAs and schools are required to observe. The first code was issued in 1994.

An LEA is required to keep under review all its arrangements for the provision of special education and if it is considered that it is inappropriate to meet the need in a school, then provision could be made to meet it elsewhere – even in another area (if necessary).

The duty to serve the needs of disabled people in a school that is not a special school is a qualified duty. Such an establishment is only responsible for the education of those with special needs if:

(*a*)   the parents of the child wish it;

(*b*)   the education is compatible to providing the special education to which the learning difficulty requires;

(*c*)   to provide the special education is compatible to meeting the needs of the other children of the school; and

(*d*)   there will be an efficient use of resources.

[*Education Act 1993, s 160*].

An LEA is required to ensure that all disabled pupils with a special need have the need met and may utilise the help of the District Health Authority to do so. A governing body of a county, voluntary or grant-maintained school that is not a special school, is required to ensure that the special educational needs of any disabled pupils are met and that all the people required to teach those pupils are made aware of that special education need.

Parents who are unhappy with the arrangements made should air grievances with the school and/or the Secretary of State. A disabled pupil with special educational needs should be allowed to engage in the same activitives as other children who do not have special educational needs.

Governing bodies are also required to issue an annual statement which details what the school has done in order to fulfil the special needs of the relevant disabled pupils.

23.15 STATUTORY ASSESSMENT OF A SPECIAL EDUCATION NEED

If a disabled child has a special education need, the LEA needs to determine the special education provision for the child in order to meet these needs, and LEA may make an assessment of the child's needs [*Education Act 1993, s 167*]. Once such an assessment has been made of the child's needs, an authority may make a statement of the child's special education need which details:

(*a*)   the needs; and

(*b*)   state what should be done to meet them; and

(*c*)   state what type of school or other institution should be used to meet them; and

(*d*)   name the most appropriate school to meet those needs; and

(*e*)   specify any measures to be taken.

That school will then have to admit the child [*Education Act 1993, s 168*].

Such a statement is only usually made if the LEA feels that the special needs of the disabled child cannot be met in an ordinary (mainstream) school and if he or she is falling seriously behind. An assessment will be made if the LEA thinks fit or if the parents request it, although an LEA can still refuse the parents' request if an assessment is felt to be unnecessary.

If an LEA declines to make such an assessment or statement under *section 167*, a parent can refer the matter to a Special Education Tribunal within two months of the decision complained of being made. If the Tribunal cannot deal with the issue, then the grievance is dealt with by the Local Government Ombudsman.

The Tribunal may find that a statement should be made, dismiss the appeal or remit the case to the LEA and tell them to reconsider the matter taking account of the Tribunal's observations.

The parents may also appeal to the Tribunal against the contents of a statement made after an assessment. The same time limit applies.

The education needs of a pupil must be continually reviewed at least once a year (and more often if asked by the parents). If an LEA decides not to review the child's case the parents may appeal to the Tribunal. An assessment of a child's special education needs may also be made upon request of a governing body of a school.

If it is found that progress has been made, then the statement may cease and a child may be sent back to an ordinary school. If a child leaves school at 16, the statement will cease. It will continue until the child is 19 if he remains in further education.

Therefore, even though there is no express provision relating to the discrimination of disabled persons in education, mainstream schools are required to be more open about the issue of educating disabled persons and face the problem head on.

23.16 Education

23.16 THE DISABILITY DISCRIMINATION ACT 1995

Under the *Disability Discrimination Act 1995*, the term 'disability' embraces a wider spectrum going beyond earlier provisions (such as the previously mentioned access provisions) which envisage disability as simply being confined to a wheelchair. Access to educational facilities will now include access for blind or deaf pupils or those with other impairments (see DISABILITY (18)).

By the *Disability Discrimination Act 1995*, teacher training agencies are required to have regard to the needs of disabled persons, increasing awareness of the problems faced by disabled persons in education.

Under *section 25* of the *Disability Discrimination Act*, the requirement for schools to disclose arrangements made for disabled persons in the annual statement are extended. The annual statement must also contain provisions as to:

(*a*) the arrangements made for the admission of disabled pupils;

(*b*) steps taken to prevent disabled pupils from being treated less favourably than other people; and

(*c*) the facilities provided to assist the access to the school by disabled people.

The provisions introduced by the *Disability Discrimination Act* in relation to the disclosure of facilities for disabled pupils do not extend to independent schools. It is these schools that frequently offer special education facilities. Parents of disabled pupils are not able to demand information about the special facilities offered by these schools. Recommendations have been made that the disclosure provisions be extended to independent schools. It has also been recommended that the requirement of disclosure of information be extended to Adult Education Colleges.

It has been argued that without further guidelines many educational establishments may still fail to cater for students with disabilities beyond the commonly perceived disabilities. However, the Government's Schools Access Initiative will set aside a limited amount of funds in order to improve access to schools for disabled pupils. Each LEA or grant-maintained school can bid for a portion of the funds (the size of the fund for each LEA being limited by the number of schools in the area). Access funds that are available include:

(*a*) those for children with sensory impairments;

(*b*) access to the curriculum; and;

(*c*) access to social activities and even to the surrounding community.

The first funds will become available after March 1996.

23.17 FURTHER AND HIGHER EDUCATION

The *Disability Discrimination Act 1995* requires that when Further Education Funding Councils provide funding for further education under the *Further and Higher Education Act 1992*, conditions may be attached to such funding which may require the governing body of the establishment to publish a 'disability statement' describing the facilities provided for disabled persons.

The council may also give funding to the body on the condition that provisions be made for disabled people. *Disability Discrimination Act s 26(4)* requires that a Council make a statement at the end of every financial year as to the provisions that have been made for disabled people, and as to any future plans in this respect.

Similarly, Higher Education Funding Councils must ensure that when exercising functions under the *Further and Higher Education Act 1992*, consideration is given to the needs of disabled persons [*DDA s 26(5)*], and when providing funding to higher education bodies, such bodies make disability statements as to the provision of education for disabled people. Conditions may be attached so that the needs of disabled persons be met when providing such funding. [*DDA s 26(6)*].

24 Employment

24.1 DEFINITION

It is unlawful to discriminate against any employee on grounds of race or sex in respect of his employment. For the purposes of discrimination legislation the definition of 'employment' is a wider one than that for employment protection legislation generally. This can be seen from a number of distinctive features.

(*a*) There is no 'qualifying period' of service; protection from the *RRA, SDA* and *EqPA* is immediate (as against a two-year service qualification for protection from unfair dismissal under the *EPCA*. However, the Court of Appeal held in *R v Secretary of State for Employment Ex parte Seymour-Smith and Perez* [1995] *IRLR 464* that the two-year service requirement was indirectly discriminatory) (see EPCA (26)).

(*b*) For the purposes of the *SDA* and *RRA* the definition of 'employment' includes self-employed persons, provided their contract requires them to execute the work 'personally'. [*RRA s 78(1); SDA s 82(1)*]. (See *Quinnen v Hovells* [*1984*] *IRLR 227*.) If the contract enables them to delegate the work to a third party, then they are outside the scope of those Acts (*Mirror Group Newspapers v Gunning* [*1986*] *ICR 145*). The *EPCA* does not extend to self-employed persons in any circumstances.

(*c*) Where the *EPCA* provides only limited protection (other than against unfair dismissal), the *RRA* and *SDA* protect the employee in every regard of the employment relationship, from the arrangements made to appoint [*RRA s 4(1)(a)(c); SDA s 6(1)(a)(c)*], through the terms of the appointment, promotion and other benefits [*RRA s 4(1)(b), (2)(b); SDA s 6(1)(b), (2)(a)*], to dismissal and 'any other detriment', which term is all-encompassing. [*RRA s 4(2)(c); SDA s 6(2)(b)*].

24.2 EXCEPTIONS

Employment outside the UK

RRA s 8 and *SDA s 10* define the meaning of 'employment at an establishment in Great Britain'. An employee is to be regarded as coming within the scope of the legislation unless he does his work 'wholly or mainly outside Great Britain'. *SDA s 7(2)(g)* also exempts employment where the job needs to be held by a man because the position 'is likely' to involve performing duties abroad in countries where restrictions are imposed by law or custom on women performing such duties. There is no such equivalent exception in the *RRA*. Aircraft, hovercraft and shipping employees are subject to all the Acts if their vessels are registered in the UK, unless they are employed exclusively outside the UK. However, seamen recruited outside the UK (not including employees on oil rigs or those engaged in exploration in UK waters) are not subject to the *RRA*. [*RRA s 9*].

24.3 Employment in a private household

The *RRA* does not apply to employment in a private household, except for discrimination by way of victimisation. [*RRA s 4(3)*]. The definition of 'employment in a private household' is a strict one. In a case where a chauffeur was paid by a company, but employed exclusively in the private household (driving the Chairman's wife), this was deemed not to be employment in a private household (*Heron Corporation Ltd v Commis* [*1980*] *ICR 713*). Any director wishing to discriminate in the appointment of his or his wife's chauffeur in future should ensure that the employment is paid for directly by the director himself and not out of the company payroll. Morally, there seems no argument to sustain such a wide exception.

The *SDA* has a more limited 'genuine occupational qualification' (GOQ) exception for employment in a private household [*SDA s 7(2)(ba)*] which might, 25 years after the first *Race Relations Act*, be more appropriate. Note that the *RRA* exception probably does not extend to advertising such a position [*RRA s 29*], as the prohibition on discriminatory advertising extends to what might reasonably be understood to be an intention to commit an act of discrimination, whether the doing by him of that act would be lawful or unlawful. For example, an advertisement for a white butler would be understood as indicating an intention to discriminate, notwithstanding the exception that exempts such an appointment from the Act.

24.4 Other exceptions

There are a limited number of exceptions whereby it is permissible to discriminate in favour of an individual on the grounds of his sex or race, where that person's sex or race is a GOQ. [*RRA s 5; SDA s 7*]. These circumstances are limited and are dealt with in full in GENUINE OCCUPATIONAL QUALIFICATION (33). As the GOQ is an exemption from the main purpose of the legislation (which is to prevent discrimination), it will be restrictively interpreted (*London Borough of Lambeth v CRE* [*1990*] *IRLR 231*).

24.5 APPOINTMENTS

Background

There is a large body of research material which shows that racial discrimination in particular is commonplace at the recruitment stage. A study in Nottingham in 1980, using a control group of 'applicants' from Indian, West Indian and white groups, found that, at short-listing stage only, one out of every two applications by the black candidates was a waste of time ('Half a Chance', CRE, 1980). Frequently, short-listing is a 'weeding' process executed by relatively junior staff working to set criteria. Often these staff will assume prejudices on the part of their employer, sometimes even if they are not themselves prejudiced but have observed an 'all white' culture at the firm. The CRE Code of Practice recommends monitoring as an effective way for an employer to be sure that there are not problems at this level (see 24.23 below).

24.6 Arrangements to appoint

Both Acts protect the employee in respect of the arrangements for making the appointment. [*RRA s 4(1)(a); SDA s 6(1)(a)*]. 'Arrangements' covers the advertising of the position, the short-listing criteria, the short-listing process itself and the entire selection, interviewing and appointment process. Where a woman or ethnic minority candidate is, on paper, better qualified or suited for the post than the successful male or white (or other race) candidate, and that individual commences an action in the industrial tribunal, the employer will be called upon to provide a satisfactory 'innocent' explanation for the apparent discrimination. The Acts cover omissions as well as actions. A failure to advertise a vacancy might, in some circumstances, constitute indirect discrimination, unless it could be justified.

24.7   Terms of the appointment

It is unlawful to offer discriminatory terms of appointment on grounds of race or sex. It would not, therefore, be lawful to offer a position which gave medical care benefits only to male employees. [*RRA s 4(1)(b); SDA s 6(1)(b)*].

24.8   Advertising

Employers are restrained from discriminatory advertising by more than just the possibility of an individual application in the industrial tribunal alleging unlawful discrimination. The CRE and EOC have the power to prosecute advertisers and publishers of discriminatory advertisements. [*RRA s 29; SDA s 38*]. (The National Disability Council is likely to have similar powers.) (See ADVERTISING (2) for a detailed analysis.) In summary, an employer should avoid using sexist terminology (e.g. waiter, barman etc.), and either use neutral terminology or stipulate the alternative (e.g. waiter/waitress). Caution should be used in advertising positions to which a GOQ applies; either the EOC or CRE will advise employers on such matters on request. Advertised criteria should be assessed to ensure that they are not unjustifiably indirectly discriminatory.

24.9   Failure to advertise

Word-of-mouth recruitment, trade union recruitment and internal advertising are all potentially indirectly discriminatory as they may reinforce the pre-existing racial or sexual composition of the workforce. Where a workforce is already balanced, this will not be the case, but otherwise employers need to consider whether they can reasonably justify such practices on non-racial grounds. Such recruitment practices will not be discriminatory where exercised in conjunction with Job Centre recruitment advertising in local newspapers or other normal recruitment practices, because then it would not be possible to show adverse impact.

24.10   Role of gate, reception and personnel staff

The CRE Code (para 1.14(a)) advises that gate, reception and personnel staff should be instructed not to discriminate. There have been successful tribunal applications where gate staff informed all black individuals seeking work that there were no vacancies and handed application forms only to white persons, unbeknown to company management. If the companies concerned had issued instructions not to discriminate, they would not have been liable.

24.11   PROMOTION

Introduction

Both the *SDA* and *RRA* expressly provide that an employer must give equal access to promotion opportunities regardless of race or sex. [*RRA s 4(2)(b);*

SDA s 6(2)(a)]. A failure to promote an individual on grounds of race or sex is a detriment covered by the catch-all 'any other detriment' wording in *RRA s 4(2)(c)* and *SDA s 6(2)(b)*.

Complaints about failure to obtain promotion are the most common basis for tribunal applications apart from complaints about dismissal and original appointment. Such complaints cause great stress for all concerned, individual and employer alike, as the employment relationship has to continue whilst the legal process grinds on, often interminably, it seems. Such applications create special problems for employers. It is not an unnatural response for a line manager accused of racial or sexual discrimination to feel hostile towards his accuser and 'take it out on him'. Any detrimental treatment so motivated would be VICTIMISATION (54) and it is important that, if an individual takes advantage of his statutory right to make a complaint to a tribunal about failure to be promoted on discriminatory grounds, appropriate advice and training is given to relevant managers and colleagues.

24.12 **Direct discrimination**

It is important for an employer to remember that it is the *cause*, not the *motive*, for any discrimination that is at issue. An employer may say: 'I am not prejudiced but I know that the workforce is, and I will have a walkout if I appoint a black/female supervisor'. In such a case, the employer's motivation is fear of industrial unrest, but the cause of the adverse treatment of the individual who is not promoted is race or sex; the individual will be entitled to damages and, probably, a recommendation that they be given the relevant position (see REMEDIES (49)).

It is possible that individuals involved in the promotion process may exercise subconscious discrimination against black or female candidates, based on subconscious racial or sexual stereotyping, which causes them to have reservations which either cannot be quantified or are disguised by vague generalisations about 'long-term potential' or the like. Whilst such criteria may be wholly legitimate they can easily disguise conscious, or subconscious, prejudice against wholly suitable black or female candidates (*Baker v Cornwall County Council [1990] IRLR 194*).

24.13 **Discriminatory encouragement to apply for promotion permitted**

SDA s 48 and *RRA s 38* permit an employer to encourage women or men only, or a particular racial group (the under-represented group) to 'take advantage of opportunities for doing particular work' if in the preceding twelve months there have been no, or comparatively few, members of the sex in question or, as the case may be, of the under-represented group doing that work (presumably higher level, or different, work). The wording of these sections is a little imprecise, and they have not been put to the test. A normal reading, however, would suggest that this clause enables an employer actively to encourage an under-represented group to seek promotion, but not actually to restrict the promotion on such a basis. In other words, if, despite not having been encouraged to apply, a man applies for a promotion for which women have been encouraged to apply, he must be considered and, if the best candidate, he must be given the post.

24.14 MATTERS RELEVANT TO BOTH APPOINTMENT AND PROMOTION

Criteria for short-listing

It is unlawful to fail to short-list candidates (or appoint them) because of their race, sex or marital status. This is straightforward direct discrimination. It is a relatively rare occurrence as most employers and, more importantly, their staff involved in recruitment, are aware that straightforward selection by virtue of race and sex is unlawful. There is some doubt as to whether this has been fully appreciated in relation to marital status.

Other, *prima facie* lawful, fixed criteria are often used for the short-listing process. Such criteria may, in particular circumstances, constitute indirect discrimination and be unlawful unless they can be justified on non-racial (or non-sexual) grounds. A requirement to have supervisory experience linked to a maximum age criterion may indirectly discriminate against otherwise suitable women who have taken a career break. Residence requirements will indirectly discriminate against certain ethnic minority groups. There are too many possible examples to list them all.

Any job criterion should be considered carefully in the light of prevailing local circumstances, and consideration given as to whether the effect of the criterion will be to exclude one or other sex, or ethnic or racial group. If it does tend to do so, that criterion should be discarded unless there is other good justification for using it. Employers should be particularly careful about imposing 'essential' criteria for positions. Only absolute criteria fall within this category. A criterion that is 'desirable', but not essential (as a matter of fact as well as assertion), cannot constitute indirect discrimination as it would not be an absolute bar (*Meer v London Borough of Tower Hamlets [1988] IRLR 399*).

The CRE Code of Practice recommends that short-listing should not be done by one individual alone, but should at least be checked by a senior (para 1.14(c)).

24.15 Qualifications

Requiring 'O' levels can constitute indirect discrimination unless overseas equivalents are permitted. There have been some cases on the point, which have not really cast the sort of helpful light on the matter that employers might wish. Whether the requirement of 'O' levels is or is not justifiable is a matter of fact for the particular tribunal to consider. Extraordinarily, the EAT accepted that two separate tribunals could come to different conclusions on this point, on the same facts (*Raval v Department of Health and Social Security [1985] ICR 685*). The likelihood on existing authority is, however, that the requirement of certain 'O' levels will be justifiable so long as the employer can show that such a requirement does relate realistically to the position in hand. Requirements as to the number of exams passed at one sitting are not likely to be found justifiable (as an absolute criterion), and there is research evidence to show that persons with an Asian background are likely to take 'O' levels at more sittings than the indigenous community.

24.16 Interview

Both the CRE and EOC Codes of Practice recommend that all staff involved in interviews should receive appropriate training about the provisions of the relevant legislation and the risks associated with making stereotyped assumptions on the basis of the sex or race of the applicant (EOC Code, para 23, CRE Code, para 1.14(b)).

24.17 **Tests**

The CRE Code (para 1.13) and the EOC Code (para 21) advise that employers should ensure that selection criteria and tests are carefully assessed to ascertain that they are job-related. The CRE Code gives the following examples.

(*a*)   Standards of English language (spoken or written) required should relate to the job in hand, and candidates should not be disqualified if they cannot complete a job application unaided unless this criterion is relevant to the position. This is potential indirect discrimination.

(*b*)   Standards of educational attainment should relate to the job in hand. This is also potential indirect discrimination.

(*c*)   Selection tests, psychometric tests and similar tests should be examined carefully to ensure that they are not culturally biased, nor put ethnic minority individuals at a disadvantage (for example, because of an inbuilt disadvantage if their English was learned rather than acquired from birth), that they are relevant to the job and, if they do have an adverse impact, are otherwise justifiable. Such tests are particularly vulnerable to what might be termed 'mother tongue bias'. The speed of completion may be adversely affected where the language of the test is an acquired one. General knowledge questions in such tests may also be culturally biased (by way of illustration, 'Trivial Pursuit' has different sets of questions in each country in which it is available, because the amount of 'universal' general knowledge is limited).

24.18 **Interview criteria**

If an individual complains of failure to be selected or promoted, then, once he has established that this failure could possibly be by virtue of unlawful discrimination, the employer is called upon to satisfy the tribunal with an explanation (*Chattopadhyay v Headmaster of Holloway School [1982] ICR 132*). The more objective the criteria employed at the interview, the easier it will be to provide this explanation.

On occasions, however, amorphous criteria such as leadership potential, ability to 'fit in', or long-term potential will be used. The Court of Appeal has recognised that these criteria can be a mask for unlawful discrimination (*Baker v Cornwall County Council [1990] IRLR 194*). It will be more difficult for the employer to satisfy a tribunal unless the criteria have been clearly set out (and preferably made known to the candidates) and the relevant staff trained in respect of the obligations of the *RRA* and *SDA*. Such criteria are not, however, unlawful. They will only be unlawful if they make a deliberate policy of discrimination on grounds of race or sex, or because their vague nature results in the interviewer unwittingly using racial or sexual stereotypes at the expense of female or black candidates (*British Gas v Sharma [1991] IRLR 101*).

24.19 **Questions relating to marital or family commitments**

The EOC Code expressly advises against interviewers asking questions about future marital and family commitments (para 23(c)). Such questions are liable to be construed as showing bias against female candidates, and even when an employer asks *all* candidates about current family commitments there are risks. Such questions are not directly discriminatory in themselves if asked of all candidates (*Simon v Brimham Associates [1987] IRLR 307* – an RRA case where all applicants were asked about their religion). If an absolute bar is imposed in respect of family responsibilities, this may be indirectly discriminatory. Provided an absolute bar is not operated, it is permissible for an employer to take into account family responsibilities on a rational basis. A tribunal is likely to draw an adverse inference of sex discrimination, however, if assumptions have been made about the family commitments of female candidates.

24.20 Disability

Employers with more than 20 employees must not discriminate against disabled persons in relation to offering employment, terms of employment, promotion and training, save where the employer's conduct is justified under the *Disability Discrimination Act 1995, s 5*. (See DISABILITY (18).)

24.21 Other unlawful criteria

It should be noted that it is also unlawful to discriminate against an individual at the appointment stage, either regarding arrangements made for the appointment, or by refusing to offer the appointment on grounds of membership, or non-membership, of a trade union. In this regard, employers should be cautious of making use of recruitment agencies that have made a record of political or trade union activities of employees.

24.22 Code of Practice recommendations

The EOC Code of Practice sets out recommended procedures for recruitment and promotion (paras 21, 23, 24 and 25). The EOC advises that employers should assess requirements of a position carefully, particularly in regard to unsocial hours and travel, and these should be discussed objectively with the job applicant. Care should be taken to consider favourably candidates of both sexes with differing career patterns and general experience. The CRE Code deals with 'selection criteria and tests' and 'treatment of applicants, short-listing, interviewing and selection' at paras 1.13 and 1.14, and contains similar advice to the EOC Code.

The Codes of Practice are not statements of the law as such, but are advisory (see CODES OF PRACTICE (8)). They may, however, be taken into account by a tribunal in considering an application. In an application before the tribunal by a woman alleging discrimination on grounds of sex because of adverse assumptions about child care responsibility, a tribunal will take into account the prohibition of marital status questions in the Codes in deciding whether or not to draw an inference of discrimination.

24.23 Monitoring

Both the CRE (paras 1.33-1.37) and (to a more limited degree) the EOC (paras 25(f) and 37) recommend monitoring in their respective Codes of Practice. In selection procedure, it is often desirable to be able to detach the information required for monitoring (race, sex, marital status details etc.) so that this information is not used in the short-listing process, but only utilised at a later stage to objectively assess the recruitment exercise.

24.24 Remedy

An employee who considers that he has been discriminated against in respect of appointment or promotion on grounds of sex or race may take a claim to the industrial tribunal within three months of the act complained of, and claim damages. The extent of those damages will depend on whether he establishes that because of the discrimination, he lost only the opportunity of the position (i.e. he had a chance of getting the job), or the position itself (i.e. he would definitely have got the job but for the discrimination). The tribunal can also make limited recommendations to the employer to reduce the adverse effect of the discrimination. (See REMEDIES (49) and, as to time limits, 24.33 below.)

24.25 CHECKLIST

1. Have a clear job specification and clear job criteria been drawn up? Is there a need for essential criteria? Do any of the criteria have an adverse impact on grounds of race or sex? If so, can they be changed, or are they justifiable?

2. Has the appointment or promotion been advertised to all staff? If not, will the method of selection favour men against women, or vice versa, or favour a particular racial group or groups? If there is a disproportionate impact, can it be justified on non-racial/sex-related grounds? Are there groups of potential appointees not already employed by the company who could complain of indirect discrimination if the position has only been advertised internally, and can this be justified?

3. Has the wording of the advertisement been checked to ensure that the terms used are not discriminatory? (Beware titles such as 'Foreman'.)

4. Have any written tests been examined to ensure that they are both relevant and free of cultural bias?

5. If the position is one to which a GOQ applies, has this been checked with the EOC or CRE?

6. Have the short-listing and interviewing staff been trained or issued with instructions about equal opportunities, and advised against making stereotyped assumptions?

7. Are all the applicants on an equal footing (i.e. in terms of knowledge of the post), and aware of the criteria to be used?

8. Has each candidate been asked about matters that might create a problem, rather than assumptions made (e.g. female candidates asked about overtime or travel commitments)?

9. Has the final selection been assessed to ensure that it satisfies objective scrutiny?

10. If there remains an under-representation of female or ethnic minority staff at the higher grade, is it appropriate to offer special training to categories of existing staff or potential recruits?

24.26 TRAINING

It is unlawful to discriminate on grounds of race or sex in the provision of training or opportunities for training. [*RRA s 4(2)(b); SDA s 6(2)(b)*]. Employers should consider carefully the arrangements that they make for training. It is possible that a training programme that, for example, only provides opportunities for training on residential weekend courses may be *prima facie* indirectly discriminatory and, if a member of staff were to challenge such a practice, the employer would have to justify the practice. A tribunal would then balance the discriminatory effect against any cost or convenience argument put forward by the employer.

24.27 Exceptions to the RRA and SDA

The *RRA* and *SDA* make provision for employers to take modest ('positive action') steps in respect of training [*RRA s 38; SDA s 48*], and a degree of discrimination in favour of disadvantaged groups is permitted. (See POSITIVE DISCRIMINATION (43).)

24.28 FACILITIES AND BENEFITS

Segregation

Providing equal, but segregated, facilities for members of different racial groups by way of employment benefits is unlawful. [*RRA s 1(2)*]. There is no such clause in the *SDA*, and provision of separate, but equal, facilities for men and women is lawful (and common-sense). In some circumstances, a failure to provide separate female (or male) toilet facilities could constitute indirect discrimination. If a position involves on-site changing and washing, and such a facility is not available to a woman, so effectively acting as a bar to her performing the duties of the position, it would, *prima facie*, be indirectly discriminatory, and probably not justifiable (except perhaps if there was no physical space for such facilities or if the cost was wholly disproportionate).

24.29 Other benefits

It is unlawful to discriminate on grounds of race or sex in the provision of any other benefits, such as private health cover, company car etc. [*RRA s 4(2)(b); SDA s 6(2)(b)*], unless they are benefits given to a woman in connection with pregnancy or childbirth. [*SDA s 2(2)*].

24.30 Benefits connected with pregnancy or childbirth

SDA s 2(2) prevents men from making any complaint about the special treatment of women in connection with childbirth or pregnancy. This covers special maternity leave, ante-natal care leave and return to work provisions. It seems unlikely that this provision extends beyond arrangements for the return to work. Employers should, therefore, ensure that 'return to work' packages are made available to both men and women wishing to take a career break for family reasons. Such a package would still be *prima facie* indirectly discriminatory, but the justification of staff turnover and the cost of the loss of trained staff should satisfy an industrial tribunal (but this cannot be guaranteed – it is a matter of fact for the tribunal).

24.31 DISMISSAL

It is unlawful to dismiss an employee by reason of his race or sex. [*RRA s 4(2)(c); SDA s 6(2)(b)*]. This includes dismissing white staff for refusal to accept discriminatory instructions (*Zarczynska v Levy* [*1979*] *ICR 184*). Employers with large numbers of ethnic minority staff, or with any staff with language difficulties, should consider ensuring that disciplinary rules and safety commands are available in translation.

Redundancy criteria should be examined to ensure that they are not unlawfully discriminatory. Employers should be especially cautious about a 'last in, first out' (LIFO) policy (which may be indirectly racially or sexually discriminatory (*Clarke v Eley (IMI Kynoch) Ltd [1982] IRLR 131*)), or a policy that involves selecting part-timers first (which will probably be indirectly sexually discriminatory). (See DISMISSAL (21).)

An employee can terminate his contract of employment if his employer is in 'repudiatory breach', which means, in essence, that the employer is in breach of a fundamental term of the contract (*Western Excavating (ECC) Ltd v Sharp [1978] ICR 221*).

If an employee is subjected to a work environment in which he is discriminated against, or subjected to racial or sexual harassment to the extent that he can tolerate it no longer, he will have a claim for constructive dismissal (as well as for race or sex discrimination). (See CONSTRUCTIVE DISMISSAL (12).)

24.32 'ANY OTHER DETRIMENT'

It is also unlawful to subject an employee to 'any other detriment' by reason of his race or sex. [*RRA s 4(2)(c); SDA s 6(2)(b)*]. This is a wide 'sweep up' phrase. In one instance, it was a detriment that an instruction had been issued to search all black staff leaving a factory (on the basis of suspicions against one black individual), even though the complainant had not actually been stopped. The existence of the instruction itself was a detriment (*British Leyland Cars v Brown [1983] ICR 143*).

24.33 TIME LIMIT

An employee must make a claim within three months of the alleged discriminatory dismissal [*RRA s 68; SDA s 76*], except where a tribunal considers it just and equitable in all the circumstances to entertain a late claim. [*RRA s 68(6); SDA s 76(5)*]. If an employee is subjected to a continuing act of discrimination, then the time limit continues to run. An example of a continuing act of discrimination is, say, a company rule that women are not eligible for senior management appointments. This applies only if there is a definite rule; there is no continuing act of discrimination if an individual fails to get a particular post, even though the consequences of that decision continue to affect the individual (see *Amies v Inner London Education Authority [1977] ICR 308, Calder v James Finlay Corporation [1989] ICR 157* and *Barclays Bank plc v Kapur [1991] IRLR 136*). The individual must prove discrimination, but if the individual can show that an explanation for his treatment could be unlawful discrimination, the employer must satisfy the tribunal as to his 'innocent explanation', or else an inference of unlawful discrimination is likely to result. (See BURDEN OF PROOF (6).)

25 Employment Agencies

25.1 SCOPE OF LEGISLATION

It is unlawful for an employment agency to discriminate against any individual in the terms on which it offers its services, or by refusing or failing to provide its services or in the way it provides its services. [*RRA s 14(1); SDA s 15(1)*].

An employment agency could also be liable by virtue of *RRA s 33* or *SDA s 42* if it accepted and acted upon discriminatory instructions from an employer, both in respect of proceedings by the relevant Commission (CRE or EOC, as the case may be) for a declaration that discriminatory instructions had been issued or discriminatory pressure applied, and by the affected individual making a complaint and seeking damages.

In 1993 the CRE investigated a Bradford company (Britannia Products Ltd) and two employment agencies (Brook Street and Network Recruitment Ltd) for alleged discriminatory instructions from the company to the employment agency. Non-discrimination notices were issued against Brook Street and Network Recruitment Ltd.

The EOC has also investigated employment agencies, and a non-discrimination notice was issued in October 1994 against Workforce Employment Agency Ltd.

25.2 DEPARTMENT OF EMPLOYMENT LICENCE

Since 3 January 1995, employment agencies have been able to operate without a licence from the DoE. This change is a result of the *Deregulation and Contracting Out Act 1994*. The standards of conduct for employment agencies are still in force, and it is now possible to apply to industrial tribunals for an order prohibiting people from running employment agencies on grounds of misconduct or other unsuitability.

25.3 EXCEPTIONS

An employment agency may discriminate where it would be lawful for an individual to discriminate, i.e. in the following instances.

(*a*)   On grounds of race only, in respect of any appointment for the purposes of a private household [*RRA s 4(3)*] (but the agency may not advertise such a post on a discriminatory basis), and on grounds of sex if such an appointment involves the post-holder in a degree of physical or social contact with, or an intimate knowledge of, an individual living in that home. [*SDA s 7(2)(ba)*].

(*b*)   Where the post to be filled by the employer is one for which there is a genuine occupational qualification. [*RRA s 5; SDA s 7*]. (See GENUINE OCCUPATIONAL QUALIFICATION (33).)

(*c*)   Where a partnership is seeking to recruit a partner, it may not discriminate on grounds of sex [*SDA s 11 (as amended)*], but partnerships of fewer than six partners are not prohibited from discriminating on racial grounds [*RRA s 10*] (although, again, such a position may not be advertised on a discriminatory basis).

(*d*)   In any other instance where the discrimination is lawful, e.g. on statutory authority [*RRA s 41; SDA s 51*], or for safeguarding national security

[*RRA s 42; SDA s 52*] – but note that by virtue of *SI 1988 No 249, SDA s 52* no longer applies to discrimination in employment or related areas.

25.4 **INSTRUCTIONS AND PRESSURE TO DISCRIMINATE**

Employment agencies are particularly likely to be the recipients of instructions or pressure to discriminate. An employer may request that an agency send no women or send no black staff. Employment agencies should consider having a special procedure to deal with such instances (as, for example, did the now defunct Manpower Services Commission, which referred such matters to a special department which then passed the information to the CRE or EOC if appropriate). If such a procedure is in force and the agency can show clearly that its staff are not permitted to accept discriminatory instructions, then it will not be liable for unauthorised acceptance of such instructions by individual staff. [*RRA s 32(3); SDA s 41(3)*]. There is no obligation to report a discriminatory instruction either to the individual or to the EOC or CRE.

The CRE and EOC usually act on any complaint and either obtain promises of future good conduct or take proceedings and obtain a declaration that the discriminatory pressure or instructions happened (there are no damages, but the CRE or EOC may obtain an injunction in respect of persistent discriminatory acts). Such reports have a salutary effect and generally the employer from whom the instruction originates, if it is an operation of any size, will not have authorised such a criterion nor have wished it to be applied in its name. An employment agency is not, however, protected from victimisation as it is a service provider and there is no provision in either Act prohibiting the service customer from discriminating on racial or sexual grounds.

25.5 **THE CODE OF PRACTICE**

The CRE Code of Practice has an entire section of extensive advice devoted to employment agencies (Part 4). The EOC Code, on the other hand, has only a brief and rather bland paragraph (para 9) devoted to employment agencies.

26   Employment Protection (Consolidation) Act 1978 (EPCA)

26.1   SCOPE AND PURPOSE

The *EPCA* (as amended) protects employees from being dismissed from their jobs without some substantial cause, such as redundancy, misconduct or lack of capability. It protects all employees who have not less than 2 years' continuous service. However, in August 1995 the Court of Appeal held that the 2-year qualifying period was indirectly discriminatory against women *(R v Secretary of State for Employment Ex parte Seymour-Smith and Perez [1995] IRLR 464)*. The Government is believed to be appealing against this decision. Until this area is clarified, employers should act cautiously and treat all employees, irrespective of the length of service, as though they are entitled to claim unfair dismissal (see 21.2 above).

Similarly, discrimination legislation protects all employees, regardless of length of service or hours worked, from dismissal on discriminatory grounds or discrimination short of dismissal; indeed, prospective employees are protected.

An employee who has been dismissed, and who has the requisite length of service, can claim unfair dismissal, and can also complain of discrimination if he or she believes that is the reason for the dismissal.

26.2   EFFECT OF PARALLEL CLAIMS

An individual can only be compensated for actual loss of earnings once. In addition to such compensation (the 'compensatory award'), a claim under the *EPCA* also attracts a 'basic award' related to length of service and age. Discrimination legislation compensates injury to feelings, which the *EPCA* does not.

26.3   FAILURE TO SPECIFY LEGISLATION ON ORIGINATING APPLICATION TO TRIBUNAL

There is no need for an individual to make express reference to the *EPCA* if he makes a complaint of race or sex discrimination in respect of dismissal. So long as it is clear that the complaint relates to dismissal, that it is in time and that the individual otherwise qualifies, then the tribunal will hear the complaint under both the *EPCA* and relevant discrimination legislation. The same is true for a complaint of unfair dismissal which makes clear at some point on the face of the originating application that racial, or as the case may be, sexual, discrimination is complained of *(Home Office v Bose [1979] ICR 481)*.

26.4   EFFECT OF COMPLAINT UNDER BOTH UNFAIR DISMISSAL AND DISCRIMINATION LEGISLATION

The burden of proof in a discrimination case is formally upon the applicant, whereas in an unfair dismissal case, it is balanced, but effectively upon the employer. The formal burden of proof in the industrial tribunal is often of more esoteric than real interest. The tribunal listens to the evidence and does its best to assess the witnesses' credibility and make a judgment in the round.

However, the formal burden does have procedural consequences. In an ordinary unfair dismissal case, the employer starts, but in a discrimination case, it is the applicant who starts. In an application under both heads of legislation, it is a matter for the tribunal which side starts. The tribunal will usually accept any agreement between the parties on the point, and it is generally accepted that in such circumstances, the employer will call his evidence first. It is, therefore, important in such cases that the employer should be certain that the applicant has been required to particularise his case fully. This can be achieved by requesting 'further and better particulars of each and every instance of discrimination relied upon specifying the date on which such discrimination is alleged to have occurred, the nature of the discrimination and the persons said to have committed such acts'. The party that gives his evidence first will be able to open and 'set the scene'. (There is no absolute right to an opening in the tribunal, and an opening is usually discouraged in an ordinary unfair dismissal claim, but tribunals usually find it helpful to be given a broad perspective of the case at the beginning of a discrimination claim.) The opening side will also have the final closing submission (except that the other side will be able to reply on any new point of law raised in closing).

Whatever the strategic or other theoretical advantages and disadvantages of opening and closing in a case brought under both heads of legislation, it will almost always serve for clarity and save time for the respondent to go first. In fact, because of the unusual nature of a claim of discrimination, which means that the evidence as to causation and motivation is always uniquely in the possession of the respondent, it is probably unfortunate that the applicant has to open in a claim brought solely in respect of discrimination. However, the tribunal does have the discretion to reverse the order of play, either of its own volition or at the request of one or both parties.

26.5 EFFECT OF FINDING OF UNLAWFUL DISCRIMINATION IN RESPECT OF UNFAIR DISMISSAL CLAIM

It is difficult to envisage a circumstance in which an individual would succeed in respect of a discrimination claim alleging race or sex as a motivation for dismissal, and not succeed in an unfair dismissal claim.

26.6 REFERENCE

The *EPCA* is otherwise outside the scope of this book. The relevant law is comprehensively dealt with in *Tolley's Employment Handbook*.

26.7 EMPLOYMENT RIGHTS BILL

In May 1995 the Employment Rights Bill was introduced. It is expected that this Bill will receive the Royal Assent in the Autumn of 1995 and come into effect in 1996. The effect of this Bill is to consolidate individual employment rights legislation under one Act. It covers a number of areas, including unfair dismissal, redundancy payments, notice rights, maternity rights, right to receive employment particulars and outside pay statements, protection of wages and Sunday working.

The Bill does not introduce any changes in existing law, but it is intended that, by having individual employment rights contained in one consolidatory statute, employers will be more aware of their statutory obligations, and employees will be more aware of their own rights.

27   Equal Opportunities Commission

27.1   HISTORY

The Equal Opportunities Commission (EOC) was established by the *Sex Discrimination Act 1975*. It is funded through the Home Office from the public purse at an annual cost of about £6 million, over half of which represents staffing costs.

27.2   DUTIES

It has a dual role reflected in its statutory duties:

(*a*)   to work towards the elimination of discrimination; and

(*b*)   to promote equality of opportunity between men and women.

[*SDA s 53(1)*].

It also has a duty to keep the *SDA* and *EqPA* under review.

There are those who consider that this dichotomy of role inhibits the function of the EOC. Like the CRE, it has both the 'carrot' role with its promotions work and a duty to wield the 'stick' by way of enforcement proceedings against transgressors.

27.3   POWERS

The EOC's powers can conveniently be divided into five distinct categories:

(i)   assisting individuals with complaints to the industrial tribunal or county court;

(ii)   conducting formal investigations;

(iii) promoting good equal opportunity practice and equality;

(iv)   promoting and encouraging equal pay; and

(v)   conducting or sponsoring research into matters of concern to equal opportunities.

27.4   ORGANISATION

The work of the EOC covers the following areas:

1.   Administrative: internal bureaucracy.

2.   Law enforcement:

(i)   provision of legal assistance to individuals, investigations and other law enforcement;

(ii)   provision of legal advice and support to other divisions.

3.   Development:

promotional work, encouraging equal opportunity policy adoption by employers, trade unions, etc., providing training resources.

4.   Public affairs divisions:

media and publicity promotional work, liaison with voluntary organisations, research, statistical and information support.

27.5 ASSISTING COMPLAINANTS

Of most frequent concern to individuals and employers alike is the power of the EOC to assist individuals in taking cases to the industrial tribunal. This power is provided by *SDA s 75* and enables the EOC to assist individuals in taking proceedings pursuant to the Act if:

(*a*)   the case raises a question of principle;

(*b*)   taking into account the complexity of the case, the relative position of the individual and the employer, or any other matter, it would be unreasonable to expect the individual to proceed unassisted; or

(*c*)   for any other reason.

This provides a wide discretion. The decision as to whether or not to provide assistance is made by a committee of Commissioners (the Legal Committee). This committee sits monthly and considers reports compiled by officers in the EOC's Complaints and Investigations Department in their Law Enforcement Division. There are two teams in the Complaints and Investigations Department, one dealing with employment matters and the other with non-employment matters. The CRE divides the function of assisting individuals from the formal investigation role, and has a special committee dealing only with individual applications for assistance with complaints. The EOC's Legal Committee, on the other hand, deals both with applications for individual assistance and formal investigations, which may well be a better organisational structure from a strategic point of view. Only about 350 formal applications are received annually and many more individuals are given telephone or other informal advice, but the EOC assists fewer individuals than the CRE. The EOC may assist an individual in drawing up an *SDA s 74* questionnaire (see QUESTIONNAIRE PROCEDURE (47)) and in drafting the application to the industrial tribunal. The reply to the questionnaire is utilised by the EOC to consider the merits of an application for assistance. It can frequently take several months for the EOC to reach a decision on assistance. An individual can (and frequently does) pursue a claim regardless of the decision of the EOC not to support it.

27.6 FORM OF ASSISTANCE GIVEN

Like the CRE, the EOC has a wide discretion as to the form of assistance given to a complainant. It may be limited to assistance with conciliation or legal representation at the industrial tribunal. The EOC may allocate a case that it is supporting to its small in-house legal team, who will usually instruct Counsel direct, or a solicitor from an approved panel may be instructed. Pending a final decision on representation, the EOC's legal staff will usually assist an applicant with tribunal correspondence and the like.

27.7 CONDUCTING FORMAL INVESTIGATIONS

The EOC is empowered by *SDA s 57* to conduct formal investigations. Such an investigation may be in relation to any matter pertaining to its general powers which, as already mentioned, are:

27.8 Equal Opportunities Commission

(*a*)   to work towards the elimination of discrimination;

(*b*)   to promote equality of opportunity between the sexes; and

(*c*)   to keep the working of the *SDA* and *EqPA* under review.

The EOC nominates one or more of its Commissioners and, subject to approval by the Secretary of State, may appoint additional Commissioners to conduct the investigation. [*SDA s 57(2)(3)*]. The actual investigation itself is conducted by EOC staff answerable to the appointed Commissioner(s). The Law Enforcement Department is divided into two teams, one to deal with employment and one to deal with everything else (housing, service provision etc.). The EOC completed a formal investigation into the recruitment of student midwives in the Southern Derbyshire Health Authority and an investigation into Workforce Employment Agency Ltd led to a non-discrimination notice being issued in October 1994. However, few investigations are embarked upon. This may be because of the onerous formal procedural requirements in conducting an investigation. (See INVESTIGATIONS (37).)

27.8   Types of investigation

There are two types of investigation:

(*a*)   a named persons investigation, and

(*b*)   a general investigation.

As the term implies, a named persons investigation is directed expressly at a company or persons who the EOC has reason to believe have been operating a discriminatory practice, whereas a general investigation is more by way of a research project into, say, employment practices in a particular industry. The powers and procedures to be followed in a formal investigation are dealt with in detail at INVESTIGATIONS (37).

27.9   OTHER ENFORCEMENT POWERS

Only the EOC has the power to take proceedings in respect of alleged discriminatory advertisements [*SDA s 38*], or instructions or pressure to discriminate [*SDA ss 39, 40*], by virtue of *SDA ss 67, 72*. It may proceed either by way of an application to the industrial tribunal for a declaration that the discrimination complained of took place (and subsequently to the county court for an injunction if it considers that there will be a repeat offence) [*SDA s 72*], or by a non-discrimination notice subsequent to, or in the course of, a formal investigation. [*SDA s 67*]. To date, the EOC has issued five non-discrimination notices, including one against an employment agency in West Yorkshire (Workforce Employment Agency Ltd), and has not infrequently commenced proceedings in the tribunal. (See ADVERTISING (2) and PRESSURE TO DISCRIMINATE (45).)

27.10 PROMOTIONAL WORK

The EOC also provides an advisory service to employers and trade unions in relation to equal opportunity practice.

27.11 CODE OF PRACTICE

As part of its promotional duties, the EOC has produced a code of practice [*SDA s 56A*] (see CODES OF PRACTICE (8)) which sets out advice to employers, trade unions, employment agencies and individuals on complying with the law and good equal opportunity employment practice. The EOC may review its code, subject to parliamentary approval [*RRA s 56(9)*]; no review is apparently contemplated at present.

In May 1995 the EOC published a draft Code of Practice on Equal Pay. The purpose of this Code is to assist employers in eliminating the consistent pay gap between male and female employees (see CODES OF PRACTICE (8)).

27.12 RESEARCH

The EOC has an internal research department and also funds external research into topics related to equal opportunities. The EOC is also under a duty to keep the *SDA* under review and produced a consultation document (and thereafter recommendations) in 1989.

27.13 OFFICES

The head office is Overseas House, Quay Street, Manchester M3 3HN (Tel: 0161-833 9244). There are also three regional offices. The addresses of these are:

LONDON (media enquiries)
36 Broadway
London SW1H 0XH
Tel: 0171-222 1110

SCOTLAND
Stock Exchange House
7 Nelson Mandela Place
Glasgow G2 1QW
Tel: 0141-248 5833

WALES
Caerwys House
Windsor Lane
Cardiff CF1 1LB
Tel: (01222) 343552

27.14 STAFFING

At the time of writing, the EOC employs approximately 170 staff nationwide; most of these are based at the Manchester office.

27.15 OTHER EQUALITY BODIES

ACAS also has a small team of equal opportunity advisers, who will provide a confidential advice service. There are a large number of 'self help' and 'civil rights' type organisations in existence. The EOC keeps an informal list of such organisations, such as The Women's Legal Defence Fund, which provide assistance to individuals and undertake research. These bodies have no formal powers and are usually unincorporated associations.

28 Equal Opportunity Policy

28.1 LEGAL BASIS

There is nothing to stop any employer from styling himself an 'equal opportunity employer', regardless of what steps he has or has not taken to achieve such a goal. There is no requirement to have any equal opportunity policy (EOP) vetted by either the CRE or EOC, or by any other statutory body. Equally, losing industrial tribunal cases is no bar to an employer styling himself an equal opportunity employer in promotional material. There is no restriction on the wording that may be used in promotional literature, except if such wording could be interpreted as positive discrimination (see ADVERTISING (2)).

28.2 LEGAL EFFECT

Although, as stated above, there is no legal check on an employer advertising himself as an equal opportunity employer, there is a form of sanction against abuse arising out of the legislation. Both Codes of Practice recommend the adoption of equal opportunity policies (CRE Code, paras 1.1-1.4, EOC Code, paras 34-36). The steps taken in regard to a provision of the applicable Code of Practice are to be taken into account by an industrial tribunal in assessing a complaint before it, if that provision is relevant. [*RRA s 47; SDA s 56A*].

An 'equal opportunity' employer with an equal opportunity policy that is in line with the recommendations of either (preferably both) the Codes of Practice will be entitled to have that fact taken into account by a tribunal, if a case is brought against him (and it is commonplace for employers to pray in aid such policies). An effective equal opportunity policy will mean that the employer will not be liable for unauthorised acts of discrimination by recalcitrant employees. [*RRA s 32(3); SDA s 41(3)*]. An employer who simply styles himself an 'equal opportunity employer', but takes no real steps to achieve that status, may well have held against him the fact that he has not conformed to the spirit of the relevant Code of Practice, and he will be liable for unauthorised acts of discrimination by his employees.

28.3 RECOMMENDED ACTION

Negotiation

Where there are trade unions or employee consultation bodies, it is advisable to negotiate the implementation of the Code with such bodies (CRE Code, para 1.4(b), EOC Code, para 36). Both Codes set out recommended action for trade unions which includes co-operating with the implementation of such Codes as well as effecting internal equal opportunity practices. Most trade unions have elaborately worded conference resolutions committing the union to negotiating equal opportunities on behalf of the membership. Regrettably, however, there have been instances where trade unions have been resistant to equal opportunity initiatives at the workplace negotiating level. (There have also been instances where trade union representatives have pressurised employers into following discriminatory practices – see, for example, *R v CRE, Ex parte Westminster City Council* [1985] *ICR 827*.) An employer will usually be able to embarrass a local trade union representative into action by suggesting referral to the head office of the union.

28.4   **Equal opportunity statement**

It is advisable for an employer wishing to adopt an equal opportunity policy to have an equal opportunity statement, which should be distributed to all members of staff. An outline statement is set out below (see 28.7). If it is not circulated to all staff, then ignorance can be pleaded. Such a statement should not only be placed in any employment handbook that is issued to staff, but should also be contained in the employer's recruitment or starters' pack.

28.5   **Equal opportunity policy**

The equal opportunity statement should be backed up by an effective policy to ensure its implementation. The degree of action required will vary, depending on the size of the employer. An employer with only a handful of staff could reasonably rely on the statement alone. Larger employers should, however, consider the following steps, as advised by the CRE Code (para 1.4):

(*a*)   allocating responsibility for the equal opportunity policy to a member of management (this will usually be the member of management responsible for personnel matters);

(*b*)   providing training and guidance for all staff involved in recruitment, promotion and supervision;

(*c*)   running a check on existing recruitment, promotion and personnel procedures to make sure that they are not discriminatory; and

(*d*)   setting up monitoring procedures to analyse the workforce, job applicants and promotion exercises.

28.6   **ADVERTISING**

Neither Code advises that employers should describe themselves as 'equal opportunity employers'. The practice has now become widespread, and a check in the recruitment section of any newspaper is likely to find the majority of larger employers describing themselves as equal opportunity employers. The wording varies from 'We are an equal opportunity employer' to a sentence or two of assurance that applications are treated without discrimination on grounds of race, sex, disability, religion or sexual orientation. Unless the wording amounts to a statement of intent to positively discriminate on grounds of sex or race (outside the permitted exceptions), there is no restriction on the wording that may be employed. Such wording in job advertisements does act as a public assurance to women, ethnic minority individuals and the disabled. It also acts as a constant reminder to all the company's existing staff involved in recruitment that, whatever those individuals' personal opinions, they must not discriminate on behalf of their employer. It is, therefore, a worthwhile exercise, and recommended.

28.7   **A RECOMMENDED EQUAL OPPORTUNITY STATEMENT**

As mentioned above, a statement on its own is, except in smaller establishments, unlikely to be sufficient, even if, as is recommended, it is circulated personally to every member of the current staff and is placed in the pack of documents given to new staff on their introduction to the company. In addition, it will be necessary to devise training programmes, particularly for management and staff involved in recruitment and promotion. In a larger

28.8   Equal Opportunity Policy

concern, it will also be practicable and advisable to have a comprehensive equal opportunity policy which covers such issues as training and special initiatives. It is beyond the scope of this book to provide such guidance, which may be obtained from the EOC, CRE, Department of Education and Employment, ACAS, professional advisers and consultants. However, a recommended equal opportunity statement is set out below.

[TITLE OF COMPANY]

Equal Opportunity Statement

The Company is committed to a policy of treating all its employees and job applicants equally. No employee or potential employee shall receive less favourable treatment or consideration on the grounds of disability, race, colour, religion, nationality, ethnic origin, sex or marital status, or will be disadvantaged by any conditions of employment or requirements of the Company that cannot be justified as necessary on operational grounds.

Every senior executive and member of management, and all employees, are instructed that:

1.   There should be no discrimination on account of disability, race, colour, religion, nationality, ethnic origin, sex or marital status.

2.   The Company will appoint, train, develop and promote on the basis of merit and ability.

3.   All employees have personal responsibility for the practical application of the Company's equal opportunity policy, which extends to the treatment of employees and customers.

4.   Special responsibility for the practical application of the Company's equal opportunity policy falls upon managers and supervisors involved in the recruitment, selection, promotion and training of employees.

5.   The Company's grievance procedure is available to any employee who believes that he or she may have been unfairly discriminated against.

6.   Disciplinary action should be taken against any employee who is found to have committed an act of unlawful discrimination. Discriminatory conduct and sexual or racial harassment will be treated as gross misconduct.

7.   In the case of any doubt or concern about the application of the policy in any particular instance, any member of staff should consult [*a named individual or function*].

28.8   Implementation of the equal opportunity policy

A comprehensive equal opportunity policy will be tailored to the individual needs of the company, and will model itself on the guidance given in the EOC and CRE Codes of Practice. The policy should be set out in simple terms so that both staff and managers can understand its requirements. The company should put particular emphasis on ensuring that all staff responsible for recruitment and promotion have proper training and a thorough knowledge of the policy. The real key to a successful equal opportunity policy is to ensure that there is a programme of training and review so as to secure its implementation.

28.9   Example of an equal opportunity policy

In Appendix 3 of this book, there is set out the text of the equal opportunity policy in use by Gardner Merchant. This is by way of an example of an equal opportunity policy in use. Gardner Merchant were known to be reviewing the equal opportunity policy at the time of writing. However, the policy in Appendix 3 is still satisfactory. Every equal opportunity policy should be tailored to the needs of the individual organisation to which it will apply, and final advice can be sought from the EOC and CRE as to content; such advice does not have to be followed but will usually be extremely useful.

29   Equal Pay

29.1   SCOPE

The *Equal Pay Act 1970 (EqPA)*, as amended by the *Sex Discrimination Acts* of 1975 and 1986 and the *Equal Pay (Amendment) Regulations 1983 (SI 1983 No 1794)*, entitles women to be paid the same as men (and vice versa) for the same work, work rated as equivalent, or work of equal value. The *EqPA* introduces an 'equality clause' (see 29.2 below) into every individual's contract, to achieve the purpose of the Act. [*EqPA s 1(1)(a)*].

The legislation is aimed primarily at redressing the historical differential in pay enjoyed by men over women. The *EqPA* extends to men who find themselves in the position of doing a broadly similar job as, or work of equal value to, a woman, but earning less. This has been of particular relevance in the pensions field (*Barber v Guardian Royal Exchange Assurance Group [1990] ICR 616*). Women have not been rushing to make claims, and those that have commenced actions have found themselves in a quagmire of procedural niceties and legal argument. Whilst the potential of the legislation is far-reaching and should be of significant impact, the reality has been one of a failure of the legislation to achieve its primary purpose of equalising the historical pay differential between men and women. Between 1970 and 1975 there was a significant reduction in that differential, but the differential remains marked and there has been no evidence of further progress. It is not possible to contract out of the statutory right to equal pay, except through the auspices of an ACAS officer by agreement with a particular employee in settling an actual or potential claim. [*SDA s 64*]. It is clear that employers must keep pay structures under constant review.

29.2   THE EQUALITY CLAUSE

EqPA s 1(1)(a) inserts an 'equality clause' into a woman's contract where:

(a)   the woman is employed on 'like work' with a man in the same employment [*EqPA s 1(2)(a)(4)*];

(b)   the woman is employed on work 'rated as equivalent', in a job evaluation study, to work done by a man in the same employment [*EqPA s 1(2)(b)(5)*];

(c)   the woman is employed on work of 'equal value' with a man in the same employment. [*EqPA s 1(2)(c)*].

The effect of an equality clause is that –

(i)   if, apart from that clause, the woman's contract has a term which is or becomes less favourable to her than a term of a similar kind in the man's contract, that term of the woman's contract will be treated as modified so as not to be less favourable, and

(ii)   if, apart from that clause, the woman's contract omits a beneficial term which is in the man's contract, the woman's contract will be treated as including such a term.

[*EqPA s 1(2)*].

In the next part of this chapter, the meanings of some of the key terms referred to above, 'employed', 'like work', 'work rated as equivalent', 'work of equal value' and 'man in the same employment' are examined. In addition, there is discussed exactly what, apart from pay, is within the scope of the equality clause. The two most important defences to an equal pay claim are then dealt with in detail. Finally, the qualification period and time limit for equal pay claims are discussed, the main exclusions from the *EqPA* are listed, the procedure in the industrial tribunal in respect of equal pay claims is outlined, and the continued impact of the EU is considered.

29.3   MEANING OF 'EMPLOYED'

EqPA s 1(6)(a) expressly defines 'employed' as meaning 'employed under a contract of service or of apprenticeship or a contract personally to execute any work or labour'. A self-employed individual will, therefore, be protected so long as the requirement is for that individual to perform the duties personally. If they are able to 'subcontract' the work they are outside the scope of the Act.

29.4   MEANING OF 'LIKE WORK'

The meaning of 'like work' is defined by *EqPA s 1(4)*:

> 'A woman is to be regarded as employed on like work with men if, but only if, her work and theirs is of the same or a broadly similar nature, and the differences (if any) between the things she does and the things they do are not of practical importance in relation to terms and conditions of employment; and accordingly in comparing her work with theirs regard shall be had to the frequency or otherwise with which any such differences occur in practice as well as to the nature and the extent of the differences.'

The proper approach of a tribunal to the question 'is the work of a broadly similar nature?' was set out by the EAT in *Capper Pass Ltd v Lawton [1977] ICR 83*:

> 'In deciding whether the work done by a woman and the work done by a man is "like work" within the meaning of *section 1(4)* of the *Equal Pay Act* the industrial tribunal has to make a broad judgment. The intention is that the industrial tribunal should not be required to undertake too minute an examination, or be constrained to find that work is not "like work" merely because of insubstantial differences. In order to be "like work" within the Act's definition the work need not be of the same nature; it need only be broadly similar.'

In that particular case, a female chef in the directors' dining room, who worked 40 hours a week, claimed equal pay with chefs in the company canteen, who did about 5 hours' overtime each week and occasionally deputised for the head chef. The EAT concluded that, within the definition in *Sec 1(4)*, the work was broadly similar.

Subject to a tribunal following the guidelines set out in *Capper Pass v Lawton*, it is a matter of fact as to whether work is 'like work', which is unlikely to be disturbed on appeal. If the tribunal concludes that the work of the comparator is not 'like work', then the degree to which any difference of pay may be unreasonable in regard to the real difference of duties is irrelevant. This is because the tribunal has no jurisdiction to adjudicate if the work is not 'like work' (unless there is an overlapping claim as to equivalence or equal value – see 29.6 below).

29.5 Equal Pay

In an old case (*Waddington v Leicester Council for Voluntary Service [1977] ICR 266*), it was held that if the tribunal found that work was not 'like work' because the applicant had more responsibility than the (better paid) comparator, it was not 'like work' and the tribunal had no jurisdiction to make an award. Many commentators have criticised this decision, but the mischief can be overcome by an equal value claim in direct reliance on *Article 119* (*Murphy and others v Bord Telecom Eireann (Case 157/86) [1988] ICR 445*), where a claim for equal pay where the applicant was found to have been doing work of greater value was upheld.

29.5 Examples of factors indicating 'like work'

Responsibility. A material level of different responsibility can defeat a claim that work is 'like work' (*Eaton Ltd v Nuttall [1977] ICR 272*), and note also a further case involving Capper Pass Ltd, where the tribunal had found that the applicant had less responsibility than the comparator; the EAT found that it was open to the tribunal to find that the work was not 'like work' (*Capper Pass Ltd v Allan [1980] ICR 194*). The responsibility factor must be 'of practical importance' (*Shields v E Coomes (Holdings) Ltd [1978] ICR 1159*).

Hours worked. The hours of work at which duties are performed should not affect the basic rate of pay, which can be dealt with by way of a night shift premium over and above the basic rate. An applicant will be able to claim 'like work' and equal pay at the basic rate (*Dugdale v Kraft Foods Ltd [1977] ICR 48*). The tribunal can, if it is asked to do so, make an allowance in its award for the unsocial hours factor, or ignore it in arriving at its substantive conclusion as to whether or not there is 'like work' (*National Coal Board v Sherwin & Another [1978] ICR 700*). In another Coal Board case, however, the EAT did uphold a tribunal decision that unsocial hours worked by a man can mean that work, otherwise identical, was not 'like work' (*Thomas v National Coal Board [1981] ICR 757*).

Actual work done. A tribunal is entitled to look at what happens, in practice, to see if the work is really 'like work'. If, notwithstanding the fact that a substantial part of the duties are the same, there are in fact some real differences, then the work is not 'like work' (*Maidment and Another v Cooper & Co (Birmingham) Ltd [1978] ICR 1094*).

29.6 MEANING OF 'WORK RATED AS EQUIVALENT' AND 'WORK OF EQUAL VALUE'

By virtue of *EqPA s 1(5)*, a woman is to be regarded as employed on 'work rated as equivalent' with that of any men if her job and their job have been given an equal value in a job evaluation study, in terms of the demands made on a worker under various headings (for instance, effort, skill, decision). Where no such job evaluation study has been carried out, a woman may nevertheless claim that her work is 'of equal value' to that of a man in the same employment, in terms of the demands made on her (for instance, under the three headings referred to above). [*EqPA s 1(3)*].

Where a job evaluation study has been carried out which has given different values to the work of the woman and the work of the man with whom she is being compared, there shall be taken to be no reasonable grounds for determining that the woman's work is of equal value to that of the man. However, this applies only if there are no reasonable grounds for determining that the evaluation contained in the study was made on a system which discriminates on grounds of sex. [*EqPA s 2A(2)*]. A system which discriminates on grounds of sex means one 'where a difference, or coincidence, between values set by that system on different demands under the same or different headings is not justifiable irrespective of the sex of the person on whom those demands are made'. [*EqPA s 2A(3)*].

Note that if the woman's work is determined not to be equivalent, or of equal or greater value, to that of the man with whom she is being compared, the tribunal has no jurisdiction in the matter however great the disparity in pay may be.

For a detailed consideration of the 'job evaluation defence' to an equal value claim, see 29.12 below.

29.7 MEANING OF 'MAN IN THE SAME EMPLOYMENT'

Any equal pay claim is dependent upon identifying a 'comparable man'. There are a number of requirements in respect of a 'comparable man', which are considered below.

(a) He must be real

A comparable man cannot be a theoretical man. This is in marked contrast with the *SDA* where an industrial tribunal, in considering whether or not a woman has been treated adversely on grounds of sex, can be asked to contemplate how a man might have been treated. It is difficult to understand the philosophical objection to the fictional man in this context. The question 'Were a man to be doing this job, would the pay be higher and, if so, how much?' would seem to be an easier one to ask than many of those thrown up by these complex provisions.

(b) The woman chooses the man

Which 'comparable man' to pick is a matter for the woman bringing the equal pay claim (*Ainsworth v Glass Tubes and Components Ltd [1977] ICR 347*). There is no need to identify the comparator specifically until after the discovery process (*Leverton v Clwyd County Council [1989] ICR 33*).

(c) There can be more than one comparable man

There is no limit on the number of comparators that a woman can choose, although the House of Lords in *Leverton* (above) urged common sense. In perhaps the best known of equal pay cases, Julie Hayward, who was a cook in the works canteen, compared herself with a painter, a thermal insulation engineer and a joiner (*Hayward v Cammell Laird Shipbuilders Ltd [1988] IRLR 257*).

(d) He may be past or present

He may be employed at the same time as the woman who is seeking to compare their jobs, or (under *Article 119* of the Treaty of Rome) he may have been her predecessor in the post (*Macarthys Ltd v Smith [1980] IRLR 210*).

(*e*)   **He must be in the 'same employment'**

The 'same employment' relates to the employer and not to geographical location. *EqPA s 1(6)* defines 'in the same employment' as being employed:

(i)   at the same establishment by the same employer; or

(ii)   at the same establishment by employers under the same control (i.e. part of the same group of companies or any company over which the other has effective control); or

(iii)   at different establishments of the same employer where common terms and conditions are observed either generally or for employees of their respective classes, i.e. employees employed under the same collective agreement (*Leverton v Clwyd County Council* [*1989*] *IRLR 28*). In *British Coal Corporation v Smith; North Yorkshire County Council v Ratcliffe* [*1994*] *IRLR 342*, the Court of Appeal held that an applicant can choose as her comparator a male employee at a different establishment of the same employer, so long as the terms and conditions of employment of men of the comparative class are common with (i.e. exactly the same as, save for pay) male employees of the relevant class employed at the applicant's establishment. The comparator should, of course, be representative of the class/group of male employees from whom he is selected, i.e. as regards the relevant terms of his contract of employment. There is no requirement that terms and conditions of employment of female employees at the comparator's establishment are the same as those of female employees at the applicant's establishment. The Court of Appeal decision was upheld by the House of Lords [*1995*] *IRLR 439*.

This case affects employers with a number of establishments, where employees' terms and conditions of employment are governed by collective agreements;

(iv)   different establishments and employers under the same control where common terms and conditions are observed.

Different local authorities are not associated employers for the purposes of the *EqPA* and so comparisons cannot be made across local authorities.

Situations in which the man would not be held to be 'in the same employment' as the woman are, for example, where they are employed:

(i)   at the same establishment, but with different employers (e.g. contractors); and

(ii)   at different establishments with the same employer, but with local negotiation of terms and conditions of service, and no national agreement.

This presents employers with the possibility of avoiding the legislation by subcontracting vulnerable work. For example, in the *Hayward* case referred to above, had Cammell Laird Shipbuilders employed contract caterers, Miss Hayward would not have been able to bring her claim as, whilst she would still have been employed at the same establishment, she would not have been employed by an 'associated employer' within the definition of the Act. This would apply, even though Cammell Laird, in setting the terms of the catering contract, would still effectively have been in control of the broad level of her remuneration. This factor may be one of the explanations for the popularity of subcontracting such work.

29.8 MEANING OF 'PAY'

It is not only wages and salaries that are covered by the *EqPA*. The Act extends to all forms of remuneration (except pensions), such as holiday pay, sickness pay or mortgage interest allowance (*Sun Alliance and London Insurance Ltd v Dudman [1978] ICR 551*). Each element of the remuneration contract is to be assessed separately when assessing pay. The argument that the pay package should be looked at and compared as a whole was considered and rejected by the House of Lords in *Hayward v Cammell Laird Shipbuilders Ltd [1988] IRLR 257*. In that case, the employer unsuccessfully tried to argue that, when taken as a whole, better holidays, sickness benefits etc. compensated for a less favourable hourly rate for female kitchen staff as against 'production worker' comparators. In that case, however, the employer had not tried to argue this point as a 'material factor' defence at the industrial tribunal which first heard the matter, and it is possible that such an argument at first instance would have succeeded. (For the 'material factor' defence, see 29.10 below.)

Although pensions are not covered by the *EqPA*, the ECJ held in the case of *Barber v Guardian Royal Exchange Assurance Group [1990] ICR 616* that contracted out occupational pension schemes are covered by the definition of 'pay' in *Article 119* of the Treaty of Rome. Female employees can rely directly on *Article 119* to claim equal pay.

29.9 DEFENCES TO AN EQUAL PAY CLAIM

There are two types of defence to an equal pay claim, the 'material factor' defence [*EqPA s 1(3)*] and the 'job evaluation' defence [*EqPA s 2A*]. Each of these defences is dealt with in turn below.

29.10 MATERIAL FACTOR DEFENCE

An employer will be able to resist a claim for equal pay, even where a woman has established that she is employed on like work, equivalent work, or work of equal value, where the employer can prove that the difference between the woman's and the comparator man's contract is 'genuinely due to a material factor which is not the difference in sex'. [*EqPA s 1(3)*]. In the case of like work or work rated as equivalent, that factor *must* be a material difference between the woman's case and the man's [*EqPA s 1(3)(a)*], and in the case of work of equal value, that factor *may* be such a material difference. [*EqPA s 1(3)(b)*]. This means that in theory, in an equal value claim, the scope of the employer's defence under *Sec 1(3)* is wider, because the defence is not confined to a material difference between the two cases.

The 'material difference' in a 'material factor' defence must be 'significant and relevant' and 'reasonably necessary' (*Rainey v Greater Glasgow Health Board [1987] ICR 129*). In that decision, the House of Lords equated the 'material factor' defence to the finding of the ECJ (in respect of *Article 119* of the Treaty of Rome) in *Bilka-Kaufhaus GmbH v Weber von Hartz (Case 170/84) [1987] ICR 110* that an employer must show that the ground on which he relies 'may be regarded as objectively justified on economic grounds'. The House of Lords also equated the 'material factor' defence with the concept of 'justification' in defending a claim of indirect discrimination:

'A difference which demonstrated unjustified indirect discrimination would not discharge the onus placed on the employer. Further, there would not appear to be any material distinction in principle between the need to demonstrate objectively justified grounds for the purpose of *EqPA s 1(3)* and the need to justify a requirement or condition under *SDA s 1(1)(b)(ii).*'

The 'material difference' defence was applied by the EAT, after direct referral to the ECJ on questions of interpretation of *Article 119*, in *Jenkins v Kingsgate (Clothing Productions) Ltd [1981] ICR 715 (EAT)* and *[1981] ICR 592 (ECJ)*. The EAT had concluded that the test under the *EqPA* was slightly higher than that required by *Article 119* and the same as the 'justifiable' test in respect of indirect discrimination. The House of Lords in *Rainey*, however, concluded that there is no such distinction in fact or substance between the approach required in considering the direct application of *Article 119* as against *EqPA s 1(3)*. Either way, an employer has to be able to show that the decision was not only untainted by any sexual bias, but also objectively justifiable on economic or other reasonable non-sexual grounds.

Whether or not a 'material difference' defence succeeds or not will, so long as the approach is consistent with the guidelines set out in *Rainey*, be a matter of fact for the industrial tribunal in each case. It is therefore important that the employer pleads the 'material difference' defence clearly in his Notice of Appearance.

As from 1 April 1994, in equal value claims, where the 'material factor' defence is raised by an employer before the tribunal decides whether to order an independent expert's report, the defence now *cannot* also be raised at the reconvened tribunal hearing. Therefore, an employer no longer has 'two bites at the cherry' (*Industrial Tribunal (Constitution and Rules of Procedure) (Amendment) Regulations 1994 (SI 1994 No 536)*).

Where an employee is claiming equal pay in circumstances of indirect discrimination, and the employer relies on the material factor defence, it is clear from the House of Lords decision in *Rainey v Greater Glasgow Health Board [1987] ICR 129* that the 'material difference' must be 'significant and relevant', as well as 'reasonably necessary'. In addition, the grounds relied on by the employer must be objectively justified.

In *Financial Times Ltd v Byrne & Others [1992] IRLR 163*, the EAT held that where the material factor defence is raised, the burden is on employers to prove that the difference in pay is genuinely due to a material factor, and also that none of the factors are related to the sex of the employee.

In *Enderby v Frenchay Health Authority and Secretary of State for Health [1993] IRLR 591*, the ECJ held that, in an equal value claim, *Article 119* of the Treaty of Rome requires an employer to *objectively* justify differences in pay between female employees and comparable male employees. Objective justification is required where an employee shows a *prima facie* case of sex discrimination. In *Enderby* the fact that the male and female employees' salary was determined as a result of separate collective bargaining processes (which were themselves not discriminatory) was not sufficient of itself to amount to objective justification.

In *Calder v Rowntree Mackintosh Confectionery Ltd [1993] IRLR 212*, the Court of Appeal upheld the tribunal decision that a pay differential was objectively justified even though it was attributable to two factors – the inconvenience of being required to work rotating shifts as well as unsocial hours – in circumstances where the applicant also worked unsocial hours. The Court of Appeal held that the fact that part of the pay differential was due to working unsocial hours (similar to the applicant) did not prevent the whole of the pay differential being objectively justified on the grounds that the premium was due to working rotating shifts.

However, the ECJ in *Enderby* held that where only part of the pay differential is objectively justified, the national court dealing with the applicant's claim (i.e. an industrial tribunal) should attempt to determine precisely the proportion of the differential that is attributable to objectively justified factors. If it is able to do this, then that proportion of the pay differential is objectively justified. However, if it is not clear what proportion of the pay differential is due to objectively justified factors, then the tribunal must assess whether market forces are significant enough to amount to objective justification for all or part of the pay difference.

29.11   Examples of material factor defences

Market forces. The decision of the House of Lords in *Rainey*, referred to above, established that 'market forces' are a legitimate 'material difference' defence. That case involved the employers paying a new female recruit less than existing male members of staff, who were recruited at a higher grade when setting up the service, in circumstances where it would otherwise have been impossible to recruit the staff. The employers established that it was their intention to recruit all new staff on to the lower grade, and thus the defence succeeded in that case. The danger of the 'market forces' argument is that 'market forces' are, historically, discriminatory against women. A 'market forces' defence that argues that the employer is paying the going rate for the job is unlikely to succeed, as it will fail the requirement of *EqPA s 1(3)*, which requires that the 'material factor' is 'not the difference in sex'.

The House of Lords decision in *Rainey v Greater Glasgow Health Board* (see above) is authority for the fact that market forces can amount to a material factor defence (so long as they are objectively justified) under *EqPA s 1(3)*.

The ECJ decision in *Enderby v Frenchay Health Authority and Secretary of State for Health* (see above) allows employers to use the market forces defence in respect of a claim under *Article 119* of the Treaty of Rome.

In the case of *Ratcliffe & Others v North Yorkshire County Council (IRLB 526)*, the House of Lords dismissed the employer's 'market forces' defence as a genuine material factor in justifying unequal pay. This was in the context of a Council employee's salary being reduced in order to enable the Council to make a competitive tender in a compulsory competitive tendering situation. The reduction in wages had not been done because of the sex of the employees, but in order to successfully tender for a contract. Despite this, the House of Lords held that the Council had paid female employees less than male comparators and that this was because they were female. Therefore, this constituted direct discrimination, and was not able to be justified on grounds irrespective of the sex of the employee concerned. It would appear that the reasoning behind this decision stems from the fact that a job evaluation study had rated the female employee's work as equivalent to that of their male comparators who did not have their salary reduced, and also held that the female employees were paid less *because they were women*. The employer had failed to show that the material factor used to justify the difference in pay was not actually based on sex.

In addition, the market forces argument must be material at the time. If the market forces that lead to the differential have disappeared, then the defence will not succeed (*Benveniste v University of Southampton [1989] IRLR 122*). A university lecturer was appointed at a time of severe financial constraints and, as a result, she agreed to accept a salary which was below that which she would normally have received, having regard to her age and qualifications. The financial constraints were lifted approximately a year later, but the University refused to regrade her. The Court of Appeal rejected the University's 'material factor' defence, based on the economic circumstances pertaining at the time of her appointment, on the grounds that after the financial constraints had been removed, there was no longer a material difference between her and her comparators engaged on like work. The case shows that the concept of 'material difference' is not a static one, and that a difference which was initially justified may cease to be so once the justification is removed as no longer current.

Difference in location. In some ways this is a variant of the 'market forces' argument. It is well-established that rates of pay vary geographically, so that if the employer can show that the reason for the difference between the pay of the complainant and the comparator is because of such a geographical variation, then the complainant's claim will fail (*NAAFI v Varley [1977] ICR 11*).

'Red circling'. This is a practice where a group of workers (or a single worker) are moved to new positions which would normally attract less remuneration than their old posts. To encourage them to accept the transfer, their pay is preserved ('red circled'). This will be deemed a 'material difference' defence (*Trico Folberth v Groves & Aiston [1976] IRLR 327*). However, a tribunal will look to see that the length of time of 'red circling' relates to good industrial practice, in considering whether this practice was 'reasonably necessary' (*Outlook Supplies Ltd v Parry [1978] IRLR 12*). The tribunal will not accept such a defence if the 'red circling' simply relates to the preservation of past discriminatory differential terms, and, indeed, the employer must show that this is not the case (*Snoxell & Davies v Vauxhall Motors Ltd [1977] IRLR 123; United Biscuits Ltd v Young [1978] IRLR 15*).

Performance of duties (merit pay), productivity pay. An employer who operates an objectively justifiable merit pay scheme, or who operates a performance-based pay review structure, will have a 'material difference' defence to an equal pay claim (*Buckland v Dowty Rotol Ltd [1976] IRLR 162*, an industrial tribunal decision). Employers should ensure, however, that the criteria operated are as clear and objective as possible, as such criteria may be considered indirectly discriminatory, contrary to EU law, and therefore may have to be justified on grounds unrelated to sex. (See the ECJ's ruling in *Handels-Og Kontorfunktionaerernes Forbund i Danmark v Dansk Arbejdsgiverforening [1991] ICR 74* ('the *Danfoss* case').) Inevitably, schemes will involve subjective judgment as to 'performance' in a general sense, and in such circumstances, it may be sensible to monitor pay levels being achieved against sex and length of service.

Hours worked. So long as the object of differential pay rates between part-time and full-time workers is not to exploit a cheap seam of female labour, a distinction based on full-time or part-time work is a material difference (*Bilka-Kaufhaus GmbH v Weber von Hartz [1987] ICR 110; Jenkins v Kingsgate*

(Clothing Productions) Ltd [1981] ICR 715). The usual reason given by employers is that encouraging full-time workers by a pay differential leads to more efficient utilisation of machinery, less administrative overheads and less absenteeism. So far, employers have not been required to prove that the reasons are true, but merely that those are the reasons upon which they relied and that they acted reasonably in doing so. However, in future, under the *Bilka-Kaufhaus/Rainey* test, employers are likely to have to demonstrate a real economic need for the differential and, unless they are able to do this, will be expected to pay part-timers on a pro rata basis.

In *Leverton v Clwyd Councy Council [1989] ICR 33,* the applicant worked 32½ hours per week compared with the comparator's 37 hours per week, and had 70 days' holiday per year compared with the comparator's 20 days' holiday. The House of Lords decided that these were genuine material factors justifying the pay differential. In support of this finding was the fact that, when converted into a notional hourly rate, there was no significant difference between the two jobs.

Experience, qualifications, skills. Subject to these criteria being relevant to the job in question, they are the most straightforward and obvious 'material difference' justifications for pay differentials. However, in *McPherson v Rathgael Centre For Children and Young People and Northern Ireland Office (Training Schools Branch) [1991] IRLR 206,* the Northern Ireland Court of Appeal ruled that a genuine but mistaken belief that an employee holds qualifications which would justify a difference in pay does not justify such a difference. The fact that an employer does not intend to discriminate on the ground of sex is irrelevant.

Length of service. Length of service was held to be a legitimate 'material difference' factor in *Shields v E Coomes (Holdings) Ltd [1978] ICR 1159,* and by the ECJ in the *Danfoss* case, referred to above. Some caution should, however, be exercised by employers in this regard. The issues are similar to those relating to drawing a distinction between full-time and part-time staff. Because of breaks in employment to raise a family, a length of service criterion is likely to have a disproportionate impact on women generally, and therefore its impact may have to be justified irrespective of sex (see *Nimz v Freie und Hansestadt Hamburg [1991] IRLR 222*).

Differences resulting from multiple union agreements. Where a difference in pay arises because of different scales negotiated by trade unions with the employer, so long as neither of these scales are themselves discriminatory in origin, then this will be a 'material factor' defence (*Reed Packaging Ltd v Boozer and Everhurst [1988] ICR 391; Enderby v Frenchay Health Authority and Secretary of State for Health [1991] IRLR 44*). It is for the employer to show that neither pay scale is discriminatory in itself.

Differences in significant terms in the contract. If there are significant differences in the terms of the contract, beneficial to the woman as against the comparator man, that 'can be translated into a notional hourly rate which yields no significant difference', then this will sustain a 'material difference' defence (*Leverton v Clwyd County Council [1989] ICR 33*), where a nursery nurse enjoyed more holiday and shorter hours than her chosen comparator).

Mistake. An employer's argument that its grading of a male employee higher than the female employee, had been in error, was held not to be a genuine material factor justifying a pay differential in *McPherson v Rathgael Centre for Children and Young People and Northern Ireland Office [1991] IRLR 206.*

29.12   Equal Pay

In *Yorkshire Blood Transfusion Services v Plaskitt [1994] ICR 74*, the employers contested the employee's claim for equal pay on the grounds that the comparator had been mistakenly put on to the wrong grade. They argued that the comparator should have been on the same grade as the employee, and this was a genuine material factor other than sex. The industrial tribunal rejected this argument. However, the EAT allowed the employer's appeal on the basis of the EAT's decision in *Calder v Rowntree Mackintosh Confectionery Ltd* (above), holding that there was no obligation on the employer to provide objectively justified grounds for the difference in pay. It was sufficient to show that the difference was not due to sex-based discrimination.

Also, in *Young v University of Edinburgh* (unreported), the EAT accepted that a genuine material factor existed when the disparity in pay had arisen from a clerical administrative error, but only in circumstances where the employer was unable to eliminate the disparity. In this case, the comparator had refused to accept a decrease in pay, and the employer was not able to increase the applicant's salary because it would create further anomalies in their system, which would increase the risk that other employees would seek equal pay with the applicant.

29.12   JOB EVALUATION DEFENCE

EqPA s 2A(2) prevents a tribunal from holding that there are reasonable grounds for determining that the work of a woman is of equal value to that of a comparator man, if a job evaluation study has been completed that has given the work of the woman and the comparator man different values. It would appear that such a study can be validly undertaken at any time prior to the industrial tribunal's determination, provided that there has not been a material change in circumstances between the time of the application and the time of the study (*Dibro Ltd v Hore [1990] IRLR 129*).

There must be no reasonable grounds for determining that the job evaluation was 'made on a system which discriminates on grounds of sex'. The evaluation must comply with *EqPA s 1(5)*, which refers to the jobs of the woman and of the comparable man being evaluated:

'. . . in terms of the demand made on a worker under various headings (for instance effort, skill, decision), on a study undertaken with a view to evaluating in those terms the jobs to be done by all or any of the employees in an undertaking or group of undertakings. . .'.

This requires that the scheme must be analytical in its approach (*Bromley & Others v H & J Quick Ltd [1988] IRLR 249*). It is not acceptable to use a 'felt fair' or 'benchmark' approach. In *Bromley* the employer had used specialists who analysed a limited number of the 'key' positions on a proper basis and then 'slotted in' the remaining positions on a 'felt fair' basis. As neither the job of the applicant, nor that of her comparator, had been evaluated on an analytical basis, this was held to be insufficient to satisfy *Sec 1(5)*. It is not, however, incumbent on the employer to analyse every single position. Positions can be grouped where there is no significant difference in the nature of those positions, and then one position can be analysed on a representative basis for that group. It will be for the employer to satisfy the tribunal that there was truly no difference between the jobs within the group, and that the chosen position was representative.

29.13 Evaluation must relate to comparator and applicant

A woman can still bring a claim, even if she has been the subject of a job evaluation study that has deemed her job as equivalent to that of a man paid the same, or not equivalent to that of a particular man, if she cites as a comparator a man not part of the particular evaluation study (*Pickstone v Freemans plc [1988] ICR 697*). Also, the evaluation must be a single exercise. It is not sufficient to undertake two exercises, for example, one relating to clerical employees and the other relating to manual employees, and attempt to rely on the two together if the applicant is a clerical worker and the comparator a manual worker.

29.14 CONDUCTING A JOB EVALUATION

ACAS have published a guide to Job Evaluation called 'Job Evaluation – an Introduction', which provides guidance on conducting a job evaluation. A job evaluation study is, however, a complex and difficult exercise, and it is wisest to employ reputable consultants to carry out such an exercise. The EOC, ACAS, professional advisers, or organisations such as the CBI will recommend suitable consultants. In their guide, ACAS set out the principal types of job evaluation study, which divide into two types, analytical and non-analytical.

ACAS state that the non-analytical schemes are 'unlikely to succeed as a defence to an equal value claim'. This is an understatement, in the authors' view; such schemes cannot succeed as a defence to an equal value claim, as they do not meet the requirements of *EqPA s 1(5)*. Unacceptable schemes are 'job ranking', 'paired comparison', 'job classification' or any similar approach which is not analytical. Acceptable schemes are 'points rating' and 'factor comparison', which are both analytical. The unacceptable schemes and acceptable schemes are dealt with in turn below.

29.15 Unacceptable evaluation methods

These methods have been summarised by ACAS as follows.

'*Job ranking.* This is a technique using job descriptions or job titles. Each job is considered as a whole and placed in a "felt fair" rank order to produce a league table. It is considered the simplest method since there is no attempt to break down or analyse the whole job in any way. It is therefore easy to understand and implement, particularly with a small number of jobs.'

'*Paired comparisons.* This is also a relatively simple technique. Each job is compared as a whole with each other job in turn and points (0, 1, or 2) awarded according to whether its overall importance is judged less than, equal to or more than the other. Points awarded for each job are then totalled and a rank order produced. This method has all the advantages of job ranking and is slightly more systematic. However it is best limited to organisations with a maximum of 30 jobs in a particular job population and, like job ranking, it does not involve any analysis of jobs nor indicate the extent of difference between them.'

'*Job classification.* This is also a "whole job" evaluation technique. In job classification the number of grades is decided first and detailed grade definitions produced. Representative (benchmark) jobs are evaluated to validate the definitions. Other non-benchmark jobs are then slotted in on the basis of the relevant grade definitions. This method may be used where groups of jobs can be clearly defined – for example, clerical and administrative employees. Again it is easy to understand and does allow for some skill content. There is, however, a temptation to grade jobs according to how they have been paid historically rather than according to their definitions, and aspects of individual jobs may straddle job definitions.'

(ACAS Guide No 1)

Any approach that can be shown to be analytical in its methodology will be acceptable, so long as the weighting within the evaluation is not in itself discriminatory. Factors over which caution needs to be exercised in this regard are traditionally male-orientated criteria such as 'requirement for muscular effort' etc.

An employer cannot rely upon a job evaluation scheme (JES) to block a claim of equal value unless the JES was undertaken in respect of employees in the company's undertaking, or group of undertakings. In *McAuley v Eastern Health and Social Services Board [1991] IRLR 467*, the Northern Ireland Court of Appeal rejected the employer's reliance on a JES undertaken in Great Britain in respect of health service ancillary workers, even though the JES evaluated workers in jobs similar to those of the applicants. The JES was not undertaken in respect of employees in Northern Ireland, and therefore the employer could not rely on it.

29.16   Acceptable evaluation methods that provide a defence

Points rating (or points assessment) was described by ACAS as follows.

'*Points rating.* This is a commonly used job evaluation technique. It is an analytical method which breaks each job down into a number of factors – for example, skill, responsibility, physical or mental requirements and working conditions, with the factors sometimes being further broken down into sub-factors such as education, decision-making, dexterity etc. These sub-factors will be further divided into degrees or levels. Points are awarded for each factor according to a predetermined scale and the total points decide a job's place in the rank order. The factors should reflect the varying degrees of importance attached to them. Care should be taken to ensure that the weightings do not result in a sex-biased scheme – for example, by attaching an unjustified weighting to the physical strength factor at the expense of manual dexterity. A points rating scheme has the following advantages:

–   it provides a rationale as to why jobs are ranked differently

–   it may be entered as a defence to an equal value claim when factors are selected and weighted to take no account of sex

–   it will be seen as generally less subjective than non-analytical techniques.

The limitations of points rating are that it is time consuming to introduce and can be complex and costly to undertake. In addition it can be seen to be inflexible in times of rapid change and can imply an arithmetical precision which is not justified.'

(ACAS Guide No 1).

In *Springboard Sunderland Trust v Robson [1992] IRLR 261*, in a job evaluation survey the applicant's job was rated at 400 points, but on appeal this was increased to 410. Her comparator's job was rated at 428 points. Following the JES, all jobs were graded according to their points rating. All jobs rated at 410 to 449 points were graded at salary Grade 4. However, the applicant only received salary at Grade 3. The EAT held that the applicant was employed on work rated as equivalent with the comparator even though the jobs received different points ratings under the job evaluation survey. This was because in determining whether two jobs are of equal value, the tribunal should have regard to the full results of the job evaluation survey, including the allocation to grades at the end of the evaluation process. Therefore, it was necessary to look further than the final points rating given to each job.

A further acceptable analytical approach is set out by the EAT in *Eaton Ltd v Nuttall [1977] ICR 272*:

'*Factor comparison*. This is also an analytical method, employing the same principles as points assessment but using only a limited number of factors, such as skill, responsibility and working conditions. A number of "key" jobs are selected because their wage rates are generally agreed to be "fair". The proportion of the total wage attributed to each factor is then decided and a scale produced showing the rate for each factor of each key job. The other jobs are then compared with this scale, factor by factor, so that a rate is finally obtained for each factor of each job. The total pay for each job is reached by adding together the rates for its individual factors.'

29.17 No obligation to undertake evaluation or accept conclusions of evaluation

There is no obligation under the *EqPA* that requires an employer to conduct a job evaluation study. If, however, a claim for equal value is made by the applicant, the tribunal will order an expert to prepare a report which will inevitably encompass such a job evaluation, and so an individual who is able to satisfy a tribunal that he has some case will in effect be able to force an evaluation (see TRIBUNALS (53)). Equally, an employer is not obliged to accept the conclusions of a job evaluation study, but must be able to make it clear that he does not accept those conclusions at the time, so as to enable him to resist any claim by an employee in reliance on such an evaluation (*Arnold v Beecham Group Ltd [1982] ICR 744*).

29.18 Employee can rely on job evaluation scheme commissioned and accepted by an employer

If an employer accepts the findings of a job evaluation study, an employee is entitled to rely on those findings, even if the employer does not actually implement them (*O'Brien v Sim-Chem Ltd [1980] ICR 573*), and can rely on *EqPA s 1(5)* to found a claim on the basis that her work has been rated as equivalent to the comparator man's.

29.19 QUALIFICATION PERIOD

There is no qualification period. *[EqPA s 2(1)]*. Thus, an individual is covered from day one of her employment, although she must actually be, or have been, employed by the employer to bring a claim against him under the *EqPA*. However, if the complaint relates to discriminatory pay in a job offer, then this can still be brought under the *SDA [SDA s 6(1)(b)]*, although it cannot be brought under the *EqPA*.

29.20 TIME LIMIT

An individual must be working for the employer, or have worked for him within the previous six months, for a claim under the *EqPA* to be referred to the industrial tribunal. [*EqPA s 2(4)*]. This does not apply to claims made under European Union law (see 29.27 below). In *British Railways Board v Paul* [*1988*] *IRLR 20*, it was held that the time limit under *EqPA s 2(4)*, referred to above, applies only to a reference to the industrial tribunal by the Secretary of State under *EqPA s 2(2)*, and not to an application to the tribunal by an employee or ex-employee under *EqPA s 2(1)* or by an employer under *EqPA s 2(1A)* (see below). The EAT therefore allowed a claim to be brought some two-and-a-half years after the complaint had arisen. However, in *Etherson v Strathclyde Regional Council* [*1992*] *IRLR 392*, the EAT held that the time limit under *EqPA s 2(4)* is six months (i.e. the applicant must have worked for the employer within the previous six months in order to be able to present a claim under the *EqPA*). The decision in *British Railways Board v Paul* was not followed; the time limit therefore applies to claims presented by ex-employees directly to the tribunal, as well as to references by the Secretary of State under *EqPA s 2(2)*. The extent to which an industrial tribunal (or other court) can award back pay is limited to two years prior to the institution of the proceedings. [*EqPA s 2(5)*].

29.21 ENFORCEMENT

Proceedings for an equal pay claim normally take place in the industrial tribunal [*EqPA s 2(1)*], and must take place in the industrial tribunal where the claim relates to equal value [*EqPA s 2A*], for which a special procedure applies (see TRIBUNALS (53)). There is nothing to prevent an individual from taking an equal pay claim (that does not involve equal value) on a contractual basis to the High Court or a county court. If the court considers it appropriate that the matter should be dealt with by an industrial tribunal, however, it may, of its own volition or on the application of a party to the proceedings, strike out the claim or refer it to an industrial tribunal. [*EqPA s 2(3)*]. It is open to an employer, as well as to an individual, to refer a dispute about equal pay to an industrial tribunal. [*EqPA s 2(1A)*].

29.22 EXCLUSIONS FROM THE ACT

The legislation is comprehensive and covers men and women, without regard to age [*EqPA s 11(2)*], who are 'employed at an establishment in Great Britain'. [*EqPA s 1(1)*]. Working 'at' an establishment encompasses working 'from' that establishment (*Hugh-Jones v St John's College, Cambridge* [*1979*] *ICR 848*). Excluded are the following.

(a)   *Employment outside the UK.* The legislation is limited to the United Kingdom. Within the rest of the EU, however, the *Equal Treatment Directive* will apply, as will similar national legislation. Elsewhere, provisions vary, but many countries have more comprehensive legislative protection (e.g. Canada).

(b)   *Members of the armed forces* [*EqPA s 1(8)(9)*]. However, *Article 6* of the *Equal Treatment Directive* requires member States to introduce legislation to enable anyone to obtain a remedy for a breach of the principle of the Directive (see *Johnston v The Chief Constable of the Royal Ulster Constabulary* [*1987*] *ICR 83*), and it seems likely that a member of the armed forces could take proceedings in the UK in reliance on the Directive itself.

(c)   *Retirement and pension provisions [EqPA s 6(1A)(b)]*. This exception is now of little relevance following the ECJ decision in *Barber v Guardian Royal Exchange Assurance Group [1990] IRLR 240*, which has had the effect of requiring the equalisation of pension arrangements by application of the *Equal Treatment Directive*. This is dealt with in full in PENSIONS (42).

(d)   *Pregnancy and maternity provisions for women. EqPA s 6(1)(b)* excludes terms 'affording special treatment to women in connection with pregnancy or childbirth'. This excludes men from claiming the right to paternity leave or the like (although there are moves within the EU to legislate for this specifically). This is an exception to the overall intention of the legislation, and will therefore be construed narrowly, consistent with general principles of statutory interpretation. Whilst it does enable employers to offer special arrangements to women to return to work after childbirth, it is unlikely to enable them to offer those women enhanced payments upon their return. Such arrangements will invite a claim from men. Similarly, this provision is unlikely to extend to financial inducements in connection with 'career breaks'.

(e)   *Steps in compliance with special laws regulating the employment of women.* The *SDA 1986* (and *Employment Act 1989*) repealed most of the protective legislation preventing women from being employed on certain shifts and in certain occupations, although some restrictions remain.

29.23 EQUAL PAY CLAIM PROCEDURE

Like work and work rated as equivalent

These claims are processed in the normal way by an industrial tribunal. An equal pay claim is commenced in exactly the same way as an ordinary claim, by way of an originating application (except that an employer, as well as an employee, can ask for a dispute to be determined). The employer is then sent a copy of the originating application, and has the usual 14 days in which to enter his reply by way of a notice of appearance (although the tribunal will invariably give extra time for this if requested to do so prior to the deadline – in an equal pay claim, it is inadvisable for an employer to put in a defence without having considered matters carefully and taken advice). There is nothing to prevent an individual mounting a claim in the High Court or county court on the basis of an equality clause where a question of equal value is not involved. If he does, however, the likelihood is that the court will strike out the claim or refer it to an industrial tribunal. [*EqPA s 2(3)*]. If a claim involves 'like work' or 'work rated as equivalent' and an equal value claim, the equal value claim will be held in abeyance whilst the 'like work' or 'work rated as equivalent' claim is disposed of. Only if this fails will the equal value claim be dealt with. The procedure is thereafter exactly the same as in any other discrimination case. The burden of proof is upon the applicant to satisfy the tribunal as to the claim.

29.24 Procedure in equal value claims

A special procedure pertains for equal value claims which is set out in TRIBUNALS (53).

29.25 COLLECTIVE AGREEMENTS

Any collective agreement that has any term that contravenes the requirement for an equality clause in all contracts of employment [*EqPA s 1*] is deemed automatically unenforceable and void [*SDA 1975, s 77; SDA 1986, s 6*], and can be referred to a county court by any individual with an interest in the relevant agreement.

In *Nimz v Freie und Hansestadt Hamburg* [*1991*] *IRLR 222*, the ECJ indicated that where a claim is made under EU law, there is power to amend a collective agreement which is discriminatory in its effect.

TURERA 1993, s 32 inserted a new *Sec 6(4A)* into the *SDA* as from 30 November 1993. It gives employees and prospective employees the right to challenge the validity of the terms of a collective agreement which applies to them, where the terms may contravene equal treatment principles. Under this new provision, the tribunal may make a declaration that the relevant term of the collective agreement is void.

29.26 THE ROLE OF ACAS

ACAS has a duty to attempt to conciliate in respect of an equal pay claim as in any other, but the tribunal will also always ask the parties if they would like the further opportunity for an adjournment to conciliate in an equal value claim. [*IT Regs, 2 Sch Rule 12 (2A)*]. Clearly, ACAS can be of considerable assistance in equal pay claims, given the time and cost involved for such cases to go through the tribunal process. However, an ACAS officer cannot be asked by the independent expert to make submissions to him. (For the role of ACAS generally, see CONCILIATION (11).)

29.27 CONTINUED IMPACT OF THE EU

An individual may also rely upon the Treaty of Rome to enforce the right to equal pay provided for by *Article 119* under EU law. This provides that:

'Each Member State shall during the first stage ensure and subsequently maintain the application of the principle that men and women should receive equal pay for equal work. For the purposes of this Article, "pay" means the ordinary basic or minimum wage or salary and any other consideration, whether in cash or in kind, which the worker receives, directly or indirectly, in respect of his employment from his employer.'

This has been held to include sick pay, compensation for unfair dismissal, redundancy pay and pensions (*Barber v Guardian Royal Exchange Assurance Group* [*1990*] *ICR 616*).

The Council of the European Union has adopted one Directive in the area of equal pay, *Directive 75/117*, which requires member States to introduce: 'such measures as are necessary to enable all employees who consider themselves wronged by failure to apply the principle of equal pay to pursue their claims by judicial process after possible recourse to other competent authorities'. (*Article 2*).

The *Equal Pay Directive (75/117)* has been held to be interpretive of *Article 119* and is therefore considered to be directly enforceable by individuals in the United Kingdom's jurisdiction (*Jenkins v Kingsgate (Clothing Production) Ltd* [*1981*] *ICR 715*). However, it is only directly effective against public-sector employers and 'emanations of the State'.

It may also, on occasions, be necessary to consider the implications of the *Equal Treatment Directive (76/207/EEC)*. This is not directly enforceable by individuals unless they are employees of the State (see *Foster v British Gas plc [1990] IRLR 353*). The application of the *Directive* to private sector employees remains doubtful. In *Duke v GEC Reliance Systems Ltd [1988] ICR 339*, the House of Lords held that the relevant domestic law (in that case, the *SDA*) should not be interpreted to give effect to European law unless domestic legislation was passed specifically to implement European law. However, in a commercial case (*Marleasing SA v La Comercial Internacional de Alimentacion (ECJ 106/89, 13 November 1990)*), the ECJ has held that domestic law should always be interpreted in line with EU directives.

A claim under *Article 119* can be brought directly in the industrial tribunal if it can be shown that the domestic equal pay legislation falls short of the terms of *Article 119* (*Barber*, above), and that the terms of the Article are clearly applicable without further definition by national legislation (*Leverton v Clwyd County Council [1989] ICR 33*). Community law will take precedence where there is an inconsistency, and the wording of UK statutes will be interpreted accordingly (*Pickstone v Freemans plc [1988] ICR 697*). A national tribunal may refer an appropriate point of law to the ECJ for determination (see for instance *Marshall v Southampton and South West Hampshire Regional Health Authority [1986] ICR 335*).

Article 119 has been held to cover directly and indirectly discriminatory pay structures (see *Rinner-Kuhn v FWW Spezialgebaudereinigung GmbH & Co [1989] IRLR 493*) and *Handels-Og Kontorfunktionaerernes Forbund i Danmark v Dansk Arbejdsgiverforening* ('the *Danfoss* case') *[1991] ICR 74*; but cf. *Enderby v Frenchay Health Authority and Secretary of State for Health [1991] IRLR 44*). This includes, for example, the provision of redundancy payments for full-time employees only (*Kowalska v Freie und Hansestadt Hamburg [1990] IRLR 447 (ECJ)*). *Article 119* has also been held to cover pay in lieu of notice, even when responsibility to make the payment is with the Secretary of State for Employment out of the National Insurance Fund where the employer is insolvent (*Clark v Secretary of State for Employment [1995] IRLR 421*).

There is no express time limit on claims brought under EU law (*Stevens v Bexley Health Authority [1989] IRLR 240*, confirmed in *Secretary of State for Scotland v Wright and Hannah [1991] IRLR 187*).

The ECJ has recently held (in the context of social security benefits) in *Johnson v Chief Adjudication Officer (No 2) [1995] IRLR 57* that it is not contrary to EU law for national law to impose time limits on the period in respect of arrears of benefits which are payable, in circumstances where a member State has failed to implement EU law correctly. In relation to pension entitlements, which are covered by the *EqPA*, this decision could have the effect of limiting the impact of the earlier ECJ decision in *Vroege v NCIV [1994] IRLR 651* (that part-time employees are potentially entitled to membership of occupational pension schemes retrospectively from 8 April 1976), so that only two years' worth of pension benefits can actually be claimed.

30   Equal Treatment Directive

30.1   SCOPE OF THE EQUAL TREATMENT DIRECTIVE

The *Equal Treatment Directive (76/207/EEC)* introduced the principle of equal treatment for men and women in relation to employment, vocational training and promotion and working conditions. The *Directive* prohibits discrimination on the grounds of sex (either directly or indirectly). However, it does allow discrimination in favour of women as regards pregnancy and maternity.

Article 3 of the Directive prohibits discrimination on the grounds of sex in the conditions of access to employment.

By *Article 4* of the Directive the principle of equal treatment was implemented as regards access to vocational training.

By *Article 5* of the Directive the principle of equal treatment was implemented as regards working conditions, including conditions relating to dismissal, and men and women 'shall be guaranteed the same conditions without discrimination on grounds of sex' (*Article 5.1*).

By *Article 6* of the Directive, member States have been required to implement into their national legal system 'such measures as are necessary to enable all persons who consider themselves wronged [by not being subject to the principle of equal treatment] to pursue their claims by judicial process'.

30.2   EFFECT OF THE EQUAL TREATMENT DIRECTIVE ON UK LAW

EU Directives have 'vertical direct effect', following the decision of the ECJ in *Van Duyn v Home Office [1975] 3 All ER 190*. This means that certain individuals are able to rely on Directives where national law is insufficient. Therefore where a member State has failed to implement correctly the terms of a Directive (or failed to implement the Directive at all), certain individuals will be able to allege breaches of EU law, where otherwise they may not have any remedy.

The concept of 'vertical direct effect' means that public sector employees are able to rely on the terms of a Directive, but not private sector employees. This is because Directives are enforceable against 'emanations of the State' (such as local authorities, health authorities and public utilities).

The *Equal Treatment Directive* has had the greatest impact on UK law in this area of direct effect, having been relied upon by public sector employees to force the Government to alter national law. The reason for this is the judgment of the ECJ in *Francovich v Italy [1992] IRLR 84*. In this case, the Italian Government had failed to correctly implement the provisions of a Directive on the protection of employees in the event of the employer's insolvency. The applicant brought proceedings directly against the Italian Government claiming damages for the losses he had incurred as a result of its failure to correctly implement the provisions of the Directive. The ECJ agreed with the claim and held that the Italian Government was under an obligation to compensate the applicant for his losses.

As a result of the decision in *Francovich*, private sector employees who lose out on a remedy open to public sector employees as a result of a Government's failure to implement the terms of a Directive are potentially able to commence proceedings directly against the Government. The possibility of such proceedings has on more than one occasion forced the Government to alter the provisions of national law in the immediate aftermath of an ECJ decision so as to prevent the possibility of any such claim being brought against it.

The Government recently settled a *'Francovich'* claim of an individual who had been supported by the Northern Ireland EOC. This was the first successful claim of this kind in the United Kingdom.

30.3   Two of the most important recent decisions in the area relating to discrimination concerned the *Equal Treatment Directive*. In *Marshall v Southampton and South West Hampshire Area Health Authority (No 2) [1993] IRLR 445*, the ECJ held that the existing provisions of the *SDA* were contrary to *Article 6* of the *Equal Treatment Directive* as regards imposing an upper limit on the amount of compensation that could be awarded in the cases of unlawful sex discrimination.

For the reasons explained above, this decision only affected public sector employees. However, faced with the prospect of *Francovich* claims by private sector employees, the Government has since amended the *SDA* by the *Sex Discrimination and Equal Pay (Remedies) Regulations 1993 (SI 1993 No 2798)*. These regulations removed the upper limit on compensation that the tribunals can award. In addition, although this decision was only in relation to sex discrimination, the Government subsequently removed the upper limit and compensation that tribunals can award in race discrimination cases – *Race Relations (Remedies) Act 1994* (see REMEDIES (49)).

A further landmark was the House of Lords decision in *R v Secretary of State for Employment, Ex parte Equal Opportunities Commission [1994] IRLR 176*. In this case, the House of Lords held that the qualifying thresholds in the *EPCA* as regards the right to claim a statutory redundancy payment or unfair dismissal were indirectly discriminatory against part-time employees, and this is contrary to the principle of equal treatment laid down in the *Equal Treatment Directive*.

As a result of this decision, public sector part-time employees were able to claim statutory redundancy payment and unfair dismissal after two years' service. The Government subsequently amended the *EPCA* so that all part-time employees can claim these rights after two years' continuous service – the *Employment Protection (Part Time Employees) Regulations 1995 (SI 1995 No 31)*. (See PART-TIME EMPLOYEES (40).)

30.4   The *Equal Treatment Directive* has been a powerful weapon for the EOC and female employees generally in promoting the principle of equal treatment. As seen in the above two cases, EU law has been at the forefront of forcing changes to national law and of furthering the principle of non-discrimination on grounds of sex. Since successive Governments' policy has been to treat matters of race and sex discrimination on the same basis, EU law has also indirectly had an impact on the law relating to race discrimination.

31   Extended Leave and Holidays

31.1   NO LEGAL ENTITLEMENT TO HOLIDAYS

Surprisingly, there is no legal entitlement to holidays in the United Kingdom. The employee's position is entirely dependent on the provisions of the individual employment contract. *EPCA ss 1(1)-(3), 2(1)* provides every employee working for more than one month with the right to written terms and conditions of employment not later than two months after the beginning of the employment, including, inter alia, any terms and conditions relating to holidays. In the absence of express provision, there is an implied term in every employment contract to reasonable holidays. An individual without a contract who is denied reasonable holidays is able to apply to the tribunal if he has no written terms, or if they are incomplete in failing to deal with holidays (or any of the other required terms). The tribunal may imply a term, but must consider all the material facts, including the way the contract has actually been operated by the parties (*Mears v Safecar Security Ltd [1982] ICR 626*).

Some employees were previously protected by orders made by the various wages councils. Since the *Wages Act 1986*, however, these orders have been repealed, although any such protected staff employed at the time those orders were effective will have had such terms incorporated by practice into their individual contracts, and will continue to enjoy that benefit. *Article 118* of the Treaty of Rome requires member States to maintain equivalent holiday schemes, and *Recommendation 75/457/EEC* of 22 July 1975 (OJ LI199/32 of 30 July 1975) provides for four weeks' minimum paid holiday, but the recommendations are not obligatory. The Social Charter adopted on 10 December 1989, to which the UK was not a signatory, also provides for the right to annual holidays, and it is likely that the matter will be covered in a future Directive.

31.2   EXTENDED LEAVE

A particular feature of newly-immigrant communities is that they may wish to return to their country of origin to visit relatives. Particularly for families from the Indian subcontinent and from the West Indies, this is an expensive and time-consuming exercise, not to be undertaken lightly or with any great frequency. For this reason, many such individuals request special extended leave, either by running their holidays through from one year to the next, or by taking additional unpaid leave on top of their normal entitlement. Over the years, employers have responded sympathetically to such schemes, but there have been problems.

31.3   Extended leave schemes must be open to all

Extended leave can cause administrative and production problems for employers and, whilst not unsympathetic to genuine applications, there is often a desire on the part of employers not to make extended leave a general practice amongst staff. Care must be taken when imposing restraints on extended leave schemes. It is unlawful to limit any such scheme to, say, employees born, or with relatives, in the Indian subcontinent. There should be no geographical or racial restraint on any such scheme, or it will be contrary to *RRA s 1(1)(a)*. The 1984 CRE Code of Practice (para 1.21) makes particular reference to the need for consistent application of extended leave schemes:

'In addition, employees may request extended leave from time to time in order to visit relations in their countries of origin or who have emigrated to other countries. Many employers have policies which allow annual leave entitlement to be accumulated, or extra unpaid leave to be taken to meet these circumstances. Employers should take care to apply such policies consistently and without unlawful discrimination.'

31.4 LAWFUL RESTRICTIONS ON EXTENDED LEAVE SCHEMES

An employer who is concerned that a universal right to extended leave will cause administrative and production problems to an excessive extent may lawfully restrict the scheme in a variety of ways. These are outlined below.

(*a*)   **No extended leave rule**

There is no obligation to give extended leave at all. It will not be discriminatory, *per se*, to refuse to give such leave. It may be, however, that a member of staff with extreme family circumstances who, without such leave would be forced to leave work, might be able to argue indirect discrimination where such an absolute bar is operated, which the employer would then have to justify. It is therefore advisable for employers to retain a discretion to grant such leave in exceptional circumstances, as the basic prohibition would no longer be an absolute bar and could not then constitute indirect discrimination (*Perera v Civil Service Commission (No 2)* [1983] ICR 428).

(*b*)   **Discretion to grant leave in exceptional circumstances**

Any such discretion must not on the face of it be discriminatory. An employer operating such a system would be advised to monitor its operation with some care. Where discretion is exercisable, there is the opportunity for a manager or supervisor, consciously or subconsciously, to discriminate on racial grounds. Any guidance given should be carefully considered to make sure that it is not itself discriminatory; geographical or nationality-based criteria are unlawful. A 'time taken to travel' criterion might constitute indirect discrimination, but would almost certainly be justifiable.

(*c*)   **Limited extended leave scheme subject to fixed criteria**

Any criterion that is non-racial, or, if potentially indirectly discriminatory, straightforwardly justifiable, is acceptable. A criterion that could not be discriminatory would be one that limits extended leave to circumstances such as the bereavement or illness of an immediate relative, but care should be taken to ensure that this benefit is given to all staff. Alternatively, it would probably be justifiable, where the employer can demonstrate that a universal scheme would lead to production or administration problems, to limit the scheme to memb   *aff with* close relations more than *x* miles abroad. Employers m conducting a survey of staff to identify the real effect of high number of indigenous employees will have relativ of the world as a legacy of the country's colonial past a emigration to Australasia.

31.5   Extended Leave and Holidays

(d)   Time served criterion

A criterion that limits extended leave to staff who have served the company for more than, for example, seven years, or limits extended leave to one such leave every seven (or some other number of) years will not, *per se*, be discriminatory. Employers would be well advised to monitor the ethnic composition of their staff against length of service to satisfy themselves that a 'time served' criterion does not, in fact, have an adverse impact on particular groups of staff. Given the pattern of immigration to the country, it is less likely today than in the recent past that such a criterion will have an adverse impact. If it does, further questions as to why it does need to be addressed. Even if there is an adverse impact, a justification on the grounds of administrative and commercial practicality would probably find favour with a tribunal.

31.5   DISMISSING OVERSTAYERS

The tribunal has addressed this question on a number of occasions. The normal dismissal rules apply. There should be a clear provision that any unauthorised overstay on extended leave is potentially a matter of gross misconduct. The individual should be invited to attend a disciplinary hearing, and given an opportunity to explain, justify or excuse his conduct. If the employee has still not returned, good practice would be to defer the disciplinary hearing on the first occasion, thereafter hear the matter in the individual's absence, dismiss the employee (if no extenuation is apparent), but offer an extended appeal date of (say) one month from the date of dismissal.

32   Fair Employment (Northern Ireland) Acts 1976 and 1989

32.1   The 1976 Act introduced unlawful discrimination on religious and political grounds as regards access to employment in Northern Ireland.

The *Fair Employment (Northern Ireland) Act 1989* established the Fair Employment Tribunal which has jurisdiction to hear claims under the *Fair Employment (Northern Ireland) Act 1976*.

These Acts are outside the scope of this book. The address of the Fair Employment Commission is:

Andras House
60 Great Victoria Street
Belfast
BT2 7BB

Tel: (01232) 240020

33 Genuine Occupational Qualification

33.1 Both the *RRA* and the *SDA* provide limited circumstances in which it is lawful to discriminate because of a 'genuine occupational qualification' (GOQ). [*SDA s 7; RRA s 5*]. There are more of such exceptions from sex discrimination than race discrimination. It is for the employer to establish that the exception applies and, as these clauses are exemptions from the main purpose of the Acts, they are strictly construed by the courts (*London Borough of Lambeth v CRE [1990] IRLR 231*).

33.2 SCOPE OF GOQ EXCEPTIONS

The exceptions apply even if only part of the job relates to the GOQ criteria. The legislation refers to 'some of the duties', which does not impose a fixed proportion (see *Tottenham Green Under Fives' Centre v Marshall (No 2) [1991] IRLR 162*). On the other hand, these exceptions only apply *if* there are not sufficient persons of the relevant sex already employed capable of carrying out the duties, who could reasonably be employed in those duties. [*SDA s 7(4); RRA s 5(4)*]. (See *Wylie v Dee (Menswear) Ltd [1978] IRLR 103*.)

It is important that employers should consider 'on the record' the option of utilising existing employees of the relevant sex, if they wish to take advantage of the GOQ exceptions. Unless clearly a sham, a tribunal is unlikely to find that it would be reasonable to utilise such employees if the matter has been carefully considered by the employer in a reasoned and open fashion. Two examples of when it would not be reasonable to utilise such employees would be if it would require a change in those employees' contracts of employment or job description which they would not be willing to accept, or if it would have an adverse effect on industrial relations.

As in so much of this area of the law, it would be a matter of fact for the 'industrial jury' (the tribunal), and so no cast iron predictions can be made; but where an employer has clearly asked himself all the right questions and come to a reasoned conclusion, 99 times out of 100 the tribunal will not upset that decision.

It is permissible to specify the sex of the post-holder as a criterion for a position in eight limited circumstances set out below, and in two of these it is also permissible to specify the race of the post-holder where it is race, rather than sex, that is relevant.

33.3 GOQ APPLICABLE TO RACE ONLY

Restaurants

There is one additional ground where race is a 'GOQ' that does not apply to sex, which is popularly known as the 'Chinese restaurant exception'. *RRA s 5(2)(c)* allows the racial group to be specified 'for reasons of authenticity' where food or drink is supplied. This would cover promotional events, as a trading situation is not a prerequisite, but actual supply of food or drink is. A French wine promotion with only French staff would be legitimate, but only if the wine was actually served!

148

33.4   **GOQ APPLICABLE TO BOTH RACE AND SEX**

It is permissible to specify the job-holder's sex or race in the following situations.

1. Dramatic authenticity

This applies to dramatic performances, modelling or other jobs where physiology (not including strength and stamina) is part of the essential nature of the job, dramatic performance or other entertainment (as the case may be), on grounds of authenticity. (This does not prevent girls from being picked for the role of principal boy, or men for the role of the wicked witch in the annual panto, or the selection of a white actor to play Othello!) The GOQ is permissive and, even when the circumstances are appropriate, not mandatory. It allows discrimination on grounds of sex or race, and there is no general requirement of consistency. [*SDA s 7(2)(a); RRA s 5(2)(a)(b)*].

2. Personal welfare services

The holder of the position provides individuals with personal services promoting their welfare or education, or similar services, which can most effectively be provided by a person of the same sex or same race. This could cover social workers, nurses, teachers etc. in certain limited circumstances. [*SDA s 7(2)(e); RRA s 5(2)(d)*]. The emphasis is on the personal nature of the services provided, and there must be an element of one-to-one. Strategic management posts are not covered by this provision (*London Borough of Lambeth v CRE [1990] IRLR 231*).

In respect of race, the terminology relates to racial group. 'Racial group' includes a group defined by reference to colour. [*RRA s 3(1)*]. A requirement for, say, a black social worker might, therefore, be legitimate, provided that the employing authority can substantiate that a significant proportion of the client group can be defined as black by virtue of their welfare needs, and that those needs 'can most effectively be provided' by a black social worker (*London Borough of Lambeth v CRE [1990] IRLR 231*). An authority that can show that it has considered these criteria carefully and concluded that they apply is likely to satisfy a tribunal that the GOQ is legitimate. An authority that cannot may have difficulties. The normal use of this clause in race cases, however, will relate to the linguistic needs of the client group (although on a strict interpretation of this exemption the appointee should be a 'mother tongue' speaker of the client group's language and of the same racial group).

33.5   **GOQ APPLICABLE TO SEX ONLY**

1. Privacy

This applies to swimming pool changing room attendants, toilet attendants and other personnel where a person of the same sex is required for the post on grounds of decency and privacy because the post involves physical contact, or the work involves being in the presence of members of that sex in a state of undress, or using lavatorial facilities. [*SDA s 7(2)(b)*].

2. Domestic nurse

This is sometimes called 'the butler exception'. It applies to a private companion, butler, nurse or other job-holder where the position involves working or living in a private home in which the individual will have close physical or social contact with, or knowledge of, intimate personal details of his employer. There is a 'reasonable objection' test within this clause. There is a line of thought that such an objection could not be reasonable. Indeed, the elderly in need of a companion are sometimes characterised in popular fiction as utterly unreasonable in their demands. This provision allows 'The Lady' magazine to function without fear of prosecution under the Act. [SDA s 7(2)(ba) inserted by SDA 1986, s 1(2)]. It is not clear what 'knowledge of intimate details of such a person's life' is meant to mean, but this clause is likely to be given considerable leeway by the industrial tribunal.

3. Lack of sleeping or toilet facilities

This covers live-in employees (year-round or for fixed spells) such as lighthouse keepers, shipmates and the like where the nature *or* location of the job makes it impractical to live elsewhere, there is no separate sleeping and sanitary accommodation *and* it would not be reasonable for the employer to make alternative arrangements or provide such accommodation. [SDA s 7(2)(c)].

The latter proviso places a substantial burden on the employer (*Hermollee v Government Communications HQ (unreported)*). Once again, an employer who can show a record of having considered this question carefully, by working out the cost of making alternative arrangements and considering the economic consequences, is far more likely to be able to convince an industrial tribunal that he is entitled to the advantage of this clause.

4. Single sex institutions

This applies to care and supervisory jobs in a single sex institution, or single sex part of an institution, such as a hospital, prison or other establishment for people in need of special care, supervision or attention. [SDA s 7(2)(d)]. The exceptional presence of an individual from the opposite sex is not a bar to taking advantage of this section. [SDA s 7(2)(d)(ii)]. The employer does have to show that it is 'reasonable', having regard to the essential character of the establishment (or relevant part of it), that the employee should be of the same sex as the inmates. Single sex schools could probably take advantage of this section, but would have to show an element of consistency.

5. Working abroad

This applies where the job is likely to involve duties outside the UK in a country whose laws and customs are such that the duties could not be performed as effectively by a woman. [SDA s 7(2)(g)]. This would cover appointments to Islamic countries, for instance.

6. Married couple

This applies where the position is one of a pair to be held by a married couple. [SDA s 7(2)(h)]. Among the attractive foibles of the SDA is this inherent philosophical inconsistency and harking back to an Edwardian world gone by. This provision relates to housekeeper and gardener/handyman situations, and is not limited to a private home, but can cover clubs, blocks of flats or similar premises. The exception is, however, limited to a requirement for married couples.

(Note that the GOQ formerly specified in *SDA s 7(2)(f)* (job needing to be held by a man because of statutory restrictions on the employment of women) is no longer applicable, that provision having been repealed by *Employment Act 1989, s 3(2)*.)

34   Harassment

34.1   DEFINITION

Surprisingly neither sexual nor racial harassment are specifically identified as distinct offences under either the *RRA* or *SDA* but have been held to be 'less favourable treatment' and a 'detriment' which are made unlawful by each of those Acts. [*RRA s 4(2)(c); SDA s 6(2)(b)*].

The European Commission issued a Recommendation and Code of Practice at the end of 1991 in relation to sexual harassment. For the first time, sexual harassment was defined as:

'conduct of a sexual nature, or other conduct based on sex affecting the dignity of women and men at work, including conduct of superiors and colleagues, is unacceptable if:

(*a*)   such conduct is unwanted, unreasonable and offensive to the recipient;

(*b*)   a person's rejection of or submission to such conduct on the part of employers or workers (including superiors or colleagues) is used explicitly or implicitly as a basis for a decision which affects that person's access to vocational training, access to employment, continued employment, promotion, salary or other employment decisions; and/or

(*c*)   such conduct creates an intimidating, hostile or humiliating work environment for the recipient; *as specified by.....*

and that such conduct may, in certain circumstances, be contrary to the principle of equal treatment within the meaning of [the *Equal Treatment Directive*]'.

Whilst this Code is not binding, it has been used by a number of industrial tribunals in harassment cases. The Code of Practice states that the essential characteristic of sexual harassment is that it is *unwanted* by the recipient. This is a subjective test, i.e. it is for each individual to determine the level of behaviour that is acceptable and unacceptable to them. Usually, sexual harassment will be persistent acts. However, this does not preclude one serious act from constituting harassment as in the case of *Insitu Cleaning Co Ltd v Heads* [*1995*] *IRLR 4*.

Various other attempts have been made to define sexual harassment. The TUC has issued guidelines in dealing with sexual harassment which suggest the following definition:

'repeated and unwanted verbal or sexual advances, sexually explicit derogatory statements made by someone in the workplace which are offensive to the worker involved, which cause the worker to feel threatened, humiliated, patronised or harassed, or which interfere with the worker's job performance, undermine job security or create a threatening or intimidating work environment'.

A single proposition by a manager for sexual favours, if associated with a fear of detriment (be it punishment or lack of promotion), will constitute sexual harassment to the same extent as will repeated but unwelcome advances. Any serious single act of harassment, that is some kind of assault or verbal abuse, will constitute harassment (*Bracebridge Engineering Ltd v Darby* [*1990*] *IRLR 3; Insitu Cleaning Co Ltd v Heads* [*1995*] *IRLR 4*).

It is clearly a difficult area for an industrial tribunal. In *De Sousa v The Automobile Association* [*1986*] *ICR 514*, the Court of Appeal held that harassment would be a detriment and contrary to the *RRA* or *SDA* not only where 'the result of the sexual or racial discrimination complained of was either dismissal or other disciplinary action by the employer, or some action by the employee such as leaving the employment on the basis of constructive dismissal', but also in other circumstances. Thus, where a 'reasonable employee could justifiably complain about his or her working conditions or environment, then whether or not these were so bad as to be able to amount to constructive dismissal, or even if the employee was prepared to work on and put up with the harassment, I think this too could contravene the subsections' (May LJ). In its judgment, the Court of Appeal indicates that the tribunal must look at the effect on the employee as much as the viewpoint of the employer. In the particular case, the applicant had not complained initially about a racially derogatory comment of which she had heard second hand, and had only mentioned the matter in the proceedings very late in the day, when answering a questionnaire. The Court of Appeal held that, in the particular circumstances, there was no detriment in that a racial insult on its own, if it was not intended that the individual should overhear it or get to hear of it, could not constitute discrimination. In this particular case, the circumstances were somewhat exceptional and it is likely that normally a racial insult will constitute a detriment.

In *B L Cars Ltd v Brown* [*1983*] *IRLR 193 (EAT)*, an instruction given to search all black people leaving the premises of the employer on the basis of a suspicion that a black person had stolen some parts was held to be a detriment not only to those staff searched, but to all black staff at the depot.

The EAT in *Stewart v Cleveland Guest (Engineering) Ltd* [*1994*] *IRLR 440* held that it was not harassment to require a woman to work in an environment where pictures of nude women were displayed even though her employer knew that such displays were offensive to her. The employer successfully argued that the pictures would have remained displayed if a male employee had also found them offensive, and therefore the fact that a male employee in the same situation as the applicant would have also been offended and treated in the same way meant that the applicant had not suffered a detriment so as to constitute a sex discrimination.

This is an odd decision by the EAT, and it should not be relied upon. The prudent employer will ban 'girlie' pin-ups. A more recent decision of the EAT, *Insitu Cleaning Co Ltd v Heads* [*1995*] *IRLR 4*, shows the stance that tribunals are increasingly taking in respect of sexual harassment. In this case, a single remark about a women's breasts was a detriment sufficient to constitute unlawful sex discrimination. Mr Justice Morison said:

'A remark by a man about a woman's breasts cannot sensibly be equated with a remark by a woman about a bald head or a beard. One is sexual the other is not.'

In *Gates v Security Express Guards* (unreported) the applicant successfully claimed unlawful discrimination when he was subjected to homosexual harassment. The tribunal decision referred to the Recommendation and Code of Practice.

In *Wadman v Carpenter Farrer Partnership* [*1993*] *IRLR 374*, the EAT stated that the definition of sexual harassment in the Recommendation could be of assistance to tribunals in considering such cases.

34.2 Harassment

It is likely that the Code of Practice and Recommendation will continue to be used by tribunals in determining whether harassment has taken place sufficient to amount to unlawful discrimination.

The task for the tribunal, once it has found there to be a detriment, is to assess what damages should be awarded.

34.2 LIABILITY OF EMPLOYERS FOR HARASSMENT

Both Acts provide for the liability of an employer for the acts of their employees, in the following terms:

'anything done by a person in the course of his employment shall be treated for the purposes of this Act as done by his employer as well as by him, whether or not it was done with the employer's knowledge or approval'. [*RRA s 32(1); SDA s 41(1)*].

The key words are 'in the course of his employment'. In *Irving & Irving v The Post Office [1987] IRLR 289 (CA)*, a case where a postman had scrawled a racist comment on the mail of one of the individuals on his delivery round, the Court of Appeal held that this was not an act in the course of his employment because he was acting outside his duties as a postman. The fact that he had the opportunity to do the discriminatory act did not mean that it was done in the course of his employment.

This concept is leading to a great deal of difficulty for industrial tribunals and some contradictory decisions are emerging. In three cases (all unreported), entirely different positions have been taken. In a Leeds tribunal case, *Wassell v Barnsley Metropolitan Borough Council*, the tribunal held that a sexual assault on a young trainee by three work colleagues was not an action in the course of their employment, whereas in a Dundee case and a London case (*Crane v V C Link Ltd* and *McVee v Smith Anderson & Co Ltd*), the opposite conclusion was reached. In *Crane*, a charge hand was found to be acting in the course of his employment when he sexually harassed one of the women he supervised although he was not authorised to behave in that way, and in *McVee*, a sales manager's harassment of one of his sales staff was held to be an action in the course of his employment. The distinguishing factor that seems to be building up, and may become a key ingredient as to whether or not the harassment is deemed to be in the course of employment, is a supervisory relationship (see *Bracebridge Engineering Ltd v Darby [1990] IRLR 3*). However, this will not always be the case. In *Insitu Cleaning*, the remark was made by an employee who was of less seniority than the female employee (although he was the son of two of the company's directors).

Employers would, in any event, be well advised to ensure that disciplinary procedures make it clear that any incident of sexual or racial harassment can be regarded as gross misconduct and can lead to dismissal.

34.3 Reasonable steps taken

An employer can avoid liability for the action of an employee in the course of their employment if he proves 'that he took such steps as were reasonably practicable to prevent the employee from doing that act, or from doing in the course of his employment acts of that description'. [*RRA s 32(3); SDA s 41(3)*]. The burden of proof is upon the employer to show that he has taken such steps (*Enterprise Glass Co Ltd v Miles [1990] ICR 787*). An employer will not be able to rely upon the fact that he has an equal opportunity policy or has taken relevant steps in the past if the equal opportunity policy, or the relevant steps taken, have fallen into disuse and lapsed.

If an employer has an effective equal opportunities policy which he is able to show he has fully implemented, then he will be able to rely upon this in avoiding any liability for unauthorised acts by his employees. A recommended equal opportunities statement is included in EQUAL OPPORTUNITY POLICY (28), and an example policy is reproduced in Appendix 3 (which was under review at the time of writing). The Employment Appeal Tribunal has also held that this section protects an employer where he has a proper system of staff supervision and had made known his policy of equal opportunities to staff but where the employer was unaware of the sexual harassment that has taken place (*Balgobin & Francis v London Borough of Tower Hamlets* [*1987*] *ICR 829*).

In *Balgobin*, two individuals were cleaners and had been harassed by a cook who worked at the same establishment. They had complained about this treatment but the employers had been unable to arrive at a conclusion and reinstated the cook, who had previously been suspended. The tribunal held that in having a proper and adequate supervisory system and in making known the equal opportunity policy, 'we do not think that there were any other practical steps which could have been taken to foresee or prevent the acts complained of'. The Employment Appeal Tribunal accepted that this was a finding of fact to which the industrial tribunal was entitled to come. Some caution should be exercised over this outcome as the decision of the EAT was very much on that basis. In many cases there may well be a wealth of evidence as to the proper steps that an employer could take in respect of implementing an equal opportunity policy, but in this case it was felt there was nothing more that the employer could do.

It would always be a matter of fact for the tribunal to determine whether or not proper steps have been taken. The equal opportunity statement provided in this book, may, or may not, be held to be sufficient. The major element that the authors would suggest recommends the equal opportunity statement, is that it puts the responsibility on both supervisor and supervised to consult if there is any doubt. In this regard, it is also important that an employer should have a grievance procedure that enables the individual concerned to 'jump' the first stage of management in respect of any allegation of racial or sexual harassment. In such circumstances, it may well be that the manager is the person who is responsible for the harassment, and it is certainly in cases where the manager is involved that the tribunal is most likely to find that the action is 'in the course of his employment' (see *Bracebridge Engineering Ltd v Darby* [*1990*] *IRLR 3*).

34.4 CONSTRUCTIVE DISMISSAL

An individual who is subjected to harassment of a racial or sexual nature will be able to claim constructive dismissal if, after having drawn it to the attention of management, nothing is done about it and as a result he resigns from the employment. It is, however, important that, before resigning, the individual should draw the harassment to the attention of management, and if he does not do so then his complaint of constructive dismissal will not succeed (*McCabe v Chicpack Ltd* [*1976*] *IRLR 38*). The test in relation to constructive dismissal is for the tribunal to identify whether or not the applicant's position was such that the trust and confidence necessary to sustain the employment relationship was at an end. Frequently, in cases of sexual harassment or racial harassment where complaints have been made and not acted upon, this will be the case.

34.5 **Steps for employer to take in potential constructive dismissal situation**

Employers who have procedures for post-termination interviews will have an opportunity to pick up the warning signs of a situation where an employee considers that he has suffered harassment and been forced to resign. It is therefore advisable for employers to interview all staff as to the reasons why they are leaving. Such a procedure can, in any event, provide very useful data for an employer in the terms of assessing his competitive situation in the employment market and the reasons for turnover of staff which can contribute significantly to staff costs.

If, either through this process, or by way of any letter or other communication from the individual, the employer is given an indication that the individual has resigned his position because he considers that he has suffered harassment of a racial or sexual nature, then the employer should take action. He would be well advised to invite the individual to specify the allegations and to conduct an investigative enquiry and, if necessary, a disciplinary interview in respect of the person alleged to have harassed that individual. If the allegations are proved, disciplinary action can be taken against the harasser, and the harassed member of staff can be invited back into employment. Whilst, strictly, such action is not relevant to a consideration of whether or not the employer had taken reasonable steps to prevent the discrimination happening (as it is action after the event), it will clearly influence the industrial tribunal in assessing the *bona fides* of the employer's equal opportunity attitudes and the basis of his conduct prior to the incident; it will also limit any damages.

34.6 **UNFOUNDED ALLEGATIONS OF HARASSMENT**

Allegations of racial or sexual harassment are extremely serious and are bound to be highly disruptive within the business environment. In such circumstances, where the complaint is unfounded, there is a temptation on the part of the employer to dismiss the individual who has made the complaint. There have been a number of applications in the industrial tribunal where such a complaint is made by an individual. Employers should exercise the greatest possible caution in taking such a step. An individual who has made a complaint with reference to the *RRA* or *SDA* is protected by virtue of *RRA s 2* or (as the case may be) *SDA s 4* from victimisation. This includes any individual who has made a complaint of harassment of a sexual or racial nature. Such an individual will be unprotected by the *RRA* or the *SDA* only if the following *two* conditions are met:

(*a*)   that the complaint is unfounded, and

(*b*)   that it is made in bad faith.

It will be a matter of fact for the industrial tribunal as to whether or not the complaint was unfounded regardless of any finding at which the employer may have arrived. In these circumstances, there is further cause for caution on the part of the employer in that, for a variety of reasons, employees who are alleged to be witnesses may not want to come forward in the employment environment. However, such employees may, under oath, confirm in the industrial tribunal that the discrimination actually took place, in which event the employer will be liable for victimising the complainant.

If, however, the circumstances are such that there is a reasonable suspicion that not only is the complaint unfounded but also made maliciously and in bad faith (by way of spite or otherwise), then the employer must also ensure that proper disciplinary procedures are followed. There must be a clear distinction between the conclusion of the grievance procedure, whereby there is a finding that the complaint is not sustained, and the commencement of disciplinary proceedings. If proper disciplinary procedures are not followed, then a finding of unfair dismissal will be made on the complainant's application, regardless of the outcome of any application pursuant to *RRA s 2* or *SDA s 4*. The employer should, after the conclusion of the grievance hearing, send the complainant a letter detailing the conclusion of that hearing. Thereafter, he may send the complainant a separate letter detailing the fact that he considers that a disciplinary offence has been committed by the complainant for making a serious allegation in bad faith and on a malicious basis. There should then be a hearing at which the complainant should have a further opportunity to substantiate the underlying allegation and also to show that he has acted in good faith. Only if the employer concludes that the allegation was false and made in bad faith should the complainant be dismissed. (See VICTIMISATION (54).)

34.7   DISCIPLINING THE HARASSER

Subject to proper procedures having been followed (see *British Home Stores Ltd v Burchell [1978] IRLR 379; Polkey v A E Dayton Services Ltd [1987] IRLR 503*), the dismissal of any individual after an employer has reasonably concluded that he has harassed another member of staff on racial or sexual grounds (or any other ground) will not be found to be unfair. In this regard, the employer has only to be reasonable. In many cases, there will be the uncorroborated statement of the individual complaining of harassment and that of the alleged harasser. There may or may not be statements from other members of staff in support of, or against the individual making the allegation. It is for the employer to weigh up everything and to try to make up his mind, on a reasonable basis, as to who is telling the truth. So long as he is reasonable in the way he carries out this exercise, there will not be any question of unfair dismissal.

In some circumstances an employer may conclude that, notwithstanding the lack of corroborative evidence, he believes the individual who has made the allegation of harassment. In relation to considering a complaint of unfair dismissal, it does not actually matter that he is in fact wrong in this, merely whether or not he was reasonable in his conclusion (*British Home Stores Ltd v Burchell [1978] IRLR 379*). There have been many cases where individuals have been dismissed in such circumstances and have taken the matter to the industrial tribunal, where the dismissal has been found to be fair. In *James v Cory Distribution [1977] IRLR 248*, a member of staff said to a temporary colleague who spoke up in favour of another colleague: 'Is he shagging you or something?'. The temporary was so upset that she left her employment immediately. Disciplinary proceedings were commenced against the individual concerned and he was dismissed. Dismissal was found to be fair.

In most cases of sexual or racial harassment, it will be appropriate to suspend the member of staff against whom the allegation is made. It does not constitute discrimination if, having investigated the matter and not having come to the conclusion that the individual has been guilty of harassment as alleged, the employer returns him to the same workplace as the individuals who have complained of harassment (*Balgobin & Francis v London Borough of Tower*

Hamlets [1987] ICR 829). Many employers may, however, consider this to be unwise. The employer *should not* move the person who has made the allegation of discrimination because, regardless of motive, this is likely to be a detriment even if it does not involve any loss of pay or material benefits (*Seide v Gillette Industries Ltd [1980] IRLR 427; Deeson v B L Cars Ltd (1981) EAT 173/80*).

34.8 **RECOMMENDED DISCIPLINARY PROCEDURE FOR INDIVIDUALS ALLEGED TO HAVE SEXUALLY OR RACIALLY HARASSED**

(*a*)   Ask the complainant for a full statement. Where a female member of staff is making a complaint of sexual harassment, it will be appropriate to have her statement taken by a female personnel officer.

(*b*)   Subject to the seriousness of the complaint, the individual complained of should be suspended pending the investigation of the complaint.

(*c*)   All the staff who may be able to provide evidence about the alleged incident or incidents should be interviewed and statements taken from them.

(*d*)   The individual accused of harassment should be invited to attend an investigatory meeting and provide a statement. It will depend on the particular circumstances as to whether or not it is appropriate to reveal the name of the complainant to him, but in most circumstances this will be unavoidable. Only in the most exceptional circumstances can it be reasonable to withhold from him such essential information as would enable him to defend himself, such as a genuine fear of violence to the complainant.

(*e*)   If there is either substance or doubt in relation to the matters complained of, then a disciplinary hearing should be held where the individual should be given full opportunity to answer the complaint or otherwise justify or excuse his conduct.

(*f*)   Subject to the conclusion of the disciplinary hearing, consideration should be given to penalty. If a finding of serious harassment is made, the likely outcome must be dismissal, as it would be a detriment to the other member of staff to have to continue working with that person. In limited circumstances it may be appropriate to transfer the individual. Where it is a matter of verbal abuse of a less serious nature, a final written warning will be appropriate.

34.9 **GRIEVANCE PROCEDURE**

As mentioned in 34.3 above, it is essential that the company grievance procedure enables anyone complaining of harassment to avoid what is normally the compulsory first stage of the procedure and take the complaint to the next stage of management. A procedure that facilitates this will be more likely to bring into the open any problems before they become impossible to contain.

34.10 **MATTERS THAT CAN BE TAKEN INTO ACCOUNT BY THE INDUSTRIAL TRIBUNAL HEARING A CLAIM**

The conduct of the applicant and her attitude with regard to matters relating to sexual conduct can be admissible in any claim brought under the *RRA* or *SDA*

(*Snowball v Gardner Merchant [1987] ICR 719*). This was a controversial decision by the Employment Appeal Tribunal which held that because compensation must relate to the degree of detriment, the question of injury to her feelings must be looked at not only objectively with reference to what an 'ordinary reasonable female' might feel, but also subjectively with reference to her as an individual. For that reason, evidence as to the conduct of the individual with regard to sexual matters was admissible. Evidence in relation to conduct by either party after the event complained of is also admissible (*Chattopadhyay v Headmaster of Holloway School [1982] ICR 132*, but see also *Wileman v Minilec Engineering [1988] IRLR 144*). One of the problems with detailing allegations in relation to an individual's conduct is that this provides salacious material for the media. A tribunal cannot normally be held in private, although a restricted reporting order may be made (see TRIBUNALS (53)).

34.11 CRIMINAL JUSTICE AND PUBLIC ORDER ACT 1994

The *Criminal Justice and Public Order Act 1994* has amended the *Public Order Act 1986*, introducing a new *Sec 4A* that creates a criminal offence of intentional harassment, alarm or distress. It came into force on 3 February 1995 and it renders racial, sexual and all other forms of harassment at work and in the street a criminal offence punishable by imprisonment. It is necessary to prove that the harasser's action was intentional, and also that someone was actually harassed. The offence carries a maximum punishment of 6 months' imprisonment or a fine.

The offence is widely drafted, and covers racial, sexual and other forms of harassment, including harassment against homosexuals and disabled persons.

Whilst this offence covers harassment in the employment context, it relates to harassment by an individual, and therefore does not affect the liability of employers for acts of employees which will remain in the civil domain.

34.12 RESTRICTED REPORTING ORDERS

In any case involving allegations of sexual harassment or other sexual misconduct, a tribunal has the power to make a restricted reporting order (see TRIBUNALS (53)).

34.13 SUMMARY

Industrial tribunals rightly consider serious cases of racial and sexual harassment to warrant the highest possible award of damages. Equally, such cases tend to attract tabloid publicity of an unhelpful kind, damaging to both the individual complainant and to the company. There is a growing awareness among individuals as to their rights in this regard and, quite properly, a growing reluctance on the part of women and black people to put up with such harassment. There are also a number of organisations apart from the Equal Opportunities Commission, such as the Women's Legal Defence Fund, which have been set up with the specific aim of facilitating complaints by women in relation to such conduct. It is no longer the case that women will be unable to take matters to the industrial tribunal because of a lack of resources.

35 Housing

DISCRIMINATION IN THE HOUSING SECTOR GENERALLY

35.1 The *SDA*, *RRA* and *Disability Discrimination Act 1995* prohibit discrimination in the disposal or management of premises. However, the provisions of the *Disability Discrimination Act 1995* are dealt with separately (see DISABILITY (18)).

By virtue of *RRA s 21* and *SDA s 30*, discrimination in the disposal or management of premises is prohibited. These provisions cover the work of estate agents, as well as landlords. In addition, discrimination in relation to the assignment of sub-letting of rented property is prohibited under *RRA s 24* and *SDA s 31*.

'Small dwellings' are exempt from these provisions. [*RRA s 22; SDA s 32*]. Small dwellings are those where a person provides accommodation in any premises in which he or a close relative resides; this exception is limited to premises where there is accommodation for only two households or six persons (in addition to the person disposing of the property).

35.2 *RRA s 21* and *SDA s 30* are identical. The provisions relate only to premises within Great Britain. A person who has power to dispose of premises cannot unlawfully discriminate on the grounds of race or sex:

(a) in the terms on which the premises are offered [*RRA s 21(1)(a); SDA s 30(1)(a)*]; or

(b) by refusing the person's application for those premises [*RRA s 21(1)(b); SDA s 30(1)(b)*] or

(c) in the treatment of the person in relation to any list of persons in need of premises of that description [*RRA s 21(1)(c); SDA s 30(1)(c)*].

These provisions apply to estate agents as well as to owners of premises, landlords, lessors and their agents. However, owners of premises which are wholly occupied by them, and which are being disposed of, are only subject to these provisions if they use the services of an estate agent, or they publish an advertisement in relation to the disposal. [*RRA s 21(3); SDA s 30(3)*].

35.3 In relation to persons with the power to manage premises, discrimination on the grounds of race or sex is unlawful as regards:

(a) the way that access to any facilities or benefits of the premises (or refusal of access) is granted [*RRA s 21(2)(a); SDA s 30(2)(a)*];

(b) eviction or any other detriment [*RRA s 21(2)(b); SDA s 30(2)(b)*].

Therefore, management companies, lessors and landlords are also unable to discriminate on the grounds of race or sex as regards communal facilities in rented premises, and as regards eviction. This latter protection is in addition to the usual security of tenure rights.

35.4 Where a landlord's consent is required to enable another person to dispose of premises or any part of premises under a tenancy, it is unlawful for the landlord to withhold that consent on the grounds of race or sex. [*RRA s 24(1); SDA s 31(1)*].

However, this prohibition does not apply if:

(*a*)   the person refusing the consent (or a near relative of that person) resides on the premises ('the relevant occupier') and intends to continue to do so [*RRA s 24(2)(a); SDA s 31(2)(a)*]; and

(*b*)   in addition to this person residing on the premises, there is also accommodation on the premises shared with other persons who are not members of the 'relevant occupier's' household [*RRA s 24(2)(b); SDA s 31(2)(b)*]; and

(*c*)   the premises are small premises [*RRA s 24(2)(c); SDA s 31(2)(c)*].

This exception applies to tenancies of residential premises, when the landlord or a near relative of the landlord also resides on the premises. 'Near relative' includes spouses, parents, grandparents, children, grandchildren and siblings (including step-relatives). However, the exception relates only to premises accommodating either one or two households, or up to six persons. [*RRA s 22(2)(a)(b); SDA s 32(2)(a)(b)*].

35.5   A further exception in the *RRA* not mirrored in the *SDA* is created by *RRA s 23(1)(b)*. By virtue of this provision, discrimination on the grounds of race is not unlawful where it relates to housing ancillary to service a private household (under *RRA s 4(3)*).

LOCAL AUTHORITIES

35.6   Introduction

A local authority has a duty to consider the housing needs within its district, including consideration of further housing accommodation. Preference must be given to people living in overcrowded/insanitary conditions, large families and homeless persons. When local authorities are allocating accommodation, they are providing services and, therefore, they are subject to the provisions of *RRA ss 20–27* and *SDA ss 29–36* (see SERVICE PROVISION (50)).

Under *RRA s 71* local authorities are under an obligation to ensure that their duties:

'are carried out with due regard to the need—

(*a*)   to eliminate unlawful racial discrimination; and

(*b*)   to promote equality of opportunity and good relations, between persons of different racial groups'.

This basically means that local authorities must have regard to the principles of equality and non-discrimination on the grounds of race in every aspect of their undertaking, including the allocation of housing.

Discrimination may occur during the allocation of housing as regards residential requirements and the exclusion of owner-occupiers from consideration for local authority housing.

35.7   Residential Requirements

Local authorities often impose residential requirements in their housing allocation policies. The reason for this is because of their obligation to assess housing needs within their own area. However, such requirements may be discriminatory, for example, against women who have left their abode to escape domestic violence. Such women may wish to set up home in a new area, and would be likely to fail a residential requirement. This is discriminatory because, in circumstances of domestic violence, it is usually the female partner who leaves.

If residential requirements are discriminatory or have discriminatory effect, it is for the local authority to justify the practice. Whether the practice is justifiable will depend on such factors as the reason the local authority has adopted the practice, whether it has considered alternative (non-discriminatory) policies, as well as the severity of the discriminatory effect of the practice.

35.8   Owner-Occupier Requirements

Local authorities may exclude from consideration for housing allocation people who are owner-occupiers. Whilst the reason for such a policy is clear – the person already has a house, and so is not in priority need for re-housing – it can still have a discriminatory effect.

For example, not all owner-occupiers live in good housing conditions, there could be overcrowding or the accommodation could be dilapidated or insanitary. Certain ethnic minority groups are more likely to be owner-occupiers, and to exclude owner-occupiers as a group from a housing list as a matter of course could have an indirectly discriminatory effect.

Such requirements could also indirectly discriminate against female occupiers, for example where the house is owned solely by the woman's spouse and the has been default on the repayment of the mortgage. In this situation, the female would be in the same position as a normal owner-occupier, and a local authority's refusal to allow her access to a housing list could be indirectly discriminatory unless it was objectively justified.

HOUSING ASSOCIATIONS

35.9   Introduction

A Housing Association is a body of trustees, a society, or a company not trading for profit, established for the purpose of instructing, improving, managing, facilitating or encouraging the construction or improvement of houses. *Housing Act 1988, s 56* introduced a new *Sec 75(5)* to the *Housing Associations Act 1985*. This reads as follows:

> '*Section 71* of the *Race Relations Act 1976* (Local Authorities: General Statutory Duty) shall apply to the [Housing] Corporation as it applies to a local authority'.

Therefore, local authorities, the Housing Corporation, and the Welsh and Scottish equivalents of the Housing Corporation (Tai Cymru and Scottish Homes) are subject to the provisions of the *RRA* to the same degree as local authorities (see above). The Housing Corporation, Tai Cymru and Scottish Homes are the bodies responsible for funding housing associations, and play an important role in ensuring that housing associations operate on a basis of racial equality in accordance with *RRA s 71*.

The Housing Corporation, Tai Cymru and Scottish Homes can publish management guidance to ensure that housing associations manage their affairs correctly. For example, the Housing Corporation is able to issue guidance as to the criteria housing associations employ in respect of their priorities in allocating houses.

35.10 **Duties of Housing Associations**

Housing associations have no obligation to consider housing conditions of the areas in which they operate; their obligations in providing housing usually arise out of the need to obtain financial assistance in the form of grants from the Housing Corporation.

However, local authorities are able to request the assistance of a housing association in the discharge of their obligations (i.e. the local authority's obligations) to homeless persons. Such assistance may extend to providing accommodation on behalf of the local authority. If so, then the housing association must have regard to the obligations of local authorities under the *RRA*.

Frequently, local authorities will have nomination arrangements with housing associations in their district. Once again, housing associations should have regard to the obligations imposed by *RRA s 71*. This may involve monitoring the ethnic origin of persons nominated by local authorities, which should roughly be in proportion to the size of that ethnic group in the local population.

Housing associations usually compile waiting lists for their accommodation, and it is possible that the criteria used by them for placing people on the waiting lists are discriminatory. The easiest way of avoiding this is for housing associations to ensure that waiting lists are open to all applicants. However, such a waiting list will usually be administratively complicated to run, given the limitations on housing associations' budgets.

Increasingly common are 'specialist' housing associations, for example dealing specifically with the housing needs of certain ethnic groups. Such groups are not contrary to the *RRA 1976* even though they apparently operate on a discriminatory basis.

35.11 **What aspects of housing association work are covered by the RRA?**

Housing associations now have regard to the *RRA* in all aspects of their undertakings. Obviously, the allocation of housing must take place on an equal basis without the taint of race discrimination. Most housing associations now operate equal opportunity policies as regards their employees, as well as ensuring that any third party contractors are equal opportunity employers, by use of the list of questions allowed under the *Local Government Act 1988* (see CONTRACT COMPLIANCE (13)).

It is also common for housing associations to use ethnic monitoring and target setting, particularly in areas with a high proportion of ethnic minorities. This monitoring should ideally not be limited to straightforward allocation of housing, but should also involve monitoring of allocation of housing according to the quality of the accommodation.

35.12 **CRE formal investigation into housing association practice**

The Commission for Racial Equality completed a formal investigation into housing associations in England, Wales and Scotland, and published its findings in 1993 ('Housing Associations and Racial Equality'). This was a general investigation into the racial equality policies of 40 housing associations, with a brief to assess the impact of published guidance on housing association practice, and also to assess the increasing role of housing associations in providing social housing (in 1991 housing associations were responsible for 85% of all new housing initiatives). The final reason for the investigation was to assess the degree to which the Housing Corporation, Tai Cymru and Scottish Homes had implemented their duty to eliminate unlawful race discrimination.

35.13   Conclusions of the formal investigation

Racial Equality Policies
Over 90% of the housing associations had adopted formal racial equality policies. However, only 25% of the associations had implementation plans to ensure that the racial equality policy was followed. Only 5% of the associations had set a timetable for the implementation of the racial equality policies.

Ethnic monitoring and targets
The vast majority of housing associations had monitoring policies, i.e. monitoring their lettings of properties by ethnic origin, as well as monitoring the ethnic origin of prospective tenants on a waiting list. However, a much smaller number of the housing associations monitored the quality of the accommodation offered to ethnic minorities (25%), and less than a quarter of the housing associations used equality targets to assess their performance. The CRE concluded that:

> 'Ethnic monitoring in many associations was a purely mechanical exercise, and no attempt had been made to use the data to improve performance in delivering a fairer housing service'.

Allocation Policies
All of the housing associations had allocation policies. However, not all of these had been 'equality proofed'. For example, some housing associations with 'closed' waiting lists failed to give any notification when the list was reopened. Some housing associations used 'word of mouth' to notify prospective tenants that the list was reopened. A number of housing associations had 'open' waiting lists, and some also printed information on their allocation policies in a number of languages.

Nominations and Referrals
In relation to referral policies, i.e. where bodies such as local authorities refer candidates to housing associations to be entered on housing lists, the CRE found that only 50% of the housing associations kept records of the ethnic origin of individuals referred to them, and only 30% analysed and reported on this information.

The CRE was also concerned over the lack of formal referral procedures between housing associations and the referral agencies, as only just over a quarter had written agreements which were capable of being monitored. Over 50% of the housing associations had no written referral agreement at all.

Employment Policies and Procedures
The formal investigation found that whilst a number of housing associations had recruited and trained ethnic minority staff for all posts (including professional and managerial posts), there were still some areas of discriminatory practice. For example, there was a low proportion of ethnic minority employees compared with their proportions in the local labour markets, and ethnic

minority staff tended to be concentrated in the manual and lower clerical grades. In addition, the investigation found that there was a lower appointment rate than application rate for ethnic minority applicants, and a low proportion of female ethnic minority managers.

Racial Harassment
80% of the associations investigated had adopted a racial harassment policy, and in addition most associations required a non-harassment clause in their tenancy agreements. Almost 50% of associations provided racial harassment training for their employees. However, only 5% of associations had actually taken possession proceedings against tenants guilty of racial harassment.

Racial Equality Training
Although nearly three-quarters of the housing associations were found to have carried out racial equality training, the investigation revealed that not all staff received training and that the contents and quality of the training varied considerably.

Management Committees
Over two-thirds of the housing associations investigated had no ethnic minority representation on their management committees even though most associations had areas with a significant proportion of ethnic minorities within their territory.

Contract Compliance
Less than half the housing associations had established a habit of questioning contractors in respect of their equal opportunities practice before admitting them on to any approved list, even though 73% of the housing associations referred to contractors and consultants in their equal opportunity policies.

Development Programmes
Over half of the associations investigated had attempted to identify the needs of ethnic minorities as part of their overall assessment of housing needs, and this was usually done through consultation with the community organisations. 35% had developed schemes to meet the specific housing needs of ethnic minority households. However, some housing associations had had difficulties in developing larger properties to meet the needs of large ethnic minority families.

35.14 Named Persons Investigation

In 1993 the Commission for Racial Equality completed a formal investigation into Oldham Borough Council's policy regarding allocation of housing, and it found unlawful racial segregation in the allocation of housing. For example, on an estate which was run down, 71% of tenants were Asian, whereas on a more modern estate nearby there was only 1 Asian tenant out of 300.

The CRE did not issue a non-discrimination notice, as the Council confirmed that it would implement the CRE's recommendations.

PRIVATE SECTOR HOUSING

35.15 Landlords and Rented Accommodation

With regard to disposal of rented accommodation, landlords are also bound by the provisions of the *RRA*. However, in limited circumstances discrimination on grounds of sex and race is permissible (see SERVICE PROVISION (50)).

35.16 Housing

35.16 Estate Agents

Estate agents are responsible for any discriminatory practices, such as discriminatory advertising of houses, or discrimination against vendors or purchasers. Estate agents are liable for discriminatory acts of their employees, and are also liable if they act upon discriminatory instructions.

35.17 Private Property Sales

Private vendors of houses are also subject to the provisions of the *RRA* and *SDA*, as regards discriminatory instructions to estate agents, discriminatory advertisements, and discriminatory acts of estate agents acting within their authority from the vendor.

However, where the private sale is completed without services of an estate agent or advertising, neither the *SDA* or *RRA* will apply.

35.18 Advertisements

Under *SDA s 38*, *RRA s 29* and *DDA s 19* it is unlawful to publish an advertisement that indicates (or is reasonably understood to indicate) an intention to discriminate on the grounds of race or sex. Only the CRE and EOC have the power to prosecute in respect of such advertisements, and, in relation to discriminatory advertisements in the housing field, proceedings must be commenced in the county court within six months of the date of the advertisement being published. Individuals do not have the right to bring proceedings for discriminatory advertisements (*Cardiff Women's Aid v Hartup [1994] IRLR 390*).

36   Indirect Discrimination

36.1   INDIRECT DISCRIMINATION (SEX AND RACE)

Indirect discrimination is one of the three forms of discrimination prohibited by the *SDA* and the *RRA* and is a more difficult concept to understand than DIRECT DISCRIMINATION (17). An employer can indirectly discriminate against an individual where there is no unlawful motive or reason for the treatment. What is important is the effect on that individual.

36.2   DEFINITION

Indirect discrimination is defined by *RRA s 1(1)(b)* and *SDA s 3(1)(b)*. Indirect discrimination takes place where an employer imposes a condition or requirement with which the individual cannot comply and which is therefore to his detriment, that condition can be shown to have a disproportionate impact in excluding others of that individual's sex (or race or marital status), and that condition cannot be justified irrespective of the individual's sex (or race or marital status). A straightforward example is a single height or weight requirement for men and women. Some women would be able to meet a 5′ 10″ height requirement but a much larger proportion of women than men would be excluded from consideration by such a criterion. The employer would then be called upon to justify the criterion. If the job involved picking fruit from 7′ bushes where ladders were not a practical option it might be justified. If the employer wanted to save money by only having one uniform size, it would not!

36.3   COMPENSATION FOR INDIRECT DISCRIMINATION

No damages are awarded to an individual if an employer is able to show that the requirement or condition imposed on the individual was not applied with the intention of treating the individual unfavourably on the grounds of race or sex (*RRA s 57(3); SDA s 66(3)*), although this has been questioned by some commentators in relation to the Equal Treatment Directive and the requirement for an 'adequate remedy' in national jurisdictions (see *Marshall (No 2)* [*1995*] *IRLR 445* for an elaboration of the principles).

In the case of *London Underground Limited v Edwards* [*1995*] *IRLR 355*, the employee was one of 21 female train operators out of a total of 2,044. The train operators worked three 8-hour shifts, and shift bonuses were payable for working in shifts during unsociable hours. The train operators were able to change their shifts for other shifts, which would result in them gaining or losing shift bonuses depending upon when they worked. The employee, who was a single parent, arranged her working pattern to enable her to combine child care responsibilities with working. The employer proposed to introduce a flexible rostering scheme as part of a cost saving initiative. This involved the scrapping of shift bonuses, and employees were able to change over their shifts as before, but this involved exchanging a shorter shift for a longer shift for the same remuneration. These new arrangements meant that it was no longer beneficial for the employee to use the changeover system to enable her to only work during the day. In effect, she had to work longer hours than previously for the same pay, and this affected her ability to look after her child. The employee refused to accept the terms and ultimately resigned on voluntary severance terms. She claimed that she had been indirectly discriminated against.

36.4 Indirect Discrimination

The industrial tribunal held that the new flexible rostering scheme was a requirement/condition, and it was such that a considerably smaller proportion of female single parents than male single parents were able to comply. The employee had suffered a detriment because she was unable to comply with the scheme, and the tribunal also held that the employer had not justified the requirement, because it would have been possible for the employer to make provision for single parents without significantly damaging the need to make savings. The employer argued that the new rostering arrangements had not been applied with the intention of treating the employee unfavourably on the grounds of her sex, and therefore, that the employee was not entitled to compensation under *SDA s 66(3)*. The tribunal rejected this argument and awarded the employee £5,000.

The employer appealed to the EAT, who held that the tribunal had selected the wrong pool of employees for comparison. The appropriate pool was all train operators to whom the new rostering arrangements applied, not all single parent train operators to whom the rostering arrangements applied. The tribunal should not have introduced a further sub-division into the pool for comparison. However, the EAT held that the requirement was not justified, and also upheld the tribunal's decision that the employer had not shown that the new rostering arrangements had been applied without the intention of treating the employee unfavourably on the grounds of her sex. The industrial tribunal was right to infer that this requirement was applied with full knowledge of its unfavourable consequences for the employee as a single parent, and from this inference it was possible to further infer that the intention to produce those consequences.

36.4 FACTORS CONSTITUTING INDIRECT DISCRIMINATION

There are a number of elements to indirect discrimination. These are outlined below as a number of questions to be considered.

(a) Is there a condition or requirement?

This is straightforward. The applicant must show that there is a condition or requirement in operation. Examples of such a condition are age, dress code, qualifications, and importantly, hours of work.

Even where the adverse impact of an employer's decision is clearly apparent, it is still necessary for the applicant to show that a condition or requirement has been applied: *Bhudi v IMI Refiners Ltd [1994] IRLR 204* (this is unlike the law of equal pay, where the ECJ in *Enderby v Frenchay Health Authority* held that indirect discrimination contrary to *Article 119* of the Treaty of Rome can be found without the applicant showing that 'a requirement or condition' has been applied to their detriment).

In *Brook v London Borough of Haringey [1992] IRLR 478*, the EAT held that the employers had not applied a 'requirement or condition' when, in a redundancy situation, they had decided that certain trades would be 'exempted' from consideration for redundancy. This is because the exempted trades were open equally to men and women, and the fact that there were in fact more men than women in the exempted trades did not make the policy a 'requirement or condition'.

In the case of *Stadt Lengerich v Helmig [1995] IRLR 216*, the ECJ held that it was not indirectly discriminatory to restrict payment of premium overtime rates to employees who worked more than the designated number of full time hours. On the face of it, this was a condition or requirement which adversely affected part-time employees, who were predominantly women, because they did not receive premium overtime payments. However, disregarding the overtime payments, part-time employees received the same hourly pay as full-time employees. The ECJ held that this fact meant that there was no difference in treatment between full-time employees and part-time employees and, therefore, no discrimination contrary to *Article 119* of the *Treaty of Rome* or the *Equal Treatment Directive*.

(*b*) **Is it an absolute?**

The condition or criterion must be absolute to constitute a 'condition or requirement' (*Perera v Civil Service Commission and Department of Customs and Excise (No 2) [1983] ICR 428; Meer v London Borough of Tower Hamlets [1988] IRLR 399*). This interpretation of the wording of the section is not conducive to achieving the aims of the Act. So long as an employer is able to say that a criterion is not an absolute bar, but only highly desirable, then it will not constitute indirect discrimination. This is likely to make a nonsense of the provision. By way of example, an employer specifying that an employee aged under 30 with supervisory experience is required for a specific post would be vulnerable to a claim from a woman who had returned to work after a career break to have a family. She would be able to show that such a criterion would exclude a greater proportion of women than men, because such a career break would be common for women. An employer who specified 'preferred' instead of 'required' would not be vulnerable to such a claim of indirect discrimination unless an applicant could show that, in fact, 'preferred' was a misstatement and an absolute bar was being operated. Employers should beware, however, of relying on the present statement of the law as it would not seem to be compatible with the European *Equal Treatment Directive*.

(*c*) **Is it applied universally?**

The criterion must be applied irrespective of race (or sex or marital status). If the criterion relates directly to sex, race or marital status, it will be a matter of direct discrimination.

(*d*) **Has the applicant established his racial group (or sex or marital status)?**

This criterion is obvious in sex or marital status cases but can be the source of difficulty where race is concerned (see RACIAL GROUP (48)). The applicant must establish membership of a particular racial group for comparison purposes.

(*e*) **Has the applicant established that the condition was applied to him to his detriment?**

The individual has to show not only that a discriminatory criterion was in operation but that it adversely affected him. Taking the example referred to in (*b*) above, a 32-year old woman who had not taken a career break to have a family would not be able to succeed in an indirect discrimination claim. She would be able to show an indirectly discriminatory criterion but not that it resulted in detriment to her (*London Borough of Tower Hamlets v*

Qayyum [*1987*] *ICR 729*). 'Detriment' has a very wide meaning. In one race relations case it was held that an instruction to search all black members of staff (exclusively) arising out of an instance of theft was to the detriment of black employees even if they were not actually searched (*BL Cars & Another v Brown* [*1983*] *IRLR 193*).

(*f*)   **Is he and his racial group (or sex) unable to comply?**

The 'can comply' test is one of common sense. In *Mandla v Dowell Lee* [*1983*] *IRLR 209* the criterion was one of school uniform, and in particular, a school cap. The applicant said he was not able to comply because of religious dictates. He was a Sikh. The school pointed out that it had Sikh pupils who did not feel so bound and that, as a matter of sheer practicality, it was easy for him to comply with its rule and not wear a turban. The House of Lords disagreed and said that, in practice, the boy could not comply with the condition. In essence, the 'can comply' test is a subjective one for the individual, so long as he can show that a significant proportion of his own racial group cannot comply on the same rationale. The test is therefore, 'can comply consistently with the customs and cultural conditions' of the group, not 'can physically comply'.

(*g*)   **Within what section of the community does the proportion comparison fall to be made?**

The tribunal must examine the right 'control' group to determine whether impact is disproportionate. The comparator group is a matter of fact for the tribunal, so long as it is reasonable. In a promotion case, the comparator group will be the persons otherwise qualified for the post. It will frequently be simpler for the tribunal to look at a restricted sample, but difficulties may arise when an external vacancy is at issue. In such cases, again, the logical approach would be to look at the reasonable catchment group for the vacancy. This can reveal significant points. Immigration patterns might lead to educational disadvantage for members of a particular racial group in a restricted locality which is not reflected in the performance of that racial group on a settled basis. The basis of comparison can be limited by other, common sense, criteria. Where an age bar is operated it will not adversely affect a greater proportion of women as a whole. The relevant group of women to consider is, however, those who have taken a career break (*Price v Civil Service Commission* [*1978*] *ICR 27*).

Further authority that the 'control' group to determine whether the impact is disproportionate is all those who satisfy the relevant criteria apart from the 'requirement or condition' was the Court of Appeal decision in *Jones v University of Manchester* [*1993*] *IRLR 218*. The applicant (a woman aged 46) argued that a job advertisement stating that the university was looking to employ somebody aged between 27 and 35 was discriminatory in that a higher proportion of female mature students would be unable to comply with the requirement than male mature students. The Court of Appeal held that the correct control group in these circumstances was all male and female graduates with the required experience. There is no need to subdivide the control group into male and female mature students (as the applicant had argued), because there was no requirement that applicants be mature students.

(*h*)   **What level of proof is required to show disproportionate impact?**

The Court of Appeal has directed that a common sense approach to this question should be adopted (*Meer v London Borough of Tower Hamlets* [*1988*] *IRLR 399*). The tribunal is not expected to wade through tomes of statistics. In the example cited in (*b*) above, there may or may not have been research as to the pattern of career breaks for women to have a family, but it is a matter of self-evident common knowledge. The clearest cases will, however, be those where the immediate comparators exhibit the relevant patterns. In that example, a woman applicant returning to work after a career break would be able to show a statistical adverse impact even if she were the only woman applicant to have taken a career break, unless it happens that a male applicant also took such a break, which is unlikely.

(*i*)   **Is there a disproportionate impact?**

The proportion of persons of the individual's sex or racial group who cannot comply with the requirement has to be 'considerably smaller' than the proportion who can comply with it, so a marginal impact will not be sufficient to lead to a finding of indirect discrimination. It has been argued that a 100% failure rate against a 100% success rate is outside the scope of the provision but this argument found no favour (*Perera v Civil Service Commission and Department of Customs & Excise* [*1982*] *ICR 350*).

In *Jones v University of Manchester* [*1993*] *IRLR 218*, the Court of Appeal held that the correct approach in determining whether there was disproportionate impact as a result of a 'condition or requirement' being imposed by an employer is by comparing the proportion of women in the control group who can comply with the proportion of men who can comply. If one is significantly smaller than the other then there will be disproportionate impact. Therefore, it will depend on the facts in each case whether there is such disproportionate impact.

(*j*)   **Can the requirement be otherwise justified irrespective of race (or sex or marital status)?**

Justification is dealt with separately below.

36.5 JUSTIFICATION

Justification is a difficult concept. It is a matter of fact for the industrial tribunal, but it must apply the correct test in making that finding of fact. There are a number of distinct elements to be considered, which are outlined below.

(*a*)   **The justification must be irrespective of race (or sex or marital status)**

The justification must be irrespective of the race (or sex or marital status) of the individual. [*RRA s 1(1)(b)(ii); SDA ss 1(1)(b)(ii), 3(1)(b)(ii)*]. In broad terms this means that it must not be a factor that is irretrievably bound up with race or sex (*Orphanos v Queen Mary College* [*1985*] *IRLR 349*, where the House of Lords determined that the 'justification' in that case 'cannot be justified irrespective of nationality' and could not, therefore, succeed).

36.5 Indirect Discrimination

(b) **The test to be applied**

The Court of Appeal considered what was meant by 'justification' in some detail in *Ojutiku and Oburoni v Manpower Services Commission [1982] IRLR 418* when it determined that it 'implies a lower standard than the word "necessary"' and 'The party applying the discriminatory condition must prove it to be justifiable in all the circumstances on balancing its discriminatory effect against the discriminator's need for it. But that need is what is reasonably needed by the party that applies the condition'.

The Court of Appeal later reviewed the *Ojutiku* case in *Hampson v Department of Education and Science [1989] ICR 179* and concluded that such an approach did not conflict with the decision by the European Court of Justice in an equal pay case that such a test must 'relate to a real need on the part of the undertaking, be appropriate with a view to achieving the objectives pursued and be necessary to that end'. (*Bilka-Kaufhaus GmbH v Weber von Hartz (No 170/84) [1987] ICR 110*). Balcombe LJ states: 'In my judgment "justifiable" requires an objective balance between the discriminatory effect of the condition and the reasonable needs of the party who applies the condition' and 'Clearly it may, as in the present case, be possible to justify by reference to grounds other than economic or administrative efficiency in a concern not engaged in business or commerce.' The Court of Appeal also held, however, that a tribunal must give its reasons for arriving at a conclusion of justification and that a tribunal must identify the standards by which it tests a respondent's justification. It is not enough for a tribunal just to assert that it found the condition justified. The matter was not argued when *Hampson* came to the House of Lords (*[1990] ICR 511*), but the only short reference seems to imply that the House of Lords agreed with the views expressed in the Court of Appeal in the *Hampson* case and *Ojutiku* is, therefore, no longer good law.

The House of Lords in *Webb v EMO Air Cargo (UK) Ltd [1993] IRLR 27* confirmed that the correct test was the one stated in *Hampson v Department of Education and Science [1989] ICR 179*.

(c) **A matter of fact for the tribunal**

Subject to the tribunal applying the right test, it is a matter of fact for it (*Mandla v Dowell Lee [1983] IRLR 209*). One tribunal might reach one conclusion and another might reach a different one. As long as both followed the guidelines set out in *Orphanos v Queen Mary College [1985] IRLR 349*, neither could be disturbed on appeal. Unless it is manifest that a tribunal's decision was unreasonable, it will not be disturbed. This is singularly unhelpful in many ways. The problem is illustrated by the conclusion of the Employment Appeal Tribunal in *Raval v Department of Health and Social Security [1985] ICR 685*. In that case an 'O' level English criterion prevented a temporary clerk being given a permanent position. This was found by the tribunal to be indirectly discriminatory but justifiable on grounds that amounted to administrative convenience. The EAT reflected that it, or another tribunal, might have concluded otherwise but that it was not perverse for that particular tribunal to have so concluded.

This leaves an unsatisfactory state of affairs where a tribunal in Birmingham might agree that the administrative convenience of an 'O' level criterion outweighs its discriminatory impact where a tribunal in Bedford would not. As is always the case, those employers who can show that before employing such a criterion, they have thought carefully about the impact and the business requirements favouring the imposition of such a criterion, are likely to convince the tribunal as to justification without difficulty. In this regard, however, employers should remember to keep such matters under review. In a tough economic climate with 200 applicants for every job, an 'O' level criterion sift may seem reasonable, but if the requirement for an 'O' level does not really relate to the requirements of the post, and has manifest adverse impact, then it is likely that a tribunal will not find it justifiable.

36.6 EXAMPLES OF JUSTIFICATION

Upheld

Health and hygiene considerations. In *Panesar v Nestlé Co Ltd [1980] ICR 144* and *Singh v Rowntree Mackintosh [1979] ICR 554* the risk of contamination from facial hair was held to justify a clean shaven rule. In *Singh v British Rail Engineering [1986] ICR 22*, the personal safety of the operative was held to justify a 'helmets not turbans' rule.

Economic considerations. In *Kidd v DRG (UK) Ltd [1985] ICR 405* the additional costs of servicing part-time labour were held to constitute justification given the tight margins in a competitive market (but see *Home Office v Holmes [1984] IRLR 299* which went the other way on a similar attempted justification).

Administrative convenience. In *Raval v DHSS [1985] ICR 685* the imposition of an 'O' level requirement as a 'sifting' tool in the light of the high number of applications received was deemed justified. (See also 24.15 EMPLOYMENT.)

Religion. In *Board of Governors of St Matthias Church of England School v Crizzle [1993] IRLR 472*, the EAT held that a requirement that a head teacher of the school be a committed communicant Christian was objectively justifiable, irrespective of the fact that this had a disproportionate impact upon people of Asian origin.

Not upheld

Uniformity. In *Mandla v Dowell Lee [1983] IRLR 209* the imposition of a 'no turbans' rule to achieve uniformity in the school uniform was not justifiable.

Custom and practice. In *Clarke and Powell v Eley (IMI Kynoch) Ltd [1982] IRLR 482* a 'last in, first out' policy which had been long accepted and originally negotiated by the unions was held not to be justification. Such 'LIFO' policies are likely to discriminate on grounds of race as well as sex.

Social policy. In *R v Secretary of State for Employment, Ex parte Equal Opportunities Commission [1994] IRLR 176*, the House of Lords held that the minimum hours qualifying periods in respect of unfair dismissal and redundancy payments were not objectively justifiable on social policy grounds, as the Government had failed to show that a reduction in the qualifying period would adversely effect employment opportunities.

36.6   Indirect Discrimination

In *R v Secretary of State for Employment, Ex parte Seymour-Smith and Perez* *[1995] IRLR 464*, the Court of Appeal held that the 2 years' qualifying period for unfair dismissal claims was not objectively justifiable on social policy grounds, as it was not possible to conclude that this qualifying period promoted the creation of job opportunities. The Court of Appeal overruled the earlier High Court decision (*[1994] IRLR 448*). It is expected that the High Court decision will be restored by the House of Lords; a decision is expected late in 1995.

37   Investigations

37.1   NATURE

One of the more innovative features of the *SDA 1975* and the *RRA 1976* was the granting of investigative powers to the newly established Commissions under those Acts, the EOC and CRE respectively. Previously, under the *RRA 1968*, the Race Relations Board had a quasi-judicial function in respect of individual complaints which it investigated as such. The new Acts gave both Commissions what were thought to be wide-ranging and general powers to investigate for any purpose connected with their duties under the relevant Act, to make a finding and, if appropriate, issue a non-discrimination notice together with recommendations for appropriate action. It was believed at the time that the Acts were introduced that these investigative powers would be used on a strategic basis to advance the purposes of each Act. In reality this has not happened; it is mostly case law involving individuals that has achieved this purpose.

The investigative powers of both Commissions were likened in 1978 by Lord Denning to the 'days of the inquisition' (*Science Research Council v Nassé [1979] ICR 921* – the remarks were made in passing and the particular case was not related to the investigative powers but to ordinary discovery). When Lord Denning had an opportunity to comment in respect of an actual case involving the investigative powers, he stated that he was 'very sorry for the Commission, but they had been caught up in a spider's web spun by Parliament from which there is little hope of their escaping', in commenting on the complexity of the provisions relating to investigations.

In fact, these complexities have now largely been resolved and the bases on which the EOC and CRE can conduct investigations are relatively clear and should not lead to further problems. Challenges to the exercise of the powers of the Commissions in respect of investigations are now failing where they used to succeed. It is interesting to note, however, that both Commissions seem reluctant to embark upon investigations in any great number and this is undoubtedly related to internal apprehension that was created by the original difficulties. After one adverse decision in the House of Lords (*CRE v Prestige Group Plc [1984] IRLR 166 HL*) the CRE abandoned approximately 30 investigations. It may be, however, that as the Commissions have greater success with the more cautious approach they have been taking, they will embark upon more investigations.

37.2   TYPES OF INVESTIGATION

There are two types of investigation:

(*a*)   a general investigation pursuant to *SDA s 58(3)* and *RRA s 49(3)*, and

(*b*)   a named investigation pursuant to *SDA s 58(3A)* and *RRA s 49(4)*.

37.3   General investigation

It is difficult to distinguish a general investigation from an ordinary research project, the only obvious difference being that a formal report is produced at the end of the investigation which may make recommendations. A report, however, does not seem to have any particular status in the hierarchy of legal precedent.

37.4   Investigations

General investigations tend to be aimed at examining wider issues in respect of discrimination. For example, a few years ago the CRE completed investigating promotion opportunities within the hotel industry, for which the co-operation of various elements of that industry had been sought and obtained. This report, and others like it, may well have strategic value in providing guidance to employers on a general basis.

It is only in relation to named investigations that the Commission has special powers to obtain evidence (unless it obtains the authorization of the Secretary of State under *SDA s 59* or *RRA s 50*). A general investigation cannot turn into a named investigation. The Commissions used to believe that if they identified any discriminatory practices in the course of a general investigation then they could issue a non-discrimination notice and make recommendations in the same way as a named investigation. This is precisely what had happened in *CRE v Prestige Group Plc [1984] 1 WLR 335*. The House of Lords held, however, that a general investigation could not, in effect, be turned into a named investigation and that where the Commission suspected any discriminatory practices or unlawful behaviour, it was required to give notice of a formal named investigation if it wished to pursue the matter further. This, in essence, would mean starting the investigation again.

37.4   Named investigation

The power of the Commissions to conduct named investigations [*RRA s 49(4); SDA s 58(3A)*] is, without a doubt, a powerful weapon. Once a named investigation has been started, the Commissions have the power to obtain information (see 37.6 below) and the power to issue a non-discrimination notice if they find that discrimination has taken place or is taking place. Such a notice may also impose other requirements upon the investigated party.

37.5   STEPS TO BE TAKEN PRIOR TO CONDUCTING A NAMED INVESTIGATION

Neither the EOC nor the CRE is allowed to embark on a named investigation unless the relevant Commission has complied with the following requirements.

(*a*)   It must suspect, or have a belief, that an act of discrimination has been perpetrated by a named individual. The extent of the belief required is not very onerous but the Commission must have some reasonable grounds for believing that there has been a contravention of the Act. This may be as a result of submissions made by members of the public, or by having seen an industrial tribunal decision adverse to the respondent where there is a suggestion that other discrimination may be taking place, or by having identified a statistical imbalance in the workforce, or a similar basis for suspicion.

The question of what was required in respect of this 'belief' was considered in some detail in *R v CRE, Ex parte Hillingdon London Borough Council [1982] AC 779*. In essence it requires actual evidence and an inference drawn from that evidence. There must be 'reasonable grounds for suspicion' but this is 'a state of mind far short of proof'. It was also suggested in the judgment that there should be 'enough material before the Commission sufficient to raise in the minds of reasonable men, possessed of the experience of covert racial discrimination that has been acquired by the Commission, a suspicion that there may have been acts by a person named of racial discrimination'. In other words the Commission needs very little information upon which to commence a named investigation.

The question was also considered in *CRE v Prestige Group Plc [1984] 1 WLR 335*, where the House of Lords stated that the Commission should have formed a suspicion that the subject of the named investigation 'may have committed some unlawful act of discrimination and had at any rate some grounds for so suspecting, albeit that the grounds upon which any such suspicion was based might, at that stage, be no more than tenuous because they had not yet been tested'. This has to be the logical approach and, in essence, the employer is going to have difficulty in challenging a decision of the Commission to investigate if it has any evidence at all.

However, the key point is that the investigation must be related to the belief. For example, the CRE cannot investigate the entire working practices of an employer because of information suggesting that black workers have difficulty in obtaining promotion. In the *Hillingdon* case, the belief related to the treatment of homeless families arriving at Heathrow Airport (after Councillor Dicks (the then Chairman of the Housing Committee of Hillingdon Borough Council, now an MP) had left such a family on the doorstep of 10 Downing Street). The CRE purported to embark upon a much wider investigation into the general housing practices of the borough. The House of Lords held that this was by way of a 'fishing expedition' and that the CRE's belief related only to the treatment of housing homeless families. Therefore, the terms of investigation were too wide and the investigation was ultra vires (that is outside the scope of its power) and the decision to investigate the London Borough of Hillingdon's housing policies was quashed.

(*b*)   It must draw up formal terms of reference for the investigation. (If the investigation has been requested by the Secretary of State, then the Secretary of State draws up the terms of reference in consultation with the Commission [*RRA s 49(2); SDA s 58(2)*] – no such investigation has ever taken place.)

(*c*)   It must inform the individual of its belief and of its proposal to investigate the act in question.

(*d*)   It must offer the individual an opportunity of making oral or written representations (or both) about the terms of reference of the investigation. These can include trying to persuade the Commission not to investigate at all or otherwise to change its terms of reference. Such representations can be by way of counsel or solicitor or by any other suitable person of his choice (suitability being a matter for the Commission who can object to an individual on reasonable grounds – for example, the CRE might object to an individual of well known political right-wing persuasion from acting on behalf of an employer).

The rules for notifying the individual as to the terms of reference are set out in the *Race Relations (Formal Investigations) Regulations 1977 (SI 1977 No 841)* and the *Sex Discrimination (Formal Investigations) Regulations 1975 (SI 1975 No 1993)*. These do not set out any time frame by which the CRE and EOC are required to give notice. It is not clear as to when the Commission must act on any underlying suspicion that it has, nor when information-gathering ceases to be just that and in reality becomes part of the investigation that has not yet started. This is an important question as the purpose of the requirement to serve a notice on the named party is to alert them to the fact that they are being investigated.

37.6 POWER TO OBTAIN INFORMATION

Once a named investigation has been commenced then the Commission has what have been described as 'draconian' powers to obtain information (Lord Denning in *Science Research Council v Nassé [1979] ICR 921*). There is a prescribed form of notice set out in *Schedule 1* to *SI 1977 No 841* and *Schedule 1* to *SI 1975 No 1993* by which the appropriate Commission may require

(*a*) information, and

(*b*) the attendance of any individual to give oral evidence and to produce documents.

The power to obtain information is a wide one. The Commission 'may require any person to furnish any such written information as may be described in the notice, and may specify the time at which, and the manner and form in which, the information is to be furnished'. [*RRA s 50(1); SDA s 59(1)*]. This is a significantly wider power than is available in discovery in a discrimination case. For an ordinary complaint, the individual can obtain discovery and statistical information so long as it has actually been collated (*West Midlands Passenger Transport Executive v Singh [1988] ICR 614*), but not if such information does not actually exist either in a collated form or in computer form capable of being collated (*Carrington v Helix Lighting Ltd [1990] ICR 125*).

The Commissions' power is slightly wider than in the industrial tribunal in that, although this power does not extend beyond the power to order the provision of information or production of documents, in similar proceedings before the High Court or the Court of Session interrogatories (a procedure for asking formal written questions of the other side) are available and can be used by the Commission to seek relevant statistical information, whereas they are not available in industrial tribunal proceedings.

The Commission must pay witness expenses, where a person is required to attend to give evidence or produce documents. There has not been any legal challenge to the Commissions' power to obtain information in the course of an investigation. Neither Commission has any power to order the preservation of any evidence and if it is destroyed before any notice from the Commission to produce it, under the present legislation such conduct would be lawful. For this reason, the CRE has called for a reform of the law in that regard.

37.7 CONDUCT OF INVESTIGATION

Both Commissions are able to nominate one or more of their number to conduct the formal investigation on behalf of the Commission and the Commission may also appoint special additional Commissioners, subject to the approval of the Secretary of State, for the purpose of a formal investigation. [*RRA s 48; SDA s 57*]. The Commissioners may delegate work to the staff at the relevant Commission but any material decisions in relation to the investigation must be theirs. In reality, investigations have taken an extremely long time to pursue even when there have been no legal complications. This is largely a result of the relatively small number of staff that either Commission has available to devote to its investigative function.

37.8 CHANGE OF TERMS OF REFERENCE

If the Commission wishes at any stage to change the terms of reference of its investigation then it must notify the subject of the investigation and give them a further opportunity to make submissions. [*RRA s 49(5); SDA s 58(4)*].

37.9 ISSUE OF NON-DISCRIMINATION NOTICE

If, in the course of a formal investigation it seems that the investigation need not have been completed, the Commission becomes satisfied that a person is committing or has committed an act of discrimination, after giving him an opportunity to make further representations (see 37.10 below), it has the power to serve on him a 'non-discrimination notice' requiring him

(*a*)   not to commit any such acts;

(*b*)   to take the necessary steps to change his practices or other arrangements in order to ensure that he does not commit any such acts;

(*c*)   to inform the Commission as to what those changes are and when those changes have been effected and take such steps as the notice reasonably requires to pass on that information to other persons concerned; and

(*d*)   to provide such information to the Commission as may reasonably be required in order to verify that the notice has been complied with.

37.10 PROCEDURE PRIOR TO ISSUE OF NON-DISCRIMINATION NOTICE

Whilst, as mentioned above, the Commission does not need to have actually finished its formal investigation before issuing a non-discrimination notice, it must have first

(*a*)   given the individual, against whom the notice is to be issued, notice of the fact that it is minded to do so, specifying the grounds on which it contemplates taking such action;

(*b*)   offered him an opportunity of making oral or written representations (or both) in the matter within a period of not less than 28 days specified in the notice; and

(*c*)   thereafter, taken account of those representations.

[*RRA s 58(5); SDA s 67(5)*].

37.11 FORM OF NON-DISCRIMINATION NOTICE

The form of the non-discrimination notice is set out in the relevant statutory instrument (*SI 1977 No 841 (RRA)* and *SI 1975 No 1993 (SDA), 2 Sch* in both cases).

37.12 PRACTICE OF FORMAL INVESTIGATIONS

As a matter of practice, the issuing of non-discrimination notices has coincided with the final report of the formal investigations. As mentioned above, the legislation does not actually seem to require this; it appears to be open to the CRE or EOC to issue a non-discrimination notice as soon as it is reasonably satisfied that discrimination has occurred. In cases where the CRE or EOC has a strong suspicion that indirect discrimination has occurred, on the basis of statistical evidence open to it, there does not seem to be any particular reason why it should not issue a 'minded' notice (see 37.10 above) in respect of the non-discrimination notice as soon as it has completed the original formalities on serving notice of intention to investigate (see 37.5 above). It would then be for the named party to make submissions to justify the alleged discrimination that has taken place and for the Commission to consider that justification and arrive at a reasonable conclusion.

37.13 REGISTER OF NON-DISCRIMINATION NOTICES

The CRE and EOC are each obliged to keep a register of non-discrimination notices which have become final (that is, they have not been appealed against or any appeal has been rejected) which can be inspected by any member of the public at the Commission's offices, who may take copies of any entry. [*RRA s 61; SDA s 70*].

37.14 APPEALING AGAINST NON-DISCRIMINATION NOTICE

The recipient of a non-discrimination notice may appeal to the industrial tribunal (or, if the subject matter of the investigation does not relate to employment-related matters, to the county court) within six weeks after the non-discrimination notice is served upon him. The burden of proof in such an appeal is upon the appellant to prove that the Commission made mistakes of fact (*CRE v Amari Plastics Ltd [1982] ICR 304*) and the appeal can be not just on the basis that the Commission conducted the investigation in an improper manner but in respect of the underlying facts themselves (*CRE v Amari Plastics Ltd [1982] ICR 304; R v CRE, Ex parte Westminster City Council [1985] ICR 827*). The procedure regulating appeals to the industrial tribunal against non-discrimination notices is set out in the *Industrial Tribunals (Non-discrimination Notices Appeals) Regulations 1977 (SI 1977 No 1094)*.

37.15 JUDICIAL REVIEW

If at any time the subject of a formal investigation considers that the CRE or EOC has exceeded its powers in its conduct of the investigation, or is about to exceed those powers, it may apply for judicial review, as both Commissions are statutory bodies. Like any other statutory body, both the CRE and EOC must exercise their powers on a proper basis and with due regard to natural justice (*Associated Provincial Picture Houses v Wednesbury Corporation [1948] 1 KB 223*).

37.16 OBSTACLES TO COMPLETING AN INVESTIGATION

As has been seen in this chapter, in order to complete an investigation, the CRE or EOC must give the employer a number of rights, which are summarised below.

(*a*)   The right to make representations about the investigation taking place at all, and its terms of reference.

(*b*)   The right to make representations if the investigating Commission wishes to change the terms of reference of the investigation.

(*c*)   The right to make representations in respect of any proposed non-discrimination notice.

(*d*) The right of appeal against a non-discrimination notice. The recipient of a non-discrimination notice may also appeal against 'any requirement' of a non-discrimination notice to provide information.

(*e*) The right to pursue the investigating Commission for judicial review if the employer considers that it has exceeded its authority at any stage during the process.

In these circumstances it is not surprising that the procedure takes some time.

37.17 ENFORCING A NON-DISCRIMINATION NOTICE

Both the CRE and EOC have the power to conduct a further investigation as to the compliance with a non-discrimination notice [*RRA s 60; SDA s 69*] or to apply to the county court for an injunction, if they believe that there will be further acts of discrimination, restraining the named individual from doing such acts of discrimination. They may also apply for a county court injunction in respect of any breach of a requirement of a non-discrimination notice. [*RRA ss 58(7), 60, 62; SDA ss 67(7), 69, 71*]. These powers are subject to specified time limits.

37.18 INVESTIGATIONS IN PRACTICE

The CRE has completed over 70 formal investigations and the EOC 14. Recently, there has been an increase in activity on this front by both Commissions. Employers should always bear in mind the powers of both the CRE and EOC to conduct such investigations, when corresponding with them.

38   Marital Status

38.1   DEFINITION

It is unlawful to discriminate against somebody on the grounds that he or she is married. [*SDA s 3*]. However, single people are not protected from discrimination on the grounds that they are not married, unless it can be shown that such discrimination really constitutes indirect discrimination in that the criterion has a greater impact on one or other sex in the particular circumstances of the case (perhaps where a supervisor of secretaries was being appointed and it so happened that the only male secretary was married and the overwhelming majority of female secretaries were not). Married persons are only protected from discrimination after marriage; surprisingly, the dismissal of a person on the basis that she or he is about to become married is not contrary to the Act (*Bick v Royal West of England Residential School for the Deaf [1976] IRLR 326*). However, if a woman who was dismissed for being about to be married can show that the same would not have happened to a man (or vice versa), this would be direct sex discrimination (*McLean v Paris Travel Service Ltd [1976] IRLR 202*).

38.2   COHABITEES

Just as *SDA s 3* does not protect single individuals, neither does it protect co-habitees. The requirement is to be married. [*SDA s 3*].

38.3   PARENTS

Discrimination against individuals with children will not be directly discriminatory unless it relates only to married people. There is a high likelihood, however, that such a criterion will indirectly discriminate against women contrary to *SDA s 1(1)(b)*.

38.4   PREGNANCY

Dismissal for reasons relating to pregnancy will always be unlawful (*Hertz v Aldi Marked K/S (sub nom Handels-Og Kontorfunktionaernes Forbund I Danmark v Dansk Arbejdsgiverforening) [1991] IRLR 31* and *Dekker v Stichting Vormingscentrum Voor Jonge Volwassenen (VJV-Centrum) Plus [1991] IRLR 27* – see PREGNANCY: MATERNITY RIGHTS (44)).

38.5   ENFORCEMENT

An individual must make a complaint within three months of the act of discrimination complained of [*SDA s 76*] by submitting an originating application to the industrial tribunal. The procedures for considering a claim and the burden of proof are the same as for an ordinary *SDA* claim.

39   Monitoring

39.1   INTRODUCTION

The process of monitoring is a necessary adjunct to an equal opportunities policy. Employers who have introduced an equal opportunity policy would be defeating the purpose of the policy if they failed to implement a structured system of monitoring the ethnic and gender make-up of their employees. In fact, both the CRE and EOC recommend in their Codes of Practice that employers should regularly monitor not only their equal opportunity policy but also job recruitment and advertisement and personnel practices and procedures.

39.2   CRE GUIDANCE

The CRE issued guidance to employers on achieving racial equality through the use of ethnic monitoring ('A measure of equality – monitoring and achieving racial equality in employment' (1991)). This is for guidance purposes only and is not obligatory. The CRE stated that monitoring policies are essential to ensure that employers are aware of the nature and extent of any inequalities in the ethnic composition of their workforce. This monitoring process enables employers to be aware of where inequalities exist and, therefore, where remedial action is required.

The CRE suggests that employers should obtain information on the ethnic origins of all their employees, and also of all job applicants. The feeling behind this is that if employers promote equality of opportunity in relation to job applicants, and regularly monitor the ethnic proportion of all job applicants, then this will have a filtering effect on the levels of ethnic minorities in the workforce.

Information regarding the ethnic origins of all employees and job applicants should be placed on personnel records. Employers should monitor the distribution of employees across their organisation, and examine the success rate of applicants/candidates for training and promotion as well as for jobs.

However, the CRE suggests that employers should go even further than this and ensure that monitoring takes place for each job and grade and within each department. The CRE also recommends that equality targets should be an integral part of the monitoring process, i.e. equality targets are to be built into management job plans. However, employers should not impose an equality quota to ensure that a certain number or percentage of ethnic minorities are appointed to jobs, but rather should treat these as aims and targets which can be attained through correct employment selection without the need for positive discrimination. The use of equality quotas could itself be discriminatory if it worked to exclude persons of certain racial groups as a matter of course.

In monitoring the ethnic composition of the workforce, the CRE recommends that employers use five ethnic categories: White, Afro-Caribbean, Indian, Pakistani/Bangladeshi and Others.

The CRE discourages the use of questions relating to place of birth, as this can be misleading as to a person's ethnic group.

However, employers may be well advised to use more than five ethnic categories, depending upon the geographical circumstances. The national census uses nine ethnic categories: White, Black African, Black Caribbean, Black Other (please specify), Indian, Pakistani, Bangladeshi, Chinese, Other (please specify).

The CRE also recommends that consultation should take place with trades unions and employee representatives before a system of monitoring is adopted; it advocates the use of a trial period of monitoring before a final version of the scheme can be put in place.

39.3 CONCLUSION

Whilst undoubtedly resulting in extra expenditure for employers, a monitoring scheme is a useful aspect of any equal opportunities policy. Without continual monitoring of the equal opportunities policy, recruitment, training and the ethnic composition of the workforce, any hopes of achieving continuing equality without discrimination will be hampered. Although the CRE guidance only deals with monitoring the ethnic composition of the workforce, employers should also monitor the general composition of their workforce to ensure that the chances of sex discrimination occurring are reduced.

In many cases involving allegations of race discrimination, a questionnaire will be served by the applicant. Usually the CRE will serve it on behalf of the applicant (see QUESTIONNAIRE PROCEDURE (47)).

It is common for these questionnaires to incorporate questions about an employer's recruitment, training and promotion policies, including reference to the ethnic origin of employees and job applicants. Without effective monitoring such information is difficult to collate, involving a considerable amount of time and administrative costs. In addition, if an employer fails to reply to any part of a questionnaire (or the response is insufficient) a tribunal is able to draw any inference it likes, including the inference that the discrimination complained of in fact took place.

Having an effective monitoring policy, including acting upon the findings of this monitoring, will reduce the chances of a questionnaire being served, and make it simpler to respond if one is.

In *West Midland Passenger Transport Executive v Singh* [1988] IRLR 186, the Court of Appeal held that the applicant was entitled to see documentation detailing the ethnic composition of employees and applicants for a particular grade and rank within the employer's undertaking, for the period from the date the employer had introduced an equal opportunity policy statement to the date of the act of discrimination complained of. The information was logically probative of whether the employer had discriminated against the applicant. The Court of Appeal specifically referred to the CRE Code of Practice, which recommends ethnic monitoring of the workforce and of applicants. If the statistics obtained as a result of monitoring showed racial or ethnic imbalance, then this could indicate racial discrimination. Balcombe LJ said:

'. . . in the absence of a satisfactory explanation in a particular case, it is reasonable to infer that the complainant, as a member of the group, has himself been treated less favourably on the grounds of race'.

In *Carrington v Helix Lighting Ltd* [1990] IRLR 6, the applicant applied for a job, was given a brief interview (2–3 minutes) and told that if she heard nothing further she had been unsuccessful. She did not hear from the respondents but the job continued to be advertised. She requested a schedule detailing the ethnic composition of the respondents' workforce. The respondents did not have this information immediately available (as they did not have a system of monitoring in force) and it would have been very costly and time consuming to prepare the information. The industrial tribunal refused the applicant's request because in effect it would have amounted to ordering answers to interrogatories, which (at that time) was not within the power of tribunals. The applicant appealed to the EAT which dismissed her appeal, because tribunals had no power to order the release of information which was equivalent to answering interrogatories. The EAT also held, however, that the CRE Code of Practice encouraged employers to monitor their workforce and keep records. Although the Code of Practice is not binding upon employers, Wood J said that:

> 'failure to comply with the provisions and spirit of the Code of Practice can be taken into account by a tribunal and when it considers the whole of the case an adverse inference may be drawn'.

These decisions show the importance of the use of monitoring policies. If an employer has a monitoring system then, if discrimination proceedings are commenced by an employee or job applicant, any information requested will be far simpler to compile. In addition, the fact that the employer has a monitoring system in place (and one which is acted upon) will prevent a tribunal from drawing an inference that the discrimination alleged has in fact taken place. It should also be noted that tribunals now have the power to order answers to interrogatories, so in circumstances like those in *Carrington* the information requested may now be ordered by a tribunal (see TRIBUNALS (53)).

40 Part-time Employees

40.1 INTRODUCTION

Until 1994, part-time employees were only able to claim a statutory redundancy payment or compensation for unfair dismissal if they worked over 8 hours per week, and even then, only when they had accrued 5 years' continuous service. However, in a landmark decision of the House of Lords the qualifying thresholds of the *EPCA* were held to be contrary to EU law (see below).

In addition, part-time employees may be able to claim the right to join an occupational pension scheme as a result of a decision of the ECJ.

40.2 REMOVAL OF THE QUALIFYING THRESHOLD IN THE EPCA 1978

In *R v Secretary of State for Employment, Ex parte Equal Opportunities Commission [1994] IRLR 176*, the EOC brought judicial review proceedings against the Secretary of State contesting his view that the UK qualifying thresholds for statutory redundancy payments and unfair dismissal compensation were not contrary to EU law.

The EOC argued that the qualifying thresholds in the *EPCA* were indirectly discriminatory against women on the grounds that approximately 90% of all part-time employees were women. The qualifying threshold prevented part-time employees claiming statutory redundancy payment or unfair dismissal compensation until they had accrued 5 years' service (those employees who worked less than 8 hours per week would never be able to claim a statutory redundancy payment or unfair dismissal). It was clear that the thresholds were indirectly discriminatory, and the Government sought to justify the thresholds on the grounds that lowering them would adversely affect employment opportunities available for part-time work.

The House of Lords held that the Government had failed to show there was justification for the qualifying thresholds in the *EPCA*, and declared that the provisions in relation to the right to a redundancy payment were contrary to *Article 119* of the *Treaty of Rome*, as well as the *Equal Treatment Directive*, and also that the *EPCA* provisions in relation to the right to claim unfair dismissal were contrary to the *Equal Treatment Directive*.

40.3 Consequences of this decision

This decision enabled all part-time employees to rely directly upon *Article 119* of the *Treaty of Rome* (which is directly enforceable by employees in both the private and public sector) once they have 2 years' continuous service, and therefore to claim redundancy payments or unfair dismissal.

As regards the right to claim unfair dismissal compensation, only part-time employees in the public sector are able to rely upon EU law to claim unfair dismissal once they have 2 years' service. This is because the House of Lords did not rule that unfair dismissal compensation was 'pay' for the purposes of *Article 119* of the *Treaty of Rome*. Rather, it held that the unfair dismissal qualifying thresholds were contrary to *Article 5* of the *Equal Treatment Directive*. The *Equal Treatment Directive* only has direct effect as regards employees in the public sector. However, while part-time employees in the private sector could not rely directly upon EU law to claim unfair dismissal once they had 2 years' continuous service, there was still the possibility of such employees commencing proceedings directly against the Government as a consequence of the ECJ decision in *Francovich v Italy [1992] IRLR 82*.

40.4 Whilst the House of Lords was not prepared to rule that unfair dismissal compensation was 'pay' for the purposes of *Article 119* of the *Treaty of Rome*, subsequently the EAT was prepared to make this ruling. In *Mediguard Services Ltd v Thame [1994] IRLR 504*, the EAT ruled that compensation for unfair dismissal was 'pay' under *Article 119* of the *Treaty of Rome* because it was consideration received by the ex-employee, albeit indirectly, from the ex-employer in respect of her employment.

The effect of this decision was that all part-time employees working over 8 hours per week were able to bring complaints for unfair dismissal once they had 2 years' service, and that such claims could rely directly upon EU law.

40.5 The decision in the *EOC* case was in respect of part-time employees who worked more than 8 hours per week. This still left the question of whether part-time employees working less than 8 hours per week were able to claim a redundancy payment or unfair dismissal compensation after 2 years' service. In *Warren v Wylie [1994] IRLR 316*, a Southampton industrial tribunal held that the 8-hour threshold in the *EPCA* was contrary to *Article 119* of the *Treaty of Rome*, and therefore all employees were able to claim unfair dismissal and a redundancy payment once they had the required 2 years' service. However, this decision was not binding on subsequent tribunals.

In any event, pressure was still mounting on the Government to remove both of the qualifying thresholds in the *EPCA* on the grounds that they were indirectly discriminatory against women.

40.6 **The Government's Response**

As stated above, the decision in the House of Lords placed the Government under considerable pressure to remove the qualifying thresholds in the *EPCA*, or face the prospect of *Francovich* claims by part-time private-sector employees.

The Government's response was to introduce the *Employment Protection (Part-time Employees) Regulations 1995 (SI 1995 No 31)*: with effect from 6 February 1995 the qualifying thresholds in the *EPCA* were removed. Consequently, *all* employees are now entitled to a written statement of terms and conditions of their employment, unless their employment is for less than one month. *All employees* are also entitled to a redundancy payment and to claim unfair dismissal once they have 2 years' continuous service.

However, the Court of Appeal held in the case of *R v The Secretary of State for Employment Ex parte Seymour-Smith and Perez [1995] IRLR 464*, that the 2 years' service requirement was itself indirectly discriminatory against female employees, as they were more likely to take career breaks and because of this more likely to move to new employers and, therefore, unable to claim unfair dismissal until they had acquired 2 years' service with each employer.

The Government is appealing against this decision. Whilst the position is still unclear, employers would be well advised to treat all employees as if they have the right to claim unfair dismissal, irrespective of the length of service, and particularly those employees with more than 12 months' service. This is because, although this decision only affects public-sector employees and does not have general application, it is possible that the Government could introduce legislation extending the scope of this decision and with retrospective effect.

In any event, in an equal opportunities environment, consistency of treatment of all employees irrespective of their length of service, is desirable to avoid the possibility of any difference in treatment being tainted with discrimination on the grounds of sex.

40.7   The *EOC* case raised the possibility of retrospective claims by ex-employees, i.e. those dismissed before the House of Lords decision. In the case of *Biggs v Somerset County Council [1995] IRLR 452* the EAT held that retrospective claims could not be brought by former part-time employees and, therefore, that the usual 3-month time limit applied. The EAT held that the claim had been brought under *Article 119* of the *Treaty of Rome*, which was directly effective in 1976, and therefore the time limit ran from this date. However, Mummery J in the EAT said that this was an issue that ought really be determined by a higher court. The *Biggs* decision is likely to be appealed.

40.8   PART-TIMERS' RIGHTS AS REGARDS BENEFITS

The House of Lords decision meant that where the exclusion of part-time employees from certain benefits is indirectly discriminatory, i.e. because a disproportionate number of part-time employees were female, then this is contrary to European law. However, just because part-time employees are denied a benefit that full-time employees are entitled to, does not mean that the exclusion is discriminatory *per se*. This is because it is possible for instances of indirect discrimination to be justified, as long as the justification is on objective factors not based on sex, such as economic necessity (see INDIRECT DISCRIMINATION (36)).

In addition, whether a decision to exclude part-time employees from certain benefits (for example, occupational pension schemes) is indirectly discriminatory will depend upon the composition of employees in that undertaking (or within a department/grade within that undertaking). For there to be indirect discrimination, a significantly smaller proportion of employees of one sex must be unable to comply with a requirement, such as an 'hours requirement'. It is possible that some employers will have more male than female part-time employees (although this is unlikely), but it will be a question of fact in each case. In any case, it is not 'numbers' but 'proportions'; therefore, if say 80% of male employees but only 40% of female employees can comply, then this is a significantly smaller proportion, and would be indirectly discriminatory unless the employer can justify it. Whether there is disproportionate effect will be a question of fact in each case.

40.9   JUSTIFICATION

In order to be able to justify the exclusion of part-time employees from certain benefits, an employer must not rely on factors tainted by sex. An employer must show that the reasons used for excluding part-time employees are appropriate for achieving the objective (e.g. economic considerations), that they relate to a real need of the employer, and that the method chosen is necessary to achieve the specified needs.

For example, if administrative costs of allowing part-time employees access to benefits are unduly excessive in comparison with the value of the benefits conferred, this may amount to an objectively justified reason.

40.10 PART-TIMER'S RIGHT AS REGARDS ACCESS TO PENSIONS

In *Vroege v NCIV [1994] IRLR 651*, the ECJ held that the right to *join* a pension scheme was covered under *Article 119* of the *Treaty of Rome*. Therefore, where access to an occupational pension scheme is limited to full-time employees, and where that employer has a considerably higher number of female than male part-time employees, those female employees will be able to contest the employer's decision to refuse them access to the scheme on the basis that it is indirectly discriminatory. It will then be for the employer to justify the decision to exclude part-time employees on grounds unrelated to sex.

The ECJ further held that the right to join a pension scheme took effect from 8 April 1976 (the date of the decision in *Defrenne v Sabena (No 2)* holding that *Article 119* of the *Treaty of Rome* was directly effective).

The Government introduced regulations confirming the ECJ decision. The *Occupational Pension Scheme (Equal Access to Membership) Amendment Regulations 1995 (SI 1995 No 1215)* came into effect on 31 May 1995, and confirmed that certain categories of workers can only be excluded from occupational pension schemes where the employer is able to objectively justify this exclusion on grounds unrelated to sex.

However, the impact of the ECJ decision in *Vroege* and of the regulations referred to above is likely to be reduced as a result of the subsequent ECJ decision in *Johnson v Chief Adjudication Officer (No 2)* [1995] IRLR 157, together with *section 62* of the *Pensions Act 1995*. This is because only two years' arrears of pension benefits will be recoverable by way of a back-dated award (see EQUAL PAY (29); PENSIONS (42)).

41 Partnerships

41.1 DISCRIMINATION BY PARTNERSHIP UNLAWFUL

(*a*) *As employers*. A partnership is treated in exactly the same way as any other employer in respect of the ordinary employment of staff, and the provisions of *RRA s 4* and *SDA s 6* apply in the normal way.

(*b*) *In respect of admission to partnership*. Partnerships must not discriminate in respect of the following [*RRA s 10; SDA s 11*]:

    (i) The arrangements they make for the purpose of determining who should be offered a position as partner in the firm (i.e. holding interviews on a Saturday might indirectly discriminate against Jewish persons, or requiring membership of, say, the Masons would discriminate against women).

    (ii) The terms in which they offer such a position (such as an equity share).

    (iii) Refusing or deliberately omitting to offer partnership.

    (iv) Where an individual already is a partner, in the way he is afforded access to any of the benefits of the partnership, or by expelling him from the partnership, or by subjecting him to any other detriment.

(Note that (i) and (iii) above do not apply to a position as partner where being of a particular sex or racial group is a genuine occupational qualification for the partnership. [*RRA s 10(3); SDA s 11(3)*].)

The basis of the burden of proof in these matters is the same as in an ordinary employment case and it is for the prospective partner to prove his case. If he is able to show that *prima facie* it would appear that he had suffered discrimination on racial or sexual grounds, then the partnership would have to furnish an explanation to the satisfaction of the industrial tribunal, where proceedings are instituted. The time limit is three months as in other employment cases. [*RRA ss 54, 68; SDA ss 63, 76*]. (The Acts have effect in relation to the formation of partnerships as well as the appointment of new partners. [*RRA s 10(2); SDA s 11(2)*].)

41.2 PARTNERSHIPS OF FIVE OR LESS EXEMPTED FROM THE PROVISIONS OF THE RACE RELATIONS ACT

Section 10 of the *RRA* does not apply to partnerships of up to five individuals. Such partners can appoint into the partnership on a discriminatory basis up to the fifth partner but not beyond. [*RRA s 10(1)*]. There used to be a similar provision in the *SDA 1975* but this was amended by *SDA 1986, ss 1(3), 9(2) Sch, Part II*. There appears to be no particular logic about exempting small partnerships from the provisions of the *RRA*. Such small partnerships are still subject to the *RRA* in respect of their ordinary employment relationships; there would be an argument open to an employee that the hope of the benefit of a partnership was an 'opportunity' arising out of his employment and the denial of access to that opportunity was a contravention of *section 4(2)* of the *RRA*. The equivalent restriction in the *SDA* was removed only after enforcement proceedings by the European Commission (*Commission of the European Communities v United Kingdom (Case No. 61/81) [1982] IRLR 333*).

42   Pensions

42.1   INTRODUCTION

Since the decision in *Barber v Guardian Royal Exchange Assurance Group* *[1990] ICR 616* threw the law relating to pensions into confusion, a number of recent ECJ decisions seem to have settled the situation once and for all. In addition to the ECJ decisions, Parliament passed the Pensions Bill, which received the Royal Assent on 19 July 1995. The bulk of the *Pensions Act 1995*, will come into force in or around April 1997, when regulations have been finalised. A key provision of the *Pensions Act* is the equalisation of state pension ages for men and women at 65. This *Act* is largely outside the scope of this book.

42.2   RETIREMENT AGE

From the year 2020 men and women will have a state pension age of 65. This equalisation will be phased in over the previous decade. (*Pensions Act 1995, s 126, 4 Sch*).

42.3   PENSIONS

In a string of decisions, the ECJ has clarified most of the issues outstanding since the *Barber* decision. The situation as regards equality in occupational pensions is as follows:

Barber v Guardian Royal Exchange Assurance Group [1990] ICR 616: unequal pension rights for men and women was sex discriminatory contrary to *Article 119* of the *Treaty of Rome*; and a pension is 'pay' within the meaning of *Article 119*. This decision only has effect for service on or after 17 May 1990.

As regards access to pension schemes, in *Fisscher v Voorhuis Hengelo BV [1994] IRLR 662* the ECJ confirmed that *Article 119* also covered the right to join an occupational pension scheme. Therefore, the refusal of access to a pension scheme for married women is direct discrimination in breach of *Article 119*. In addition, the ECJ held that this right was not limited in time by the Barber decision, and therefore the right of access to a pension scheme on an equal basis dates from 8 April 1976 (the date of judgment in *Defrenne v Sabena*).

Further, in *Vroege v NCIV [1994] IRLR 651*, the ECJ held that where a pension scheme excluded access to part-time workers this could amount to indirect discrimination where a far greater number of women than men were affected, and where the exclusion could not be objectively justified on grounds not related to sex. In such circumstances part-time employees are entitled to join the pension scheme, as from 8 April 1976.

Where the scheme is a contributory scheme, however, an employee wishing to join the scheme retroactively must pay all contributions that she would have had to pay had she been a member from that date. This will deter many employees from proceeding in this way.

The Government introduced regulations which came into force on 31 May 1995 confirming the effect of the ECJ decision in *Vroege*. Employers are not able to impose rules on membership of occupational pension schemes which indirectly discriminate against more members of one sex than another, which would include a requirement that members must work a minimum number of hours before being able to join such a scheme. Employers are able to impose an indirectly discriminatory requirement only if it can be objectively justified.

The ECJ decision in *Vroege v NCIV* provided for analogous national limitation periods to apply to claims for equal access. The decision in *Johnson v Chief Adjudication Officer (No 2) [1995] IRLR 157* confirmed the validity of such limitation periods in EC law. Employers and pension scheme trustees may well be able to argue that the two year limit on equal pay awards under *EqPA s 2(5)* also applies to pension benefits and pension access (see EQUAL PAY (29)).

42.4 A number of decisions have also clarified the situation as regards the types of pension scheme that are covered by the equality principle in *Article 119*.

It is clear that social security schemes covered directly by statute are not covered by *Article 119*. However, pension schemes based on agreement between employer and employee, or private sector contracted-out pension schemes will be covered by *Article 119*. In the *Ten Oever* case *[1993] IRLR 601*, the ECJ held that a pension providing benefits for the employees' survivors is 'pay' for the purposes of *Article 119*.

In *Coloroll Pension Trustees v Russell [1994] IRLR 586*, the ECJ held that occupational pension schemes run by trustees are also covered by *Article 119*.

However, single-sex pension schemes are not covered by the equality principle. This is on the basis that it is impossible to establish equal pay for equal work because only one sex has ever been involved in the work in question.

Separate AVC schemes are not covered by the equality principle, as they are based solely on the contributions made by the employee and, therefore, the benefits are not calculated by reference to the sex of the employee.

It was also decided in the *Coloroll* case that the use of sex-based actuarial factors (whereby the fact that women usually live longer than men is taken into account in determining how much an employer must contribute to a scheme) is not contrary to *Article 119* in defined-benefit schemes where the retirement ages under the scheme are the same. This confirmed the decision in *Neath v Hugh Steeper Ltd [1994] IRLR 91*, a case in which the ECJ ruled that sex-based actuarial factors were not contrary to the principle of equal treatment in *Article 119*, provided they were in relation to defined-benefit pension schemes.

If an employee transfers from one occupational pension scheme to another (for example where there is a change of employer), and the transfer payment is not calculated on the basis of equality, then the new pension scheme must remedy this inequality. Although this might appear to be detrimental to the new pension scheme, there is a possibility that the courts will allow trustees of the new pension scheme to recover from the previous pension scheme in respect of this inequality, although such recovery would be limited to the date of the *Barber* judgment (i.e. in respect of benefits for service on or after 17 May 1990). However, the trustees of the pension scheme or the employer usually have a discretion whether to accept the transfer payment.

In *Birds Eye Walls Ltd v Roberts [1994] IRLR 29*, the ECJ clarified the situation as regards bridging pensions. These are paid to employees who retire before the state pension age. The amount paid under the bridging pension is reduced once the state pension age is attained; once women have reached 60, therefore, the amount of their bridging pension is reduced compared with that of male employees (who are only entitled to a state pension at 65). The ECJ held that this was not contrary to the principle of equal pay, because *Article 119* presupposes that both men and women are in identical situations. Under existing law the state pension ages were not equal, and so if the bridging pensions were required to be equal, between the ages of 60 and 65 women would be at an unfair advantage as compared with men.

In relation to the equalisation of pension benefits and ages, the ECJ held in *Smith v Avdel Systems Ltd [1994] IRLR 602* that it is not contrary to *Article 119* to equalise pension benefits to the detriment of the previously advantaged class, i.e. equalising for future service benefits the pension age upwards for women to the same age as that of men. However, for service from the date of the *Barber* judgment (17 May 1990) to the date of equalisation of benefits, men's entitlement must be calculated on the same basis as women's, and not vice versa.

42.5 PENSIONS ACT 1995

In December 1994 the Government issued a Pensions Bill, which proposed substantial reforms to the law relating to pensions, including the equalisation of state pension age at 65 from the year 2020 onwards. This will be implemented progressively over the previous decade. The Pensions Bill received the Royal Assent on 19 July 1995. Most of the Provisions of the *Pensions Act* come into force in or around April 1997.

In addition, it contains a number of amendments to *EqPA 1970*, which will apply the 2-year limit on equal pay awards to pension benefits and pension access (see EQUAL PAY (29)).

43   Positive Discrimination

43.1   THE FUNDAMENTAL RULE

The *SDA* and *RRA* are Acts of Parliament introduced to prohibit discrimination on grounds of race and sex. This includes discrimination against white people and against men. Positive action of any kind is, therefore, unlawful unless it comes within the scope of the (limited) exceptions allowed by those Acts. These exceptions are construed narrowly as they are contrary to the fundamental purpose of the legislation (see *London Borough of Lambeth v CRE [1990] IRLR 231* and *Tottenham Green Under Fives' Centre v Marshall [1989] ICR 214*).

These exceptions can be broadly divided into two categories:

(*a*)   where race or sex is a GENUINE OCCUPATIONAL QUALIFICATION (33); and

(*b*)   where there is under-representation of ethnic minorities or women in a particular grade, or type of job, employers may take steps especially designed to attract applications from the under-represented 'class' and to provide training opportunities limited to that 'class' of individuals.

These lawful exceptions are dealt with below at 43.4 onwards. There are various other forms of positive action which are dealt with in turn.

43.2   QUOTAS

An employer would be imposing a quota if because women or ethnic minority staff were, in his opinion, under-represented in a particular grade (or for any other reason), he decided to fill positions only with women, or, as the case may be, ethnic minority staff until he had achieved the desired proportion or appointed the desired number of women or ethnic minority staff. Such a step would be a straightforward breach of the legislation as the criterion clearly employed to fill the vacancy or make the promotion would be the race or sex of the appointee. [*RRA s 1(1)(a); SDA s 1(1)(a)*].

43.3   TARGETS

A target differs from a quota in that it is a stated aspiration and not a requirement. An employer may set a target for achieving the same percentage of ethnic minority staff in his employment as the local community, or of female managers as male. Providing that this does not operate as a *de facto* quota this will not be unlawful. If targets are being set, however, staff involved in recruitment should be expressly reminded (preferably by written instruction) that they must not use race or sex as a criterion in making an appointment.

An employer could offer special training (see 43.8 below) as part of a lawful programme to achieve targets. As part of an equal opportunity policy, it is also not unlawful to set targets for the balance of race and sex within the workforce or within supervisory grades, and to monitor the outcome of appointments against those targets. However, care has to be exercised in taking such a step, so as to ensure that appointments are not made in order to achieve those targets, otherwise in such circumstances the targets would have become quotas. The monitoring process should, therefore, ideally be completely separate from the actual interviewing process.

Appointments must be made on the basis of suitability for the position on offer. If monitoring reveals a continued failure to meet relevant targets, then the employer can re-examine procedures so as to identify any failure to attract female or ethnic minority applicants. If the statistics show equally qualified applicants but an imbalance in appointments, the employer may consider additional training for individuals on appointments panels.

43.4   LAWFUL POSITIVE ACTION

The discrimination legislation has limited provisions for positive discrimination. These are exceptions to the basic purpose of the legislation and so will be construed narrowly by the courts (*London Borough of Lambeth v CRE [1990] IRLR 231 (CA)*). The *RRA* has slightly more scope for positive action measures than the *SDA*. Both Acts permit discrimination where race or sex (respectively) is a 'genuine occupational qualification' (GOQ) [*RRA s 5; SDA s 7*] (see GENUINE OCCUPATIONAL QUALIFICATION (33)).

These exceptions only apply if there are not already in that employment sufficient persons of the relevant sex, capable of carrying out the duties, who could be reasonably employed in those duties (see *Wylie v Dee & Co (Menswear) Ltd [1978] IRLR 103*). It is important that employers should consider this question 'on the record' if they wish to take advantage of the exception. Unless clearly a sham, a tribunal is less likely to find against an employer who has acted in an open, reasonable manner, clearly asked himself all the right questions and come to a considered conclusion.

43.5   GOQ and sex discrimination

The GOQ can be used to justify the appointment of a woman (subject to the above) where the holder of the position provides individuals with personal services promoting their welfare, education or similar services which can most effectively be provided by a woman. This could cover social workers, nurses, teachers, etc. in certain limited circumstances. [*SDA s 7(2)(e)*].

In *Salisbury v Philip and Judy Calvert t/a Aster House and Nursing Home*, the refusal to employ a man as a nightcare assistant on the grounds of sex was held to be not unlawful, in circumstances where the job potentially involved intimate contact with elderly female residents who would object to the presence of a man.

However, in *Moult v Nottinghamshire County Council*, a tribunal rejected the Council's argument that it was a GOQ that a teaching post on a women-only course run by an all-woman organisation had to be taken by a female.

In the case of *Cropper v UK Express Ltd*, it was a GOQ that a position on a 'chatline' be given to a woman.

The emphasis is on the personal nature of the services provided and there must be an element of one-to-one contact (*London Borough of Lambeth v CRE [1990] IRLR 231*). For example, an advice centre could appoint a woman worker if they could show that female clients had problems which they would prefer to discuss with a woman.

It is important that the employer should show that he has given active consideration to establishing the need and to deciding whether or not existing female employees were sufficient to meet that need.

There are seven other special circumstances where sex can be a genuine occupational requirement. These are less likely to be of relevance to affirmative action. They are set out in full in GENUINE OCCUPATIONAL QUALIFICATION (33).

43.6 Positive Discrimination

43.6 GOQ and racial discrimination

The GOQ can be used to justify an appointment on grounds of race where the holder of the position provides the type of personal services referred to in 43.5 above [*RRA s 5(2)(d)*], except, of course, that race is the relevant consideration (again see GENUINE OCCUPATIONAL QUALIFICATION (33)).

Once again the emphasis is on the personal nature of the services provided and there must be an element of direct interaction with the client group (*London Borough of Lambeth v CRE [1990] IRLR 231*). For example, an advice centre could appoint a black worker if it could show that black clients had problems which they would prefer to discuss with a member of their own race. A GOQ will be valid even if only a very small part of the job is involved (*Tottenham Green Under Fives' Centre v Marshall (No 2) [1991] IRLR 162*).

It is important that the employer should show that he has given active consideration to establishing the need and to deciding whether or not existing black employees were sufficient to cover that need.

The individual must be of the same racial group as the client group. Whilst the definition of racial group is wide [*RRA s 3*] (see RACIAL GROUP, RACIAL GROUNDS, NATIONAL AND ETHNIC ORIGIN (48)) there are dangers in adopting this as a racial group for the purposes of *RRA s 5(2)(d)*. Frequently the needs of, for example, the Asian sub-group may be materially different from those of the West Indian sub-group. The group can be defined on the basis of colour (*London Borough of Lambeth v CRE [1990] IRLR 231*).

This section can also be employed where language is a criterion, although, strictly, any appointment would be limited to the particular racial group (for instance, in the case of a Welsh language criterion, the post would have to go to a Welsh-speaking Welsh person not a Welsh-speaking Englishman!).

43.7 POSITIVE ACTION RACE, SEX AND ADVERTISING

Most frequently the issue of positive action arises in respect of advertising vacancies and making appointments. Only the CRE and EOC can take legal action in respect of unlawful advertisements (*Cardiff Women's Aid v Hartup [1994] IRLR 390*). To date, the CRE and EOC appear to have used their power sparingly and prefer to deal with matters by agreement and to get employers to agree not to place unlawful advertisements in the future. There have been prosecutions, however, most recently in *London Borough of Lambeth v CRE [1990] IRLR 231*, which has been mentioned above (see ADVERTISING (2)).

Regardless of action against the advertisement, however, an individual who believes himself to have been denied an employment opportunity as a result of positive action can take the matter to an industrial tribunal and so it is important to exercise care when taking advantage of the limited provisions of the Acts for affirmative action. These are dealt with below.

43.8 TRAINING AND ADVERTISING

Current staff, and other individuals living locally

Both the *RRA* and the *SDA* permit employers to offer special training to existing employees [*RRA s 38; SDA s 48*] (see also EMPLOYMENT (24)), or to encourage members of a particular group of potential employees in the local area to take up particular employment with them if, within the past twelve months, there have been no members of that racial group doing the particular job, or only a small proportion of that racial group employed at that workplace or within the local recruitment area. [RRA s 37; SDA s 47].

An employer can take advantage of this section to limit advertising of a position to, say, the local Council for Racial Equality or to aim an advertisement at members of the black community, or just women, in the local paper. The section can also be used to limit access to special training courses to women or ethnic minority members exclusively (subject, of course, to the criteria above being met).

The sections do not permit discrimination in the appointment itself. Any persons who replied to the job advertisement but were not members of the target racial group should be properly considered and appointed if it turns out that they are, objectively, the best candidates.

RRA s 37 also permits trade unions to conduct advertising campaigns aimed at members of a particular racial group or groups, and to offer special training exclusively to those groups.

43.9   National considerations

RRA s 37 and SDA s 47 also enable employers to discriminate in providing training facilities or opportunities limited to a particular ethnic group, or just to women (or men), if they identify that there are no members, or few members, of that group (or of that sex) doing that work nationally (as against locally – see 43.9 above). Employers previously had to obtain designation as an authorised training body from the Secretary of State if they wanted to look beyond their own direct locality and take the view that, nationally, there was, say, a shortage of female engineers or West Indian police officers and offer special training or targeted advertising for such groups. Employment Act 1989, s 7(3) amended RRA s 37 and SDA 1986 amended SDA s 47 and now no designation is required. These amendments, however, also provided expressly that these sections do not exempt any employer from liability in respect of discrimination against an applicant for a job [RRA s 4(1)] or an existing employee. [RRA s 4(2)]. As with the exemptions dealt with in 43.8 above, these provisions do not permit discrimination in the appointment itself.

43.10   RACE RELATIONS ACT: OTHER PROVISIONS

RRA s 35 provides a general exemption from the provisions of the Act for anything 'done in affording persons of a particular racial group access to facilities or services to meet the special needs of that racial group in regard to their education, training or welfare, or any ancillary benefits'. Some commentators have suggested that this provides an opening for positive action initiatives. The section has not been subjected to litigation. The wording of the section mirrors that for genuine occupational qualification (see 43.5 above) and the two should probably be read in conjunction. For example, where a local authority has decided to make special provision for, say, the Asian elderly and has appointed Asian care staff (as permitted by GOQ), this section would permit the authority to allocate certain places at a home, or a home itself, to members of the Asian community, which would otherwise be unlawful. Guidance published by the Commission for Racial Equality accords with this view.

197

43.11 Positive Discrimination

43.11 DISCRIMINATORY SERVICE PROVISION

Both the *SDA* and *RRA* extend to the provision of services. It is unlawful to discriminate on grounds of race or sex in providing a service of almost any kind. [*RRA s 20; SDA s 29*]. There are a limited number of exceptions to the general rule which largely relate to welfare provision. (See SERVICE PROVISION (50)).

44   Pregnancy: Maternity Rights

44.1   INTRODUCTION

There have been significant developments in the last few years in the area relating to female employees' rights to maternity leave, as well as their rights during these periods of maternity leave. There was also a significant ruling of the ECJ in *Webb v EMO Air Cargo (UK) Ltd [1994] IRLR 482*. In addition, the *Trade Union Reform and Employment Rights Act 1993 (TURERA 1993)* substantially amended *EPCA* in line with the *Pregnant Workers Directive (No 92/85)*. Most significant of the changes was the introduction of the right of all female employees, regardless of their length of service, to 14 weeks' maternity leave.

44.2   ANTENATAL RIGHTS

An employee who (*a*) is pregnant, (*b*) has, on medical advice, made an appointment to receive antenatal care, and (*c*), if requested to do so, has produced to the employer relevant certificates showing that she is pregnant together with evidence of the appointment, should not be unreasonably refused time off to enable her to receive that antenatal care. [*EPCA s 31A(1)(2)*]. The right of the employer to request the production of a certificate and an appointment card does not apply to the first appointment that she makes. [*EPCA s 31A(3)*].

An employee taking such time off is entitled to continue to be paid at the appropriate rate for the period of absence (piece work and the like should be averaged out over the previous twelve-week period). *EPCA s 31A(5)* details the precise nature of the calculations, but an employer who continues to pay the employee on a normal basis will comply with these provisions.

If the employer unreasonably refuses to allow the employee to attend such an appointment, she can complain to the industrial tribunal, but must do so within three months of the date of the appointment. The tribunal, if it upholds the complaint, must order that she be paid compensation equivalent to the amount of money to which she would have been entitled had she taken the time off and been paid. [*EPCA s 31A(6)(7)*]. There is no qualification period for this right and the entitlement is immediate as soon as the employee starts work.

44.3   RIGHT TO 14 WEEKS' MATERNITY LEAVE AND TO RETURN TO WORK

The amendments to *EPCA* in relation to maternity rights introduced by *TURERA 1993* came into force on 16 October 1994. All female employees due to give birth on or after this date are entitled to 14 weeks' maternity leave, irrespective of their length of service or the number of hours that they usually work. Employees who have 2 years or more continuous service at the start of the 11th week before the expected week of childbirth (EWC) are entitled to a longer period of up to 40 weeks' maternity leave. Technically, this is not called maternity leave but 'the right to return to work up to 29 weeks after the week of birth'. It causes less confusion to refer to this period as 'the extended period of maternity leave'.

Consequently, there is now a two-tier system in operation. The requirements in respect of notification, and the benefits that the employee is entitled to, are different for each system of maternity leave.

44.4 Pregnancy: Maternity Rights

44.4 Right to 14 weeks' maternity leave

All employees irrespective of length of service or the hours they usually work are entitled to 14 weeks' maternity leave, subject to certain requirements relating to notification. This means that an employee can tell her employer on her first day of work that she is pregnant and that she intends to take maternity leave, and the employer is obliged to let the employee take advantage of these provisions. The employee is also entitled to receive all her contractual entitlements (save for remuneration) for this 14-week period, together with the right to return to work after the period of maternity leave.

The period of maternity leave cannot begin before the 11th week before the EWC (the week of birth). However, the period will automatically commence if the employee is absent from work for a pregnancy-related reason at any time after the start of the 6th week before the EWC, save for absences from work in attending antenatal appointments. If the maternity leave is automatically triggered, then this will override any previous notice given by the employee.

In order to be able to take 14 weeks' maternity leave, the employee must comply with certain notice requirements. The employee must:

(*a*) inform her employer *in writing* at least 21 days before her maternity leave period is to begin (if this is not reasonably practicable, she must notify the employer as soon as is reasonably practicable) of the fact that she is pregnant, of the EWC (or if she has already given birth, the date of birth); and

(*b*) provide at least 21 days' notice to her employer (or as much notice as is reasonably practicable) of the date on which she intends to commence her maternity leave.

The employer can also require that the employee provides a certificate from a registered G.P. or midwife stating the EWC.

As stated above, the maternity leave period cannot commence prior to the start of the 11th week before the EWC. However, the maternity leave period will automatically commence where childbirth occurs before the date on which the employee has notified the employer when she intends to commence her maternity leave (and also when the employee is absent from work for a pregnancy-related reason at any time after the start of the 6th week before the EWC).

These are the only notice requirements for employees entitled to 14 weeks' maternity leave.

44.5 The Right to Return to Work

The *EPCA* contains no express right for employees to return to work after the 14-week maternity leave period. However, the employment contract is treated as subsisting throughout the maternity leave period under *EPCA s 33(1)*, and therefore the employee continues to be employed throughout the maternity leave period. The employee need only present herself for work on the first day after the expiry of the 14 weeks.

If the employee wishes to return to work before the expiry of the 14-week period, she is obliged to give her employer 7 days' notice of the day on which she intends to return. If she fails to give such notice, the employer is able to postpone her return to a date which would ensure that she has given the required 7 days' notice. The employer cannot delay the employee's return beyond the end of the 14-week period. If the employer postpones the employee's return but nonetheless the employee arrives for work, there is no obligation on the employer to remunerate the employee until adequate notice has been given or the 14-week period has expired (whichever is sooner).

Unlike the extended period of maternity leave, the employee need not give notice of her intention to return to work, even if requested to do so by the employer (see 44.9 below).

44.6   Return to What?

An employee who is entitled to 14 weeks' maternity leave is also entitled to 'return to work'. Although there is no express right in the *EPCA* for the employee to return, the wording of *EPCA s 33(1)* makes it clear that the employee's contract is treated as still subsisting throughout the period of her maternity leave. Therefore, upon expiry of her 14 weeks' maternity leave the employee is entitled to return to the same job.

44.7   Postponement of Return to Work

Under the *Maternity (Compulsory Leave) Regulations 1994 (SI 1994 No 2479)*, since 19 October 1994 there has been a prohibition on female employees working in the 2 weeks immediately after the date of birth. This prohibition is enforced by the Health and Safety Executive or local authorities, and an employer who breaches this provision is liable on conviction to a fine of up to £500. In practice the effect of this prohibition is limited to employees entitled only to 14 weeks' maternity leave. The 2-week period will usually be included in the 14-week maternity leave period itself, unless this period expires within the 2 weeks immediately after the date of birth.

If the employee has used her 14-week leave period before she has given birth, her period of leave is automatically extended until the birth of the child. In these circumstances, the employee will not be able to return to work for a further 2 weeks by reason of the above Regulations.

Under *EPCA s 60(d)*, where the employee is unable to return to work because of illness or disease and, before the end of her maternity leave period, she provides a doctor's certificate stating that she is unable to return to work at the end of her maternity leave, the employee is protected from dismissal (within the 4-week period immediately following the end of her maternity leave) where she is still incapable of returning to work, and that medical certificate is still current.

Although this is not strictly a provision allowing an employee to postpone her return to work, it will provide an employee with some protection against dismissal in circumstances where she is unable to work. However, this is limited to the 4-week period immediately following the expiry of the maternity leave period, or the period for which the medical certificate is current (whichever is shorter).

44.8   RIGHT TO THE EXTENDED PERIOD OF MATERNITY LEAVE

All female employees who have 2 years' or more continuous service at the beginning of the 11th week before the EWC are entitled to a maximum of 40 weeks' maternity leave, together with the supplemental right to return to work at any time up to the beginning of 29 weeks after the week of birth.

44.9   Pregnancy: Maternity Rights

Where an employee is entitled to the extended period of maternity leave, the first 14 weeks of this leave will count as the 14-week maternity leave period under the new scheme detailed above. This has an effect in relation to the employee's entitlements for the first 14 weeks and the subsequent weeks of maternity leave.

The employee must comply with the notice requirements detailed above (see 44.4) in respect of notifying the employer that she is pregnant, the EWC, and that she intends to take maternity leave. As with the 14-week maternity leave period, the extended period of maternity leave can be automatically triggered (see above).

44.9   RIGHT TO RETURN TO WORK

Employees who are entitled to the extended period of maternity leave also have the 'right to return to work' at any time from the end of the initial 14-week maternity leave period until 29 weeks after the beginning of the week of birth. However, before an employee is able to exercise her right to return to work, she must have complied with the notification procedures:

(*a*)   the employer is entitled to make a written request to the employee that she confirm in writing that she intends to exercise the right to return to work. The employer is not entitled to make this request until 21 days before the end of the 14-week maternity leave period. If this request has been made in the required time limit, then the employee must respond in writing within 14 days;

(*b*)   the employee must also notify her employer in writing of the date she intends to return to work, giving at least 21 days' notice of this date. This date is called the 'notified day of return' (NDR). If the employee fails to comply with these notice requirements, she will lose her statutory right to return to work. An employee in any doubt would be well advised to reply to the employer's request by stating that she intends to return to work – she can always retract this notice of intention at a later date.

Therefore, the NDR can be any day up to the beginning of the 29th week after the week of the birth. This is subject to the 2-week prohibition on the employee returning to work under the *Maternity (Compulsory Leave) Regulations 1994 (SI 1994 No 2479)* (see 44.7).

If the employee fails to comply with the notice requirements, she will lose her *statutory* right to return to work. However, this does not necessarily mean that the employee will not be able to return to work, as she may have a *contractual* right to return to work.

In *Hilton International Hotels (UK) Ltd v Kaissi [1994] IRLR 270*, the EAT held that where the employer had terminated the employment of the employee when she had failed to comply with the notification requirements, this was an unfair dismissal. The employee had a 'contractual' right to return to work which had not been affected by her failure to comply with the notification requirement. The EAT held that there was nothing in the parties' actions to indicate that there had been an agreement to treat the employment contract as terminated. Therefore, the employee's contract had continued up to the point of dismissal (despite her failure to comply with the statutory notice requirements). The employer's failure to investigate the reasons for the employee's continued absence and failure to comply with the notification requirements meant that her dismissal was unfair.

44.10 POSTPONEMENT OF RETURN

Unlike the 14-week maternity leave period, the 2-week prohibition on the employee's return to work is unlikely to be of any relevance for employees on extended maternity leave.

However, employees who are entitled to the extended period of maternity leave are entitled to postpone their return to work by up to 4 weeks from the NDR or from the end of the 29-week period (i.e. 29 weeks from the week of birth) on medical grounds. The absence need not be related to pregnancy or childbirth, but the employee must provide her employer with a medical certificate stating that she will be incapable of work at the NDR or at the end of the 29-week period.

If the employee fails to comply with these requirements and is absent from work on medical grounds after the NDR or end of the 29-week period, then she will have lost her statutory right to return to work. However, as seen above in *Hilton International Hotels (UK) Ltd v Kaissi*, she might still have a contractual right to return to work.

The right to postpone the return to work on medical grounds can be exercised only once, so if the employee is still unable to return to work at the end of the postponed period, she will have lost her statutory right to return to work. It is always open for the parties to agree that this period be extended, notwithstanding that the employee has lost her statutory right to return for the purposes of *EPCA s 39*.

44.11 Postponement by the Employer

An employer can postpone the employee's return to work for up to 4 weeks after the NDR, so long as the postponement is for a 'specified reason' – *EPCA s 42(2)*. There is no need for this notification to be in writing. 'Specified reasons' are not defined or clarified in the *EPCA*.

44.12 EMPLOYEE'S RIGHT TO RETURN

Where the employer refuses to let the employee return to work at the end of the 14-week maternity leave, it is possible that she would not have the required amount of service to claim unfair dismissal or redundancy. However, *TURERA 1993* amended the existing *section 60* of the *EPCA 1978* to make dismissals for pregnancy, or a pregnancy-related reason, automatically unfair. In view of the decision of the ECJ in *Webb v EMO Air Cargo (UK) Ltd [1994] IRLR 482* that a dismissal for a pregnancy-related reason is direct discrimination, an employee who is refused the right to return to work following maternity leave could also claim unlawful sex discrimination.

44.13 Refusal of the right to return to work

Where the employer refuses to allow the employee to return to work following an extended period of maternity leave, and the employee has complied with the notification procedure described above, there will be a 'deemed' dismissal as at the date she was refused the right to return to work. It does not mean that unfair dismissal will necessarily follow – an employer may have acted reasonably in using the reason for the dismissal as sufficient reason to dismiss the employee. However, there is always the possibility of a claim for unlawful discrimination by the employee in such circumstances on the basis of the ECJ decision in *Webb v*

EMO Air Cargo (UK) Ltd [1994] IRLR 482 if the detrimental treatment (i.e. her dismissal) was because of the consequences of her pregnancy. This is a matter of direct discrimination, and therefore the employer will not be able to show any justification for the decision. It is important for employers to be able to prove that any dismissal was in no way connected with the employee's pregnancy, or the consequences of pregnancy.

44.14 Exclusions

There are two instances whereby the statutory right to return to work is excluded. These are set out in *EPCA s 56A*, and are outlined below. (Note that if an employer relies on either of these exclusions in defending a complaint of unfair dismissal, the burden of proof is on him to show that the exclusion relied on was satisfied in relation to the complainant.)

First, the right to return does not apply to an employer with less than five employees (including those employed by any associated employer), where it is not reasonably practicable for him to permit the employee to exercise her right to return to work, or for him or an associated employer to offer her employment under a contract of employment satisfying the conditions specified in *EPCA s 56A(3)* (see below).

Second, the right to return does not apply to any employer where (*a*) it is not reasonably practicable, for a reason other than redundancy, for him to permit the employee to exercise her right to return to work, (*b*) he or an associated employer offers her employment under a contract of employment satisfying the conditions specified in *EPCA s 56A(3)* (see below), and (*c*) she accepts or unreasonably refuses that offer.

The conditions specified in *EPCA s 56A(3)*, which are applicable to both the exclusions referred to above, are:

(*a*)   that the work to be done under the contract is of a kind which is both suitable in relation to the employee and appropriate for her to do in the circumstances; and

(*b*)   that the provisions of the contract (as to capacity, place of employment and other terms and conditions) are not substantially less favourable to her than if she had been able to exercise her statutory right to return.

44.15 Suspension from Work on Maternity Grounds

The *Pregnant Workers Directive (No 92/85)* required member States to implement legislation protecting pregnant women (and those who have recently given birth or are breast-feeding) in health and safety matters. The provisions enacted by the Government to implement this aspect of the *Pregnant Workers Directive* are contained in *EPCA ss 45 and 47* (as amended by *TURERA 1993*) and the *Management of Health & Safety at Work (Amendment) Regulations 1994 (SI 1994 No 2865)*.

Employers must already assess the health and safety risks of various jobs within their undertaking, but from 1 December 1994, employers must specifically assess the health and safety risks to all pregnant employees (or those who have recently given birth, or are breast-feeding). If any such employee is exposed to any risk (e.g. chemicals or heavy lifting), then the employer must take all reasonable action to prevent the employee from being exposed to the risk. Reasonable action may include altering the working hours and conditions of the employee. If this is not possible, the employee should be offered alternative work until either the risk is removed or until she is no longer susceptible to the risk.

If neither of the above stated alternatives are possible, then the employee must be given leave of absence until she is no longer at risk. During the period of suspension from work, the employee is entitled to receive all of her contractual entitlements, including payment of salary.

An employer should consult the employee over possible courses of action, indicating whether there is any alternative work that she could carry out until the period of suspension is over, and let the employee decide which option she wishes to take. The employer should not force the employee to be suspended without pay, or to commence her maternity leave early.

If the employee is dismissed during her period of suspension (and the principal reason for the dismissal is the suspension) then dismissal will be *automatically* unfair – *EPCA s 60(e)*.

44.16 Employee's Entitlement During Maternity Leave

Employees who are entitled to only 14 weeks' maternity leave are entitled to the benefit of their normal contractual terms and conditions of employment save for remuneration. This applies also in respect of the first 14 weeks of the extended maternity leave period for those employees who qualify.

44.17 What is remuneration?

Remuneration covers the financial aspects of the employment contract, i.e. wages and salary. It may also include contractual bonuses and commission. However, business expenses and other financial benefits (such as pensions) do not fall within the definition of remuneration.

This means that during the 14-week maternity leave period, the employee is entitled to all of her contractual benefits save for wages/salary. For example, if she has a company car she will be entitled to use this throughout the 14-week period. Similarly, the employee will be entitled to other contractual benefits, such as health insurance and membership of gymnasiums and so on.

The employee will also continue to accrue holiday entitlement.

In relation to any occupational pension scheme operated for the benefit of employees, employers are obliged to make contributions to the pension funds as though the employee were earning her usual salary. The employee is required only to contribute according to the amount of statutory maternity pay or contractual maternity pay that she is receiving. However, these provisions apply only to periods of *paid* maternity leave (i.e. when the employee is receiving contractual maternity pay or statutory maternity pay).

The 14-week maternity leave period will count towards the employee's continuity of service, and will also count towards her length of service.

44.18 The Extended Maternity Leave Period

An employee's entitlement for the remainder of the extended period is slightly different from that for the 14-week period. The *EPCA* does not *expressly* state that an employee's contract continues when she is absent from work on extended maternity leave; rather it states that she has a statutory right to return to work.

This creates some problems if the employee's contract is deemed to cease during her period of maternity leave, especially in respect of continuity and length of service. The EAT held in *Institute of the Motor Industry v Harvey [1992] IRLR 343* that if an employee has notified her intention to return to work following her maternity leave, then her contract is likely to continue during the period of her leave. Also, in *Hilton International Hotels (UK) Ltd v Kaissi [1994] IRLR 270,* the EAT ruled that even where the employee has lost the statutory right to return to work, her employment contract will subsist unless there is express indication to the contrary. Therefore, in the absence of any such indication, her employment contract will be deemed to subsist throughout the period of her maternity leave.

During the extended period of maternity leave (i.e. all leave after the first 14 weeks of maternity leave) the employee is not entitled by statute to any of her contractual benefits save as are mentioned below. However, her contract may state that she is entitled to certain or all of her contractual benefits during any period of maternity leave.

While the employee is on paid maternity leave (i.e. in receipt of contractual maternity pay or statutory maternity pay), the employer must maintain payments to any occupational pension scheme as if the employee was earning her usual salary.

After the 14-week maternity leave period, employees on extended maternity leave will continue to accrue holiday entitlement and length of service. Their continuity of service remains unaffected.

It is an anomaly that employees are entitled to more benefits for the initial 14 weeks of the maternity leave. It may be possible for employees who would otherwise lose out as a result of this anomaly to claim these extra rights during the extended period by way of an equal pay claim. For example, when a sickness absence scheme allows an employee on long-term sick leave to continue to have the use of contractual benefits such as a company car, and the contractual maternity scheme does not allow this, it may be possible for the employee to challenge this by way of an equal pay claim (under *EqPA*).

The fact that employees on maternity leave are not entitled to receive wages/ salary has been challenged in Northern Ireland in *Gillespie v Northern Ireland Health and Social Services Board and Others [1995] IRLIB 524.* In this case, the employees were not entitled to receive full pay whilst they were on maternity leave, nor were they entitled to receive a back-dated salary increase incorporated into their salary at this time (which employees not absent on maternity leave did receive). The employees claimed that this was less favourable treatment on the grounds of sex and, therefore, directly discriminatory contrary to *Article 119* of the Treaty of Rome, the *Equal Pay Directive* and the *Equal Treatment Directive.*

The industrial tribunal dismissed the applications on the grounds that the 'package' of benefits given to female employees during maternity leave did not amount to less favourable treatment, because it was a package not available to male employees. The employees appealed to the Northern Ireland Court of Appeal, who referred a number of questions to the ECJ:

1. Does *Article 119* of the Treaty of Rome, the *Equal Pay Directive* or the *Equal Treatment Directive* require that a woman on maternity leave be paid the full salary that she would have received if she had been working normally?

2. If the answer to 1. is 'No', do these provisions require that the salary a woman receives whilst on maternity leave be determined by reference to certain criteria?

3. If the answer to 2. is 'Yes', what are the criteria?

4. If the answers to 1. and 2. are 'No', do these provisions have any application as respects the amount of pay to which a woman on maternity leave is entitled?

The decision of the ECJ is awaited with interest, as there is a likelihood that, if the employees are successful, all employees on maternity leave will be entitled to full salary during their maternity leave. This would be a controversial ruling by the ECJ, and would result in difficult policy decisions for employers.

The Advocate-General of the ECJ has recently given his opinion in *Gillespie*. In his opinion, neither *Article 119* of the *Treaty of Rome*, the *Equal Pay Directive*, or the *Equal Treatment Directive* require that a female employee on maternity leave should receive full pay. In the opinion of the Advocate-General, none of these provisions require that certain criteria be produced to ascertain the level of salary that a female employee is entitled to whilst on maternity leave and, therefore, the amount of maternity pay that female employees are entitled to receive is left to be determined by member States.

44.19 STATUTORY MATERNITY PAY

There are 2 types of statutory maternity benefits available to pregnant women: statutory maternity pay (SMP) and maternity allowance (MA). The provisions relating to SMP and MA are contained in the *Social Security Contributions and Benefits Act 1992*, which was amended by the *Maternity Allowance and Statutory Maternity Pay Regulations 1994 (SI 1994 No 1230)* in compliance with the relevant provisions of the *Pregnant Workers Directive (No 92/85)*. The new arrangements for SMP and MA apply to all women expecting to give birth on or after 16 October 1994.

The arrangements for SMP are that any employee who has been continuously employed for 26 weeks at the Qualifying Week (i.e. the start of the 15th week before the EWC) is entitled to up to 18 weeks' SMP provided her weekly earnings are at or above the lower earnings limit (from April 1995 this is £58 per week). There is no minimum working hours requirement to be eligible for SMP. An eligible employee will receive the higher rate SMP for the first 6 weeks of her absence. The higher rate SMP is equal to 90 per cent of the employee's 'normal weekly earnings'. After this, the employee is entitled to a maximum of 12 weeks' SMP at the lower rate, which is £52.50 per week, in line with the maximum rates for statutory sick pay.

Employees who do not qualify for SMP may be eligible to receive up to 18 weeks' MA, provided they have paid at least 26 weeks' National Insurance contributions in the 66-week period before the EWC. If a woman is eligible for MA, then she will receive £52.20 per week if she is employed at the Qualifying

44.20 Pregnancy: Maternity Rights

Week, and £45.55 per week if she is self-employed or not employed at the Qualifying Week.

If the employee is not eligible to receive either SMP or MA, then she may be eligible for sickness benefit or income support.

44.20 Eligibility for SMP

The woman must actually be an 'employee' and have:

(*a*) 26 weeks' continuous service at the start of the Qualifying Week (i.e. the 15th week before the EWC);

(*b*) become pregnant and have reached the start of the 11th week before the EWC;

(*c*) average earnings of at least the lower earnings limit (£58 per week) for the 8 weeks ending with the Qualifying Week;

(*d*) given 21 days' notice (in writing if her employer so requests) of her intention to cease work because of her pregnancy;

(*e*) produced a medical certificate showing the EWC; and

(*f*) ceased working for the employer because of the pregnancy.

44.21 The Maternity Pay Period (MPP)

This is the period of a maximum of 18 weeks in which SMP is payable. As stated above, SMP is payable in 2 tiers. For the first 6 weeks of the MPP, SMP is paid at 90 per cent of the employee's usual earnings; and for the remainder of the MPP, SMP is payable at £52.50 per week.

Where the employee does not have 2 years' continuous employment at the start of the 11th week before her EWC, she will only be entitled to 14 weeks' maternity leave. Such an employee will also be entitled to only 14 weeks' SMP, and will lose out in respect of 4 weeks' SMP at the standard rate of £52.50 per week, unless she does not intend to return to work following her maternity leave (in which case she will be entitled to the maximum of 18 weeks' SMP.)

Where an employee is unable to return to work at the end of the maternity leave period because of sickness, provided she is absent under a medical certificate and has not exhausted her SMP entitlement, she will be entitled to receive SMP for this period of absence.

Where the employee has 2 years or more continuous employment at the start of the 11th week before the EWC, she will be entitled to the maximum 18 weeks' SMP.

The MPP can commence at any time from the beginning of the 11th week before the EWC; at the latest it will commence on the first Sunday following the date of birth. It will usually start on the Sunday after the employee has started her maternity leave having given the employer the notice as required above.

If the employee attends work in any week (even if it is only for half a day) at any time after the start of the MPP, she will lose one week's SMP for every week or part week involved. The SMP that she loses first will be at the standard rate SMP.

As with the 14-week maternity leave period and extended maternity leave period, the MPP can be automatically triggered if the employee is absent from work at any time after the start of the 6th week before the EWC for a pregnancy-related reason. In such a case, the MPP will automatically commence on the first Sunday following the employee's absence. If this occurs and the employee subsequently attends work, she will lose her entitlement to SMP for any such week, as discussed above.

The Maternity Allowance Period is also 18 weeks. Like the MPP, it will not usually start before the 11th week before the EWC; the latest that it can start is the first Sunday after the date of birth. Similarly, the Maternity Allowance Period will be reduced where the employee worked at any time after it commenced, or where it is automatically triggered.

44.22 Effect of dismissal or resignation on SMP entitlement

What is the situation where, having qualified for SMP (i.e. having satisfied the above requirements at the start of the Qualifying Week), the employee has resigned, or is dismissed on grounds unrelated to her pregnancy? It would appear that in these circumstances the employee does not lose her entitlement to SMP. The MPP would begin on either the start of the week after the employment ended, or the start of the 11th week before the EWC.

If the employment relationship ends as a consequence of the employee's resignation, she is under no duty to give the 21 days' notice.

44.23 Relationship between employee and contractual maternity pay

If an employee is entitled to receive contractual sick pay, she is not entitled to receive SMP as well. Usually, the employer will simply pay the amount of the contractual sick pay, or will pay both contractual sick pay and SMP and deduct from the contractual sick pay a sum equivalent to SMP.

44.24 DISMISSAL DURING MATERNITY LEAVE OR FOR A MATERNITY RELATED REASON

Pregnancy-related dismissal is automatically unfair

TURERA 1993 amended *section 60* of the *EPCA 1978* so that all pregnancy-related dismissals are *automatically* unfair. This provision operates irrespective of the employee's length of service or the number of hours she usually works per week. This provision was introduced to bring UK law into line with *Article 10* of the *Pregnant Workers Directive (No 92/85)*, and provides that dismissal will be automatically unfair where:

(*a*)   the reason for the dismissal is that the employee is pregnant or any other reason connected with that pregnancy – *EPCA s 60(a)*;

(*b*)   the employee's maternity leave period is ended by the dismissal and the reason for the dismissal is that the employee has given birth or any other reason connected with her having given birth – *EPCA s 60(b)*;

(*c*)   where her employment is terminated after the end of the maternity leave period, and the reason for the dismissal is that the employee took maternity leave or took advantage of the benefits of maternity leave – *EPCA s 60(c)*;

(*d*)   where the employee is absent from work at the end of her maternity leave period having provided a doctor's certificate stating that she is unable to return to work, and the dismissal takes place within the 4-week period immediately following maternity leave (or during the currency of the medical certificate), and the reason for the dismissal is that she has given birth, or any other reason connected with the fact that she has given birth – *EPCA s 60(d)*;

(*e*)   the reason for the dismissal is because of a requirement which requires the employee to be suspended from work on maternity grounds – *EPCA s 60(e)*;

(*f*)   the employee's maternity leave is ended by the dismissal and the reason for the dismissal is that she is redundant, and the employer has failed to offer a suitable alternative vacancy – *EPCA s 60(f)*.

Where the employer refuses to allow the employee to return to work after the extended period of maternity leave, there is a 'deemed' dismissal. Provided that the employee has complied with the notification requirements governing her return to work, and the employer refuses to allow her to return to work, the employee is treated as being employed until the NDR, with the dismissal taking effect from that date. This will be the case even where the employer has notified the employee before this date that he will not allow her to return to work.

The reason for the dismissal is the reason that the employer gives for not allowing the employee to return to work. This does not necessarily mean that the dismissal will be an unfair dismissal – it will depend on the reason given and the reasonableness of the employer in using that reason as sufficient to dismiss the employee.

An employee is unable to claim a dismissal unless she has complied with the notification requirements. It is because the employee must show that her dismissal took place while she was attempting to return to work that she must comply with the notification requirements (if she has not complied with these requirements, there is no presumption that she was intending to return to work).

Any dismissal for one of the above reasons (referred to as 'inadmissible reasons') will be automatically unfair. The burden of proof in such circumstances is with the employer. The employee only has to provide evidence showing a presumption that the dismissal was for a pregnancy or related reason; it is then up to the employer to show that the dismissal was not for an 'inadmissable reason'. If the employer cannot do this, the dismissal will be automatically unfair.

44.25 Redundancy dismissals automatically unfair

TURERA 1993 also amended *EPCA s 59* thereby rendering any dismissal by way of redundancy – where the reason for the redundancy is one of the 'inadmissible reasons' – an automatically unfair dismissal.

In addition, under *EPCA s 60(f)*, where the employee's maternity leave is ended by reason of redundancy, and the employer fails to offer the employee any suitable alternative vacancy, then the dismissal will be automatically unfair.

44.26 Pregnancy and Sex Discrimination

It is clear that any detrimental treatment (such as dismissal, and failure to promote) on the grounds of an employee's pregnancy, or for other maternity related reasons, is direct discrimination contrary to the *SDA*. Therefore, there is no need for a comparison with a male employee in similar circumstances. Once a female employee has established that her treatment amounted to direct discrimination, no question of justification for this treatment can arise. This principle was firmly established by the ECJ in *Webb v EMO Air Cargo (UK) Ltd [1994] IRLR 482*.

In this case the ECJ held that any unfavourable treatment on the grounds of pregnancy or maternity is contrary to the *Equal Treatment Directive*. This Directive has direct effect in relation to public-sector employees. Such employees dismissed on pregnancy related-grounds can therefore rely directly upon European law to claim unlawful sex discrimination.

Private-sector employees, however, will not be able to rely directly upon the *Equal Treatment Directive*, and must bring a claim under *SDA*.

The House of Lords has yet to make its final decision in *Webb* and must decide whether it can interpret the *SDA* in compliance with the *Equal Treatment Directive*. If it finds that it is unable to do so, legislation will be necessary to amend the *SDA* in accordance with the ECJ decision. However, it is likely that the House of Lords will be able to interpret the provisions of the *SDA* in accordance with the *Equal Treatment Directive*, so that all pregnancy and maternity related discrimination will be treated as direct discrimination.

If the House of Lords is unable to interpret the *SDA* in accordance with the *Equal Treatment Directive*, a private-sector employee may bring an action against the Government for its failure to correctly implement EU law; i.e. a *Francovich* claim. It may well have the effect of expediting legislation to amend the *SDA* in line with the *Equal Treatment Directive*.

As a consequence of the decision in *Webb*, any employee dismissed for a pregnancy-related reason is able to claim both unfair dismissal and sex discrimination. An employee in such a situation would be advised to claim both of these, as there is no limit on the maximum award in respect of unlawful sex discrimination, whereas the maximum compensatory award for unfair dismissal is £11,300 (see REMEDIES (49)).

In giving its decision, the ECJ emphasised the fact that Mrs Webb was taken on by EMO Air Cargo on an indefinite contract. This would suggest that where the employee is taken on for a fixed period, for example as a replacement for another employee on maternity leave, her subsequent dismissal might not amount to direct discrimination.

The Scottish Court of Session have stepped away from what was believed to be the established position following *Webb*, in its decision in *Brown v Rentokil Ltd [1995] IRLR 211*. In this case, the employer operated a rule whereby any employee absent on sick leave for 26 continuous weeks was dismissed. This rule had been applied by the employer in respect of male employees in the past. The female employee became pregnant, and had not attended work because of a pregnancy-related illness from August 1990 until her dismissal in February 1991. An industrial tribunal and the EAT dismissed her application. The Court of Session followed the reasoning in *Webb* and also referred to the ECJ decision in *Hertz [1992] ICR 332*. In this case (i.e. *Hertz*) the ECJ held that where an illness arose after maternity leave, this was the same as any other illness. The fact that certain illnesses were specific to one sex was irrelevant. The only relevant factor was whether the dismissal of a woman on the grounds of illness occurred in the same circumstances as a man – if so, then there was no direct discrimination on the grounds of sex.

44.27   Pregnancy: Maternity Rights

The Court of Session held that *Webb* did not distinguish *Hertz* from the female employee's situation in the present case, because *Webb* was about a pregnancy dismissal, not about an illness dismissal. The tribunal, and the EAT, had therefore been correct in dismissing the employee's application. The employer's treatment of the employee did not amount to direct discrimination contrary to the *SDA* or the *Equal Treatment Directive*.

This decision is clearly inconsistent with the ECJ approach in *Webb*, and is to be doubted. In the author's view it will almost certainly be overruled on appeal.

44.27 Armed Forces Pregnancy Dismissals

Before August 1990, female members of the armed forces who became pregnant were either told to resign or were dismissed. Under *SDA s 85* the armed forces were not subject to the provisions of the *SDA*. However, in December 1991 the Ministry of Defence conceded that this policy contravened the *Equal Treatment Directive (76/207/EEC)* and that *SDA s 85* was inconsistent with the *Equal Treatment Directive*. As a result of this concession, an estimated 4,500 ex-servicewomen dismissed between 1978 and August 1990 (the date that the dismissal policy was altered) brought sex discrimination proceedings.

In all of these cases, usually referred to as 'Ministry of Defence' cases, the sole issue was the level of compensation (liability was admitted). However, as a consequence of the decision in *Marshall v Southampton and South West Hampshire Area Health Authority (No 2) [1993] IRLR 445*, the compensation limit on awards in sex discrimination cases was removed, with effect from 22 November 1993 (*Sex Discrimination & Equal Pay (Remedies) Regulations 1993*) (see REMEDIES (49)).

The direct consequence was that the level of awards received by some ex-servicewomen was astronomical, the largest award being an estimated £350,000, which included loss of pension rights and loss of the prospect of promotion or further/extended commissions. The Ministry of Defence estimates that the total cost of settling all the cases brought was in the region of £100 million.

The Ministry of Defence appealed against the level of some of the awards, and the EAT gave guidance for industrial tribunals in determining awards in these cases (*Ministry of Defence v Cannock and Others [1994] IRLR 509*). As a result of this guidance, the level of awards has generally fallen. However, the average award in these 'Ministry of Defence' cases is over £35,000, double the present maximum award (basic and compensatory award) for unfair dismissal.

The Government introduced the *Sex Discrimination Act 1975 (Application to Armed Forces etc) Regulations 1994 (SI 1994 No 3276)*, which came into force on 1 February 1995, amending the *SDA* so that it is now of general application to the armed forces.

44.28 PATERNITY LEAVE

There is no statutory provision requiring employers to grant paternity leave. The *SDA* expressly excludes any benefits given to women in respect of pregnancy or childbirth, and so men cannot use the *SDA* to claim any equivalent benefit to give them paternity leave. There is a recommendation from the EEC in respect of paternity (as part of a new *Parental Leave Directive*), but this is not enforceable.

44.29 Paternity leave is not unlawful

Any benefit in respect of men relating to the birth of their children is theoretically within the scope of the *SDA*, but in reality would not be, because there would be no circumstances where women would be able to show that they were not getting a similar (or, in reality, greatly enhanced) benefits.

44.30 Paternity leave in practice

Employers have long been willing to allow fathers to take their holiday to coincide with the birth of their children when perhaps business convenience would dictate otherwise. It is also a growing practice for employers to provide set paternity leave for fathers. There is no limitation on the type of policy an employer might operate. It can be discretionary or otherwise, and the leave offered might be for as little as a day or as much as a month.

44.31 Potential problems

In practice, problems may arise over employers' policies for giving leave to deal with responsibilities for children. For example, an employer may operate a policy which allows mothers special leave, or leave at short notice, in response to domestic emergencies relating to children, but which does not allow the same benefit to fathers. Any such policy would be directly discriminatory [*SDA s 1(1)(a)*], and employers should ensure that either there is a policy of universal application, or, perhaps more practically, a discretionary policy where the limits of discretion are clearly set out.

44.32 Non-returners

It is not safe to assume that, simply because a woman has not returned after either the 14-week or the 29-week maternity scheme that she will not return and can be sent a P45. At the end of this period it is recommended that employers treat continued absence in the same way as any other member of staff who is absent without leave. The safest course is to enquire whether the individual is planning on returning and, if so, why she has not done so. Bear in mind that any continued sickness starts from the date of return. It is not (probably) normal to dismiss someone after one-days' sickness!

44A   MATERNITY CHECKLIST FOR EMPLOYERS

(1) Introduction

This is no more than an attempt to give a brief outline of those matters that employers should be aware of in relation to pregnant employees. You must be aware not only of the length of maternity leave an employee is entitled to, but also of your obligations in respect of allowing the employee to return to work. In addition, you need to be aware of an employee's right to take time off for antenatal care and her entitlements during maternity leave. The consequences of dismissal or redundancy during maternity leave must also be fully understood.

(2) Time off for antenatal care

Once satisfied that your employee is pregnant, you must not unreasonably refuse her time off to attend antenatal appointments. You are entitled to request a certificate stating that the employee is pregnant and that she has an appointment (except for the first appointment). The employee is entitled to be paid at her usual rate for the entire period that she is absent from work attending antenatal care.

You are entitled to request that employees arrange antenatal appointments outside their working hours, or close to the beginning or end of their working day, if they are able to do so.

(3) How much maternity leave?

To be able to calculate how much leave an employee is entitled to, you must ascertain what the expected date of birth is. From this date, you should work back to the Monday at the beginning of that week (this is the EWC), and then work back a further 11 weeks. If the employee has been continuously employed by you for 2 or more years at this date, she is entitled to up to 40 weeks' maternity leave. If she has not, then she is entitled to 14 weeks' maternity leave.

(4) Notice requirements

An employee cannot commence maternity leave before the start of the 11th week before the EWC. Maternity leave will automatically be triggered if the employee is absent from work for a pregnancy-related reason (other than to attend an antenatal appointment) at any time after the start of the 6th week before the EWC. Subject to this, before being able to take maternity leave, the employee must notify you in writing of the fact that she is pregnant, the EWC and the date she intends to commence her maternity leave, giving at least 21 days' notice of this (unless it is not reasonably practicable for her to provide 21 days' notice).

An employee must give this notice whether she is entitled to maternity leave of 14 weeks or up to 40 weeks. Ask the employee when she expects to return and which scheme she intends utilising (the 14-week scheme is open to everyone, including those entitled to longer maternity leave).

(5) Right to return to work

(a)   *14 weeks' maternity leave*
An employee who has been absent from work on 14 weeks' maternity leave need only present herself for work on the first working day after the

expiry of the 14-week period, and she is entitled to return to the job she was doing before she went on maternity leave. If the employee wishes to return to work before the 14-week period has expired, she need only give you 7 days' notice of the day she intends to return to work following her period of maternity leave, and you are only entitled to delay her return to work if she has not given 7 days' notice. However, once the 14-week maternity leave period has expired, you are not entitled to postpone her return on the ground that she has given inadequate notice.

You should ensure that the employee is allowed to return to the same job that she performed before maternity leave, as her contract subsists during the period of the leave.

You should not allow the employee to return to work until 2 weeks after the date of birth, even if the employee wishes to return to work, as you may be liable for a fine of up to £500. However, in most circumstances the 2-week period immediately following the birth will be part of the 14-week maternity leave period.

If the employee is unable to return to work for medical reasons following the expiry of her 14-week maternity leave, and she provides a medical certificate which states that she is unable to return to work, you are unable to fairly dismiss her for the duration of the medical certificate (subject to a 4-week maximum period).

(b)   *40 weeks' maternity leave*
An employee having the benefit of an extended period of maternity leave has the right to return to work at any time up to 29 weeks after the week of birth. However, the employee must comply with notice requirements before being able to return to work. You are entitled to request confirmation from the employee that she intends to return to work. However, you cannot make this request until 21 days before the end of the 14-week maternity leave period. The employee must respond to your request within 14 days. She must also notify you in writing of the date she intends to return to work, giving at least 21 days' notice of this.

If the employee fails to comply with these notice requirements, she will lose her statutory right to return to work. This does not necessarily mean that she is not entitled to return to work, unless it has been expressly agreed between you and the employee that, should she fail to comply with the notice requirements, her employment will automatically terminate (*Hilton International Hotels (UK) Ltd v Kaissi [1994] IRLR 270*).

You should note that employees on 40 weeks' maternity leave are able to postpone their return for up to 4 weeks on medical grounds in the same way as employees entitled to 14 weeks' maternity leave. However, you are entitled to postpone the employee's return for up to 4 weeks as long as the postponement is for a 'specified reason'. There are no limits on the reasons you may give, but they must be specified.

(6) Entitlements during maternity leave

During the initial 14-week period, all employees are entitled to receive all their contractual entitlements, such as use of a company car, pension benefits, and health insurance, with the exception of remuneration (i.e. wages, salary and commission).

Employees entitled to up to 40 weeks' maternity leave are entitled to the above contractual benefits for the first 14 weeks of their maternity leave. For the remainder of their maternity leave they are not entitled to any contractual benefits – your obligations to pay such benefits are suspended. However, in some circumstances the non-payment of benefits may amount to sex discrimination.

Periods of maternity leave count towards an employee's period of service, and her continuity of service will not be broken.

(7) Statutory Maternity Pay/Maternity Allowance

An employee whom you have continuously employed for 6 months at the start of the 15th week before the EWC is entitled to up to 18 weeks' SMP as long as her weekly earnings are above the lower earnings limit. She will receive higher rate SMP for the first 6 weeks of her absence (which amounts to 90 per cent of her normal weekly earnings), followed by up to 12 weeks' lower rate SMP (which is the same as the rates for Statutory Sick Pay). If an employee is not entitled to receive SMP, she may be entitled to receive up to 18 weeks' Maternity Allowance, so long as she has paid 26 weeks' National Insurance contributions in the 66-week period before the EWC. If she is eligible, she will receive Maternity Allowance equivalent to lower rate SMP if she is employed, or lower rate Maternity Allowance if she is unemployed or self-employed.

(8) Dismissal during maternity leave

If you dismiss an employee for a pregnancy-related reason, the dismissal will be automatically unfair. It will also be unlawful sex discrimination. The maximum amount of compensation that a tribunal can award in respect of unfair dismissal is £11,300 (compensatory award); there is no limit on the amount that it can award in sex discrimination cases (see REMEDIES (49)).

(9) Redundancy during maternity leave

If you make an employee redundant whilst she is on maternity leave, and the redundancy relates to her maternity, then this dismissal will be automatically unfair. The dismissal is also likely to be unlawful sex discrimination, for which there is no limit on the amount of compensation that a tribunal can award (see REMEDIES (49)).

45 Pressure to Discriminate

45.1 It is unlawful to give instructions to a person to discriminate, or to exert pressure to discriminate, on grounds of either race or sex. [*SDA ss 39, 40; RRA ss 30, 31*].

45.2 ENFORCEMENT PROCEEDINGS

Only the CRE or EOC (as appropriate) may take proceedings for contravention of the sections referred to above, by way of an application for a declaration that the act of discrimination has occurred. [*SDA s 72; RRA s 63*]. The pressure or instructions complained of, however, may well give rise to an individual complaint. An individual who has pressurised another to discriminate, or who has instructed another to discriminate, will be liable for that discrimination by virtue of *SDA s 42* and *RRA s 33*, whereby any person knowingly aiding an unlawful act is to be treated for the purposes of the *SDA* and *RRA* as though they themselves did the unlawful act. The only exception to this is if, in aiding the unlawful act, that person was reasonably relying on the statement of another that that act was exempt from the provisions of the *SDA* or *RRA*. [*SDA s 42(3); RRA s 33(3)*].

In a case where there is both the question of pressure to discriminate and an individual complaint, the two cases would normally be held simultaneously in the industrial tribunal. However, there would seem to be no requirement that they should be and, indeed, the time limits in relation to the individual complaint and the action by the CRE or EOC are different (see below). In a case where the CRE or EOC has already obtained a finding against an individual or employer, they may seek an injunction to restrain further acts of discrimination if they consider that such is likely. [*SDA s 72; RRA s 63*].

45.3 TIME LIMIT

The time limit for either Commission to take action (i.e. present a case to the tribunal) in relation to pressure or instructions to discriminate is six months. [*SDA s 76(4); RRA s 68(5)*]. An individual who wishes to name as a respondent the person or company who instructed the discriminator to discriminate, or who pressurised the discriminator to discriminate, must take such action within three months. [*SDA s 76(1); RRA s 68(1)*]. In order to be in time, the individual or company alleged to have pressurised or instructed the discriminator should also be clearly named as a respondent.

45.4 DEFINITION OF 'PRESSURE TO DISCRIMINATE'

In some ways, it is strange that 'instructions to discriminate' and 'pressure to discriminate' are identified separately, as it is difficult to contemplate a situation where an instruction to discriminate would not constitute pressure to discriminate.

The requirements of proving a case against an individual in relation to instructions are much more onerous than in relation to pressure. To make out a case in relation to instructions to discriminate, the EOC or CRE must show

(*a*)   that the individual pressurising or instructing had authority over the pressurised or instructed individual [*SDA s 38(a); RRA s 30(a)*]; or

45.5 Pressure to Discriminate

(b)   that the latter was accustomed to acting in accordance with the former's wishes. [SDA s 38(b); RRA s 30(b)].

The meaning of the wording in (b) above was considered by the Employment Appeal Tribunal in *CRE v Imperial Society of Teachers of Dancing* [1983] IRLR 315. The wording implies a pre-existing relationship, but the EAT held that this could be an institutional relationship. The fact that particular individuals had not communicated previously was not relevant, if the individual to whom instructions had been given worked for an organisation which had previously acted in accordance with the wishes of the other. In this particular case, the principal of the Society had approached a school and stated that 'she would rather the school did not send anyone coloured'. The EAT determined that there was no pre-existing relationship, in that there was no evidence that the school was accustomed to act on the wishes of the Society in relation to the selection of staff. The words used were therefore not sufficient to constitute an instruction, but they were held to be an attempt to 'induce' an act of discrimination (see below).

Instructions also include 'to procure or attempt to procure' the doing of any act in contravention of the *RRA* or *SDA*. In this context, the words 'procure' and 'attempt to procure' have been deemed to have 'a wide meaning and are apt to include the use of words which bring about or attempt to bring about a certain course of action' (*CRE v Imperial Society of Teachers of Dancing* [1983] IRLR 315).

There is no such requirement for an 'authority' relationship in respect of the unlawful act of 'pressure to discriminate'. The definition of 'pressure to discriminate' is much wider. It is unlawful to induce, or attempt to induce, a person to do any act which is made unlawful by either Act. The inducement does not have to be made directly to the individual concerned, but must be made in such a way that he is likely to hear of it. The words 'induce or attempt to induce' do not imply any element of 'stick or carrot', but take their ordinary meaning, which is 'to persuade or prevail upon to bring about' (*CRE v Imperial Society of Teachers of Dancing* [1983] IRLR 315 (see above), in which a request not to send any black staff was deemed to be an 'attempt to induce' an act of discrimination).

The mere giving of information, however, does not constitute an inducement to discriminate. In *CRE v Powell and City of Birmingham District Council EOR 7, 31*, the Employment Appeal Tribunal held that the mere passing on of the information that the employer discriminated does not constitute pressure to discriminate, but in certain circumstances could do so. 'Now the giving of information may or may not amount to an attempt to persuade some people. That is a pure question of fact and, looking at whether it is persuasion or information, the intention of the parties is clearly a matter which a court would take into account.' It would therefore be a matter for the industrial tribunal to assess whether or not the provision of the information was, in fact, an attempt to procure an act of discrimination.

45.5 SCOPE OF THE PROVISION

The most obvious area of application for these provisions of the *RRA* and *SDA* is in respect of the activities of employment agencies and job centres. Of the prosecutions conducted by the CRE (in 1986, it dealt with 51 instances of alleged pressure to discriminate), the majority are referred to them by the local Jobcentre and involve relatively small employers. Relatively few references are made by commercial employment agencies. Interestingly, the CRE Code of Practice has a special section on the responsibilities of employment agencies (Part 4), but does not recommend to employment agencies that they should report to the CRE clients who issue discriminatory instructions. The Code does recommend that they should 'report a client's refusal to interview an applicant for reasons that are directly or indirectly discriminatory to a supervisor, who should inform the client that discrimination is unlawful. If the client maintains this refusal the agency should inform the applicant of his or her right to complain to an industrial tribunal and to apply to the CRE for assistance. An internal procedure for recording such cases should be operated.' If an employment agency conforms to discriminatory instructions, then, should the individual become aware of this, they will be equally liable for aiding unlawful acts of discrimination by virtue of *SDA s 42* and *RRA s 33*.

45.6   OTHER SITUATIONS WHERE PRESSURE MAY TAKE PLACE

As well as the more obvious situation where an employer asks a job centre not to send any black or female staff, pressure to discriminate will take place if employees put pressure on management not to appoint a black or female supervisor, or indeed, not to allow a black or female member of staff to join a shift. Other examples where pressure may be applied include

(*a*)   where, in a job specification for a position, the interviewing panel are provided with a criterion that is discriminatory, for instance 'male preferred'; and

(*b*)   where a customer informs an employer that he does not want a particular salesman allocated to his account.

Clearly, the legislation is likely to be ineffective in most of these situations, given the commercial reality of the relationship between those exerting pressure and those being pressurised. In the second example referred to above, for instance, a report to the EOC to the effect that the customer had pressurised the employer to appoint a man (and not a woman) to a particular account would inevitably result in the loss of the account (with no remedy other than the purely contractual, as such action would be outside the framework of the victimisation provisions of the *SDA*). There have been such instances, however, and certainly the (now defunct) Manpower Services Commission had a set procedure in respect of discriminatory practices; any employer who declined to retract discriminatory instructions was vulnerable to being reported to one of the Commissions, with a view to proceedings. There have been instances of the commercial employment agencies taking similar action.

45.7   SANCTIONS

It is surprising that there is no financial penalty resultant upon a finding that an employer or individual has issued instructions to discriminate, or has applied pressure to discriminate. Only the CRE or EOC may take proceedings, and the tribunal can only make, or decline to make, a declaration that the act of discrimination complained of has taken place. [*SDA s 72; RRA s 63*]. Only if there is a repeat offence (and there must be a finding in respect of the original offence), can an injunction be applied for. The requirement that there must be such a finding can give rise to considerable problems, illustrated by the example of the London Borough of Lambeth, which, in an advertisements case (where the powers of the tribunal are the same), appealed the matter to the House of Lords. In the meantime, a further 15 cases of discriminatory advertisements had

45.7 Pressure to Discriminate

built up, which could otherwise have been dealt with by the injunctive proceedings about to be described (*London Borough of Lambeth v CRE [1990] IRLR 231*). Where there is such a finding, either Commission may apply to the county court for an injunction restraining future contravention of the *RRA* or *SDA*, provided that they are of the view that such further contraventions are likely to take place. [*SDA s 72; RRA s 63*].

It is difficult to identify whether or not the absence of a financial penalty was simply a mistake on the part of Parliament, or whether it was felt that the individual remedy that could be taken simultaneously by an aggrieved individual would be sufficient. In respect of legislation that is meant to have a deterrent effect, however, the only deterrent effect that these provisions have are in relation to the publicity that is invariably generated when such a case is heard, certainly in the local papers and, if the employer is big enough, in the national press. It may be, however, that in a future amendment of the legislation, the industrial tribunal will be given the power to fine in such cases which would seem to be logical and appropriate.

46 Qualifying Bodies

46.1 **DEFINITION**

Any body or authority which can confer an authorisation or qualification (i) to take part in a particular profession or trade, or (ii) which is required for taking part in that profession or trade, or (iii) which facilitates taking part in that profession or trade or confers a qualification for the same purpose, is covered by the provisions of both Acts. [*RRA s 12; SDA s 13*]. A qualifying body has been held to 'cover all cases where the qualification in fact facilitates the woman's employment, whether or not it is intended by the authority or body which confers the authorisation or qualification so to do' in a *SDA* case, *British Judo Association v Petty* [*1981*] *ICR 660* (the wording of the *RRA* provision is identical).

Not included within the provisions of these sections are educational establishments [*RRA s 17; SDA s 22*] nor local education authorities [*RRA s 18; SDA s 23*]. Educational establishments are clearly defined in *RRA s 17* and *SDA s 22*, so as to include any maintained local school and any university. The exclusion is important as the time limit for proceedings in an industrial tribunal (where complaints against qualifying bodies are heard) is three months whereas in the county court (where complaints against the educational establishments and local education authorities will be heard), the time limit is six months which can be further extended by up to three months by applying to either the CRE or EOC for assistance with the case. The procedures in the county court are also more formal and frequently more time-consuming.

Included within the definition of 'qualifying body' are such qualifying bodies as the Law Society and the Council of Legal Education, the qualifying body for the Bar (see *Bohon-Mitchell v Common Professional Examination Board and Council of Legal Education* [*1978*] *IRLR 525*), referees associations (*British Judo Association v Petty* [*1981*] *ICR 660*) and the Secretary of State for Education in relation to the qualification as a teacher [*Hampson v Department of Education and Science* [*1989*] *ICR 179 (CA)*, [*1990*] *ICR 511 (HL)*].

The distinction of forum could cause confusion and, if an applicant is in doubt, he would be best advised to commence proceedings in both the industrial tribunal and the county court to preserve his rights.

46.2 **DISCRIMINATION BY QUALIFYING BODY UNLAWFUL**

The qualifying body must not discriminate against a person on grounds of race or sex:

(*a*) in the terms on which it is prepared to confer the authorisation or qualification; or

(*b*) by refusing or deliberately omitting to grant the application for it; or

(*c*) by withdrawing it from him or varying its terms.

If such a body is required by law to satisfy itself as to an individual's good character before conferring an authorisation or qualification on him, then they must have regard to any evidence which would indicate that the individual has, in the past, practised unlawful discrimination in connection with the carrying on of any profession or trade. [*RRA s 12(2); SDA s 13(2)*]. 'Authorisation or qualification' includes recognition, registration, enrolment, approval and certification. The burden of proof in such matters is the same as in other discrimination cases and the complaint must be made to the industrial tribunal within three months of the doing of the act of which complaint is made.

46.3 POSITIVE ACTION

A qualifying body may discriminate in relation to the provision of training opportunities by providing such opportunities to only women or men, or only to members of a particular ethnic minority group, where it had identified that there were few (or no) persons of the particular sex or race doing the particular work. [*RRA s 37; SDA s 47*]. Previously this provision was limited to designated bodies and designation had to be acquired from the Secretary of State but there is now no requirement for designation. The exemption is very limited and would enable, say, the Law Society to arrange a special training course for members of a particular racial group whom it felt to be unrepresented. However, it would not enable them in any way to interfere with the relevant pass mark or level of attainment required in the solicitors' qualifying examinations.

47   Questionnaire Procedure

47.1   THE QUESTIONNAIRE

Discrimination legislation is unique in its provision of pre-litigation interrogatories, usually referred to as the questionnaire procedure. [*RRA s 65; SDA s 74; Disability Discrimination Act 1995, s 25*].

47.2   TIME LIMIT FOR SERVING

A questionnaire may be served at any time prior to commencing proceedings, within 21 days of such proceedings having been taken, or at any later stage with the leave, and at the discretion, of the industrial tribunal. [*SI 1977 No 842* and *SI 1975 No 2048, Reg 5*].

47.3   PURPOSE

Questionnaires are primarily designed to enable the individual to decide whether to institute proceedings. [*RRA s 65(1); SDA s 74(1); Disability Discrimination Act 1995, s 25(2)*]. For example, an individual who has failed to get a promotion may consider that he has been discriminated against and was the best candidate, but may change his mind upon being given the details of the best candidate, in answer to the questionnaire, and realising that the other candidate was, in fact, better qualified for the post.

47.4   PENALTY FOR FAILURE TO REPLY

There is no compulsion to answer the questionnaire, but a failure to answer or an evasive or equivocal answer can be taken into account in any proceedings in the industrial tribunal (or county court) and the tribunal can draw any inference from the failure to reply or equivocation, including the inference that the discrimination complained of took place (see *Virdee v ECC Quarries* [*1978*] *IRLR 295*). [*RRA s 65(2)(b); SDA s 74(2)(b); Disability Discrimination Act 1995, s 25(3)(b)*]. It is therefore always advisable to reply to the questionnaire. As the burden of proof is formally with the applicant, the questionnaire may be used to justify an adverse inference if the respondent fails to take any part in the proceedings.

47.5   USE OF QUESTIONNAIRE PROCEDURE BY THE CRE AND EOC

The questionnaire is frequently drafted and sent on behalf of individuals by the CRE or, in a sex discrimination case, by the EOC. The Commissions then take advantage of the questionnaire procedure to assist them in deciding whether or not to grant legal assistance to the individual involved. It is, therefore, particularly important to reply to the questionnaire when one of these agencies is involved.

47.6   TIME LIMIT FOR REPLY

Although an applicant has to serve a questionnaire within a specified time, there is no set time limit in which the employer has to reply. Usually the CRE or EOC request a reply within a stated period (14 days for the CRE). In reality they do not expect a reply within such a short time, particularly as the questionnaire frequently asks for involved statistical information. It is advisable, however, to keep the agency (or complainant) appraised of progress with the replies.

47.7 Questionnaire Procedure

47.7 FORMAT

The formats of the questionnaires are identical in substance and are prescribed by the respective statutory instruments. [*SI 1977 No 842 (RRA)* and *SI 1975 No 2048 (SDA)*]. The Regulations provide, however, that 'forms to the like effect with such variation as the circumstances may require' are also prescribed, so there is no requirement to abide rigidly by the format set by the Regulations. A letter headed 'Questions and Replies Procedure – Section 65 Race Relations Act' setting out the relevant questions and the consequences of failure to answer would suffice so long as it could be shown that this was reasonable in the circumstances. Applicants are, however, best advised to use the standard form, although an employer should treat an appropriately headed letter as though it were a questionnaire.

The standard forms (reproduced in Appendix 4) are obtainable, in theory, from any job centre, from the Department of Education and Employment, or from the EOC and CRE respectively. Some citizens advice bureaus, law centres and Councils for Racial Equality may have forms. In fact, job centres rarely carry a stock whereas the EOC and CRE do. The forms are very badly laid out and, in fact, do not adhere to the numbering provided for in the statutory instruments, which can cause confusion. The response to question 6 is, for instance, answer number 4!

47.8 GENERAL QUESTIONS PERMITTED

The most important element from the applicant's point of view is Question 6 of the form which is for 'any other questions you want to ask'. These questions should be relevant to the issue.

47.9 GUIDANCE FOR PREPARING A QUESTIONNAIRE

The Commission for Racial Equality has published guidance for completing the questions section of the questionnaire in their '*Guide to Presenting Race Cases in the Industrial Tribunal*' which is set out below. These guidelines are equally appropriate for the *SDA* questionnaire (the EOC has published a similar guide '*How to prepare your own case for an Industrial Tribunal*').

RR 65(a)

Name of person to be questioned

This is the person being complained about. Even if the complainant is alleging discrimination by a particular person such as the manager, foreman or other *employee*, the company is responsible so write the Company's name and address here.

Question 2: Give details briefly but clearly of what is being complained about. Here are some examples of the way you might do this.

(*a*) 'On 15 November 199– at about 11.30 a.m. I saw an advertisement in your shop window at 40 Fifth Street, asking for a full-time sales assistant. I went in and spoke to a Mrs Grey who told me there were no vacancies. When I telephoned later at about 3.30 p.m. and spoke to Mrs Grey she told me the vacancies were still available. I believe I was rejected on racial grounds.'

(*b*) 'On 25 July 199– I went to an Industrial Tribunal hearing as a witness for a fellow-employee who was complaining of racial discrimination. Since that time, the foreman Mr Y has harassed me by always criticising me, insulting me and giving me the dirtiest job or jobs no-one else wants to do. I believe Mr Y has been treating me in this way because I gave evidence at the tribunal hearing.' or

(*c*) 'In January of this year, a new benefit was added to the company's pension plan and any employee whose parent had worked with the company for at least 10 years was entitled to apply. I do not qualify for this new benefit and I believe very few people of my ethnic origin would qualify.'

Question 3: Unless you are sure of your law, cross out 'because' and leave this paragraph as it is.

Questions 4 and 5: There is no need to alter or add to these paragraphs.

Question 6: Our examples of the kind of questions we suggest you may ask here relate to the examples of the three situations set out in paragraph 2 above.

(*a*) 'Please state how many persons applied/were shortlisted for the post of full-time assistant.'
'What were their racial origins, qualifications, experience?'
'What criteria did you use for shortlisting/selection?'
'What were the qualifications, experience and racial origins of the successful candidate?'
'Please supply a copy of any notes made at the interviews of applicants.'
'Please state the reasons for my rejection/not being shortlisted'.
'Why did Mrs Grey tell me at first that there were no vacancies, and then later say there were?'
'Please state how many sales assistants you employ, and give their racial origins.'
'Please state how many full-time assistants you have employed since 15 November 199–; when they took up employment with you; and their racial origins.'

(*b*) 'Were there any problems between the foreman and myself before 25 July? If yes, what were they?'
'Have I complained to you on numerous occasions since 25 July about his treatment of me?'
'Please state what steps, if any, you have taken to improve the situation.'

(*c*) 'Please state how many people the company employs, and what ethnic groups are represented.'
'Please state how many employees of my racial group have parents who have worked for the company for ten years or more.'
'Please state how many persons in each ethnic group listed by you are entitled to apply for the new benefit.'
'Please explain how you justify this condition in the new benefit scheme.'
'Please supply a copy of the company's pension plan as amended by the new condition.'

> *Question 7:* Normally the representative's name and address should be entered here (otherwise cross out 'the following address', and the respondent will write to the complainant at the address given in paragraph 1). Once tribunal proceedings have started and your name as representative appears on the record, it should appear here also. Finally, *the complainant* should sign and date the form. You can post or deliver the questionnaire to the respondent. It may, however be worth sending it by registered post. This is proof of delivery. Alternatively you can send it recorded delivery and if you do not receive a reply within 21 days, for a small additional fee you can get a confirmation of delivery slip from the post office bearing the recipient's signature. You can therefore prove to the tribunal that the respondent received the questionnaire.

The CRE guidelines include a request for documentation which is not properly a function of interrogatories but is really part of the discovery process once a matter is before the industrial tribunal.

47.10 ANSWERING THE QUESTIONNAIRE

It is not possible to give direct guidance on the specifics of answering the questionnaire as this is dependent upon the questions asked. It is, however, essential to take great care in preparing answers and to ensure that any replies are accurate and can be substantiated. This will almost certainly entail taking a detailed statement from the individuals involved, prior to finalising the answers. This is particularly important if the questionnaire asks what criteria were used in an appointment or promotion. It is open to a tribunal to draw the inference that discrimination took place if the questionnaire turns out to have been incorrectly completed in any material respect. Some questions may involve an unreasonable amount of expense in providing an answer and other questions may not appear to be relevant to the complaint, but it is advisable to provide an explanation if a question is not to be answered (and the standard form has provision for this refusal).

47.11 SECOND QUESTIONNAIRE

In cases where statistical information may be in issue, for example, to rebut a defence by the employer that he has generally applied good employment practice, the applicant is at liberty to apply to the tribunal to issue a second questionnaire (*Carrington v Helix Lighting Ltd [1990] ICR 125*).

47.12 STATISTICAL INFORMATION

The industrial tribunal has no power to order discovery of statistical information that could be provided but is not, in fact, in existence. An applicant can use the questionnaire, however, to seek such statistical information (*Carrington v Helix Lighting Ltd [1990] ICR 125*). If the tribunal hearing the case takes the view that the request for such information was reasonable, then they may draw an adverse inference (including the inference that the discrimination complained of occurred) from any refusal to provide the information. Where the employer is declining to provide the information for legitimate administrative reasons, however, it is unlikely that any such inference will be drawn, and it is doubtful if it would be reasonable to draw such an inference in such circumstances.

48   Racial Group, Racial Grounds, National and Ethnic Origin

48.1   DEFINITION

Discrimination on 'racial grounds', either directly or indirectly by applying a criterion that has an adverse impact on a particular 'racial group', is unlawful by virtue of *RRA s 1*.

RRA s 3 defines 'racial grounds' and 'racial group' as follows:

' "racial grounds" means any of the following grounds, namely colour, race, nationality or ethnic or national origins;

"racial group" means a group of persons defined by reference to colour, race, nationality or ethnic or national origins, and references to a person's racial group refer to any racial group into which he falls.'

48.2   EVERYONE PROTECTED BY THE RRA

Whether black or white, an individual is protected by the *RRA*. The primary purpose of the *RRA* was, of course, to deal with unlawful discrimination exercised by the majority population against the immigrant groups who came to Britain, frequently as a result of express recruitment operations by UK concerns and with the blessing of the Government. These groups, mostly West Indian or from the Indian subcontinent, were then faced with shameful discrimination. The legislation has succeeded in eliminating the overt manifestations of this discrimination, and open 'no blacks' manifestations are, thankfully, a thing of the past. Regrettably, however, there is considerable evidence that covert prejudice is as bad as it ever was, and various studies conducted by the Policy Studies Institute and the Commission for Racial Equality (i.e. 'Black and White Britain', PSI, 1985; 'Half a Chance', CRE) indicate that discrimination on racial grounds in recruitment and promotion remains a major problem. The wording of the Act is (deliberately) universal. A surprisingly high number of white people have, in fact, used the Act, and until 1988 the highest damages awarded for injury to feelings was to three white people in Liverpool, who lost their jobs because a Nigerian company wished to employ their own nationals. This wording also has the effect of making unlawful positive action initiatives, except where permitted by the Act in a limited number of cases (see POSITIVE DISCRIMINATION (43)) (*London Borough of Lambeth v Commission for Racial Equality [1990] IRLR 231*).

48.3   'ON RACIAL GROUNDS' INCLUDES DISCRIMINATION BECAUSE OF ANOTHER'S COLOUR

'On racial grounds' encompasses *any* racial discrimination against an individual. The significance of this is that it is unlawful to discriminate against someone because of someone else's racial origins. This is illustrated by two cases, *Zarczynska v Levy [1978] IRLR 532* and *Showboat Entertainment Centre Ltd v Owens [1984] IRLR 7*. The underlying facts in both these ca
A white individual was given discriminatory instructions ('d
refused to comply with those instructions and, as a result,
EAT held, in both cases, that this was discrimination withi
Act. The finding was concisely expressed in the latter case:

227

48.4 Racial Group, Racial Grounds, National and Ethnic Origin

'*Section 1(1)(a)* covers all cases of discrimination on racial grounds whether the racial characteristics in question are those of the person treated less favourably or of some other person. The only question in each case is whether the unfavourable treatment afforded to the claimant was caused by racial considerations.' (Browne-Wilkinson J in *Showboat Entertainment Centre Ltd v Owens* [*1984*] *IRLR 7* at p 10).

48.4 COLOUR

As has been seen above (see 48.1), the Act expressly includes 'colour' within the meaning of 'racial grounds' to deal with discrimination at its most base. It is relatively unusual for cases to be brought where there have been expressly prejudicial comments made. (An example of such a case was *Alexander v Home Office* [*1988*] *IRLR 190* where Alexander, a prisoner, complained of the refusal to permit him to work in the kitchens. His prison record carried the words: 'He shows the anti-authoritarian arrogance that seems to be common in most coloured inmates'.) On the 'shop floor', however, what is sometimes referred to as 'shop floor banter' often involves racial abuse. Such abuse is frequently tolerated for a variety of obvious reasons. Employers should be aware, however, that toleration does not make such conduct lawful, and would be well advised to ensure that clear instructions are given making it plain that such language is unacceptable, and that any complaints are taken seriously and acted upon swiftly. Finally, colour has also been relevant in cases such as where a white individual has refused to obey instructions based on the colour of customers (e.g. *Showboat Entertainment Centre Ltd v Owens* [*1984*] *IRLR 7*).

48.5 RACE

'Race' has a potentially very wide meaning, and the Act has been criticised for its use of 'rubbery and elusive language' and such an 'imprecise a concept as "race" in its popular sense' (*London Borough of Ealing v Race Relations Board* [*1972*] *1 AER 105* at *115, per* Lord Simon of Glaisdale). 'Race' has been held to encompass 'Jewish', but not by argument: 'both sides accept and the tribunal accepted that "Jewish" could mean that one was a member of a race or a particular ethnic group as well as being a member of a particular religious faith' (*Seide v Gillette Industries Ltd* [*1980*] *IRLR 427*). Some commentators have suggested that 'race' carries 'a connotation of common stock'; however, the dictionary definition incorporates 'any recognisable group sharing certain characteristics', which would make it indistinguishable from 'ethnic origin'. The definition of 'race' is, however, largely redundant, given the wider 'ethnic or national origins' wording in *RRA s 3(1)*, which has been given a relatively wide interpretation.

48.6 NATIONALITY

'Nationality' was expressly included in the definition of 'racial origins' following a decision under *RRA 1968* that 'national origins' did not include 'nationality', and that discrimination solely on the grounds of nationality was outside the scope of the Act (*London Borough of Ealing v Race Relations Board* [*1972*] *1 AER 105*).

It is still a problematic area, and in *Tejani v Superintendent Registrar for the District of Peterborough* [*1986*] *IRLR 502*, the Court of Appeal held that 'nationality' did not include within its meaning 'coming from abroad', and that there had to be a racial connotation. Mr Tejani was a British national born abroad and, as was required in Peterborough of all persons born abroad, had to produce his passport prior to marriage. His complaint of discrimination failed on the basis that this was a general administrative procedure applied to all persons born abroad by the Superintendent Registrar (there was no legal requirement for him to do so) and, as there was no racial connotation (i.e. only Indian nationals etc.), it was outside the scope of the Act.

Considerable doubt has been cast on this decision, however, and it is almost certainly wrong, given that in *Orphanos v Queen Mary College* [1985] *IRLR 349* the House of Lords accepted, and agreed with, a concession that, for the purposes of the case (which concerned overseas tuition fees), the complainant belonged to three racial groups, being Cypriot, non-British and non-EEC. In his judgment, Lord Fraser states: 'I agree that Mr Orphanos belongs to each of these racial groups, and that each is a racial group as defined by *s 3(1)* (of the *RRA*) as extended by *s 3(2)*'. *Orphanos* was apparently not cited in *Tejani*, and the issue must remain unclear. The question was argued in *Tejani* in the Court of Appeal, whereas it was a concession in the House of Lords in *Orphanos*, but it was a concession that went (to some degree) to the root of the questions at issue, and these were carefully considered by the House of Lords. It is likely, therefore, that conditions or requirements that have an adverse impact on all non-UK nationals are within the scope of the Act, and that the relevant 'racial group' is 'non-British'.

48.7   ETHNIC OR NATIONAL ORIGIN: DEFINITION

Consideration of the definition of 'ethnic or national origins' will usually lead to consideration of that question by reference to 'racial group'. The question was first looked at in detail by the House of Lords in *London Borough of Ealing v Race Relations Board* [1972] *1 All ER 105*, where Lord Simon of Glaisdale employed unusually poetic language in defining 'national origins':

> '"Origin", in its ordinary sense, signifies a source, someone or something from which someone or something else has descended. "Nation" and "national", in their popular in contrast to their legal sense, are also vague terms. They do not necessarily imply statehood . . . The Scots are a nation because of Bannockburn and Flodden, Culloden and the pipes at Lucknow, because of Jenny Geddes and Flora Macdonald, because of frugal living and respect for learning, because of Robert Burns and Walter Scott. So too are the English a nation – because Norman, Angevin and Tudor monarchs forged them together, because their land is mostly sea-girt . . . By the Act of Union English and Scots lost their separate nationalities, but they have retained their separate nationhoods; and their descendants have thereby retained their separate national origins. So, again the Welsh are a nation – in the popular but not in the legal sense . . . To discriminate against Englishmen, Scots or Welsh, as such, would in my opinion, be to discriminate against them on the ground of their "national origins".'

The framework and 'test' for deciding whether a particular group constitutes an ethnic group has been set out in detail by the House of Lords in *Mandla v Dowell Lee* [1983] *IRLR 209*. In that case the House of Lords had to determine whether or not Sikhs constituted a racial (as well as religious) group. The school to which Mr Mandla wished to send his son operated a strict school uniform rule which specified school caps but did not permit turbans. Mr Mandla and his family were strict adherents to the faith, and this was a condition with which, as a matter of practice, they could not comply. Although it was accepted that there were Sikh families whose observance of their religion was such that they did not have problems with the uniform requirement, it was accepted that the rule had a disproportionate impact on Sikhs in comparison to the indigenous population (who had no problems with the school cap rule at all). Lord Fraser gave the central judgment and concluded that, whilst the word 'ethnic' conveyed a 'flavour' of race it could not, within the meaning of the Act, be defined 'in a strictly racial or biological sense', but that it had an 'extended sense to include other characteristics which may be commonly thought of as being associated with common racial origin'. Lord Fraser then defined these characteristics in detail:

'For a group to constitute an ethnic group in the sense of the 1976 Act, it must, in my opinion, regard itself, and be regarded by others, as a distinct community by virtue of certain characteristics. Some of these characteristics are essential; others are not essential but one or more will be commonly found and will help to distinguish the group from the surrounding community. The conditions which appear to me to be essential are these:-
(1) a long shared history, of which the group is conscious as distinguishing it from other groups, and the memory of which keeps it alive; (2) a cultural tradition of its own, including family and social customs and manners, often but not necessarily associated with religious observance. In addition to these two essential characteristics the following characteristics are, in my opinion, relevant; (3) either a common geographical origin, or descent from a small number of common ancestors; (4) a common language, not necessarily peculiar to the group; (5) a common literature peculiar to the group; (6) a common religion different from that of neighbouring groups or from the general community surrounding it; (7) being a minority or being an oppressed or a dominant group within a larger community, for example a conquered people (say, the inhabitants of England shortly after the Norman conquest) and their conquerors might both be ethnic groups.'

In summary:

Essential criteria: 1. Long shared and remembered history.
                    2. A distinct cultural tradition.

Indicative criteria: 1. Common ancestry.
                    2. Common language.
                    3. Common literature.
                    4. Common religion.
                    5. History as oppressor, or oppressed, group.

The House of Lords concluded that the Sikhs met these criteria and did constitute a racial group (a decision given more prominence in the newspapers of India than Britain, and possibly of greater consequence in India). Since that time, gypsies have been deemed a racial group by the Court of Appeal (*CRE v Dutton* [*1989*] *IRLR 8*), although the Court of Appeal has held that Rastafarians are not a distinct racial group (*Dawkins v Department of Environment* [*1993*] *IRLR 284*). Jewish people certainly constitute a distinct group, and it is probable that members of other distinct and closely-knit religious groups would pass 'the *Mandla* test'.

An industrial tribunal held that Mirpuries from the Kashmir region of Pakistan do not form a separate racial group for the purposes of the *RRA*, because they could not be said to have had a long shared history distinguishing them from other people from the Kashmir region (*Bhatti v Sandwell Muslims*

Organisation). Similarly, Pushtuns have been held not to be a distinct racial group under the *RRA* (*Khayum v Pakistan Muslim Centre*). Sylhetis have also been held not to be a separate racial group for the purposes of the *RRA* (*Kabir v Bangladesh Womens Association*).

48.8   A RACIAL GROUP CAN INCLUDE CONVERTS

The House of Lords, in the *Mandla* case, concluded that a convert could also legitimately be part of a racial group: 'A group . . . would be capable of including converts, for example, persons who marry into the group, and of excluding apostates. Provided a person who joins the group feels himself or herself to be a member of it, and is accepted by other members, then he is, for the purposes of the Act, a member.' Therefore, a convert to the Jewish faith is protected from discrimination against Jews (notwithstanding the fact that the Jewish racial group goes beyond religious adherence, indeed has to go beyond the simply religious, to qualify as an ethnic group).

48.9   LANGUAGE ON ITS OWN NOT ENOUGH

The EAT overruled an industrial tribunal which concluded that there were two distinct racial groups, those that spoke Welsh and those that did not (the tribunal was composed of a Welsh speaking Welshman, a non-Welsh speaking Welshman and an Englishman!). The case concerned the imposition of a Welsh language criterion by Gwynedd County Council for obtaining employment with the Council. The applicants did not speak Welsh. The EAT, by reference to *Mandla*, held that language was not one of the essential criteria, and that the two essential criteria were not met in a fashion that permitted such a division of the Welsh people. 'This concept seems to us to be as artificial as the proposition that 5,000 or so spectators at Cardiff Arms Park who are fluent in Welsh are a different group from the 45,000 or so whose command of the Welsh tongue is limited to the rendering of the Welsh national anthem'. (*Gwynedd County Council v Jones [1986] ICR 833*).

Some caution should be exercised over this decision, however, as the EAT's decision was based on the finding of fact made by the tribunal at first instance that language was the key factor. It is certainly open to argument that mother tongue Welsh speaking Welsh people form a separate racial group, and that others may become members of that group by learning the language and adopting the cultural norms. As it is, the somewhat strange situation has arisen whereby an English person can allege indirect discrimination arising out of a language requirement by Gwynedd County Council, but a non-Welsh speaking Welsh person cannot. In reality, the cause of the Welsh language would have been furthered if the EAT had upheld the tribunal decision at first instance.

48.10   MULTIPLE RACIAL GROUPS

An individual may belong to a number of racial groups. A Sikh will, for instance, be a member of the Sikh racial group, but might also be classified more broadly as of 'Indian' origin. The fact that a racial group may constitute a sub-division of a wider racial group, or be capable of further sub-division into distinct racial groups, is not material for the purposes of the *RRA*. The significant racial group will be the one against whom the alleged discrimination operates. In the example above, it might be that the employer operated a policy of not employing any people originating from the Indian subcontinent, in which event the relevant racial group is 'Indian'. Alternatively, he may operate a uniform requirement that does not permit turbans. In that event it would be the fact that the individual was a member of the Sikh racial group which would be the material factor.

48.11 RELIGION NOT ENOUGH ON ITS OWN

Discrimination on religious grounds is not, *per se*, unlawful. Religious adherence on its own is not sufficient to make an individual a member of a particular racial group with reference to the Act, although it will frequently do so. This question will only arise in indirect discrimination cases. Religious discrimination will never constitute direct discrimination, but will frequently constitute indirect discrimination because a particular religious practice will mean that a smaller proportion of a particular racial group than the host community will be able to comply with a particular criterion. Obvious examples are questions of dress with Sikhs (*Mandla v Dowell Lee [1983] IRLR 209*), dress requirements for Muslims and working hours for Jewish people; but note that in certain circumstances such discrimination can be justified on health or other grounds (*Panesar v Nestlé Co Ltd [1980] ICR 144*).

Discrimination on religious grounds is, however, prohibited in Northern Ireland by the *Fair Employment (Northern Ireland) Act 1976*. This is, however, beyond the scope of this book (see FAIR EMPLOYMENT (NORTHERN IRELAND) ACTS 1976 & 1989 (32)).

48.12 BENIGN MOTIVE NOT RELEVANT

The key test is whether the racial origin is the basis for the relevant treatment. Discrimination on racial grounds encompasses treatment that is otherwise benign, but for which the basis is the individual's racial origin. An employer will, for instance, discriminate on racial grounds if he removes an employee from a work situation in which he is suffering from racial abuse, notwithstanding that his motivation was to save the individual from further abuse. The treatment that is to the individual's detriment must have a racial basis (*Din v Carrington Viyella [1982] IRLR 281*; see also the *SDA* cases of *R v City of Birmingham Council, Ex parte EOC [1989] IRLR 173* and *James v Eastleigh Borough Council [1990] IRLR 288*). The racial origin must be the 'activating cause' (*Seide v Gillette Industries Ltd [1980] IRLR 427*), but it need not be the whole cause, just a material factor (*Owen & Briggs v James [1981] IRLR 133*).

49   Remedies

49.1   FRAMEWORK

The remedies available to an industrial tribunal are identical for both the *SDA* and the *RRA [RRA s 56; SDA s 65]* in respect of an individual complaint which is upheld. These are as follows.

(a)   An order declaring the rights of the complainant and the respondent in relation to the act to which the complaint relates. *[RRA s 56(1)(a); SDA s 65(1)(a)]*.

(b)   An order requiring the respondent to pay compensation. *[RRA s 56(1)(b); SDA s 65(1)(b)]*. There is no limit on the amount of compensation that tribunals can award in discrimination cases *[Sex Discrimination and Equal Pay (Remedies) Regulations 1993 (SI 1993 No 2798); Race Relations (Remedies) Act 1994]*.

(c)   A recommendation that the respondent take, within a set period, practical steps to eliminate or reduce the adverse effect on the complainant of any act of discrimination to which the complaint relates. *[RRA s 56(1)(c); SDA s 65(1)(c)]*.

Note. The *Disability Discrimination Act 1995* gives tribunals the power to award compensation for injury to feelings for breaches of its provisions. Awards will be made on the same basis as for breaches of the *SDA* or *RRA*, that is without any upper limit.

49.2   THE COMPENSATORY AWARD

As stated above, there is no longer a limit on the amount of compensation that can be awarded by a tribunal. Where, for example, dismissal has resulted from discrimination, this may give rise to a claim both under the *RRA* or *SDA* and under the *EPCA*. In these circumstances, there is no limit on the amount of compensation that can be awarded by the tribunal in respect of any unlawful discrimination that it finds. However, the tribunal is still bound by the present statutory limit of £11,300 in respect of compensation for any unfair dismissal that it has found.

49.3   Compensatory award in practice

The tribunal is required to decide whether or not it is 'just and equitable' to make an award of compensation *[RRA s 56(1); SDA s 65(1)]*. Once it has decided to make such an award, then the basis of its decision as to the amount of that award should be that of the damages that could be awarded in a county court at common law, and not what they consider 'just and equitable'. This means that the tribunal must assess any quantifiable loss and then make an assessment of the extent of injury to feelings (see 49.6 below). The tribunal is able to take into account the general conduct of the applicant and respondent in assessing whether or not it would be 'just and equitable' to award damages at all. However, once they have concluded that damages are awardable, their task is to assess the extent of actual loss and the extent of injury to feelings on an ordinary basis. (See *Hurley v Mustoe (No 2) [1983] ICR 422*, in which a derisory award of

50p on the basis of what was 'just and equitable' was held to be inappropriate, and an award of £100 was substituted.)

49.4 Compensation of actual loss

The industrial tribunal will compensate for any actual loss suffered by the applicant, but such loss must relate directly to its findings. In order, for instance, to obtain compensation in relation to actual loss for not being appointed to a particular position, the tribunal must be satisfied that the applicant would have actually been appointed to that position. If it is unable, on the evidence, to determine that the applicant would have been appointed, then it may only award compensation for loss of the opportunity of applying for that appointment. In assessing loss of opportunity in relation to promotion, or indeed in respect of any other matters (such as loss of any benefit), the tribunal must attempt to assess the percentage chance of success that the applicant would have had in obtaining that promotion or that benefit (*Calder v James Finlay Corporation Ltd [1989] ICR 157*). If the tribunal concludes that the applicant was dismissed because of a discriminatory reason, then they will award compensation for the loss of that position on the ordinary basis and will assess the loss of wages to the date of the application, and future loss, on a reasonable basis. In assessing the award, they must have regard to the steps the applicant has taken to mitigate his loss and his duty to mitigate his loss in the future.

49.5 No concept of contributory fault

In making an award for actual loss, the tribunal cannot reduce the award relating to a discrimination claim by any factor related to contributory fault, as it can in an unfair dismissal case. [*EPCA s 74(6)*]. In addition, the recoupment provisions in relation to unfair dismissal and other claims under the *Employment Protection (Consolidation) Act 1978, (the Employment Protection (Recoupment of Unemployment Benefit and Supplementary Benefit) Regulations 1977 (SI 1977 No 674), as amended by SI 1980 No 1608)*, which enable the State to recover any social security benefits paid from an industrial tribunal award under the *EPCA*, have no application in respect of such an award made by an industrial tribunal in a discrimination case.

49.6 Basis for compensating injury to feelings

Both the *RRA* and the *SDA* specifically state that 'for the avoidance of doubt it is hereby declared that damages in respect of an unlawful act of discrimination may include compensation for injury to feelings whether or not they include compensation under any other head'. [*RRA s 57; SDA s 66*]. The general basis for awarding damages in tort for injury to feelings was considered in such cases as *Rookes v Barnard [1964] AC 1129* and *Broome v Cassell & Co Ltd [1972] AC 1027*. The amount to award in respect of injury to feelings in discrimination cases is a difficult question, and there have been a number of cases addressing this point. All remain good authority.

The matter was first considered by the Court of Appeal in *Skyrail Oceanic Limited v Coleman [1981] ICR 864*. In that case, the Court of Appeal substituted an award of £100 for an award of £1,000 for injury to feelings (in addition to £666 actual loss) originally made by the industrial tribunal. The £1,000 award had been cut to £500 by the Employment Appeal Tribunal. The Court of Appeal held that the tribunal must compensate only for the actual injury flowing from the discrimination, and not for unrelated matters. The claim related to the dismissal of a woman because of a concern that confidential information might be passed on when her husband joined a competitor, after discussion with the competitor, on the basis that the man was the 'breadwinner'. In its judgment the Court of Appeal made it clear that it was not impressed with the claim at all. 'This was so unmeritorious a case on the facts that I deplore the encouragement given to the appellant to pursue what was at best a phantom claim'.

The question of damages has been reviewed more recently in *Alexander v The Home Office* [1988] *ICR 685*, a race relations case where a prisoner complained of racial discrimination after he had not been allowed to work in the kitchen and his prison record had discriminatory comments entered in it. He had been awarded £50 for injury to feelings by the county court at first instance after the judge concluded that the discriminatory comments meant that the plaintiff had been treated not as an individual, but as a racial stereotype, whilst in prison. However, the judge took the view that the prisoner had not suffered any substantial injury, and took into account the fact that he had been vindicated by the court. In giving the judgment of the Court of Appeal, May LJ concluded that 'on the facts and circumstances which I have outlined, the instant case was not one of the most serious', but considered that £500 would be a more appropriate figure. May LJ set out the following guidance in relation to the award of damages in such cases.

'As with any other awards of damages, the objective of an award for unlawful racial discrimination is restitution. Where the discrimination has caused actual pecuniary loss, such as the refusal of a job, then damages referrable to this can readily be calculated. For the injury to feelings, however, for the humiliation, for the insult, it is impossible to say what is restitution and the answer must depend on the experience and good sense of the judge and his assessors. Awards should not be minimal, because this would tend to trivialise or diminish respect for the public policy to which the Act gives effect. On the other hand, just because it is impossible to assess the monetary value of injured feelings, awards should be restrained. To award sums which are generally felt to be excessive does almost as much harm to the policy and the results which it seeks to achieve as do nominal awards. Further, injury to feelings, which is likely to be of a relatively short duration, is less serious than physical injury to the body or the mind which may persist for months, in many cases for life.'

In another case in the same year, *Noone v North West Thames Regional Health Authority* [1988] *IRLR 195*, the Court of Appeal, in allowing the complainant's appeal from the Employment Appeal Tribunal, substituted an award of £3,000 for injury to feelings in a case where a consultant doctor had been discriminated against in regard to a consultancy appointment (there was no actual loss). In that case, the tribunal at first instance had awarded £5,000; the EAT allowed the health authority's appeal, but would have reduced the award to £1,000. The Court of Appeal, in its judgment, canvassed the level of awards that had been made by industrial tribunals. The court noted that the individual had given evidence that she was 'quite devastated' by the extent of injury to her feelings and concluded that there was 'no doubt that she had suffered severe injury to her feelings'; it also took into account that this was not a case which involved aggravated damages (see 49.17 below).

Within this guidance, industrial tribunals must award such compensation as they think appropriate for injury to feelings. It is clear that the level of damages awarded in sexual harassment cases tends normally to be of a higher level than other sorts of cases, and in such cases awards as high as £6,000 have been made in respect of injury to feelings.

However, in another case in 1988, the Employment Appeal Tribunal held that an award of £50 made by an industrial tribunal in respect of sexual harassment was a proper award, in that the tribunal had clearly considered the extent to which it felt that the applicant had suffered injury to her feelings by virtue of the conduct about which she had complained. In that case, the EAT also held that it was not relevant to take into account evidence relating to the conduct of the applicant after the conclusion of the case in assessing damages; such evidence would not be relevant, probative or likely to have an important influence on the result of the case (*Wileman v Minilec Engineering Limited* [*1988*] *ICR 318 (EAT)*).

It would only be in the most exceptional cases that no damages at all would be awarded in respect of a case of direct discrimination (and no such cases have been dealt with on appeal). However, the actual award for damages is a matter for the industrial tribunal to assess having heard the evidence of the applicant in respect of the extent of the injury to feelings arising directly out of the discrimination of which complaint is made.

49.7   **Effect of EU law as to award of compensation and interest**

There are no longer limits on the compensatory award that can be awarded by an industrial tribunal in discrimination cases. In *Marshall v Southampton and South West Hampshire Area Health Authority (No 2)* [*1993*] *IRLR 445*, the ECJ held that the compensation limits under *SDA* were contrary to *Article 6* of the *Equal Treatment Directive*. The ECJ also held that it was contrary to *Article 6* for interest to be excluded from a compensatory award.

This decision meant that public-sector employees could rely directly on European law in sex discrimination claims to claim compensation above the then limit, although private-sector employees were not able to rely upon *Article 6* (it only has direct effect in relation to employees of public bodies). However, this decision opened the way for private-sector employees to sue the Government by way of *Francovich* claims for its failure to correctly implement European law.

Consequently, there was immense pressure on the Government to amend the *SDA* in accordance with this decision. The *Sex Discrimination and Equal Pay (Remedies) Regulations 1993 (SI 1993 No 2798)* amended the *SDA* in line with the *Marshall (No 2)* decision, with effect from 22 November 1993. These regulations relate to all awards made by tribunals after this date, not simply to acts of discrimination after this date.

The *Marshall (No 2)* decision had no effect in relation to racial discrimination. The Government's policy has always been to treat matters of sex and racial discrimination on the same basis. However, as racial discrimination is not an issue affected by the *Equal Treatment Directive*, it was necessary for primary legislation to be enacted in order to remove the compensation limits. The *Race Relations (Remedies) Act 1994*, which came into force on 3 July 1994, amended the *RRA* in exactly the same form as the amendments to the *SDA*. Therefore, from this date, tribunals were not bound by any maximum limit on the amount of the compensatory award in discrimination cases.

Since 15 May 1995, there is no limit on the amount of compensation that can be awarded for religious or political discrimination under the *Fair Employment*

(Northern Ireland) Act 1976, as a result of the *Fair Employment (Amendment) (Northern Ireland) Order 1995 (SI 1995 No 758)*.

49.8   Interest on Compensatory Award

As stated above, the ECJ in *Marshall (No 2)* held that it was contrary to European law to exclude interest on the amount of a compensatory award. The amending legislation (both in sex and racial discrimination cases) has given effect to this part of the decision, as follows:

(*a*)   Interest on awards for injury to feelings is now awarded from the date of the contravention of the statute (i.e. the act of discrimination) complained of.

(*b*)   Interest on the complainant's pecuniary loss is awarded from the mid-point of the date between the act of the discrimination complained of and the date that the amount of interest is calculated by the industrial tribunal. However, the tribunal has a discretion to calculate interest for a different period in 'exceptional circumstances' where 'serious injustice would be caused' (see below).

(*c*)   Interest after the date of the award will accrue from the day after the date that the tribunal's decision is sent to the parties, unless the award is paid in full within 14 days after this date (when no interest under this heading will accrue).

Since February 1993 the interest rate on tribunal awards has been 8 per cent.

Tribunals have been prepared to exercise their discretion under (*b*) above on a number of occasions:

In *MacDonald v Seldon*, the complainant was subjected to sexual harassment over a continuing period, culminating in her resignation. The tribunal held that interest would run from the date of the final incident of harassment.

In *Skellon v Secretary of State for Defence*, the discrimination had occurred from August 1980 to April 1983. Interest was calculated in December 1993, and on the usual basis of the rules the mid-point would have been August 1988. However, the tribunal exercised its discretion and awarded interest from the mid-point between the start and finish of the discriminatory act (which in fact increased the amount of interest awarded to the complainant by approximately £5,000).

In some of the 'Ministry of Defence' pregnancy dismissal cases, tribunals have used the 'exceptional circumstances' provisions to reduce the award of interest payable. However, the EAT in *Ministry of Defence v Cannock and Others [1994] IRLR 509* held that the interest period would only be reduced where the complainant was responsible for the delay in commencing proceedings.

49.9   Compensation in cases of indirect discrimination

The industrial tribunal is able to award compensation in respect of indirect discrimination unless the respondent *proves* that the requirement or condition in question was not applied with the intention of treating the applicant unlawfully on the grounds of his sex, marital status or race, as the case may be. [*RRA ss 56(1)(b), 57(3); SDA ss 65(1)(b), 66(3)].* It is a matter for the respondent to satisfy the industrial tribunal that there was no intention to discriminate. If the tribunal is satisfied that there was no intention to discriminate against the complainant, compensation cannot be awarded. In addition, the complainant cannot claim restitution under *SDA s 77* or *RRA s 72* (validity and revision of contracts) since such an order is outside the terms of those provisions. (*Orphanos v Queen Mary College [1985] IRLR 349 (HL)*).

Whilst compensation for unintentional indirect discrimination is not usually awardable by a tribunal, the *Marshall (No 2)* decision has been relied on by two recent industrial tribunals as justification for awarding such compensation.

In *Mulligan v Eastern Health and Social Services Board*, a Northern Ireland Industrial Tribunal held that the *Marshall (No 2)* decision applied equally to indirect discrimination as to direct discrimination, because indirect discrimination is an act prohibited by *Article 6* of the *Equal Treatment Directive*. Under *Article 6*, all people have the right to obtain an effective remedy – therefore victims of indirect discrimination are entitled to be compensated directly under *Article 6*. By using this argument, the tribunal held that the complainant was entitled to compensation directly under European law. However, this decision is not binding, and in any event the reasoning is effective only in respect of public-sector employees (*Article 6* of the *Equal Treatment Directive* only has direct effect in respect of public-sector employees).

Similarly in *Tickle v Riverview School and Surrey County Council*, the tribunal awarded the applicant £4,000 compensation even though the respondents did not intend to discriminate against her.

These decisions are not binding on subsequent tribunals. In any event, the applicants were public-sector employees. However, private-sector employees may be able to rely upon these decisions in an action against the Government under the *Francovich* principle (i.e. for the Government's failure to correctly implement European law as required).

The EAT held in the case of *London Underground Limited v Edwards [1995] IRLR 355*, that a tribunal is able to draw an inference that the discriminatory effect of a requirement was intentional where it was imposed with the knowledge of its effect.

49.10 THE DECLARATION

The power of the tribunal to make a declaration simply relates to rights of the parties in relation to the finding by the tribunal of discrimination, either direct or indirect. *[RRA s 56(1)(a); SDA s 65(1)(a)].* A county court is empowered to modify or remove any unenforceable contractual terms. *[RRA s 72; SDA s 77].* (See *Orphanos v Queen Mary College [1985] IRLR 349 (HL); Meade-Hill v The British Council [1995] IRLR 478*).

49.11 THE RECOMMENDATION

The tribunal also has the power to make 'a recommendation that the respondent take within a specified period action appearing to the tribunal to be practicable for the purpose of obviating or reducing the adverse effect on the complainant of any act of discrimination to which the complaint relates'. *[RRA s 56(1)(c); SDA s 65(1)(c)].* The primary purpose of this provision clearly relates to cases of indirect discrimination where the tribunal has identified a condition or requirement which has been applied to the detriment of the complainant, and without justification. In such cases, it may well be that the tribunal has found that the discrimination was unintentional and has not awarded compensation; therefore the recommendation will be important as being, in effect, the only remedy for the complainant.

It might be thought that this provision is equivalent to that in the *EPCA* relating to reinstatement or re-engagement following a finding of unfair dismissal [*EPCA s 69*], but it has not been treated as such by industrial tribunals. In *Noone v North West Thames Regional Health Authority (No 2)* [*1988*] *IRLR 530*, the Court of Appeal held that it was not open to an industrial tribunal to make a recommendation that a health authority should dispense with the normal requirements in relation to the appointment of consultant doctors and offer the next available post to the complainant. The Court of Appeal held that this was outside the powers of the industrial tribunal because the appointment of such consultants was regulated by a statutory instrument.

The decision in *Noone* has since been relied upon in *British Gas plc v Sharma* [*1990*] *IRLR 101* in holding that it was outside the powers of the tribunal to make such a recommendation at all. In this particular case the tribunal had not, as required by *RRA s 56(1)(c)*, specified a period in which the action should have been taken; in any event the matter was academic, as the respondent had actually taken the relevant action and promoted the complainant whilst the appeal was still pending. The EAT also considered that such a recommendation would itself be contrary to the *RRA*. It seems likely that the Employment Appeal Tribunal are wrong in this decision, and that it is within the power of an industrial tribunal to make such a specific recommendation. Such a recommendation could not be directly discriminatory, as suggested by the EAT, because a white person is as able to bring a case under the Act as a black person. This would not stop it being a matter of indirect discrimination, but it would clearly be justifiable on the basis of compliance with a tribunal order. There could be no simpler way for an employer to obviate the adverse effect of any act of discrimination when a complainant has failed to be promoted to a position than by so promoting him. It may be that in a future case, *Sharma* can be distinguished. The recommendation in *Sharma* was to appoint the complainant to the next available position rather than to the position to which the discrimination related, whereas a strict application of the wording of *RRA s 56(1)(c)* would suggest that it is only an appointment to the position to which the discrimination related that is permissible. This matter remains unresolved.

49.12 Failure to comply with the recommendation

If an employer fails without reasonable justification to comply with the recommendation made by an industrial tribunal, then if the tribunal thinks it just and equitable, it may make a further award to the applicant either by increasing any compensatory award already made or by making a compensatory award. [*RRA s 56(4); SDA s 65(4)*].

49.13 REMEDIES IN RESPECT OF ENFORCEMENT BY EOC OR CRE

Where the EOC or CRE has taken proceedings in respect of an unlawful advertisement [*RRA s 29; SDA s 38*], or instructions or pressure to discriminate [*RRA ss 30, 31; SDA ss 39, 40*], then the tribunal will, if satisfied that such is the case, make a finding that the act of discrimination complained of has occurred. [*RRA s 63; SDA s 72*]. For reasons that are not at all clear, there is no further power in respect of such proceedings for the tribunal to make an award of compensation, nor to make any recommendations (but see 49.14 below). However, the relevant Commission may take further action where a finding that a person has contravened one of the provisions referred to above has become final (i.e. any appeal against it has been dismissed, abandoned or withdrawn, or the time limit for appealing has expired without an appeal having been brought [*RRA s 78(4); SDA s 82(4)*], and the Commission takes the view that that person is likely to commit further acts of unlawful discrimination in contravention of that provision. In such a case, the Commission may apply to the county court for an injunction restraining that person from doing any such act, which the court may grant (in the terms applied for or in more limited terms) if it is satisfied that the application is well-founded. [*RRA s 63(4); SDA s 72(4)*].

49.14 Preliminary action by EOC or CRE

With a view to taking action under *SDA s 72(4)* or *RRA s 63(4)* (see 49.13 above) in relation to a person, the EOC or CRE may present to an industrial tribunal a complaint that he has done an act within its jurisdiction. If the tribunal considers the complaint to be well-founded, it will make a finding to that effect. In addition, in the case of an act contravening any provision of *SDA Part II* or *RRA Part II* (discrimination in employment), the tribunal may also, if it thinks it just and equitable to do so, make a declaration pursuant to *SDA s 65(1)(a)* or *RRA s 56(1)(a)*, or a recommendation pursuant to *SDA s 65(1)(c)* or *RRA s 56(1)(c)* (see 49.1 above), as if the complaint had been presented by the person discriminated against. [*RRA s 64(1); SDA s 73(1)*].

49.15 INVESTIGATIONS

Either the EOC or CRE may serve a non-discrimination notice upon an individual if, in the course of a formal investigation (see INVESTIGATIONS (37)), it becomes satisfied that he is committing or has committed an act of discrimination. Such a notice may require that individual not to commit any such act of discrimination; it may also require that individual to change his practices or other arrangements in order not to discriminate, to inform the Commission that he has done so, and what those changes are, and to provide the Commission with information in order to verify that the notice has been complied with. A non-discrimination notice may only be issued against any person provided that the Commission has:

(*a*)   given him notice that it is minded to issue such a non-discrimination notice, specifying the grounds;

(*b*)   offered him an opportunity to make oral or written representations within a period of not less than 28 days specified in the notice; and

(*c*)   taken into account those representations.

[*RRA s 58; SDA s 67*].

(See *R v CRE, Ex parte Hillingdon London Borough Council* [1982] *AC 779*, *CRE v Prestige Group Plc* [1984] *1 WLR 335*, and INVESTIGATIONS (37).)

49.16 RESTRICTION OF PROCEEDINGS FOR BREACH OF SDA OR RRA

Remedies in respect of the *RRA* and the *SDA* are limited to those provided by the Acts themselves, and no other proceedings are available in respect of any act that is unlawful by virtue of those Acts. [*RRA s 53(1); SDA s 62(1)*]. This restriction does not prevent any individual from making an application for judicial review against the EOC or CRE, as a public body, if it has acted unlawfully, either by doing something outside its power, or by failing to do something that it should properly do; judicial review is also available to prohibit a public body from doing something outside its powers which it is about to do. [*RRA s 53(2); SDA s 62(2)*].

49.17 AGGRAVATED DAMAGES

The Court of Appeal in *Alexander v The Home Office* [*1988*] *ICR 685*, held that aggravated and exemplary damages could be awarded in a discrimination case. Aggravated damages could be awarded (even when not pleaded, although they should be specifically pleaded – *Bradford City Metropolitan Council v Arora* [*1989*] *IRLR 442*). Aggravated damages are appropriate if 'the defendant may have behaved in a high-handed, malicious, insulting or oppressive manner in committing the act of discrimination' (*Alexander v The Home Office* (above)). Because the consideration of injury to feelings is the same as in respect of any other tort, principles relating to the award of such damages are governed by the principles set out in the common law cases such as *Rookes v Barnard* [*1964*] *AC 1129* and *Broome v Cassell & Co* [*1972*] *AC 1027*. The conduct of the proceedings themselves can lead to the award of aggravated damages (*Alexander v Home Office* [*1988*] *ICR 685*).

Aggravated damages are likely to be awarded as an additional element of the award for injury to feelings where the tribunal concludes that there is evidence that the employer has behaved in an offensive, insulting or malicious manner.

In *Patel v Leeds Metropolitan University*, the applicant was awarded £1,500 in respect of aggravated damages where a member of an interview panel had failed to disclose to the other members of the panel the fact that the applicant had a relevant qualification which the rest of the panel were clearly not aware of.

Similarly, in *Patel and Harewood v T & K Home Improvements Limited and Johnson* the applicants were each awarded £1,750 in respect of aggravated damages where the employers refused to apologise to them and had treated the presence of racially abusive material at the work place, which was insulting to the applicants, as little more than a joke.

49.18 EXEMPLARY DAMAGES

Exemplary damages cannot be awarded as damages in race or sex discrimination cases. This is a result of the decision of the EAT in *Deane v London Borough of Ealing* [*1993*] *IRLR 209*, which followed the decision of the Court of Appeal in *AB and others v South West Water Services Ltd* [*1993*] *1 All ER 609*. In the *South West Water Services* case, the Court of Appeal held that the House of Lords decision in *Rookes v Barnard* [*1964*] *AC 1129* (which decided that exemplary damages were awardable for breaches of tort) is limited to all torts that were recognised before 1964. Unless a statutory tort was recognised before the date of the decision in *Rookes v Barnard*, exemplary damages were not awardable.

Thus in *Deane v London Borough of Ealing* [*1993*] *IRLR 209*, the EAT held that exemplary damages are not awardable under *RRA*. By analogy, they are also not awardable under *SDA*. This is because the torts created by these Acts were clearly not recognised at the time of the House of Lords decision in *Rookes v Barnard*.

49.19 Remedies

At the end of 1993, a Law Commission Consultation Paper recommended that exemplary damages be retained in discrimination cases, and that they be put on a more principled basis. To date there have been no further developments on this point.

49.19 Level of Awards

In discrimination cases, compensation is awardable for any pecuniary losses suffered by the applicant, and also for injury to feeling. In the case of *Sharifi v Strathclyde Regional Council [1992] IRLR 259*, the EAT held that an award of £500 for injury to feelings is at or near the minimum level of award under this head. This decision was confirmed by the EAT in *Deane v London Borough of Ealing [1993] IRLR 209*.

Since the removal of the compensation limits, average tribunal awards have increased by 45 per cent to over £4,300. The average award for injury to feelings has increased by 42 per cent to over £1,900. Generally speaking, awards in race discrimination cases are almost double those in sex discrimination cases, and the highest awards are those in harassment cases (therefore awards in racial harassment cases are generally the highest awards granted).

In one case a black employee was awarded £34,000 in damages, which included £6,000 for injury to his feelings, and in a further case, an Asian planning officer was awarded £10,000 compensation for injury to feelings.

Aggravated damages are awarded in less than 3 per cent of cases. Where aggravated damages are awarded, the average award is over £1,100.

49.20 Religious Discrimination

At the same time as announcing its intention to remove the limits on compensation in race discrimination cases, the Government also announced that it would remove the limit on compensation awardable in cases of religious discrimination under the *Fair Employment (Northern Ireland) Act 1976*. From 16 May 1995, the limits on compensation awardable in cases of religious and political discrimination were removed, by the *Fair Employment (Amendment) (Northern Ireland) Order 1995 (SI 1995 No 758)*.

50   Service Provision

50.1   INTRODUCTION

Both the *SDA* and *RRA* contain provisions prohibiting discrimination in the provision of goods, facilities or services. [*SDA ss 29–36; RRA ss 20–27*]. The Acts provide that it is unlawful for any person who provides goods, facilities or services to the public to discriminate against a person seeking to obtain/use those goods, facilities or services:

(*a*)   by refusing or deliberately omitting to provide him with any of them [*RRA s 20(1)(a); SDA s 29(1)(a)*];

(*b*)   by refusing to provide him with goods, facilities or services of the same quality, in the same manner or on the same terms as are provided to other members of the public. [*RRA s 20(1)(b); SDA s 29(1)(b)*].

Note. The provisions of the *Disability Discrimination Act 1995* in relation to the prohibition of discrimination in service provision are somewhat different from those of the *SDA* and *RRA*, and are dealt with separately (see DISABILITY (18)).

50.2   GOODS, FACILITIES AND SERVICES

The Acts do not define what is meant by 'facilities' and 'services'. However, they do provide examples of facilities and services, including:

(*a*)   access to and use of any place which members of the public are entitled to enter [*RRA s 20(2)(a); SDA s 29(2)(a)*];

(*b*)   hotel (or other) accommodation [*RRA s 20(2)(c); SDA s 29(2)(c)*];

(*c*)   facilities for education (see EDUCATION (23));

(*d*)   facilities for entertainment, recreation or refreshment;

(*e*)   facilities for transport or travel;

(*f*)   services of a profession or trade, local or public authority.

The statutes also prohibit discrimination in the disposal or management of premises [*RRA s 21; SDA s 30*]; this covers the work done by estate agents as well as landlords and tenants. In addition it is an offence to discriminate in the assignment or subletting of rented property. [*RRA s 24; SDA s 31*].

Both *Acts* provide an exception in respect of small dwellings – where a person provides accommodation in any premises in which he or a close relative resides, discrimination is allowed. This exception is usually limited to premises where there is accommodation for only 2 households or 6 persons (in addition to the person disposing of the property).

In the *SDA* there are further exceptions in relation to the provision of goods, facilities or services. Under *SDA s 33* the prohibition on sex discrimination in *section 29* does not apply in relation to any men-only or women-only provisions in the constitution, organisation or administration of a political party. The Labour Party's policy of women-only shortlists for certain parliamentary constituencies has been referred by the EOC for counsel's opinion as to its validity in the light of the provisions of *SDA s 37*. Counsel has concluded that it comes within the protection afforded by *SDA s 33*. There is no corresponding exception in the *RRA*.

50.3   Service Provision

The *SDA* contains a similar exception with regard to the work of charities [*SDA s 34*] which is not mirrored in the *RRA*.

In respect of a hospital (or other similar establishment) or premises occupied for the purposes of a religion, sex discrimination is allowed on doctrinal grounds or where the presence of a member of the opposite sex would be likely to cause serious embarrassment. [*SDA s 35*].

Similarly, there are provisions in the *RRA* which are not mirrored in the *SDA*. Under *RRA s 25*, race discrimination by associations with over 25 members (such as trade unions and leisure clubs) is prohibited as regards the terms of admission for membership of the association. In relation to people who are already members of such associations, race discrimination is prohibited as regards access to any benefits, facilities or services, or termination of membership (or variation of terms of membership).

Under *RRA s 26*, race discrimination by certain associations is not prohibited where the main object of the association is for benefits of membership to be enjoyed by persons of a particular racial group which is not defined by reference to colour.

50.3   DISCRIMINATION RELATING TO BARRISTERS

Under *SDA s 35A* and *RRA s 26A*, discrimination relating to the offering of pupillages or tenancies is prohibited. Further, discrimination is prohibited as regards benefits, facilities or services, training opportunities, or termination. Pressure to leave the chambers or other detriment is also prohibited.

50.4   DISCRIMINATORY ADVERTISEMENTS

Under *RRA s 29* and *SDA s 38*, it is unlawful to publish advertisements which indicate (or which can be understood to indicate) an intention to discriminate on the grounds of sex or race. Only the CRE and EOC are able to prosecute such advertisements (*Cardiff Women's Aid v Hartup* [*1994*] *IRLR 390*). In relation to discriminatory advertisements in the field of the provision of goods and services, proceedings are in the county court and must be commenced within 6 months of the publication of the advertisement.

Job advertisements which discriminate against disabled persons are also unlawful, under *Disability Discrimination Act 1995, s 11*. The provisions are different than those in the *SDA* and *RRA* (see DISABILITY (18)).

50.5   CLAIMS UNDER THESE PROVISIONS

By virtue of *RRA s 59* and *SDA s 66*, claims relating to discrimination in the provision of facilities, services or other benefits are commenced in the county court. The court can award any remedy that is within the power of the High Court, including damages for injury to feelings. Claims in the county court must be commenced within 6 months of the discriminatory act complained of. [*SDA s 76; RRA s 68*].

If the individual is alleging race discrimination, and an application for assistance is made to the CRE, the time limit is automatically extended by a further 2 months to enable investigations to be carried out. [*RRA s 68(3)*]. If the CRE write to the applicant (i.e. to the individual) confirming that the application for assistance is being considered, this time limit is automatically extended by a further month. [*RRA s 66(4)*]. The CRE will usually send such a letter out as a matter of course. There are no equivalent provisions in the *SDA* or *Disability Discrimination Act*.

Note. The time limits relating to claims of discrimination in education are slightly different (see EDUCATION (23)).

50.6   **Examples of these provisions in practice**

Claims under *SDA ss 29–36* and *RRA ss 20–27* are far less common than claims for discrimination in the employment context. Nevertheless, both the CRE and EOC will assist individuals in such proceedings.

James v Eastleigh Borough Council [1990] ICR 554 – The council operated a special discount scheme for pensioners in respect of admission to its swimming pools. This was related to the state retirement age, and women could therefore take advantage of the discount scheme at 60, whilst for men the scheme only took effect when they were 65. This policy amounted to unlawful indirect discrimination contrary to *SDA s 29(1)(b)*.

Bain v Bowles [1991] IRLR 356 – The plaintiff, who lived in Italy, sought to place an advertisement in the defendants' magazine for a housekeeper/cook. The defendants had a policy that advertisements for employees outside the United Kingdom would only be accepted where the employer was a woman and resident in the household concerned. This policy had been developed to deal with a problem in the past of sexual harassment and molestation of girls who had responded to advertisements. The Court of Appeal held that this was unlawful direct discrimination contrary to *section 29* of the *SDA*. It was direct discrimination because if the plaintiff had been a woman, he would have been able to place his advertisement.

McConomy v Croft Inns Ltd [1992] IRLR 561 – The plaintiff was ejected from the defendant's pub because he was wearing earrings contrary to the defendant's dress code. This amounted to unlawful direct discrimination contrary to the *Sex Discrimination (Northern Ireland) Order 1976* (whose provisions are identical to those of the *SDA*).

In *Fox v Proprietors of the Tudor Rose Hotel*, a county court awarded a newly married couple £4,000 damages each when they were refused a honeymoon suite in a hotel. Mr Fox, who was of Afro-Caribbean origin, was treated in a hostile manner by the proprietor from the moment he went to the hotel reception.

In *Jensen v Fellowship of the Services*, Mr Jensen, who was white and of Danish origin, was refused membership of the Fellowship even though he had fought in the Royal Armed Corps for 6 years during World War Two. The Fellowship settled his claim, paying £1,000 compensation to Mr Jensen, and removed from its Articles a clause that required British parentage for all its members.

In *Rowe v Moben Kitchens*, Mrs Rowe (a widow) made an appointment for advice on refurbishing her kitchen, and was questioned about her marital status and about whether her husband would be present at the consultation. A male friend of Mrs Rowe then contacted Moben Kitchens and asked for a similar appointment, but was not asked if his spouse would be present. He was told that it was company policy to question female customers in this way. The EOC backed Mrs Rowe's case, and Moben Kitchens settled her claim and also agreed to remind all managers and agents of their responsibilities under the *SDA*.

51   Sexual Orientation

51.1   Surprisingly, homosexuals, lesbians and transsexuals ('gay' individuals) are not protected by any special legislation. They are not protected by the *SDA* either unless they can show that their treatment was motivated by a prejudice against, in the case of a man, his homosexuality, which would not have been shown against an equivalent lesbian woman, and vice versa. This proposition has not been tested on appeal, but two women won a case of sexual discrimination at the industrial tribunal after being subjected to a lesbian assault by their supervisor. The tribunal found that there was no evidence that the harasser would have treated men in the same way and that there was therefore a difference on the grounds of sex (*Johnson & Garbutt v Gateway Food Markets (1990) No. 5, EOR Law Digest*). Although this is the converse of being dismissed because of being a lesbian, the principle is the same in terms of the application of the *SDA*. In such circumstances, the sex of the individual will be the key ingredient as to the prejudice. The complainant must be able to show that a man would have been treated differently from a woman or vice versa. Otherwise the prejudice is motivated by the complainant's sexuality, not his sex, and this is not something within the compass of the *SDA*.

The *Criminal Justice and Public Order Act 1994* introduced a new *section 4A* to the *Public Order Act 1986*, creating a criminal offence of intentional harassment. This is expressed in wide terms, and covers harassment of homosexuals. However, homosexuals and transsexuals are still not protected against discrimination under any specific legislation within the employment context. The EU Code of Practice on protecting the dignity of women and men at work (see Appendix 2) covers sexuality but has no legal force.

51.2   DISMISSING AN EMPLOYEE ON THE BASIS OF SEXUAL PREFERENCES

There have been a number of cases where employers of individuals with the care of children have dismissed them after they have been found guilty of offences of gross indecency (homosexual practice in a public lavatory or similar acts) (i.e. *Wiseman v Salford City Council [1981] IRLR 202*, where a drama teacher of 16- to 19-year olds was dismissed after a public lavatory offence). It is, however, always for the employer to assess, on a proper and reasonable basis, the extent of the risk that he perceives arises out of this. Employers are required to conduct a fair procedure and come to reasonable conclusions as to both findings of fact and penalty (*British Home Stores Ltd v Burchell [1978] IRLR 379; Polkey v A E Dayton Services Ltd [1987] IRLR 503*). Therefore, in the event that an employer has discovered that an employee is a homosexual and considers it undesirable that he should continue in employment, the employer should follow the procedure outlined below:

(*a*)   Arrange a disciplinary hearing and, beforehand, set out in detail the reasons which it is considered make it unsuitable for him to continue in employment.

(*b*)   Hold that disciplinary hearing and give the employee every opportunity to argue his case either in relation to the question of his homosexuality or as to its detrimental effect on the performance of his duties.

(*c*)   Consider reasonably what the proper penalty should be and whether it is really necessary to dismiss the individual in such circumstances.

It is difficult to understand the rationale behind some of the arguments in these matters. There seems no particular reason why a homosexual male is any more dangerous to 16- to 19-year old boys than a heterosexual male is to 16- to 19-year old girls. However, as the EAT pointed out (*Wiseman v Salford City Council [1981] IRLR 202*), it is a matter for the tribunal at first instance to decide whether or not the employer has been reasonable in all the circumstances. Tribunals have held comparable dismissals to be fair where an employer has taken an adverse view of an individual's, otherwise lawful, heterosexual activities. (See *Whitlow v Alkanet Construction Limited [1975] IRLR 321* where an employee had sex with the wife of the chief executive at her invitation and was dismissed as a result, and the dismissal was found to be fair.)

Note. Employees are only guaranteed to be protected against unfair dismissal once they have two years' service, as the situation regarding the qualifying periods is still unresolved – *R v Secretary of State for Employment, Ex parte Seymour-Smith and Perez [1995] IRLR 464* (which is likely to proceed to the House of Lords) (see DISMISSAL (21) para 21.2). For employees with less than two years' service, there is no statutory obligation on the employer to behave fairly. A dismissed individual would only be able to sue for wrongful dismissal in respect of his contractual rights in relation to the notice period to which he was entitled. However, if his contract also contained provision for disciplinary proceedings, he might also be able to obtain damages in respect of the period which would have been required to implement those.

51.3 CONSTRUCTIVE DISMISSAL

An employer is always under a duty to provide a safe system of work and if he fails to do so then the employee can claim constructive dismissal. An employer is also under a duty to provide basic support (see *Turner v Vestric Ltd [1981] IRLR 23*). If a homosexual was employed by the company and he was subjected to unreasonable ridicule by his colleagues to the extent that he felt it intolerable to continue in that employment then, provided that he had reported his complaints to the management, naming the individuals involved, and no action had been taken to prevent the conduct complained of, on repetition of the events he would be able to claim damages for constructive dismissal.

The principles in relation to this are set out clearly in a case involving disability (*T J McCabe v Chicpack Limited [1976] IRLR 38*). This case involved an individual who had a number of disabilities and was subjected to ridicule by his work colleagues. However, although he complained about this behaviour, he was unwilling to name the perpetrators so it was not possible to take individual disciplinary action. The conduct continued and he eventually resigned. The tribunal held that he was not entitled to claim constructive dismissal, having failed to name the relevant employees so as to enable the company to take the relevant action. The tribunal did hold that an employee is entitled to ask his employer to maintain discipline in the workforce, to ensure that staff are not baited and to do what he can in the circumstances to prevent such action. This was only an industrial tribunal decision but the basic principles involved have been upheld in subsequent sex discrimination cases in the Employment Appeal Tribunal such as *Balgobin and Francis v London Borough of Tower Hamlets [1987] IRLR 401*.

51.4 Sexual Orientation

51.4 DISMISSALS RESULTING FROM PRESSURE FROM OTHER WORKERS

In some cases, an employer may wish to dismiss an individual on account of the disruptive effect of his employment on other workers because of prejudice in relation to his sexuality or a matter related to that sexuality. It is unlawful to dismiss any such person as a result of racial or sexual prejudice shown by the workforce but, subject to the overall reasonableness, it may not be unfair to dismiss an employee where his work colleagues are opposed to his sexuality, personal behaviour or some related factor and this could constitute 'some other substantial reason' pursuant to *EPCA s 57*. What the tribunal must assess is whether 'the employer acted reasonably or unreasonably in treating it as a sufficient reason for dismissing the employee; and that question shall be determined in accordance with equity and the substantial merits of the case'. [*EPCA s 57(3)*]. In some circumstances, if the entire production of the company has come to a halt then dismissal may well be reasonable. However, many tribunals would expect the employer to try to use other methods of resolving the matter and educating the workforce.

51.5 AIDS

There is no formal prohibition on preventing an employer from declining to employ any individual with AIDS or indeed for adopting an AIDS test as part of the general medical screening for employment, subject to the universal application of the test to men and women. Questions of dismissal are the same as those set out above. In some circumstances, it might be reasonable to dismiss somebody with AIDS, but in many other circumstances it would not be.

It is possible that an individual could mount a claim of indirect discrimination on grounds of sex in relation to a dismissal or failure to appoint relating to AIDS. It is a statistical fact that more men than women suffer from AIDS and are HIV-positive. In such a circumstance it would then be for the employer to justify the dismissal (see INDIRECT DISCRIMINATION (33)). No such case has yet been taken up, but the Terrence Higgins Trust, a trust created to look after the interest of individuals who suffer from AIDS, has, over a period, been taking an intense interest in the employment situation of persons with AIDS and it may be that they will sponsor such a case in due course. In this regard, a matter employers may also wish to take into consideration is the fact that any such circumstances are likely to be of considerable interest to the media and possibly lead to adverse publicity. There is no requirement to be employed for a certain period for claims under the *SDA* as against the two-year length of service rule for claims of unfair or constructive dismissal. *Note*: the effect of the Court of Appeal decision in the *Seymour-Smith and Perez* case is as yet unclear (see DISMISSAL (21)).

In July 1992, the National Aids Trust launched a Charter ('Companies Act!') encouraging employers to introduce non-discriminatory practices in relation to employees and potential employees with HIV and AIDS. The signatories to the Charter include Marks & Spencer, Midland Bank, National Westminster Bank, Sainsburys and IBM.

51.6 SUMMARY: PROTECTING STAFF FROM DISCRIMINATION ON THE GROUNDS OF THEIR SEXUALITY

There is nothing to prevent an employer from introducing into his disciplinary code rules that prohibit discrimination against fellow employees on the grounds of their sexuality or related reasons. Many employers also include a promise not to discriminate on such grounds within their equal opportunity policy. As there is no legal provision in relation to sexuality there is no legislative framework around such matters. If there is such a provision in the disciplinary code and a member of staff does harass an individual on the basis of his sexuality, then, provided that proper disciplinary proceedings are taken against them and the harassment is sufficiently serious to warrant dismissal, that dismissal will be fair in the normal way (*British Home Stores Ltd v Burchell [1978] IRLR 379*).

52   Trade Unions and Employers' Organisations

52.1   SCOPE

Both the *RRA* and the *SDA* make it unlawful for a trade union or employers' organisation to discriminate in the terms on which it accepts members, or in the service that it provides for those members. [*SDA s 12; RRA s 11*].

52.2   TERMS OF ENTRY

A trade union or employers' organisation must not discriminate against a person on grounds of sex, or on racial grounds, in respect of membership of the organisation

(*a*)   by refusing, or deliberately omitting to accept, his application for membership; or

(*b*)   in the terms on which it is prepared to admit him to membership (for instance, by refusing to allow a woman to use club premises associated with the trade union).

52.3   MEMBERSHIP TERMS

It is also unlawful for a trade union or employers' organisation to discriminate, on grounds of sex, or on racial grounds, against a member of the union or organisation

(*a*)   in the way it gives the member access to membership benefits; or

(*b*)   by refusing or deliberately omitting to allow him access to those benefits; or

(*c*)   by depriving the member of membership or varying the terms on which he is a member; or

(*d*)   by subjecting the member to any other detriment.

There have been two instances where trade unions have been taken to an industrial tribunal in respect of membership rights and where the matter has been appealed (*Furniture, Timber and Allied Trades Union v Modgill* [*1980*] *IRLR 142* and *Weaver v National Association of Teachers in Further and Higher Education* [*1988*] *ICR 599*). The issue in both cases was broadly similar, in that in each case, the complaint was that the union had failed to provide proper representation in respect of allegations of discrimination, and had thereby discriminated against the individual. In *Weaver*, the trade union expressly pleaded the fact that it did not take up any case which endangered the livelihood of a member, neither did it wish to be involved on both sides of a dispute. The industrial tribunal at first instance had held that this was indirectly discriminatory, but justifiable. The EAT held that the tribunal's conclusion was not unreasonable and was a conclusion which, on the particular facts, the tribunal was entitled to come to; it was a matter of fact for the tribunal on each occasion.

The implication of this decision is that there may be occasions on which a tribunal would find that it was not justifiable to operate such a policy. Most trade unions do in fact represent individuals complaining of racial discrimination, and there is a trend for them not to represent the alleged discriminator. There is clearly a problem for trade unions in relation to these matters; at the very least, they should try to ensure that if they are going to represent both sides, then there should be different individuals involved.

The Rail Union RMT was investigated by the CRE in 1993 for allegedly discriminatory practices and procedures, where 8 Asian guards had unsuccessfully applied for places on a drivers' course but were not assisted by the union. In the light of this investigation RMT agreed to alter its practices and procedures, including the introduction of monitoring the ethnic origins of its officials and members and acting to deal with any under-representations found; producing a guidance book on equal opportunities; training officials in tackling race discrimination and setting up an ethnic minority advisory committee. The National Black/Ethnic Minority Advisory Committee has been established within RMT.

52.4   CRE CODE OF PRACTICE

The Code of Practice issued by the CRE, which came into force in 1984 (by virtue of *SI 1983 No 1081*), gives specific guidance in respect of the responsibilities of trade unions. The Code urges that trade unions should make unlawful discrimination a disciplinary offence. It also deals with steps that a trade union can take with regard to positive action. A trade union is allowed to encourage or provide training for members of particular racial groups that have been under-represented in trade union membership or in trade union posts. [*RRA s 38(3)–(5)*]. The Code recommends that there should be special recruitment campaigns for black staff (permissible by virtue of *section 38*), and provision of training and information regarding the *RRA* to officers, shop stewards and members alike. It also urges trade unions to co-operate actively in relation to equal opportunity policy development by employers.

52.5   PRESSURE BY TRADE UNIONS

Regrettably, there have been a number of instances where trade unions have in fact been involved in pressurising managements to discriminate. For example, the CRE served a non-discrimination notice on the union branch chairman of the Transport and General Workers' Union at Westminster City Council after the CRE had investigated the refusal of Westminster City Council to employ any black dustmen. The investigation concluded that this resulted from pressure from the white workforce through the trade union. Westminster City Council unsuccessfully appealed against the non-discrimination notice which had also been served against them (*R v CRE, Ex parte Westminster City Council* [*1985*] *ICR 827*).

There have been other such cases, for example in relation to pre-entry closed shops. These are now illegal (by virtue of the *Employment Act 1990*). Previously, such a pre-entry closed shop could constitute indirect discrimination if it could be found to have a disproportionate effect on women or ethnic minorities. However, a policy whereby an employer makes an informal approach to the trade union about appointees would not be discriminatory on an indirect basis, because it would not be an absolute bar (*Perera v Civil Service Commission and the Department of Customs & Excise (No 2)* [*1983*] *ICR 428*).

52.6   TRADE UNION PRACTICE

Nearly all national trade unions have passed equal opportunity resolutions in relation to both race and sex at their national conferences, and are committed by way of policy resolutions to the implementation of equal opportunity policies and the negotiation of such policies with employers. Regrettably, the reality of that rhetoric is rarely applied at the factory floor level. Employers who wish to implement equal opportunity policies and are faced with local opposition from the trade union branch may well wish to consider involving the national officials of that union, who will then assist in persuading the local branch to comply with national union policy.

52.7   ENFORCEMENT

If a member wishes to take proceedings against a trade union for failing to admit him into membership, or for discrimination in relation to the terms of that membership or the benefits offered, the same procedure applies as in cases of discrimination in employment. Thus, he must take action within three months of the date on which the act of discrimination occurred, by entering an originating application in the industrial tribunal setting out his complaint and naming the trade union involved. As well as or instead of awarding compensation, the tribunal can make a recommendation as to action by the respondent and declare the rights of the parties (see REMEDIES (49)). The burden of proof is upon the complainant in the same way as in a case relating to discrimination in employment (see BURDEN OF PROOF (6)). A trade union member may serve a *RRA* or a *SDA* questionnaire against a union in the same way as he may against an employer (see QUESTIONNAIRE PROCEDURE (47)). A trade union against which a complaint is brought must enter a notice of appearance within 14 days unless granted an extension by the industrial tribunal, and the rules in relation to the conduct of the case are identical to those applying in relation to a case relating to discrimination in employment.

Section 32 of *TURERA 1993* introduced into the *SDA 1986* the right for individuals to challenge the terms of collective agreements that are sexually discriminatory. This action is done by an application to an industrial tribunal, but is not limited to employees, as people who 'are genuinely and actively seeking to become employees' are also able to present the application. If the tribunal finds the complaint to be well founded, it will make an order declaring the term to be void. One area where this new right could be used is in the use of a policy of 'last in first out' for redundancy selection. This is because such a policy may often have an adverse impact on female employees; if it cannot be objectively justified on grounds unrelated to sex, then it may be unlawfully discriminatory.

52.8   TRADE UNION COMMISSIONER

Since the *Employment Act 1988* there has been a trade union ombudsman (the Commissioner for the Rights of Trade Union Members) who has the power to assist trade unionists with the taking of proceedings in respect of the abuse of power by trade unions. It would appear that the Commissioner cannot assist trade union members in cases relating to the *RRA* or *SDA*, except where a member is complaining about the union's failure to provide representation or assistance in relation to such a complaint against his employer.

53   Tribunals

53.1   INTRODUCTION

All claims relating to the employment field must be made in the industrial tribunal. [*SDA s 63; RRA s 54; Disability Discrimination Act s 8*]. Claims which relate to discrimination falling outside the employment field (i.e. in relation to the provision of services, housing and the like) are made in the county court. [*SDA s 66; RRA s 57; Disability Discrimination Act s 16*].

Industrial tribunals hear applications in respect of the following:

(*a*)   claims under the *Race Relations Act 1976* against employers, trade unions, qualifying bodies, employment agencies and partnerships;

(*b*)   claims under the *Sex Discrimination Act 1975* against employers, trade unions, qualifying bodies, employment agencies and partnerships;

(*c*)   claims under the *Disability Discrimination Act 1995* against employers;

(*d*)   claims under the *Equal Pay Act 1970*;

(*e*)   direct enforcement of the Treaty of Rome;

(*f*)   proceedings by the CRE or EOC in respect of discriminatory advertisements, or pressure or instructions to discriminate;

(*g*)   appeals against non-discrimination notices served by the EOC or CRE;

(*h*)   unfair dismissal claims under the *Employment Protection (Consolidation) Act 1978*; and

(*i*)   claims arising from employment and related contracts, as a result of the *Industrial Tribunals Extension of Jurisdiction (England and Wales) Order 1994 (SI 1994 No 1623)*;

An industrial tribunal also has jurisdiction in respect of the *Wages Act 1986*, various aspects of the *Health and Safety at Work etc. Act 1974* and certain other matters outside the scope of this book.

Although industrial tribunal procedure is more informal than that of the county court or High Court, it is still an inferior court within the Rules of the Supreme Court. This means that superior courts, such as the High Court, have the power to intervene and rule on any breaches of procedure. For example, in *Peach Grey & Co v Sommers, [1995] IRLR 363*, the High Court had jurisdiction to punish an applicant (who had sought to persuade a witness to withdraw his evidence) for contempt of an industrial tribunal. The applicant was imprisoned for one month.

53.2   OUTLINE OF PROCEDURE

In outline, the sequence of events in the tribunal is as follows:

(1)   The applicant submits an Originating Application (Form IT1) to the Central Office of the Industrial Tribunals in Bury St. Edmunds.

(2)   The tribunal gives the application a case number and sends it to the appropriate regional office, which then sends a copy to the named respondent.

(3)   The respondent replies with a Notice of Appearance (Form IT3).

(4)   Either party may apply to the other party for discovery of documents or may seek further particulars of the Originating Application or Notice of Appearance. If these are not forthcoming, that party may seek an order from the tribunal for discovery or for further particulars. Such an order may be given without a hearing, but either side may apply to have the order varied or set aside.

(5)   Either party, or the tribunal on its own initiative, may order a pre-hearing review to determine the strength of each party's case. Following this, the tribunal will then determine whether to order the payment of a deposit by either party as a pre-condition for continuing with the proceedings. (See 53.15 below).

(6)   Either party, or the tribunal on its own initiative, may require a party to provide a written answer to any question if the answer may help to clarify any relevant issue, and the progress of the proceedings would be helped by the answer being available before the full hearing. (See 53.16 below).

(7)   The tribunal will send out a notice of hearing date. This must be at least 14 days prior to the hearing. Either party can apply to have the matter postponed.

(8)   The hearing will take place. If the respondent failed to submit a Notice of Appearance, he will not be allowed to take part except with the leave of the tribunal.

(9)   The tribunal will either give an immediate decision or, as is much more likely in a discrimination case, reserve its decision and send it to the parties by post at a later date (usually in about six weeks). A decision given orally will be confirmed in writing. The written decision is dated and the time for appeal is taken from that date.

(10)   Either party may ask for a review of the decision within 14 days of its being sent to him. A review should be on the ground that some new fact has come to light (not previously known or available), that a mistake has been made by the tribunal's staff, that the decision was made in the absence of a person entitled to be heard (i.e. a party failing to get a Notice of Hearing) or in the interests of justice.

Each of the matters outlined above is dealt with in detail in this chapter (except discovery, inspection and further particulars, which are dealt with in DISCOVERY (19)). At the end of this chapter are two checklists, which provide guidance for the applicant and respondent respectively, in relation to tribunal procedure.

The procedure in relation to applications before industrial tribunals in England and Wales is governed by the *Industrial Tribunals (Constitution and Rules of Procedure) Regulations 1993 (SI 1993 No 2687)* (the 'IT Regs'). The Rules are set out in Schedule 1 to the Regulations. There are complementary rules relating to equal value claims which are set out in Schedule 2 to the Regulations (see 53.35 below).

53.3   SUBMISSION OF FORM IT1

The originating application to the tribunal should be on the specified form, known as Form IT1. An outline Originating Application is included in the applicant's checklist at the end of this chapter. These are available from Jobcentres, from most Citizens' Advice Bureaux and from the industrial tribunal itself. If the form is not used, that does not matter so long as the letter to the central office of the tribunal contains:

(*a*)   the name and address of the applicant;

(*b*)   the name and address of the company or person against which or whom relief is sought; and

(*c*)   the grounds of the complaint.

[*IT Regs, Rule 1(1)*].

The theory which underpins the tribunal system is that it should be open to the layman without the legal formality of the normal judicial process. As a result (and however unrealistic this may be in discrimination cases), the requirements of the Originating Application are minimal. The grounds do not have to be set out in any great detail, but must make clear, in general terms, the nature of the complaint. There is no requirement to 'plead' the particulars of the legislation relied upon (*Smith v Automobile Proprietary Ltd [1973] ICR 306; Dodd v British Telecommunications plc [1988] ICR 116*). A respondent can always seek an order for further particulars from an applicant if this is appropriate. Individuals are best advised, however, to use the approved form and complete it with great care. The evidential detail of the complaint does not have to be set out (indeed should not be) but the key events which gave rise to the complaint, and key background details, should be set out.

53.4   Specific legislation need not be pleaded

As long as the body of the Originating Application includes a discernable complaint of discrimination on grounds of sex, and/or of race, and/or unfair dismissal, it will not matter that the Application fails to name the *EPCA, RRA, Disability Discrimination Act* or *SDA* as the legislation relied upon (*Home Office v Bose [1979] ICR 481*).

53.5   Individual discriminator may be named as well as the employer

The *RRA* and *SDA* both provide for the liability of individuals for acts done in the course of their employment [*SDA s 42(2); RRA s 33(2)*], even if the employer is able to escape vicarious liability for the act of discrimination. In a case of harassment, therefore, it is particularly important that the applicant names the individual discriminator as a respondent, as well as the employer, in case the employer is able to rely on the defence to vicarious liability that he took reasonable steps to prevent the act of discrimination taking place. [*SDA s 41(3); RRA s 32(3)*].

53.6   QUALIFICATION AND TIME LIMITS

Sex and race discrimination

There is no qualification period of employment to enable an individual to make a complaint of race or sex discrimination. Thus, an individual can complain to a tribunal about failure to be considered for a position or promotion, or of dismissal, regardless of the length of time employed or hours per week worked. The time limit for commencing tribunal cases in the employment field is universally, for individual complaints, three months from when the act complained of was done. [*SDA s 76; RRA s 68*]. The tribunal does, however, have a discretion to allow a complaint 'out of time' if it considers it 'just and equitable' to do so. [*SDA s 76(5); RRA s 68(6)*]. This is essentially a matter of absolute discretion for the industrial tribunal who can weigh up any factor they reasonably consider relevant, including the underlying merits of the case, the availability of appropriate advice and the speed with which the applicant acted when he became aware that he might have a time limit problem. Unless it can be shown that the tribunal took into account some extraneous factor or could not have reasonably arrived at the decision made, which is unlikely, an appeal against a tribunal decision on this point will not succeed (*Hutchinson v Westward Television Ltd [1977] ICR 279*).

Problems can arise over the relevant date for a promotion or appointment. Strictly, the time limit should run from the date of the decision on the promotion or appointment itself. Frequently, an individual will not be told the decision for some time afterwards and tribunals have, as a matter of practice, viewed the date the decision was communicated to the individual as the date of the 'relevant act'. In dismissal cases, it is the date of the dismissal itself, (rather than the date on which notice of dismissal was given) which is the relevant date (*Lupetti v Wrens Old House Ltd [1984] ICR 348*).

In *Swithland Motors plc v Clarke and Others [1994] IRLR 275*, in circumstances where a car dealership went into receivership, a prospective purchaser (Swithland) interviewed 4 of the existing employees to determine whether they would be taken on. Almost immediately following the interviews, it was decided that they would not be taken on. However, Swithland prevented the receivers from relaying this information on to the employees until the date of the purchase. The employees believed that they were not taken on because of Swithland's policy of only employing female employees. They presented sex discrimination complaints to a tribunal within 3 months of the date of dismissal by the receiver, but more than 3 months from Swithland's decision not to employ them. An industrial tribunal held that the applications were made out of time, as the employees' cause of action arose at the date of the decision not to offer them employment (i.e. almost immediately following their interviews), but that nevertheless it would be just and equitable to entertain the complaints. The EAT overruled the industrial tribunal's construction and held that a deliberate omission to offer employment does not take place until the employer is in a position to offer such employment (i.e. the date of the transfer).

Disability

In respect of claims for unlawful discrimination on the grounds of disability, the *Disability Discrimination Act 1995* imposes a 3-month time limit on claims, together with jurisdiction for tribunals to hear claims brought outside this 3-month time limit where it is just and equitable to do so (*Disability Discrimination Act 1995, 3 Sch 3*). Where the act of discrimination is continuing, as with race and sex discrimination, the 3-month time limit does not begin to run until the end of the act complained of.

53.7   Continuing discrimination

Both the *SDA* and *RRA* provide that 'any act extending over a period shall be treated as done at the end of that period'. [*SDA s 76(6)(b); RRA s 68(7)(b)*]. Any continuing rule which is discriminatory will constitute a continuing act of discrimination, for example, a rule that women are not eligible for mortgage relief in a company benefit scheme (*Calder v James Finlay Corporation [1989] ICR 157*), or a rule that overseas service in a particular country does not count towards pension entitlement (*Barclays Bank v Kapur [1991] IRLR 136*). However, a single act of discrimination with continuing consequences does not constitute continuing discrimination. An example of an act of discrimination with continuing consequences would be the decision not to promote an individual on discriminatory grounds. Whilst the consequence of this runs on, the act itself would only continue if there was a standing rule not to promote women or ethnic minorities, as the case may be (*Amies v Inner London Education Authority [1977] ICR 308*). An individual may choose to rely on a past act of discrimination to show that a later act, say a dismissal, was discriminatory because it was reliant on that earlier discriminatory act (*Yaseen v Strathclyde Regional Council and another (1991) unreported*).

53.8 Equal pay

For an individual to be able to make a claim for equal pay, he must actually have been employed by the employer; a job offer is not enough. There is no time limit on making a claim whilst the employment subsists, but once it has ceased, any claim must be referred to the tribunal within six months of the employment coming to an end. [*EqPA s 2(4)*]. In *British Railways Board v Paul [1988] IRLR 20*, it was suggested that the time limit under *EqPA s 2(4)* applies only to a reference to the tribunal by the Secretary of State under *EqPA s 2(2)*, and not to an application to the tribunal by an ex-employee under *EqPA s 2(1)*, or by an employer under *EqPA s 2(1A)* (see 29.21 EQUAL PAY), although there is some doubt as to whether this view is correct. A tribunal cannot award back-pay beyond two years before the date of the complaint, which provides an effective two-year time period for bringing proceedings. [*EqPA s 2(5)*]. In relation to claims made under European Community law, if there is no time limit specified in the legislation, domestic time limits will apply unless it can be shown that they are less favourable than claims of a similar nature under domestic law (*Biggs v Somerset County Council [1995] IRLR 452*).

53.9 Unfair dismissal

In a claim of unfair dismissal pursuant to the *EPCA*, the time limit is three months from the effective date of dismissal. The time limit is stricter than in a race or sex discrimination claim as the rule is that a late claim will only be allowed if it was not 'reasonably practicable' for the applicant to submit a claim on time, and that the claim was submitted as soon after the expiry of the time limit as was reasonably practicable. This means that on occasion, a tribunal might permit the race or sex discrimination element of a 'mixed jurisdiction' claim to be heard on the grounds that it was just and equitable to do so, but not permit the ordinary unfair dismissal claim to go forward because it would have been reasonably practicable to present the claim in time.

53.10 CRE and EOC enforcement proceedings

The EOC and CRE have six months in which to commence proceedings in respect of pressure or instructions to discriminate and against discriminatory advertisements. [*SDA ss 38–40, 72, 73, 76(3)(4); RRA ss 29–31, 63, 64, 68(4)(5)*]. An appeal to a tribunal against a non-discrimination notice issued by one of the Commissions must be made within six weeks of the service of the notice. [*SDA s 68(1); RRA s 59(1)*].

53.11 NOTICE OF APPEARANCE

After an Originating Application setting out a complaint has been received by the tribunal, it will 'forthwith' send a copy to the named respondent (there is no set time in which they must do this, but it is generally done quickly). The respondent has 14 days after receiving the copy Originating Application in which to reply. Such a reply (known as a Notice of Appearance) must set out:

(*a*)   his full name and address;

(*b*)   whether or not the claim is resisted; and

(*c*)   if so, the grounds on which it is resisted.

[*IT Regs, Rule 3(1)*].

The tribunal will send the specified Notice of Appearance form (IT3) with the copy of the Originating Application setting out the complaint. The employer need not use that form but should ensure that the points above are covered. It is usually preferable to use the form. An outline Notice of Appearance is set out in the respondent's checklist at the end of this chapter.

53.12 Time limit for completion

The time limit for returning the Notice of Appearance is 14 days, as mentioned above. In reality, the tribunal recognises that this is frequently insufficient. If an IT3 is received 'out of time' it is deemed to include an application under *Rule 15(1)* to extend the time in which to provide the notice [*Rule 3(3)*]. If the IT3 is only a matter of days late, the current practice appears to be that the tribunal will validate it of its own volition. Should the IT3 be submitted very late, it ought to be accompanied by a formal application for an extension and an explanation for the delay. If an employer writes prior to the expiration (or shortly after) and asks for a fixed period extension, the current practice of the tribunal appears to be to grant that extension. This contrasts sharply with the treatment of 'out of time' originating applications but this is because the tribunal rules provide a wide discretion whereas the time limit for the Originating Application is set by statute.

As a standard precaution, an employer would be well advised to seek extra time from the tribunal in which to enter the Notice of Appearance in a discrimination claim. It is very important to complete a thorough internal investigation into the allegations prior to completing the Notice. It is inadvisable to have to seek to amend the application at a later stage, although it is possible to do so with the leave of the tribunal.

If a Notice of Appearance is not submitted, the respondent will not be permitted to take part in the proceedings, except to ask for leave to enter a late Notice, for further particulars, or for discovery, or be a witness, be sent a copy of the decision or ask for a review of the tribunal's decision. The tribunal hears proceedings in public [*Rule 8(2)*] and so he can attend but not take part.

53.13 INTERIM APPLICATIONS

Either party may make an interim application for:

(*a*)   the tribunal to determine whether it has jurisdiction to hear the claim;

(*b*)   a pre-hearing review;

(*c*)   inspection and discovery of documents;

(*d*)   further particulars of the Originating Application or Notice of Appearance; or

(*e*)   witness orders.

53.14 Jurisdiction

The tribunal may have an interim hearing to consider the question of jurisdiction (for example, that the complaint is out of time, or that the individual is not an 'employee' within the meaning of the relevant legislation). The tribunal may, however, decide that the question of jurisdiction is so interlinked with the main issue that it should be considered at the substantive hearing.

53.15 Pre-hearing review (PHR)

The tribunal may order a PHR on the application of either party or its own initiative [*IT Regs, Rule 7*]. At the PHR, the tribunal will usually consist of a chairman sitting alone. The purpose of a PHR is for the tribunal to consider the Originating Application and the Notice of Appearance, and determine the strengths of each party's case. No oral evidence can be heard at a PHR. However, each party is allowed to give submissions to the tribunal. Any party does not attend the PHR who is entitled to submit written representations which the tribunal must take into account.

If the tribunal considers that one party's case has 'no reasonable prospect of success', the tribunal will order that party to pay a deposit (not exceeding £150) as a condition of continuation by that party in the proceedings. Before making a deposit order, the tribunal must ascertain the party's ability to pay. Any deposit ordered to be paid will be used to offset any costs ordered against that party at the full hearing (if any such costs order is ultimately made).

53.16 Interrogatories

The power of tribunals to order interrogatories is a new power granted by *IT Regs, Rule 4(3)*. On the application of either party or of its own initiative, the tribunal can require a party to provide written answers to any questions, if the answer would clarify any relevant issues and the proceedings would be assisted by the answer being available before the full hearing. The order will specify a time limit within which the written answers must be furnished. The tribunal has power to extend this time limit under *Rule 15(1)*.

A party required to comply with an order for interrogatories may apply to have the order set aside or varied [*Rule 4(5)*]. If a party fails to comply with an interrogatories order, the tribunal has power to strike out the Originating Application or Notice of Appearance (whichever is relevant).

Once the answers to interrogatories have been provided, the tribunal will take the answers into account in the same way as any other evidence.

53.17 Inspection, discovery, further particulars

Inspection and discovery is dealt with in detail in DISCOVERY (19).

53.18 Witness orders

The tribunal will make a witness order, on the application of a party, for the attendance of a witness at the hearing. Any such request should set out why the evidence the witness will give is relevant and why it is believed that he will not attend without an order, or otherwise why an order should be made. In a discrimination claim it is sensible to ask for, and serve, witness orders as a matter of course, since there is a natural reluctance for individuals to take part in such cases. Also, many employers will not release their staff without a witness order. The witness order is sent to the party asking for the order, who is responsible for serving it on the witness. If a witness fails to comply with an order, he is liable to summary prosecution in the magistrates' court for which the maximum penalty is currently a £1,000 fine. [*IT Regs, Rule 4(6)*]. The party calling a witness is not allowed to cross-examine his own witness unless the witness is declared to be a hostile witness (he would be hostile if, in giving evidence as a witness, he contradicted what he had stated in his signed proof of evidence). It is generally unwise to serve a witness order on an individual who will not provide a proof of evidence and of whom one cannot be sure as to what he will say in evidence.

53.19 Restricted Reporting Orders

In any case involving allegations of sexual harassment or other sexual misconduct, under *IT Regs, Rule 14*, the tribunal may of its own initiative, or on the application of either party, make a restricted reporting order. Such an order will not be given unless each party has had an opportunity to make oral representation on this point.

A restricted reporting order will specify the person who is not to be identified. The order will remain in force until the tribunal has 'promulgated' its decision (i.e. the date that the tribunal's decision is sent to the parties).

Where a restricted reporting order is in force, a notice of this fact will be placed on the list displayed at the tribunal, and also on the door of the tribunal.

53.20 THE HEARING

Adjournment

The hearing will be fixed by the tribunal giving at least 14 days' notice to the parties. [*Rule 5(1)*]. Some of the regional offices will consult with the parties in writing as to convenient dates, but there is no consistent practice on this. The tribunal will usually grant one adjournment to each party, but may not necessarily do so. Any request for an adjournment should be in writing and set out the reasons for the request, and should be made as soon after the notification of the hearing date as possible. Tribunals are most impressed with an application to adjourn because of a real prospect of resolving the matter by settlement, and are least impressed by a request which is motivated by the fact that the party's chosen representative is not available.

53.21 The bundle of documents

The tribunal likes the parties to have an agreed bundle of documents before them. Sometimes there may be a dispute as to whether a particular document should be before the tribunal; any such item should be left out of the main bundle and a request made to the Chairman to decide on its admissibility, either at a preliminary hearing or at the start of the main hearing. There are no requirements about the presentation of documents, but it is common sense that they should be clearly indexed, numbered and well presented, with sufficient copies for the members of the tribunal, the parties, and the witness.

53.22 Procedure at the hearing

The tribunal consists of a legally qualified Chairman and two assessors. If one of the members is unavailable or cannot sit for some reason, a tribunal can consist of two where the parties agree. These assessors are appointed by the Department of Employment from the two 'sides' of industry and one will be nominated by an employers' organisation (the CBI, Association of Local Authorities or the like) and one by the Regional TUC. The assessors are nominees, not representatives, and are not in any way accountable to their nominating bodies. As a matter of practice, in a sex discrimination claim, there should be at least one woman on the tribunal, and in a race discrimination claim, a member of the race relations panel of the tribunal. Members of this panel are deemed to have a special expertise in race relations matters (in one instance, an immigration officer, which might seem a surprising choice). Some are members of the ethnic minorities, but not many. This is not a statutory requirement and a tribunal decision made without such an assessor will not be invalidated.

A party to the tribunal can be represented by any person of his choice and there is no restriction on the 'right of audience' in the industrial tribunal. If a party is represented, he cannot conduct the case himself. The level of formality in the tribunal is less than in an ordinary court, but it is still a formal proceeding. Custom on entering the tribunal, standing for the tribunal members and so forth varies by region. In general, the further north one travels, the more formal the tribunal becomes! There is a clerk to the tribunal but he plays no part in the hearing except to assist with administering the oath for witnesses. He does not take a note of the hearing; the note is taken in long-hand by the Chairman. The tribunal has a wide discretion in the conduct of the proceedings. [*IT Regs, Rule 9*].

53.23 Order of presentation

The burden of proof is upon the applicant in a discrimination or equal pay claim. For this reason, the applicant will normally start. This is the opposite to an unfair dismissal claim where the employer starts. The tribunal is master of its own procedure and can dictate who starts. If the parties agree to switch the order, the tribunal is unlikely to oppose such a move. Either party can make an application that the order in which the parties give their evidence be altered. It is frequently more convenient for the respondent to go first where the applicant's case is clearly pleaded. On the whole it is the respondent's witnesses who provide the material facts. The party who starts will usually 'open' the case by setting out the salient facts and explaining briefly the outline of the law relied upon. There is no right to an opening and the tribunal may decide that it does not want to hear an opening. In a discrimination case, however, the tribunal will normally expect a brief opening to help it understand the case before it hears the evidence. The order in which the applicant or respondent calls his witnesses is a matter for that party. The tribunal may agree to interpose a witness into the other side's case, or during the evidence of another witness, if that is the only way that the individual will be able to give his evidence.

53.24 Calling a witness

Witnesses may swear on the appropriate religious text, or may affirm. The party who calls a witness is not allowed to 'lead' him but must ask open questions that enable him to give his evidence to the tribunal in his own words. This is called 'examination-in-chief'. If contemporary notes were taken at the time of the events, the witness is allowed to refer to these (but these should have been disclosed to the other side prior to the hearing). The witness may also be referred to the bundle of documents but is not permitted any other aide-memoire. Once examination-in-chief is complete, then the other party may 'cross-examine' the witness. That party must 'put' to the witness all material disagreements of fact between the evidence of that witness and the evidence that the witnesses that he proposes to call will give. He may suggest other matters not arising out of the evidence of the witness but that might reasonably be inferred from the underlying facts. The Chairman and the tribunal members will then have their opportunity to ask questions (although the Chairman will frequently ask questions throughout). The party calling the witness then has a final opportunity to ask further questions arising out of the cross-examination ('re-examination'). Sometimes re-examination takes place before the tribunal asks its questions, but if a matter of importance arises, the tribunal will allow re-examination on that point.

53.25 Affidavit evidence and unsworn statements

If a witness has good reason not to attend the hearing, an affidavit (statement sworn in front of a solicitor) should be completed and served on the other party prior to the hearing. It is a matter for the tribunal as to whether it will take affidavit evidence into consideration and it will not be given the weight of oral evidence. An unsworn statement may also be admitted but a tribunal is unlikely to give such a statement much weight and should not do so.

53.26 Unrepresented parties

Where a party is unrepresented, he will be asked to make a statement to the tribunal (on oath or otherwise). There is no obligation to give evidence. The tribunal Chairman will help an unrepresented party with the procedural niceties of the hearing.

53.27 Closing the case

In closing, the representative, or individual conducting the case, should briefly remind the tribunal of the key evidence and, if necessary, relate the relevant law to that evidence. Most cases involve an assessment by the tribunal as to who is telling the truth. In a discrimination case, the tribunal may also have to consider whether witnesses suffered from subconscious prejudice at the expense of the applicant. It should not be assumed, however, that the tribunal is familiar with the basic principles of the law, as discrimination cases are unusual and one of the members may not have taken part in one before. The party opening the case also closes it, except only in respect of any point of pure law. The closing speech should also deal with the question of remedy, unless the tribunal indicates that it wants to reserve that to a separate hearing dependent on the outcome of the claim.

53.28 The decision

The tribunal will either give its decision on the day of the hearing or, more usually in discrimination claims, reserve its decision and post it to the parties. In unfair dismissal claims the tribunal may give a short decision, but in all discrimination claims it must give a full decision. The tribunal will sometimes reserve its decision on remedy where it finds for the applicant, in the hope that the parties can agree the compensation. If agreement is not reached, the tribunal will arrange a further hearing (see also REMEDIES (49)).

53.29 Costs

Costs are not usually awarded in an industrial tribunal hearing. If, however, a party has acted 'frivolously, vexatiously or otherwise unreasonably' in taking the proceedings or in the conduct of them, the tribunal may award costs up to £500 (*IT Regs, Rule 12(3)(a)*). Costs will be awarded only if the case manifestly should not have been brought (or defended), where a costs warning has been ignored, where unnecessary expense has been incurred with irrelevant evidence or witnesses or submissions, or some similar reason. Costs may also be awarded if a hearing has to be adjourned. [*IT Regs, Rule 12*].

53.30 Review

A party may apply for a review of the decision within 14 days of receiving it. The application must be in writing, stating the grounds for the review in full. The review can only be on the grounds that:

(*a*)   the decision was wrong because of a clerical error; or

(*b*)   a party never received notice of the proceedings; or

(*c*)   the decision was made in the absence of a party entitled to be heard; or

(*d*)   new evidence has come to light since the hearing which was not previously available; or

(*e*)   the interests of justice require a review.

[*IT Regs, Rule 11*].

In practice tribunals are reluctant to review their own decisions and a review will usually be a waste of resources.

53.31 Appeal

Appeal is to the Employment Appeal Tribunal within 42 days of the decision of the industrial tribunal having been sent to the parties, and only on a point of law (see APPEALS (5)).

53.32 Interest

After 42 days following the decision of the industrial tribunal being sent to the parties, interest accrues on any tribunal award at a (current) rate of 8%. [*Employment Act 1982; Industrial Tribunals (Interest) Order 1990 (SI 1990 No 479)*].

In respect of awards of compensation in unlawful discrimination cases, in addition to any awards of interest made by the tribunal in respect of injury to feelings or pecuniary loss, interest will also accrue (after the date of the award) from the day after the date that the tribunal's decision is sent to the parties. However, if the amount of compensation is paid in full within 14 days of this date, no interest will accrue under this head (see REMEDIES (49)).

53.33 **Jurisdiction in respect of claims for breach of contract**

Since 11 July 1994, industrial tribunals have had the power to deal with matters arising out of employment and related contracts – *Industrial Tribunals Extension of Jurisdiction (England and Wales) Order 1994 (SI 1994 No 1623)* (in Scotland, *SI 1994 No 1624*).

Under this provision tribunals are given the power to deal with claims arising from an employment contract, or are outstanding upon termination of employment, and which relate to:

(*a*)   damages for breach of a contract of employment or any other connected contracts;

(*b*)   any sums due under such a contract;

(*c*)   recovery of a sum in pursuance of any enactment relating to the performance or terms of such a contract.

Certain categories of claim are excluded from the tribunal's jurisdiction:

(i)   claims for recovery of damages in respect of personal injuries;

(ii)   claims relating to a breach of a term requiring the employer to provide living accommodation;

(iii)   claims relating to a breach of a term relating to intellectual property;

(iv)   claims relating to a breach of a contractual term imposing obligations of confidence;

(v)   claims relating to breaches of restrictive covenants.

Provided that the claim is within the tribunal's jurisdiction, an employee can always bring such a claim. However, employers' claims under this jurisdiction can only be by way of a counterclaim, as they can only bring a claim in the tribunal if it is in response to one brought by an employee.

A claim relating to breach of contract is brought by an Originating Application, and is subject to the usual time limits. Where an employer seeks to file a counterclaim under this jurisdiction, his counterclaim must be presented within six weeks from the date of receipt of the employee's Originating Application in respect of the claim for breach of contract.

Contract claims will be heard by a chairman of the tribunal sitting alone unless he determines otherwise.

As with all other tribunal applications, ACAS conciliation is available. Where the employee's claim comprises other tribunal applications, any settlement must comply with the terms for compromise agreements in *TURERA 1993, s 39*. (See CONCILIATION (11).)

The maximum amount that a tribunal can award in relation to contract claims is £25,000 (i.e. £25,000 maximum per contract which is the source of dispute claimed).

53.34 **Equal pay claims**

Except for a claim involving equal value, the procedure in an equal pay claim is the same as any other. Where the claim involves an equal value claim the procedure is different, and is outlined below.

53.35 **PROCEDURE IN AN EQUAL VALUE CLAIM**

The first hearing

In any claim raising a question of equal value, a first hearing is held at which the tribunal will dismiss the application if it is 'satisfied that there are no reasonable grounds for determining that the work is of equal value as so mentioned'. [*EqPA s 2A(1)(a)*]. This is to ensure that hopeless or 'fishing' cases are not able to continue at great expense to the employer and the State. If the tribunal is not so satisfied, the matter proceeds by way of the tribunal ordering an independent expert's report.

In normal circumstances, the individual will have established the comparator or comparators upon which he or she relies, although in *Dennehy v Sealink UK Ltd* *[1987] IRLR 120*, the EAT held that the applicant did not necessarily have to plead the particular comparator in her originating application (she pleaded a class of employees). In some cases, the applicant will only be privy to relevant information after the discovery process (wage-related information often being confidential by its very nature) and in such cases, it would be sensible to deal with discovery prior to the first hearing.

53.36 **Grounds for dismissing a claim at first stage**

There are no specific grounds set out for dismissing an equal value claim at first stage beyond the wording of *section 2A(1)(a)* of the *EqPA* (see 53.35 above) but such a claim will be dismissed if any of the following apply.

(*a*)   The employer can show that the applicant's work and that of the comparator(s) have been subjected to an appropriate job evaluation study, and have been given different values [*EqPA s 2A(2)*] (see 29.13 EQUAL PAY).

(*b*)   The employer can establish a material factor defence (see 29.10 EQUAL PAY). On the application of a party, the tribunal may, if appropriate, hear evidence as to the material factor defence before it requires an expert to prepare a report (see 53.37 below). [*IT Regs, 2 Sch, Rule 8(2E)*]. This means that the employer can run the material factor defence at the first hearing. However, he is not obliged to do so, although it should have been clearly pleaded in the Notice of Appearance (*Hayward v Cammell Laird Shipbuilders Ltd [1988] IRLR 257*). The burden of proof in respect of the material factor defence is the same at the first hearing as at the full hearing (*McGregor v GMBATU [1987] ICR 505*). This was a surprising decision of the EAT given the wording of *section 2A(1)(a)* referred to in 53.35 above, which effectively requires the tribunal to conclude that the individual has no prospect of casting doubt at the later hearing after the preparation of the independent expert's report. If it is unclear whether there are reasonable grounds for determining whether the applicant's work is of equal value, then the applicant is permitted to proceed.

An employer is no longer able to rely on the genuine material factor defence once an independent expert's report has been ordered, if this argument had been relied on at the first hearing – this is the effect of the *Industrial Tribunals (Constitution and Rules of Procedure) (Amendment) Regulations 1994 (SI 1994 No 536)* which amended the *IT Regs 1993, 2 Sch, Rule 9(2E)* as from 1 April 1994. This means that an employer can only rely upon the material factor defence on one occasion, i.e. at the first hearing when the tribunal is deciding whether to appoint an independent expert, or at the reconvened hearing when the independent expert is giving his report.

(*c*)   The employer can show that the claim is simply misguided and manifestly has no prospect of success (taking an extreme example, the managing director's secretary comparing herself to the managing director), or where the complaint is frivolous and/or vexatious.

53.37 The independent expert's report

If an equal value claim is to proceed then, before the main hearing, the tribunal must order an independent expert's report [*EqPA s 2A(1)(b)*] from an expert on an approved panel of experts designated by the conciliation service ACAS [*EqPA s 2A(4)*].

The report must comply with the requirements of the *IT Regs, 2 Sch, Rule 7A*. The expert must prepare what amounts to an evaluation study but he must also take into account all information supplied and representations made by the parties.

Rule 7A enables a party to apply to the tribunal after 42 days to require the expert to explain the delay in preparing his report and the tribunal may revoke the expert's appointment if it is dissatisfied with his explanation. [*Rule 7A(5)*]. However, in reality, the preparation of reports inevitably takes considerably longer.

The expert can require any person to submit information and to produce documents, if necessary, by way of requesting an order from the tribunal [*IT Regs, 2 Sch, Rule 4(1A)*], but is not empowered to require a witness to attend him for the purpose of oral questioning.

The expert must, prior to drawing up a final report, send the parties a written summary of the representations and documentation that he has received and invite their further comments. He must attach this summary, and any submissions received arising from it, to the final report. [*IT Regs, 2 Sch, Rule 7A(3)*]. The tribunal pays for the expert, although a party can be asked to pay his costs in exceptional circumstances. [*IT Regs, 2 Sch, Rule 11(1A)*].

Under *IT Regs, 2 Sch, Rule 8A*, an independent expert must give written notice of the date by which he expects to send his report to the tribunal. He must supply this date within 14 days of his being instructed to prepare a report. If it is likely that the report will not be submitted on time, the independent expert must notify the tribunal. The tribunal is entitled to ask for a 'progress report'. [*IT Regs, 2 Sch, Rule 8A(9)*].

53.38 Grounds for challenging the expert's report

(*a*)   The expert has not complied with the regulations governing its production. [*IT Regs, 2 Sch, Rule 7A(8)(a)*]. For instance, the report is tainted by sexual bias [*Rule 7A(3)(d)*], or did not take into account information supplied and representations made. [*Rule 7A(3)(a)*].

(*b*)   The conclusion arrived at could not reasonably have been reached. [*Rule 7A(8)(b)*].

(*c*)   For some other material reason, the report is unsatisfactory (for example, it has transpired that the expert had an undisclosed relationship with one of the parties). [*Rule 7A(8)(c)*].

In deciding whether any of the grounds in (a) to (c) above are made out, the tribunal is required to take account of any representations made by the parties. In that connection, the tribunal may permit any party to give evidence, and to call and question witnesses, on any relevant matter. [*Rule 7A(9)*].

The expert can be required to submit himself to cross-examination on his report [*IT Regs, 2 Sch, Rule 8(2A)*], and if he declines to co-operate, his report can be rejected (*Allsop v Derbyshire Police Authority* (*1990*), *unreported*). The tribunal can also ask the expert to clarify elements of his report in writing [*IT Regs, 2 Sch, Rule 7A(10)(11)*] in which event further representations may be made by the parties. [*Rule 7A(12)*].

53.39 Tribunal procedure subsequent to expert's report

The parties are not permitted to challenge a matter of fact upon which a conclusion of the expert's report is based unless (i) the matter of fact relates to the determination of a 'genuine material factor' defence, or (ii) the report has failed to come to a conclusion on the central question of the equal value claim, because of a refusal by one of the parties (or any other person so required) to comply with an order requiring him to furnish information or documentation. [*IT Regs, 2 Sch, Rule 8(2C)(2D)*].

After the tribunal has received the expert's report, either party may commission his own report and call a single expert (who may be cross-examined) to give evidence on the substantive question(s). The tribunal cannot order either party to be interviewed by the other party's expert witnesses (*Lloyds Bank PLC v Fox* [*1989*] *ICR 80*).

In practice, both parties are now in the habit of commissioning their own expert reports. In some cases, this may give the employer an advantage in that he may have the resources to employ an expert where the applicant has not. What is universally agreed is that the complexity of the procedure is leading to cases lasting into years and carrying over many days of tribunal time in a way that is of no benefit or justice to either side, and there have been many calls for the system to be reformed.

Apart from the consideration of the expert's report, which the tribunal must take into account, and the limit of one expert witness on each side, the procedure for an equal value claim at the final hearing is the same as for any other type of tribunal claim, except that the final burden is on the applicant. Thus, except by agreement between the parties or at the discretion of the tribunal, the applicant will state his case first.

53.40 Decision and remedy

In an equal value claim, the tribunal must give reasons for its decision in the full form [*IT Regs, 2 Sch, Rule 9*] and, in practice, it will normally give full reasons in any claim under the *EqPA*. The tribunal will make a finding as to whether the applicant's position is 'work rated as equivalent', 'like work' or 'work of equal value', as appropriate, and in respect of all subsidiary questions leading to that conclusion (such as a 'genuine material factor' defence). If the tribunal finds in favour of the applicant, it will then make an award of up to two years' arrears in respect of the difference in pay. [*EqPA s 2(5)*]. Thereafter, the applicant has a contractual right to that equal pay.

53.41 Review of Independent Expert Procedure

In 1994, the Government announced that some changes to the independent expert system would be necessary, largely because of the delay in producing reports (11 months on average). The Government proposed a number of options:

(*a*)　abolish the independent expert system, so that tribunals make their own decisions on the evidence;

(*b*)　appoint full-time experts whose sole occupation is to produce reports upon request by tribunals;

(*c*)　give tribunals a discretion as to whether an expert's report is required in any given case; and

(*d*)　amend the present system to speed up the production of the expert's report, such as introducing performance bonuses if the report is on time.

53.42 Costs

The rules as to costs in an *EqPA* claim that does not involve equal value are the same as in any other type of claim before the tribunal. That is, costs are not normally awarded except on the usual grounds that the conduct has been frivolous, vexatious or unreasonable. If the claim is an equal value claim, the rule is the same. If, however, costs are awarded in an equal value claim, these can include the cost of expert evidence and in co-operating with the expert in preparing the expert's report. [*IT Regs, 2 Sch, Rule 11(1A)*].

53.43 Addresses of industrial tribunal offices

For the addresses of the central and regional offices of the industrial tribunals in England and Wales, and in Scotland, see Appendix 5.

53.44 GOVERNMENT REFORM PROPOSALS

In December 1994 the Government issued a Green Paper – *Resolving Employment Rights Disputes – Options For Reform*. This made wide-ranging proposals for reform of the industrial tribunal system, with a view to addressing the problem of growing costs and delays in having applications heard – a consequence of a substantial increase in the number of applications to industrial tribunals. These more than doubled between 1989/1990 and 1993/1994. Although fewer than one-third of all applications reach a full hearing, this still means that in 1993/1994 over 25,000 matters proceeded to a full hearing. This growth is largely a reflection of the increased jurisdiction of tribunals, such as under the *Wages Act 1986*, the *Sunday Trading Act 1994*, and employment and related contract disputes.

The proposals in the Green Paper fall under five main headings:

(*a*) **Internal Resolution of Disputes**

These proposals are aimed at reducing the workload of tribunals and ACAS, by promoting good internal industrial relations practice. A key proposal is the suggestion that, before a tribunal is able to consider an application, the employee must have taken all reasonable steps to resolve the grievance internally, such as formally stating the nature of the grievance in writing, all relevant facts and the remedy sought. It is proposed that employers be given 14 days to respond, and only following this period would the employee be allowed to proceed with a tribunal application.

The Green Paper also proposes the increased use of compromise agreements (see CONCILIATION (11)) and suggests an amendment which would mean that the employee would not be required to take independent legal advice from a qualified lawyer before he could be bound by the terms of such an agreement. It would be sufficient if he has received advice from a trade union, for example.

(*b*) **Arbitration and Conciliation**

The Green Paper suggests that ACAS conciliation be available in redundancy payment disputes. It also suggests that there be access to independent binding arbitration as an alternative to tribunals.

(*c*) **Reform of tribunal procedure**

A number of reforms of tribunal procedure were proposed by the Green Paper, including giving the secretary of industrial tribunals the right to delay registering and processing an application where it appears that the applicant is not entitled to relief. In these circumstances the applicant must be advised in writing why his application has not been registered, and informed that it will not be registered unless the applicant confirms in writing that he wishes to proceed.

The Green Paper suggests that in these circumstances a tribunal chairman should automatically consider whether to hold a hearing relating to the tribunal's jurisdiction to hear the claim.

It also suggests that where the employer fails to enter a Notice of Appearance, the tribunal should have the power to make a decision without holding a full hearing (e.g. to find in favour of the applicant).

If it is clear at a pre-hearing review that one party has no prospect of success, the Green Paper proposes that tribunals should have the power to decide or dismiss a case. Also, where the material facts are undisputed, and there is sufficient written information, the Green Paper suggests that tribunals should be entitled to determine the case with the consent of the parties solely on this written evidence.

As regards the discretion of tribunal chairmen to determine certain matters sitting alone, the Green Paper suggests that this discretion be altered to become a requirement, unless there are related proceedings which the chairman is not entitled to hear alone. It also suggests that tribunal chairmen be allowed to sit alone in all proceedings except those involving discrimination or unfair dismissal.

In relation to the conduct of tribunal proceedings, the Green Paper suggests that there should no longer be a general requirement for exchange of written evidence before the full hearing. It should be within the discretion of the chairman to issue directions on this point. It is also suggested that applicants be required to state whether they have found a new job, and if so, the rate of pay, as well as providing details of the level of compensation they are seeking.

The Green Paper includes a proposal that the time limit for serving a Notice of Appearance be extended to 28 days from the present 14 days, with further extensions to be granted only rarely. It proposes also that the tribunal be able to set time limits as to the hearing of evidence with a discretion to extend these if necessary, and also that interrogative chairmanship should be encouraged. The tribunal should also have the power to stop the hearing and dismiss the application at any time where it is clear that the applicant's case will fail.

A key proposal under this heading is that tribunals should have the power to award costs against an applicant where he has unreasonably refused the respondent's offer of compensation which was larger than the amount awarded by the tribunal. Therefore, even if the applicant is successful, there will be the possibility of a costs order against him. This reflects the 'payment into court' provisions in the civil courts.

In equal value claims, the Green Paper proposes that the tribunal should have a *discretion* to seek an independent expert's report, rather than the *requirement* as at present. Also, it suggests that in equal value claims the applicant should be entitled to name only one comparator.

(*d*) **Administrative Support**
In line with general policy, the Green Paper proposes that tribunal administrative staff be given greater responsibility, or possibly that their work be contracted out. Also, the Green Paper suggests that interlocutory work could be performed by legal officers to relieve the workload of chairmen.

(*e*) **Miscellaneous**
The Green Paper recommends widening the jurisdiction of industrial tribunals, to include cases involving discrimination against disabled people, and also the unlawful deduction of political fund contributions from wages.

In May 1995 the Government introduced the Industrial Tribunals Bill, but at the time of writing had yet to obtain parliamentary approval. The Bill is a consolidatory piece of legislation, and does not introduce any new rules of practice or procedure. The rules of practice and procedure for industrial tribunals shall remain in the form of regulations.

53A   CHECKLIST FOR AN EMPLOYEE CLAIMING IN THE INDUSTRIAL TRIBUNAL

(1) Introduction

It is not possible, within the scope of this handbook, to give more than an outline of the important points for preparing and presenting a case in the industrial tribunal. This checklist is designed as a practical guide through the tribunal procedures for an employee bringing a claim in an industrial tribunal.

(2) Apply in time

Your claim must be received by the tribunal three months less one day from the date of the discriminatory act or omission. If you are late, the tribunal may still be able to consider your claim if it thinks it 'just and equitable'; however, *don't delay*. Submit your claim immediately. The form on which to register a claim is an IT1; you can obtain it from a Jobcentre or Citizens' Advice Bureau, but a letter setting out the essential details of the complaint will do. The tribunal will send you an acknowledgment and a case number which you should keep and to which you should refer if you need to contact the tribunal.

(3) Set out essential details in the IT1

  (i)   Your name and address.

 (ii)   The name and address of the *employer* of whom you are complaining, and if appropriate, the *individual(s)* of whom you are complaining (particularly if you think that the employer will argue that he did everything that he reasonably could to stop the individual behaving as he did).

(iii)   The nature and date(s) of the complaint(s) and a (concise) note of background events.

 (iv)   The legislation relied on. For example, if you are complaining of an unfair dismissal which you consider may have been racially motivated and you had more than two years' service when you were dismissed, plead both the *RRA* and the *EPCA*. Or, to give another example, if you are a black woman and you do not know whether the motivation for the discrimination against you was race or sex, you should plead both the *RRA* and *SDA* in the alternative.

In cases involving both dismissal and discrimination, you should allege *both* unfair dismissal and racial or sexual discrimination, because there is no limit on the amount of compensation that a tribunal can award for the latter. (See REMEDIES (49).)

The actual tribunal form looks like this:

Received at COIT	For Office Use	
	Case Number	
	Code	
	Initials	ROIT

Industrial Tribunals

Application to an Industrial Tribunal

0070/1

- This form has to be photocopied. If possible, please use BLACK INK and CAPITAL letters
- Where there are tick boxes, please tick the one that applies

1 Please give the type of complaint you want the tribunal to decide *(for example: unfair dismissal, equal pay).* A full list is given in booklet ITL1. If you have more than one complaint please list all of them.

2 Please give your details.

Mr ☐   Mrs ☐   Miss ☐   Ms ☐

Surname

First Names

Date of Birth

Address

Postcode

Telephone

Daytime Telephone
(If we or ACAS need to contact you)

Please give an address to which we should send documents, if different from above.

Postcode

3 If a representative is acting for you, please give details.

Name

Address

Postcode

Telephone

Reference

4 Please give the dates of your employment.

From

To

5 Please give the name and address of the employer, other organisation or person against whom this complaint is being brought.

Name of employer, organisation or person

Address

Postcode

Telephone

Please give the place where you worked or applied to work, if different than above.

Name of employer, organisation or person.

Address

Postcode

6 Please say what job you did for the employer (or what job you applied for). If this does not apply, please say what your connection was with the employer.

272

7   Please give the number of normal basic hours worked each week.

hours per week

8   Please give your earning details.
Basic wage/salary

£   :   p   per

Average take home pay

£   :   p   per

Other bonuses/benefits

£   :   p   per

9   **Unfair dismissal applicants only**

Please indicate what you are seeking at this stage, if you win your case:

☐   *Reinstatement: to carry on working in your old job as before. (An order for reinstatement normally includes an award of compensation for loss of earnings)*

☐   *Re-engagement: to start another job or new contract with your old employer. (An order for re-engagement normally includes an award of compensation for loss of earnings)*

☐   *Compensation only: to get an award of money*

10   If your complaint is **not** about dismissal, please give the date when the action you are complaining about took place.

11   Some types of case are heard by a Chairman alone unless a Chairman decides otherwise. All types of case can be heard by a Chairman alone if the parties agree.

If you have any views on this matter indicate them here.

☐   *I would like my case to be heard by a Chairman alone.*

☐   *I would like my case to be heard by a Chairman and lay members.*

If you wish, give reasons for your preference.

12   Please give details of your complaint.
If there is not enough space for your answer, please continue on a separate sheet and attach it to this form.

13   Please sign and date this form, then send it to the address given on page 2.

Signed   Date

IT1(E/W) ───────────────── 4 ─────────────────

You do not have to use the form and could set out your complaint on plain paper like this:

Originating Application

1. I apply for a decision of the tribunal as to whether I have been discriminated against contrary to the [Race Relations Act] [Sex Discrimination Act] [and been unfairly dismissed [not been given reasons for my dismissal] contrary to the Employment Protection (Consolidation) Act].

2. My name is: [*Name*]

    Tel:

3. My representative is:

    [*Specify only if you have a definite representative*]

4. The respondent is:

    [*Here name company and/or individual complained of*]

    Tel:

5. My job title was: [*Specify*]

6. My normal basic weekly hours were: [*Specify*]

7. My basic salary was: [*Specify*], [*also specify additional benefits*]

8. [*If appropriate*] I commenced employment on the [*Date*]. My employment was terminated on [*Date*] effective from [*Date*]

9. The date on which the act of discrimination took place was: [*Specify dates*]

10. The grounds of my complaint are as follows:

    [*Here set out clear outline details of the complaint and key supporting facts*]

Signed ....   Dated ....

---

(4) Serve a questionnaire

Do you want to serve a questionnaire to get further details of the complaint or other related matters? This must be done either before you register your claim or within 21 days of doing so, unless you have the permission of the tribunal to serve the questionnaire later. For full details see QUESTIONNAIRE PROCEDURE (47).

(5) Get help

You can get advice from your local Citizens' Advice Bureau or the Equal Opportunities Commission (EOC) for an *SDA* claim, or from the CAB, the local Council for Racial Equality, or the Commission for Racial Equality (CRE) for advice in an *RRA* case, or from the National Disability Council in a *Disability Discrimination Act* case. Some solicitors displaying the 'legal aid' sign will be willing to give you advice for a fixed fee. If you have a legal insurance policy for employment matters you will probably be able to get your legal fees paid by the insurers, but get your solicitor to check this first.

(6) Use ACAS

Once you lodge a claim with the tribunal, the conciliation service (ACAS) will be notified and it will contact you. If you have a representative it will contact him. You don't have to talk to ACAS but if you have a firm idea of what you want from the case, you can tell ACAS, whose aim is to secure a settlement.

(7) The Notice of Appearance

The other side (the respondent) must reply to your claim, with a 'Notice of Appearance' which looks like this:

53A   Tribunals

Industrial Tribunals | Case Number: |

Notice of Appearance by Respondent

1 Please give the following details

Mr ☐   Mrs ☐   Miss ☐   Ms ☐

Other title _____
(or give the name of the company or organisation)

Name _____

Address _____
_____
_____

Telephone _____

Reference _____

5 If a representative is acting for you

please give his/her name and address

(NOTE: All further communications will be sent to him or her, not to you)

Name _____

Address _____
_____
_____

Telephone _____

Reference _____

2 Do you intend to resist the application made by
_____

YES ☐   NO ☐

3 Was the applicant dismissed?

YES ☐   NO ☐

If YES what was the reason?

6 Are the details given by the applicant about wages/salary or other payments or benefits correct?

YES ☐   NO ☐

If NO or if details were not given, please give the correct details:

Basic wage/salary

£ ___   per   [ ]

Average take home pay

£ ___   per   [ ]

Other bonuses/benefits

£ ___   per   [ ]

4 Are the dates of employment given by the applicant correct?

YES ☐   NO ☐

If NO please give the correct dates

Began on _____

Ended on _____

7 Maternity rights cases only

When the applicant's absence began did you have more than five employees?

YES ☐   NO ☐

(please continue overleaf)

IT3

276

8 If you answered YES to question 2 please give below sufficient details to show the grounds on which you intend to resist the application: *(continue on a separate sheet if there is not enough space for your answer)*

9

Signed _____

Dated _____

10   Please send this form to:

THE REGIONAL SECRETARY
INDUSTRIAL TRIBUNALS
SOUTHGATE STREET
BURY ST EDMUNDS
SUFFOLK, IP33 2AQ
TEL: 01284 762171
FAX: 01284 706064

FOR OFFICIAL USE ONLY

Date received _____   Initials _____

IT3 (REVERSE)

The respondent may be given extra time to complete his Notice of Appearance. This is usual; you will be sent a letter confirming that this has happened. Even if the other side do not ask for an extension, there will be an interval of about one month before you receive the employer's defence.

Once you receive the Notice of Appearance you do not have to reply to it, but consider the following points.

(i)   Do you need more information as to how the employer is defending his case? If so, you can write to the employer or his representative and ask for 'further particulars'. You should set out exactly which points you want clarified and if you get no response, you can write to the tribunal to ask for an order that the particulars be provided.

(ii) If you need to obtain documents to support your case, (such as, for example, other application forms if you were denied promotion), you can write to the employer or his representative and ask for 'discovery'. You should set out exactly which documents you want and if you get no response, you can write to the tribunal to ask for an order that the documents be provided. If the tribunal will not grant that order, you are entitled to a hearing to ask it to review its decision. Equally, the other side can challenge a decision to make an order for discovery and ask for a hearing (see DISCOVERY (19)).

(8) What the other side may do

(i)   The other side might write to you asking for further particulars of your claim. You should reply giving the particulars if it is reasonable to do so, or, if you do not want to provide them, explain why not. A tribunal may order you to provide the particulars, but you can ask for the order to be set aside (before it expires) if you do not think it is fair.

(ii) The other side might write to you asking for certain documents in your possession. You should provide the documents if it is reasonable to do so, or, if you do not want to provide them, explain why not. A tribunal may order you to provide the documents, but you can ask for the order to be set aside (before it expires) if you do not think it is fair.

(9) Who to talk to on the other side

If you see from the Notice of Appearance that the other side has a solicitor or some other representative you should communicate with him and not the other party direct. If there is no representative, and particularly if you are still employed by the other party, it may be useful to communicate through ACAS, although properly it is only obliged to assist you (and the other side) with settling the case.

(10) 'Without prejudice' discussions

In order to try to resolve the dispute it is usual for 'without prejudice' discussions and correspondence to occur. Any letter (or conversation) which relates to discussions about settling the claim is usually headed 'Without prejudice' and cannot be referred to if the matter does go to the tribunal. If you want to talk or write 'off the record', you should be express about doing so. Other correspondence will be admissible in the tribunal so you should be cautious about what you write.

(11) Pre-hearing review

If you think the other party cannot possibly succeed in defending your claim, you can ask for a pre-hearing review (PHR). Equally, the other party can ask for a PHR if he thinks you cannot possibly win, or the tribunal can decide to have a PHR itself. A special hearing will be held (which is not public). No oral evidence is heard and the tribunal just considers the Originating Application and Notice of Appearance and any points which the parties put to it in written or oral submissions. The tribunal can order a deposit of up to £150 to be paid before allowing an applicant to proceed. If a costs order is made, and you go on with your case and then lose, the money will be used to offset any costs that may be awarded against you at the full hearing. You should think very carefully, however, about proceeding in the face of a costs order.

(12) The Notice of Hearing

A notice giving the hearing date will be sent to you at least 14 days before the proposed hearing date. Some tribunals (but not all) ask you what your convenient dates are before they send out a hearing date. If you have not been consulted beforehand, the tribunal will usually grant one adjournment but you should write applying for it immediately. If you consider that not enough time has been set aside for the case, you should also let the tribunal know immediately. If you are near to settling the dispute, the tribunal will usually agree to postpone the hearing, but not always. It is a good idea to agree an application to postpone with the other side, if you can.

(13) An interlocutory hearing

If one or other side has refused to provide documents, there may be a hearing at which the tribunal considers that one issue.

(14) A preliminary hearing

Some tribunals like to get the two sides together for a short hearing to decide how the case will be conducted, deal with orders for discovery and the like, and set dates for the hearing. This is not a universal practice. A preliminary hearing may also be requested by either party, or by the tribunal itself, where there is a preliminary matter to be determined, such as whether the application was made within the time limit.

(15) Witnesses and witness orders

You should make sure that your witnesses can attend on the date arranged. It is your responsibility to arrange for them to attend. You should know what they are going to say beforehand and have taken a statement from them. If someone cannot attend, you could arrange for him to swear an 'affidavit' before a solicitor, or make an ordinary statement, but the tribunal will not attach nearly as much weight to this as to hearing the witness. It is advisable to ask for witness orders in a discrimination case, even if the individuals have agreed to attend.

(16) Compiling the bundle of documents

You should try to agree with the other side, before the hearing, what papers are to be put before the tribunal. 'Without prejudice' correspondence cannot be included in the bundle, nor should you include witness statements in the bundle.

If, however, any of your witnesses (or you) made an immediate note of events, then this should be included. You should make sure that there are six copies of all documents: three for the tribunal, one for you, one for the witnesses and one for the other side. The bundle should have an index. Usually you can ask the employer to do all this.

(17) Using the press

The press is entitled to attend and report any industrial tribunal hearing. In the London tribunals and at other major centres, there are frequently freelance journalists looking for interesting cases to report. If, however, you want the press to be present, then you should send the press a copy of the originating application and notice of appearance, and tell it the date of the hearing. Normally only your local paper will be interested, but if you are employed by a large, or public, company there may be an interest on the part of the national newspapers. You should be aware that if your case contains salacious details, the tabloid press will wish to exploit it for its own ends. You cannot control the nature of the press coverage you receive. It is, however, always best to be polite to journalists but not to make statements to them unless you are experienced in such matters.

If your case involves allegations of sexual harassment or other sexual misconduct, you or the respondent can apply for a restricted reporting order. If such an order is made, reports of the tribunal proceedings may not identify the person specified in the order until the tribunal's decision has been sent to both parties.

(18) Getting representation

Statistics show that you are better off being represented by a lawyer or by another adviser. The earlier you obtain representation, the better. If, however, you are short of funds, it may be best to instruct a lawyer just for the hearing. You could also ask the CAB to arrange for the Free Representation Unit (FRU) to conduct your case. FRU consists mainly of trainee barristers, it is free, and the trainees are generally enthusiastic and committed to your cause. Your case provides them with valuable training.

The structure of the proceedings means that it is generally better not to have to present your own case. The original idea was that individuals should present their case but, particularly with discrimination cases, the employer will be represented by lawyers. If you are unrepresented, the tribunal Chairman will ensure that you are given a fair hearing.

(19) Preparing for a tribunal hearing

The best way to prepare for a tribunal case is to go and watch another case. Tribunals are public and anyone can watch. Witnesses will feel more at ease if they know what is going to happen because they have watched another case previously.

(20) Attending the hearing

You, and your witnesses, should dress smartly. Tribunals are not as formal as ordinary courts, but they are legal proceedings. Impressions count.

The tribunal is usually laid out as illustrated overleaf.

Plan of an industrial tribunal

If you are unrepresented, the Chairman of the tribunal will go out of his way to help you find your way through the proceedings. You should have a friend with you to take a detailed note if you can and he should write down *everything* that is said.

In a discrimination case, the applicant usually starts. This can be varied by agreement of the parties, subject to the tribunal also agreeing, or by the direction of the tribunal.

The tribunal may ask you to introduce the background of the case briefly. Some do, some do not. You are not *entitled* to both an opening and a closing speech and you should not, therefore, insist on an opening speech.

The Chairman (not the clerk) keeps a full note of the evidence and you should always keep 'an eye on the Chairman's pen' to make sure that the evidence is being recorded. You should control the speed of all your questions and your witnesses' answers to suit the speed of the Chairman's pen (or, in one case, typewriter). If the Chairman fails to record a particular passage of evidence, a polite way of raising the point is to ask the Chairman if you could have the benefit of his note of the witness's last answer as you failed to catch it!

You will normally give evidence yourself. You don't have to give sworn or affirmed evidence (i.e. promising to tell the truth); you can simply make a statement. However, it is best to give evidence having affirmed, or sworn on a holy book, to tell the truth, because sworn or affirmed evidence carries more weight with the tribunal. If you give such evidence you can be cross-examined, whereas if you make a statement you cannot be. If you are unrepresented you can either just give your account of events, or ask the Chairman to help you through it by asking questions. You can then be cross-examined by the other side. You should listen carefully to the question and answer it. Do no less and no more. You should avoid saying 'but' – almost by definition, 'but' is not an answer to the question asked! If you don't understand the question, ask for it to be repeated.

After cross-examination has finished, you will have a chance to give further evidence if you think that the way in which answers came out in cross-examination may have confused the tribunal. It is at this point you deal with all the 'buts' that came into your head during the cross-examination!

(21) Calling your witnesses

If you have witnesses to call, now is the time. When you call your witnesses you take them through 'examination-in-chief' and you cannot 'lead' them. Your questions must not prompt the answers.

For example:

WRONG APPROACH (LEADING QUESTION):

Q: Did you feel very hurt when you were called a 'black bastard' on 1 March?

A: Yes.

CORRECT APPROACH

Q: Were any comments made to you on 1 March?

A: I was called a black bastard.

Q: How did you feel about this?

A: That sort of thing had never happened to me before, I felt completely devastated and couldn't sleep for thinking about it. It meant I was finished at that job so far as my career was concerned.

If you let your witnesses give their answers in their own words, they will be more credible and you are likely to get a more forceful response. You should have their statements in front of you (but they cannot refer to them unless they are notes which were taken at the time – you can, however, refer them to documents in the bundle which may prompt their memory).

After each witness has given evidence-in-chief, he may be cross-examined by the other party, the tribunal can ask questions and then there is re-examination, where matters arising in cross-examination can be dealt with further.

You should make sure that your evidence covers all the facts on which you want to rely. The other party must put to your witnesses all the evidence that he intends to produce which is in conflict with or contrary to what you or your witnesses have said.

(22) Dealing with the employer's witnesses

After you have called your evidence, it is the other party's turn. He is not permitted an opening statement. He calls his witnesses. After their evidence-in-chief you can cross-examine them. You don't have to worry about 'leading' questions when cross-examining; you should 'put' your evidence to them whenever there is a conflict. In the above example:

Q: You upset Miss X on 1 March, didn't you?

A: I don't recall her being upset.

Q: You called her a black bastard, didn't you?

A: (looking uncomfortable) No, I never did.

You are very unlikely to get admissions from the respondent's witnesses. The tribunal knows this and will be making its judgment upon the demeanour of each witness, and how credible his evidence is in the light of other facts, in deciding whether it thinks that he is telling the truth. You may be firm but you should be polite. Don't get into a situation where the witness is asking you questions back! If this happens, ask the tribunal Chairman to direct the witness.

After the employer has given his evidence, he (or his representative) will 'sum up' first. He will go through the evidence highlighting the ways in which the evidence supports his denials. He will refer to the law if he considers it appropriate to do so.

You then 'sum up' your case. You should not go into every little detail but should just highlight the key points in your favour. If need be, you can also refer to relevant case law. You should set out the remedy, the damages and/or the recommendations you want the tribunal to make. On the whole, the tribunal is not interested in previous judicial authority. Usually it simply has to decide whether the employer and his witnesses were telling the truth, and also whether you and your witnesses were. In a discrimination case, however, usually the facts you will present will be relatively uncontroversial – for example, a failure to get a job despite high qualifications. It will be for the employer to provide an explanation to the tribunal, and for the tribunal to decide if, on balance, it believes the explanation offered. In a harassment case, however, there will probably be wide areas of conflict in the evidence and the tribunal will be deciding which 'side' is telling the truth (see BURDEN OF PROOF (6)).

(23) The decision

The decision will sometimes be given immediately, but in a discrimination case, it will more often be reserved. This usually takes about six weeks. The decision will be sent to you in writing and the reasons set out in full. If an award of compensation or a recommendation has been made, it will be set out. Sometimes, compensation is left to be agreed between the parties. If agreement cannot be reached, the tribunal holds a further hearing to decide the compensation. Costs are only awarded if one or other party has behaved vexatiously or unreasonably in bringing the case or in its conduct.

(24) How to appeal

You have 42 days, from the date on which the decision was sent to you, within which to make an appeal if the decision goes against you. You can get legal aid, subject to the usual criteria, for an appeal to the Employment Appeal Tribunal. You will be given a guidance leaflet, with the decision, on how to appeal. You could also ask for the same tribunal to review its decision in certain limited circumstances but this is not generally worthwhile. The employer can also appeal if he has lost; sometimes, both sides want to appeal! If an award has been made and an appeal lodged, interest accumulates which will be paid in addition to the award itself if the employer's appeal fails. (See APPEALS (5).)

53B CHECKLIST FOR AN EMPLOYER OR OTHER RESPONDENT DEFENDING A CLAIM IN THE INDUSTRIAL TRIBUNAL

(1) Introduction

It is not possible, within the scope of this handbook, to give more than an outline of the important points for preparing and presenting a case in the industrial tribunal. This checklist is designed as a practical guide through the tribunal procedures for an employer or other respondent defending a tribunal claim.

(2) Treat any questionnaire you receive seriously

The industrial tribunal can draw an adverse inference from a failure to reply, or a misleading or delayed reply, to a questionnaire (see QUESTIONNAIRE PROCEDURE (47)). It is, therefore, important to answer the questionnaire even if you consider the case put forward to be wholly unsustainable. If a questionnaire is served on you, you should carry out the following procedure.

(i) Check that it has been served in time (either prior to tribunal proceedings having been issued, or within 21 days of the date of issue of the proceedings, or otherwise with leave of the tribunal). If the questionnaire is out of time, it is better to write back to the individual and ask how he maintains that it has been properly served. If proceedings have actually been issued, you may wish to consider replying anyway, as the questionnaire can clarify the issues between the parties.

(ii) Acknowledge receipt of the questionnaire and try to give some indication as to how long it will take to reply (there is no time limit on replying, but the tribunal can draw an adverse inference from inordinate delay).

(iii) Take great care with the answers. If it turns out that any answer is misleading or wrong and the matter goes to a tribunal hearing, the tribunal can draw an adverse inference against you, including the inference that the discrimination complained of took place. The questionnaire is frequently utilised by organisations able to assist individuals (such as the Commission for Racial Equality or Equal Opportunities Commission) to decide whether or not to provide help to an individual. A concise covering letter setting out the outline details in clear terms can resolve the matter. You may wish to instruct solicitors to prepare the answer.

(iv) If proceedings have not been issued by the individual, try to ensure that you reply before he runs out of time in which to issue proceedings. Your reply may satisfy him. If, however, he has not had your reply and issues proceedings in order to protect his position, he may be more inclined to see matters through.

(3) When you receive an Originating Application

You will receive a dated notice from the tribunal that a complaint has been made. Attached to the notice will be the individual's complaint (the Originating Application or IT1) and a form, the Notice of Appearance (IT3), for you to complete. The IT1 and IT3 will look like this:

53B Tribunals

For Office Use

Case Number

Code

Initials   ROIT

Application to an Industrial Tribunal

0070/1

- This form has to be photocopied. If possible, please use BLACK INK and CAPITAL letters
- Where there are tick boxes, please tick the one that applies

1 Please give the type of complaint you want the tribunal to decide *(for example: unfair dismissal, equal pay).* A full list is given in booklet ITL1. If you have more than one complaint please list all of them.

4 Please give the dates of your employment.

From

To

2 Please give your details.

Mr ☐   Mrs ☐   Miss ☐   Ms ☐

Surname

First Names

Date of Birth

Address

Postcode

Telephone

Daytime Telephone
(If we or ACAS need to contact you)

Please give an address to which we should send documents, if different from above.

Postcode

5 Please give the name and address of the employer, other organisation or person against whom this complaint is being brought.

Name of employer, organisation or person

Address

Postcode

Telephone

Please give the place where you worked or applied to work, if different than above.

Name of employer, organisation or person.

Address

Postcode

3 If a representative is acting for you, please give details.

Name

Address

Postcode

Telephone

Reference

6 Please say what job you did for the employer (or what job you applied for). If this does not apply, please say what your connection was with the employer.

IT1(E/W) ————————— 3 ————————— Over ▶

286

7 Please give the number of normal basic hours worked each week.

_____ hours per week

8 Please give your earning details.
Basic wage/salary

£ ____ : ____ p per ____

Average take home pay

£ ____ : ____ p per ____

Other bonuses/benefits

£ ____ : ____ p per ____

9 Unfair dismissal applicants only

Please indicate what you are seeking at this stage, if you win your case:

☐ _Reinstatement: to carry on working in your old job as before. (An order for reinstatement normally includes an award of compensation for loss of earnings)_

☐ _Re-engagement: to start another job or new contract with your old employer. (An order for re-engagement normally includes an award of compensation for loss of earnings)_

☐ _Compensation only: to get an award of money_

10 If your complaint is **not** about dismissal, please give the date when the action you are complaining about took place.

_____

11 Some types of case are heard by a Chairman alone unless a Chairman decides otherwise. All types of case can be heard by a Chairman alone if the parties agree.

If you have any views on this matter indicate them here.

☐ _I would like my case to be heard by a Chairman alone._

☐ _I would like my case to be heard by a Chairman and lay members._

If you wish, give reasons for your preference.

_____

12 Please give details of your complaint.
If there is not enough space for your answer, please continue on a separate sheet and attach it to this form.

13 Please sign and date this form, then send it to the address given on page 2.

Signed _____ Date _____

IT1(E/W) ———————— 4 ————————

Industrial Tribunals   Case Number:

Notice of Appearance by Respondent

1 Please give the following details

Mr ☐   Mrs ☐   Miss ☐   Ms ☐

Other title _____
(or give the name of the company or organisation)

Name _____

Address _____

_____

_____

_____

Telephone _____

Reference _____

2 Do you intend to resist the application made by

_____

YES ☐   NO ☐

3 Was the applicant dismissed?

YES ☐   NO ☐

If YES what was the reason?

4 Are the dates of employment given by the applicant correct?

YES ☐   NO ☐

If NO please give the correct dates

Began on _____

Ended on _____

IT3

5 If a representative is acting for you

please give his/her name and address

(NOTE: All further communications will be sent to him or her, not to you)

Name _____

Address _____

_____

_____

_____

Telephone _____

Reference _____

6 Are the details given by the applicant about wages/salary or other payments or benefits correct?

YES ☐   NO ☐

If NO or if details were not given, please give the correct details:

Basic wage/salary

£ ☐   per ☐

Average take home pay

£ ☐   per ☐

Other bonuses/benefits

£ ☐   per ☐

7 Maternity rights cases only

When the applicant's absence began did you have more than five employees?

YES ☐   NO ☐

(please continue overleaf)

8   If you answered YES to question 2 please give below sufficient details to show the
    grounds on which you intend to resist the application: (*continue on a separate
    sheet if there is not enough space for your answer*)

9	10 Please send this form to:
Signed _____	THE REGIONAL SECRETARY
	INDUSTRIAL TRIBUNALS
Dated _____	SOUTHGATE STREET
	BURY ST EDMUNDS
	SUFFOLK, IP33 2AQ
	TEL: 01284 762171
	FAX: 01284 706064

FOR OFFICIAL USE ONLY

Date received _____   Initials _____

IT3 (REVERSE)

There will be a reference number that you should use in all correspondence. The documentation will tell you that you must complete the Notice of Appearance within 14 days.

You should do the following.

(i)   Check that the claim has been made within three months less a day from the date of the discriminatory act or omission. If it is 'out of time', write to the tribunal and ask for this to be determined as a preliminary issue. In addition, ask for an extension of time in which to enter your Notice of Appearance until after this issue has been resolved. The tribunal may still agree to consider the applicant's claim if it thinks it 'just and equitable' to do so, but usually the tribunal declines to hear 'out of time' applications.

(ii)   Unless the issues are very simple and all the facts are to hand, write to the tribunal immediately asking for additional time in which to complete the Notice. This is an administrative decision and extra time is given as a matter of course by the tribunal at first instance.

(iii) Conduct a thorough investigation into the claim and speak to all the relevant individuals prior to completing the IT3.

(iv)   Consider whether or not you want to obtain professional help and instruct solicitors to handle the matter for you. As these claims are not very common, the local firm of solicitors may not have dealt with a discrimination claim before and will probably want to consult a specialist barrister at an early stage. There are a number of firms that handle this sort of work, particularly if the firm has a large employment department. Details of such firms can be found by consulting the Law Society or publications like 'The Legal 500'. If you are going to use specialist advice, it is sensible to do so as early as possible.

(4) Preparing the Notice of Appearance

You are not obliged to use the form provided and it may be more convenient not to do so. You should answer all the questions posed on the form (see overleaf).

Case No. 123/91

Notice of Appearance

Assistant Secretary of the
   Industrial Tribunal
Address of
   Tribunal

OFFICIAL USE

Date   Initials

1. We are [*Name*] of [*Address*].
2. We intend to resist the application made by [*Applicant's name*].
3. The applicant was not [*set out simple refutation of allegation of discrimination, unfair dismissal etc.*].
4. The dates of employment are (not) correct [*specify dates if incorrect*].
5. Our representatives are [*Name and address of solicitors, representative or n/a if none*].
6. The applicant's pay details are (not) correct [*set out details if incorrect*].
7. [*Maternity rights cases only*] We (do not) employ more than 5 persons.
8. We intend to resist the application on the following grounds:

[*Set out clear chronology of the facts and a point by point answer to the applicant's complaint. There is no requirement to (indeed you should not) set out all the evidence, but the nature of the defence should be fully apparent*].

Signed ....   Dated ....

FOR OFFICIAL USE
Date received ....   Initials ....

(5) Other points to consider on receipt of Originating Application

(i)   Do you need more information as to how the applicant puts the case? If so, you can write and ask for 'further particulars'. You should set out exactly what you want clarified and if you get no response you can write to the tribunal to ask for an order that the particulars be provided, i.e.:

'Please provide full particulars of "I was sexually harassed", specifying each and every occasion on which you allege that you were harassed, and stating by whom, upon what date, the precise nature of the harassment alleged and where it is said to have taken place.'

(ii)   If you need obtain documents to support your case (e.g. notes the individual may allege to have taken at the time), you can write to the applicant or his representative and ask for 'discovery'. You should set out exactly what documents you want and if you get no response, you can write to the tribunal to ask for an order that the documents be provided. If the tribunal will not grant that order, you are entitled to a hearing to ask it to review its decision. Equally, the other side can challenge a decision to make an order for discovery and ask for a hearing (see DISCOVERY (19)).

(6) What the other side may do

(i)   The other side might write to you asking for further particulars of your defence. You should reply giving the particulars if it is reasonable to do so, or, if you do not want to provide them, explain why not. A tribunal may order you to provide the particulars, but you can ask for the order to be set aside (before it expires) if you do not think it is fair.

(ii)   The other side might write to you asking for certain documents in your possession. Discovery is very important to discrimination cases and the tribunals tend to make the order for discovery requested by the applicant as long as it is not unreasonable (see DISCOVERY (19)). You should provide the documents if it is reasonable and you think it fair to do so, or, if you do not want to provide them, explain why not. A tribunal may order you to provide the documents but you can ask for the order to be set aside (before it expires) if you do not think it is fair.

(7) Using ACAS

Once an individual lodges a claim with the tribunal, the conciliation service (ACAS) will be notified and it will get in touch with you as well as the applicant. If you have a representative, ACAS will get in touch with him. You don't have to talk to ACAS but if you are willing to settle the matter, ACAS will help. (See CONCILIATION (11).)

(8) Who to talk to on the other side

If you see from the Originating Application that the other side has a solicitor or some other representative, you should communicate with him and not the applicant. If there is no representative, it may be easier to talk through ACAS, although properly it is only obliged to assist you (and the other side) with settling the case. Sometimes the CRE or EOC or another advice agency will be involved without being 'on the record'. Binding agreements can be made without ACAS involvement, provided that they comply with the requirements laid down by *TURERA 1993, s 39* (see CONCILIATION (11)).

(9) 'Without prejudice' discussions

In order to try to resolve the dispute it is usual for 'without prejudice' discussions and correspondence to occur. Any letter (or conversation) which relates to discussions about settling the claim is usually headed 'Without prejudice' and cannot be referred to if the matter does go to the tribunal. If you want to talk or write 'off the record', you should be express about doing so. Other correspondence will be admissible in the tribunal so you should be cautious about what you write.

(10) Pre-hearing review

If you think the applicant cannot possibly succeed with the claim, you can ask for a pre-hearing review (PHR). Equally, the other party can ask for a PHR if he does not think that you can resist his claim, or the tribunal can decide to have a PHR itself. A special hearing will be held (which is not public). No oral evidence is heard and the tribunal just considers the Originating Application and Notice of Appearance and any points which the parties put to it in written or oral submissions. The tribunal can order a deposit of up to £150 to be paid before allowing a party to proceed. Costs warnings are much more unusual against respondents and if one is made you should certainly obtain professional advice.

If a costs order is made against you and the applicant is successful, the money held on deposit will be used to offset any costs that may be awarded against you at the full hearing.

(11) The Notice of Hearing

A notice giving the hearing date will be sent to you at least 14 days before the proposed hearing date. Some tribunals (but not all) ask you what your convenient dates are before they send out a hearing date. If you have not been consulted beforehand the tribunal will usually grant one adjournment but you should write applying for it immediately. If you consider that not enough time has been set aside for the case, you should also let the tribunal know immediately. If you are near to settling the dispute the tribunal will usually agree to postpone the hearing, but not always. It is a good idea to agree an application to postpone with the other side, if you can.

(12) An interlocutory hearing

If one or other side has refused to provide documents, there may be a hearing at which the tribunal considers that one issue.

(13) A preliminary hearing

Some tribunals like to get the two sides together for a short hearing to decide how the case will be conducted, deal with orders for discovery and the like and set dates for the hearing. This is not a universal practice. A preliminary hearing may be arranged on a request by either side, or at the behest of the tribunal itself, to determine some preliminary issue, such as whether the tribunal application was made in time.

(14) Witnesses and witness orders

You should make sure that your witnesses can attend on the hearing date arranged. It is your responsibility to arrange for them to attend. You should know what they are going to say beforehand and have taken a statement from them. If someone cannot attend, you could arrange for him to swear an 'affidavit' before a solicitor, or make an ordinary statement, but the tribunal will not attach nearly as much weight to this as to hearing the witness. If an order is made upon one of your staff to attend the tribunal, you should release him to attend, but you are not obliged to pay him for the lost day(s) work. With discrimination cases, it is generally advisable to seek a witness order even where the individual has indicated a willingness to attend.

(15) Compiling the bundle of documents

You should try to agree with the applicant, before the hearing, what papers are to be put before the tribunal. 'Without prejudice' correspondence cannot be included in such a bundle, nor should you include witness statements in the bundle. If, however, any of your witnesses (or you) made an immediate note of events, then this should be included. You should make sure that there are six copies of all documents, three for the tribunal, one for you, one for the witnesses and one for the other side. The bundle should have an index. Usually you, as the respondent, will have most of the documents in your possession and so will produce the bundle of documents. The bundle should have a clear index and be smartly presented.

(16) The press

The press is entitled to attend and report any industrial tribunal hearing. In the London tribunals and at other major centres, there are frequently freelance journalists looking for interesting cases to report. It is advisable to have thought about your approach to the press before the tribunal hearing. Normally only your local paper will be interested, unless the case raises an unusual issue or has 'titilating' aspects to it of interest to the tabloid press. You cannot control the nature of the press coverage you receive. It is, however, always best to be polite to journalists but not to make statements to them prior to the case. It is, however, sensible to have prepared statements anticipating the possible result of the case, for use after the decision. If you provide no comment then the story will almost inevitably be one-sided.

If your case involves allegations of sexual harassment or other sexual misconduct, you or the applicant can apply for a restricted reporting order. If such an order is made, reports of the tribunal proceedings may not identify the person specified in the order until the date that the tribunal's decision is sent to both parties.

(17) Getting representation

Statistics show that you are better off being represented by a lawyer or by another adviser. The earlier you obtain representation, the better. The structure of the proceedings makes it generally better not to have to present your own case. If you are a personnel officer otherwise uninvolved in the case, this is not a factor to be concerned about. If, however, you are in the position of having to present the case and give evidence, this can present difficulties. The original idea was that individuals and employers should present their own cases. In discrimination claims, however, the individual may have the backing of one of the Commissions and in such cases (and with discrimination claims generally) the employer will be much better off represented by lawyers. If you are representing yourself or your company, are not legally qualified, and are against a lawyer, the tribunal Chairman will ensure that you are given a fair hearing.

(18) Preparing for a tribunal hearing

The best way to prepare for a tribunal case is to go and watch another case. Tribunals are public and anyone can watch. Witnesses will feel more at ease if they know what is going to happen because they have watched another case previously.

(19) Attending the hearing

You, and your witnesses, should dress smartly. Tribunals are not as formal as ordinary courts, but they are legal proceedings. Impressions count.

The tribunal is usually laid out as illustrated overleaf.

Plan of an industrial tribunal

If you are unrepresented the Chairman of the tribunal will go out of his way to help you find your way through the proceedings. You should have a member of your staff with you to take a detailed note if you can and he should write down *everything* that is said.

The Chairman (not the clerk) keeps a full note of the evidence and you should always keep 'an eye on the Chairman's pen' to make sure that the evidence is being recorded. You should control the speed of all your questions and your witnesses' answers to suit the speed of the Chairman's pen (or, in one case, typewriter). If the Chairman fails to record a particular passage of evidence, a polite way of raising the point is to ask the Chairman if you could have the benefit of his note of the witness's last answer as you failed to catch it!

In a discrimination case, the applicant usually starts. This can be varied by agreement of the parties, subject to the tribunal also agreeing, or by the direction of the tribunal.

The tribunal may ask the applicant (and, rarely) the employer as well, to introduce the background of the case briefly. Some do, some do not. The applicant is not *entitled* to both an opening and a closing speech.

The applicant will normally give evidence. It does not have to be sworn or affirmed evidence and can simply be an unsworn statement, in which case you cannot cross-examine him at all. You will, however, be able to draw to the attention of the tribunal the fact that the applicant chose not to give evidence in the normal way, and that therefore his version of events should not be given credibility. If the applicant gives sworn (or affirmed) evidence, you can cross-examine him or her. In the course of cross-examination, you must 'put' to the applicant, or to his witnesses, any evidence that your witnesses will give which is contrary to what the applicant, or his witnesses, have said.

You don't have to worry about 'leading' questions. You should 'put' your evidence to them whenever there is a conflict. For example:

> Q: You suggest that Mr Roberts told you that he would never promote a woman?
>
> A: That's right.
>
> Q: That's untrue, isn't it?
>
> A: (looking uncomfortable) No, it isn't.
>
> Q: He praised your work and said that if you carried on like that you would be promoted, didn't he?
>
> A: No, he never.

You are very unlikely to get admissions from the applicant or his witnesses. The tribunal knows this and will be making its judgment upon the demeanour of each witness, and how credible his evidence is in the light of other facts, in deciding whether it thinks that he or she is telling the truth. You may be firm but you should be polite. Don't get into a situation where the witness is asking you questions back! If this happens, ask the tribunal Chairman to direct the witness. The Chairman and the other tribunal members may also wish to ask questions. Unlike 'examination-in-chief', you don't have to know the answer to each question you ask, but asking too many questions may make the applicant's case. Unless you have spoken to, and have available, every supervisor that has been involved with an employee, an example of an unsafe question would be:

Q: You have never complained to a supervisor about discrimination, have you?

A: Oh, yes I have, to . . .

If the applicant is represented, he can be re-examined by his representative after your cross-examination.

The applicant will have the opportunity to call more witnesses to go through the same process. Witnesses must .give evidence under oath or affirmation; they cannot make statements. At the discretion of the tribunal, statements from witnesses not present may be admitted, but they will not be afforded any great credibility.

(20) Calling your witnesses

Once the applicant has finished calling his witnesses it is your turn to present your evidence. You should call only those witnesses that are relevant to the case. When you call your witnesses you take them through 'examination-in-chief' and you cannot 'lead' them. Your questions must not prompt the answers.

For example:

WRONG APPROACH (LEADING QUESTION)

Q: You didn't say you would never employ a woman, did you?

A: No, certainly not.

CORRECT APPROACH

Q: Were any comments made by you to Mrs Smith on 1 March?

A: Yes, I praised her for her work and told her that if she carried on, she might get promoted.

It is legitimate to repeat what the applicant (or one of his witnesses) has said on the witness stand and ask for your witness to comment. For example:

Q: You heard Mrs Smith say that you said to her that you would never appoint a woman to a management post?

A: I said no such thing.

Q: Did you talk to her at all that day?

A: Yes, I did.

Q: What did you say?

A: I told her that her work was good and that if she carried on like that, she would get promoted.

If you let your witnesses put the answers in their own words they will be more credible and you are likely to get a more forceful response. You should have their statements in front of you (but they cannot refer to them unless they are notes which were taken at the time – you can, however, refer them to documents in the bundle which may prompt their memory).

After each witness has given evidence-in-chief, he may be cross-examined by the other side, the tribunal can ask questions and then there is re-examination. Re-examination is another opportunity for you to ask your witness questions, but only where matters have arisen in cross-examination which need to be dealt with further.

You should make sure that your evidence covers all the facts on which you want to rely.

After you have presented your evidence, you will 'sum up' first. You should go through the evidence highlighting the ways in which the evidence supports your denial of the applicant's claim, or otherwise discredits his evidence. You should refer to the relevant law if you consider it appropriate to do so. On the whole, the tribunal is not interested in previous authority. Usually it simply has to decide whether the applicant and his witnesses were telling the truth, and also whether you and your witnesses were. In a discrimination case, however, usually the facts the applicant will present will be relatively uncontroversial – for example, a failure to get a job despite having high qualifications. It will be for you to provide an explanation to the tribunal, and for the tribunal to decide if, on balance, it believes the explanation offered. In a harassment case, however, there will probably be wide areas of conflict in the evidence and the tribunal will be deciding which 'side' is telling the truth (see BURDEN OF PROOF (6)).

The applicant will then 'sum up' his case. You have a right to reply on any point of law, but not on the evidence.

(21) The decision

The decision will sometimes be given immediately, but in a discrimination case, it will more often be reserved. This usually takes about six weeks. The decision will be sent to you in writing and the reasons set out in full. If an award of compensation or a recommendation has been made, it will be set out. Sometimes, compensation is left to be agreed between the parties. If agreement cannot be reached, the tribunal holds a further hearing to decide the compensation. Costs are only awarded if one or other party has behaved vexatiously or unreasonably in bringing the case or in its conduct.

(22) How to appeal

You have 42 days, from the date on which the decision was sent to you, within which to make an appeal if the decision goes against you. You will be given a guidance leaflet, with the decision, on how to appeal. You could also ask for the same tribunal to review its decision in certain limited circumstances but this is not generally worthwhile. The applicant can also appeal if he has lost; sometimes, both sides want to appeal! If an award has been made and an appeal lodged, interest accumulates which you will have to pay in addition to the award itself if your appeal fails. (See APPEALS (5).)

54   Victimisation

54.1 DEFINITION

The third form of discrimination recognised by the *RRA*, the *SDA* and the *Disability Discrimination Act* is victimisation (see also DIRECT DISCRIMINATION (17) and INDIRECT DISCRIMINATION (36)). The statutory meaning of the word is not that in common parlance (which is, in essence, the same as direct discrimination), and some individuals will complain to the industrial tribunal of 'victimisation' in express terms, when really they mean direct discrimination. Victimisation only arises as a result of an individual being treated adversely because he has taken, or is believed to have taken, or is thought to be intending to take, a protected action; this means an action specified in *RRA s 2(1)* or *SDA s 4(1)*. These are set out in 54.2 below.

54.2 PROTECTED ACTIONS

The individual has:

(*a*)   brought proceedings under the *RRA, SDA, Disability Discrimination Act* or *EqPA*; or

(*b*)   given evidence or information in connection with such proceedings (this includes potential proceedings); or

(*c*)   taken any steps short of proceedings under, or by reference to, the *SDA, RRA, Disability Discrimination Act* or *EqPA* (i.e. issued a questionnaire); or

(*d*)   alleged a contravention of that legislation.

54.3 MUST BE IN GOOD FAITH

An individual is not protected if the original allegation was false *and* not made in good faith. [*SDA s 4(2); RRA s 2(2); Disability Discrimination Act s 24(4)*]. Employers should take care in relying on this provision. Individuals may lose proceedings and even have costs awarded against them, and in such circumstances an employer may well be tempted to dispense with their services as a disruptive influence; however, they are still protected from victimisation unless it can be shown that they did not act in good faith. This requires an express finding of bad faith, or of untruthfulness, by the original tribunal.

54.4 WHAT IS THE COMPARISON?

A considerable amount of confusion has been caused by the way in which the wording of the relevant provisions is phrased. A person victimises another if he treats him less favourably 'than in those circumstances he treats or would treat other persons'.

In one of the early cases on this point, a job centre clerk 'shopped' an employer for giving discriminatory instructions, and was thereafter taken away from public contact and given a backroom job (*Kirby v Manpower Services Commission [1980] IRLR 229*). He claimed victimisation, but the MSC said that he was moved because he disclosed confidential information, not because he reported discrimination; therefore, he was treated in the same way as anyone else who disclosed confidential information would have been treated. This rationale was accepted by the Employment Appeal Tribunal in that case, but has since been doubted by the Court of Appeal in *Aziz v Trinity Street Taxis [1988] IRLR 204*.

In *Aziz*, the Court of Appeal held that the comparison should be with someone who has not taken proceedings in the tribunal, or taken other protected action. The first hurdle is therefore easy for an applicant to clear. The applicant must then show, however, that his treatment was 'by reason of' his having taken a protected action. There is a subtle difference in this approach. It is no longer enough for an employer to say 'anyone taking us to court would be dismissed'. Much as in direct discrimination cases, the employer has to satisfy the tribunal with an 'innocent' reason for his conduct. Mr Aziz had made secret tape recordings for the purpose of collecting evidence for a case under the *RRA*. When his colleagues found out, he was expelled from the company. The Court of Appeal determined that making the tape recordings was a protected act, but Mr Aziz had failed to show that the protected act was the reason for his expulsion, as the tribunal had accepted the evidence that the reason was breach of trust in making such secret recordings, irrespective of the fact that this was a protected act. It seems that *Kirby* would also have resulted in the same decision, but on a different rationale, following the *Aziz* decision.

Examples of four cases where an individual has successfully claimed victimisation under either the *SDA* or the *RRA*:

Jenkins v The Governing Body of Thanet Technical College: the applicant, a black college lecturer, had commenced two sets of tribunal proceedings alleging racial abuse. Before the hearing of these claims, he was informed that he would be required to attend a teacher training course which he refused. He was subjected to disciplinary proceedings for his refusal to attend the teacher training course, and was ultimately threatened with a final warning. The tribunal held that he had been unlawfully victimised. He had taken a 'protected action' under the *RRA*, and he had suffered a detriment as a result of taking such action. The reason for the employer's action was undoubtedly the fact that the applicant had instituted tribunal proceedings, and so he had been unlawfully victimised.

Pedelty v Rotherham Metropolitan Borough Council: following her complaint of sexual harassment by a male colleague, the applicant was not told whether her fixed-term yearly contract was to be renewed (all other employees had been told) and she was also excluded from a number of meetings. She was subsequently offered two positions, both of which were unacceptable, and she ultimately resigned. The tribunal upheld her complaint of victimisation as she had taken a 'protected action' (her complaint of sexual harassment) and had been treated less favourably by her employer as a consequence. There was a clear causative link between her complaint and the employer's actions, and so she had been unlawfully victimised.

Winstanley v Bolton Branch of the Pre-School Playgroup Association: the applicant successfully claimed unlawful victimisation when she was dismissed after she had given evidence in an industrial tribunal in respect of another employee's claim. The 'protected act' in this case was the giving of oral evidence.

Nagarajan v Agnew and Others [1994] IRLR 61: the EAT held that an individual could successfully claim unlawful discrimination only during the subsistence of the employment relationship. Therefore, where the former employer had given a negative reference for the employee in relation to his application for employment elsewhere, there was no unlawful victimisation. The EAT also held that for there to be unlawful victimisation, it is not enough that there merely be victimisation alone; there must also be a knock-on effect in other parts of the legislation, such as discrimination during the employment relationship, or in access to education (i.e. anything covered under the *SDA*, *RRA* or *Disability Discrimination Act*).

54.5   THE PROPER APPROACH

An employer who has lost a claim under either Act should ensure that relevant staff are made aware of the danger of victimisation. Equally, however, this provision was not designed to (and certainly does not in effect) protect individuals who have taken a protected action from being subject to normal management discipline and employment criteria.

54.6   SCOPE

Victimisation is one of the statutory definitions of discrimination and, therefore, has the same scope as direct and indirect discrimination. Therefore, the full range of the employment relationship is covered.

Appendix 1: CRE Code of Practice – Race Relations

(This Code came into effect on 1 April 1984, and is reproduced by kind permission of the Commission for Racial Equality.)

PART 1: THE RESPONSIBILITIES OF EMPLOYERS

1.1 Responsibility for providing equal opportunity for all job applicants and employees rests primarily with employers. To this end it is recommended that they should adopt, implement and monitor an equal opportunity policy to ensure that there is no unlawful discrimination and that equal opportunity is genuinely available.

1.2 This policy should be clearly communicated to all employees — e.g. through notice boards, circulars, contracts of employment or written notifications to individual employees.

1.3 An equal-opportunity policy aims to ensure:

(a) *that no job applicant or employee receives less favourable treatment than another on racial grounds;*

(b) *that no applicant or employee is placed at a disadvantage by requirements or conditions which have a disproportionately adverse effect on his or her racial group and which cannot be shown to be justifiable on other than racial grounds;*

(c) *that, where appropriate and where permissible under the Race Relations Act, employees of under-represented racial groups are given training and encouragement to achieve equal opportunity within the organisation.*

1.4 In order to ensure that an equal opportunity policy is fully effective, the following action by employers is recommended:

(a) allocating overall responsibility for the policy to a member of senior management;

(b) discussing and, where appropriate, agreeing with trade union or employee representatives the policy's contents and implementation;

(c) ensuring that the policy is known to all employees and if possible, to all job applicants;

(d) providing training and guidance for supervisory staff and other relevant decision makers, (such as personnel and line managers, foremen, gatekeepers and receptionists) to ensure that they understand their position in law and under company policy;

(e) examining and regularly reviewing existing procedures and criteria and changing them where they find that they are actually or potentially unlawfully discriminatory;

(f) making an initial analysis of the workforce and regularly monitoring the application of the policy with the aid of analyses of the ethnic origins of the workforce and of job applicants in accordance with the guidance in paragraphs 1.34-1.35.

SOURCES OF RECRUITMENT

Advertisements

1.5 *When advertising job vacancies it is unlawful for employers:*
to publish an advertisement which indicates, or could reasonably be understood as indicating, an intention to discriminate against applicants from a particular racial group. (For exceptions see the Race Relations Act).

1.6 It is therefore recommended that:

    (*a*) employers should not confine advertisements unjustifiably to those areas or publications which would exclude or disproportionately reduce the numbers of applicants of a particular racial group;

    (*b*) employers should avoid prescribing requirements such as length of residence or experience in the UK and where a particular qualification is required it should be made clear that a fully comparable qualification obtained overseas is as acceptable as a UK qualification.

1.7 In order to demonstrate their commitment to equality of opportunity it is recommended that where employers send literature to applicants, this should include a statement that they are equal opportunity employers.

Employment Agencies

1.8 *When recruiting through employment agencies, job centres, careers offices and schools, it is unlawful for employers:*

    (*a*) *to give instructions to discriminate, for example by indicating that certain groups will or will not be preferred. (For exceptions see the Race Relations Act);*

    (*b*) *to bring pressure on them to discriminate against members of a particular racial group. (For exceptions, as above).*

1.9 In order to avoid indirect discrimination it is recommended that employers should not confine recruitment unjustifiably to those agencies, job centres, careers offices and schools which, because of their particular source of applicants, provide only or mainly applicants of a particular racial group.

Other Sources

1.10 *It is unlawful to use recruitment methods which exclude or disproportionately reduce the numbers of applicants of a particular racial group and which cannot be shown to be justifiable.* It is therefore recommended that employers should not recruit through the following methods:

    (*a*) recruitment, solely or in the first instance, through the recommendations of existing employees where the workforce concerned is wholly or predominantly white or black and the labour market is multi-racial;

    (*b*) procedures by which applicants are mainly or wholly supplied through trade unions where this means that only members of a particular racial group, or a disproportionately high number of them, come forward.

SOURCES FOR PROMOTION AND TRAINING

1.11 *It is unlawful for employers to restrict access to opportunities for promotion or training in a way which is discriminatory.* It is therefore recommended that:

— job and training vacancies and the application procedure should be made known to all eligible employees, and not in such a way as to exclude or disproportionately reduce the numbers of applicants from a particular racial group.

1.12 *It is unlawful to discriminate, not only in recruitment, promotion, transfer and training, but also in the arrangements made for recruitment and in the ways of affording access to opportunities for promotion, transfer or training.*

Selection Criteria and Tests

1.13 In order to avoid direct or indirect discrimination it is recommended that selection criteria and tests are examined to ensure that they are related to job requirements and are not unlawfully discriminatory. For example:

(a) a standard of English higher than that needed for the safe and effective performance of the job or clearly demonstrable career pattern should not be required, or a higher level of educational qualification than is needed;

(b) in particular, employers should not disqualify applicants because they are unable to complete an application form unassisted unless personal completion of the form is a valid test of the standard of English required for safe and effective performance of the job;

(c) overseas degrees, diplomas and other qualifications which are comparable with UK qualifications should be accepted as equivalents, and not simply be assumed to be of an inferior quality;

(d) selection tests which contain irrelevant questions or exercises on matters which may be unfamiliar to racial minority applicants should not be used (for example, general knowledge questions on matters more likely to be familiar to indigenous applicants);

(e) selection tests should be checked to ensure that they are related to the job's requirements, i.e. an individual's test markings should measure ability to do or train for the job in question.

Treatment of Applicants, Shortlisting, Interviewing and Selection

1.14 In order to avoid direct or indirect discrimination it is recommended that:

(a) gate, reception and personnel staff should be instructed not to treat casual or formal applicants from particular racial groups less favourably than others. These instructions should be confirmed in writing;

(b) in addition, staff responsible for shortlisting, interviewing and selecting candidates should be:

— clearly informed of selection criteria and of the need for their consistent application;

— given guidance or training on the effects which generalised assumptions and prejudices about race can have on selection decisions;

— made aware of the possible misunderstandings that can occur in interviews between persons of different cultural background;

(c) wherever possible, shortlisting and interviewing should not be done by one person alone but should at least be checked at a more senior level.

Genuine Occupational Qualification

1.15 *Selection on racial grounds is allowed in certain jobs where being of a particular racial group is a genuine occupational qualification for that job.* An example is where the holder of a particular job provides persons of a racial group with personal services promoting their welfare, and those services can most effectively be provided by a person of that group.

Transfers and Training

1.16 In order to avoid direct or indirect discrimination it is recommended that:

(*a*) staff responsible for selecting employees for transfer to other jobs should be instructed to apply selection criteria without unlawful discrimination;

(*b*) industry or company agreements and arrangements of custom and practice on job transfers should be examined and amended if they are found to contain requirements or conditions which appear to be indirectly discriminatory. For example, if employees of a particular racial group are concentrated in particular sections, the transfer arrangements should be examined to see if they are unjustifiably and unlawfully restrictive and amended if necessary;

(*c*) staff responsible for selecting employees for training, whether induction, promotion or skill training should be instructed not to discriminate on racial grounds;

(*d*) selection criteria for training opportunities should be examined to ensure that they are not indirectly discriminatory.

Dismissal (including redundancy) and Other Detriment

1.17 *It is unlawful to discriminate on racial grounds in dismissal, or other detriment to an employee.*

It is therefore recommended that:

(*a*) staff responsible for selecting employees for dismissal, including redundancy, should be instructed not to discriminate on racial grounds;

(*b*) selection criteria for redundancies should be examined to ensure that they are not indirectly discriminatory.

Performance Appraisals

1.18 *It is unlawful to discriminate on racial grounds in appraisals of employee performance.*

1.19 It is recommended that:

(*a*) staff responsible for performance appraisals should be instructed not to discriminate on racial grounds;

(*b*) assessment criteria should be examined to ensure that they are not unlawfully discriminatory.

1.20 *It is unlawful to discriminate on racial grounds in affording terms of employment and providing benefits, facilities and services for employees.* It is therefore recommended that:

(*a*)   all staff concerned with these aspects of employment should be instructed accordingly;

(*b*)   the criteria governing eligibility should be examined to ensure that they are not unlawfully discriminatory.

1.21   In addition, employees may request extended leave from time to time in order to visit relations in their countries of origin or who have emigrated to other countries. Many employers have policies which allow annual leave entitlement to be accumulated, or extra unpaid leave to be taken to meet these circumstances. Employers should take care to apply such policies consistently and without unlawful discrimination.

1.22   *It is unlawful to discriminate in the operation of grievance, disputes and disciplinary procedures,* for example by victimising an individual through disciplinary measures because he or she has complained about racial discrimination, or given evidence about such a complaint. Employers should not ignore or treat lightly grievances from members of particular racial groups on the assumption that they are over-sensitive about discrimination.

1.23   It is recommended that:
in applying disciplinary procedures consideration should be given to the possible effect on an employee's behaviour of the following:

— racial abuse or other racial provocation;

— communication and comprehension difficulties;

— differences in cultural background or behaviour.

1.24   Where employees have particular cultural and religious needs which conflict with existing work requirements, it is recommended that employers should consider whether it is reasonably practicable to vary or adapt these requirements to enable such needs to be met. For example, it is recommended that they should not refuse employment to a turbaned Sikh because he could not comply with unjustifiable uniform requirements.

Other examples of such needs are:

(*a*)   observance of prayer times and religious holidays;

(*b*)   wearing of dress such as sarees and the trousers worn by Asian women.

1.25   *Although the Act does not specifically cover religious discrimination, work requirements would generally be unlawful if they have a disproportionately adverse effect on particular racial groups and cannot be shown to be justifiable.*

1.26   Although there is no legal requirement to provide language training, difficulties in communication can endanger equal opportunity in the workforce. In addition, good communications can improve efficiency, promotion prospects and safety and health and create a better understanding between employers, employees and unions. Where the workforce includes current employees whose English is limited it is recommended that steps are taken to ensure that communications are as effective as possible.

1.27   These should include, where reasonably practicable:

(*a*)   provision of interpretation and translation facilities, for example, in the communication of grievance and other procedures, and of terms of employment;

(*b*)   training in English language and in communication skills;

(*c*)   training for managers and supervisors in the background and culture of racial minority groups;

(*d*)   the use of alternative or additional methods of communication, where employees find it difficult to understand health and safety requirements, for example:

— safety signs; translation of safety notices;

— instructions through interpreters;

— instruction combined with industrial language training.

1.28 *It is unlawful to instruct or put pressure on others to discriminate on racial grounds.*

(*a*)   An example of an unlawful instruction is:

— an instruction from a personnel or line manager to junior staff to restrict the numbers of employees from a particular racial group in any particular work.

(*b*)   An example of pressure to discriminate is:

— an attempt by a shop steward or group of workers to induce an employer not to recruit members of particular racial groups, for example by threatening industrial action.

1.29 *It is also unlawful to discriminate in response to such instructions or pressure.*

1.30 The following recommendations are made to avoid unlawful instructions and pressure to discriminate:

(*a*)   guidance should be given to all employees, and particularly those in positions of authority or influence on the relevant provisions of the law;

(*b*)   decision-makers should be instructed not to give way to pressure to discriminate;

(*c*)   giving instructions or bringing pressure to discriminate should be treated as a disciplinary offence.

1.31 *It is unlawful to victimise individuals who have made allegations or complaints of racial discrimination or provided information about such discrimination, for example, by disciplining them or dismissing them.*

1.32 It is recommended that:

— guidance on this aspect of the law should be given to all employees and particularly to those in positions of influence or authority.

1.33 It is recommended that employers should regularly monitor the effects of selection decisions and personnel practices and procedures in order to assess whether equal opportunity is being achieved.

1.34 The information needed for effective monitoring may be obtained in a number of ways. It will best be provided by records showing the ethnic origins of existing employees and job applicants. It is recognised that the need for detailed information and the methods of collecting it will vary according to the circumstances of individual establishments. For example, in small firms or in firms in areas with little or no racial minority settlement it will often be adequate to assess the distribution of employees from personal knowledge and visual identification.

1.35 It is open to employers to adopt the method of monitoring which is best suited to their needs and circumstances, but whichever method is adopted, they should be able to show that it is effective. In order to achieve the full commitment for all concerned the chosen method should be discussed and agreed, where appropriate, with trade union or employee representatives.

1.36 Employers should ensure that information on individuals' ethnic origins is collected for the purpose of monitoring equal opportunity alone and is protected from misuse.

1.37 The following is the comprehensive method recommended by the CRE.

Analyses should be carried out of:

(a)   the ethnic composition of the workforce of each plant, department, section, shift and job category, and changes in distribution over periods of time;

(b)   selection decisions for recruitment, promotion, transfer and training, according to the racial group of candidates, and reasons for these decisions.

1.38 Except in cases where there are large numbers of applicants and the burden on resources would be excessive, reasons for selection and rejection should be recorded at each stage of the selection process, e.g. initial shortlisting and final decisions. Simple categories of reasons for rejection should be adequate for the early sifting stages.

1.39 Selection criteria and personnel procedures should be reviewed to ensure that they do not include requirements or conditions which constitute or may lead to unlawful indirect discrimination.

1.40 This information should be carefully and regularly analysed and, in order to identify areas which may need particular attention, a number of key questions should be asked.

1.41 Is there evidence that individuals from any particular racial group:

(a)   do not apply for employment or promotion, or that fewer apply than might be expected?

(b)   are not recruited or promoted at all, or are appointed in a significantly lower proportion than their rate of application?

(c)   are under-represented in training or in jobs carrying higher pay, status or authority?

(d)   are concentrated in certain shifts, sections or departments?

1.42 If the answer to any of these questions is yes, the reasons for this should be investigated. If direct or indirect discrimination is found action must be taken to end it immediately.

1.43 It is recommended that deliberate acts of unlawful discrimination by employees are treated as disciplinary offences.

1.44 *Although they are not legally required, positive measures are allowed by the law to encourage employees and potential employees and provide training for employees who are members of particular racial groups which have been under-represented in particular work.* Discrimination at the point of selection for work, however, is not permissible in these circumstances.

1.45 Such measures are important for the development of equal opportunity. It is therefore recommended that, where there is under-representation of particular racial groups in particular work, the following measures should be taken wherever appropriate and reasonably practicable:

(*a*)   job advertisements designed to reach members of these groups and to encourage their applications: for example, through the use of the ethnic minority press, as well as other newspapers;

(*b*)   use of the employment agencies and careers offices in areas where these groups are concentrated;

(*c*)   recruitment and training schemes for school leavers designed to reach members of these groups;

(*d*)   encouragement to employees from these groups to apply for promotion or transfer opportunities;

(*e*)   training for promotion or skill training for employees of these groups who lack particular expertise but show potential: supervisory training may include language training.

PART 2: THE RESPONSIBILITIES OF INDIVIDUAL EMPLOYEES

2.1   While the primary responsibility for providing equal opportunity rests with the employer, individual employees at all levels and of all racial groups have responsibilities too. Good race relations depend on them as much as on management, and so their attitudes and activities are very important.

2.2   *The following actions by individual employees would be unlawful*:

(*a*)   *discrimination in the course of their employment against fellow employees or job applicants on racial grounds*, for example, in selection decisions for recruitment, promotion, transfer and training;

(*b*)   *inducing, or attempting to induce other employees, unions or management to practise unlawful discrimination*. For example, they should not refuse to accept other employees from particular racial groups or refuse to work with a supervisor of a particular racial group;

(*c*)   *victimising individuals who have made allegations or complaints of racial discrimination or provided information about such discrimination*.

2.3   To assist in preventing racial discrimination and promoting equal opportunity it is recommended that individual employees should:

(*a*)   co-operate in measures introduced by management designed to ensure equal opportunity and non-discrimination;

(*b*)   where such measures have not been introduced, press for their introduction (through their trade union where appropriate);

(*c*)   draw the attention of management and, where appropriate, their trade unions to suspected discriminatory acts or practices;

(*d*)   refrain from harassment or intimidation of other employees on racial grounds, for example, by attempting to discourage them from continuing employment. Such action may be unlawful if it is taken by employees against those subject to their authority.

2.4   In addition to the responsibilities set out above individual employees from the racial minorities should recognise that in many occupations advancement is dependent on an appropriate standard of English. Similarly an understanding of the industrial relations procedures which apply is often essential for good working relationships.

2.5 They should therefore:

(*a*) where appropriate, seek means to improve their standards of English;

(*b*) co-operate in industrial language training schemes introduced by employers and/or unions;

(*c*) co-operate in training or other schemes designed to inform them of industrial relations procedures, company agreements, work rules, etc;

(*d*) where appropriate, participate in discussions with employers and unions, to find solutions to conflicts between cultural or religious needs and production needs.

PART 3: THE RESPONSIBILITIES OF TRADE UNIONS

3.1 Trade unions, in common with a number of other organisations, have a dual role as employers and providers of services specifically covered by the Race Relations Act.

3.2 In their role as employer, unions have the responsibilities set out in Part 1 of the Code. They also have a responsibility to ensure that their representatives and members do not discriminate against any particular racial group in the admission or treatment of members, or as colleagues, supervisors, or subordinates.

3.3 In addition, trade union officials at national and local level and shopfloor representatives at plant level have an important part to play on behalf of their members in preventing unlawful discrimination and in promoting equal opportunity and good race relations. Trade unions should encourage and press for equal opportunity policies so that measures to prevent discrimination at the workplace can be introduced with the clear commitment of both management and unions.

3.4 *It is unlawful for trade unions to discriminate on racial grounds:*

(*a*) *by refusing membership;*

(*b*) *by offering less favourable terms of membership.*

3.5 *It is unlawful for trade unions to discriminate on racial grounds against existing members:*

(*a*) *by varying their terms of membership, depriving them of membership or subjecting them to any other detriment;*

(*b*) *by treating them less favourably in the benefits, facilities or services provided.* These may include:

training facilities;

welfare and insurance schemes;

entertainment and social events;

processing of grievances;

negotiations;

assistance in disciplinary or dismissal procedures.

3.6 In addition, it is recommended that unions ensure that in cases where members of particular racial groups believe that they are suffering racial discrimination, whether by the employer or the union itself, serious attention is paid to the reasons for this belief and that any discrimination which may be occurring is stopped.

3.7   It is recommended that deliberate acts of unlawful discrimination by union members are treated as disciplinary offences.

3.8   *Although they are not legally required, positive measures are allowed by the law to encourage and provide training for members of particular racial groups which have been under-represented in trade union membership or in trade union posts.* (Discrimination at the point of selection, however, is not permissible in these circumstances.)

3.9   It is recommended that, wherever appropriate and reasonably practicable, trade unions should:

(*a*)   encourage individuals from these groups to join the union. Where appropriate, recruitment material should be translated into other languages;

(*b*)   encourage individuals from these groups to apply for union posts and provide training to help fit them for such posts.

3.10 Training and information play a major part in the avoidance of discrimination and the promotion of equal opportunity. It is recommended that trade unions should:

(*a*)   provide training and information for officers, shop stewards and representatives on their responsibilities for equal opportunity. This training and information should cover:

the Race Relations Act and the nature and causes of discrimination;

the backgrounds of racial minority groups and communication needs;

the effects of prejudice;

equal opportunity policies;

avoiding discrimination when representing members.

(*b*)   ensure that members and representatives, whatever their racial group, are informed of their role in the union, and of industrial relations and union procedures and structures. This may be done, for example:

through translation of material;

through encouragement to participate in industrial relations courses and industrial language training.

3.11 *It is unlawful for trade union members or representatives to induce or to attempt to induce those responsible for employment decisions to discriminate:*

(*a*)   *in the recruitment, promotion, transfer, training or dismissal of employees;*

(*b*)   *in terms of employment, benefits, facilities or services.*

3.12 For example, they should not:

(*a*)   restrict the numbers of a particular racial group in a section, grade or department;

(b)   resist changes designed to remove indirect discrimination, such as those in craft apprentice schemes, or in agreements concerning seniority rights of mobility between departments.

3.13   *It is unlawful to victimise individuals who have made allegations or complaints of racial discrimination or provided information about such discrimination.*

3.14   *Where unions are involved in selection decisions for recruitment, promotion, training or transfer, for example through recommendations or veto, it is unlawful for them to discriminate on racial grounds.*

3.15   It is recommended that they should instruct their members accordingly and examine their procedures and joint agreements to ensure that they do not contain indirectly discriminatory requirements or conditions, such as:

unjustifiable restrictions on transfers between departments or irrelevant and unjustifiable selection criteria which have a disproportionately adverse effect on particular racial groups.

3.16   It is recommended that:

(a)   unions should co-operate in the introduction and implementation of full equal opportunity policies, as defined in paras 1.3 & 1.4;

(b)   unions should negotiate the adoption of such policies where they have not been introduced or the extension of existing policies where these are too narrow;

(c)   unions should co-operate with measures to monitor the progress of equal opportunity policies, or encourage management to introduce them where they do not already exist. Where appropriate (see paras 1.33-1.35) this may be done through analysis of the distribution of employees and job applicants according to ethnic origin;

(d)   where monitoring shows that discrimination has occurred or is occurring, unions should co-operate in measures to eliminate it;

(e)   although positive action is not legally required, unions should encourage management to take such action where there is under-representation of particular racial groups in particular jobs, and where management itself introduces positive action representatives should support it;

(f)   similarly, where there are communication difficulties, management should be asked to take whatever action is appropriate to overcome them.

PART 4: THE RESPONSIBILITIES OF EMPLOYMENT AGENCIES

4.1   Employment agencies, in their role as employers, have the responsibilities outlined in Part 1 of the Code. In addition, they have responsibilities as suppliers of job applicants to other employers.

4.2   *It is unlawful for employment agencies: (For exceptions see Race Relations Act)*

(a)   *to discriminate on racial grounds in providing services to clients;*

(b)   *to publish job advertisements indicating, or which might be understood to indicate, that applications from any particular group will not be considered or will be treated more favourably or less favourably than others;*

(c)   to act on directly discriminatory instructions from employers to the effect that applicants from a particular racial group will be rejected or preferred or that their numbers should be restricted;

(d)   to act on indirectly discriminatory instructions from employers i.e. that requirements or conditions should be applied that would have a disproportionately adverse effect on applicants of a particular racial group and which cannot be shown to be justifiable.

4.3   It is recommended that agencies should also avoid indicating such conditions or requirements in job advertisements unless they can be shown to be justifiable. Examples in each case may be those relating to educational qualifications or residence.

4.4   It is recommended that staff should be given guidance on their duty not to discriminate and on the effect which generalised assumptions and prejudices can have on their treatment of members of particular racial groups.

4.5   In particular staff should be instructed:

(a)   not to ask employers for racial preferences;

(b)   not to draw attention to racial origin when recommending applicants unless the employer is trying to attract applicants of a particular racial group under the exceptions in the Race Relations Act;

(c)   to report a client's refusal to interview an applicant for reasons that are directly or indirectly discriminatory to a supervisor, who should inform the client that discrimination is unlawful. If the client maintains this refusal the agency should inform the applicant of his or her right to complain to an industrial tribunal and to apply to the CRE for assistance. An internal procedure for recording such cases should be operated;

(d)   to inform their supervisor if they believe that an applicant, though interviewed, has been rejected on racial grounds. If the supervisor is satisfied that there are grounds for this belief, he or she should arrange for the applicant to be informed of the right to complain to an industrial tribunal and to apply to the CRE for assistance. An internal procedure for recording such cases should be operated;

(e)   to treat job applicants without discrimination. For example, they should not send applicants from particular racial groups to only those employers who are believed to be willing to accept them, or restrict the range of job opportunities for such applicants because of assumptions about their abilities based on race or colour.

4.6   It is recommended that employment agencies should discontinue their services to employers who give unlawful discriminatory instructions and who refuse to withdraw them.

4.7   It is recommended that employment agencies should monitor the effectiveness of the measures they take for ensuring that no unlawful discrimination occurs. For example, where reasonably practicable they should make periodic checks to ensure that applicants from particular racial groups are being referred for suitable jobs for which they are qualified at a similar rate to that for other comparable applicants.

EU Code of Practice

Appendix 2: EU Code of Practice – EU Recommendation and Sexual Harassment Code

(Reproduced from the Official Journal of the European Communities.)

COMMISSION RECOMMENDATION ON THE PROTECTION OF THE DIGNITY OF WOMEN AND MEN AT WORK

THE COMMISSION OF THE EUROPEAN COMMUNITIES

Having regard to the Treaty establishing the European Economic Community and the second indent of Article 155 thereof;

Whereas unwanted conduct of a sexual nature, or other conduct based on sex affecting the dignity of women and men at work, including the conduct of superiors and colleagues, is unacceptable and may, in certain circumstances, be contrary to the principle of equal treatment within the meaning of Articles 3, 4 and 5 of Council Directive 76/207/EEC of 9 February 1976 and the implementation of the principle of equal treatment for men and women as regards access to employment, vocational training and promotion and working conditions[1], a view supported by case law in some Member States;

Whereas, in accordance with the Council Recommendation of 13 December 1984 on the promotion of positive action for women[2], many Member States have carried out a variety of positive action measures and actions having a bearing, *inter alia*, on respect for the dignity of women at the workplace;

Whereas the European Parliament, in its resolution of 11 June 1986 on violence against women[3], has called upon national governments, equal opportunities committees and trade unions to carry out concerted information campaigns to create a proper awareness of the individual rights of all members of the labour force;

Whereas the Advisory Committee on Equal Opportunities for Women and Men, in its opinion of 20 June 1988, has unanimously recommended that there should be a Recommendation and code of conduct on sexual harassment in the workplace covering harassment of both sexes;

Whereas the Commission in its Action Programme relating to the implementation of the Community Charter of Basic Social Rights for workers undertook to examine the protection of workers and their dignity at work, having regard to the reports and recommendations prepared on various aspects of implementation of Community law[4];

Whereas the Council, in its Resolution of 29 May 1990 on the protection of the dignity of women and men at work[5], affirms that conduct based on sex affecting the dignity of women and men at work, including conduct of superiors and colleagues, constitutes an intolerable violation of the dignity of workers or trainees, and calls on the Member States and the institutions and organs of the European Communities to develop positive measures designed to create a climate at work in which women and men respect one another's human integrity;

[1] *OJ No. L 39, 14.2.76, p. 40.*
[2] *OJ No. L 331, 19.12.84, p. 34.*
[3] *OJ No. C 176, 14.7.86, p. 79.*
[4] *COM (89) 568 final, 29.11.89. For example, 'The dignity of women at work; a report on the problem of sexual harassment in the Member States of the European Communities', October 1987, by Michael Rubenstein (ISBN 92–825–8764–9).*
[5] *OJ No. C 157, 27.6.90, p. 3.*

Whereas the Commission, in its Third Action Programme on Equal Opportunities for Women and Men, 1991–1995 and pursuant to paragraph 3.2 of the said Council Resolution of 29 May 1990, resolved to draw up a code of conduct on the protection of the dignity of women and men at work[1], based on experience and best practice in the Member States, to provide guidance on initiating and pursuing positive measures designed to create a climate at work in which women and men respect one another's human integrity;

Whereas the European Parliament, on 22 October 1991, adopted a Resolution on the protection of the dignity of women and men at work;

Whereas the Economic and Social Committee, on 30 October 1991, adopted an Opinion on the protection of the dignity of women and men at work;

RECOMMENDS AS FOLLOWS:

Article 1

It is recommended that the Member States take action to promote awareness that conduct of a sexual nature, or other conduct based on sex affecting the dignity of women and men at work, including conduct of superiors and colleagues, is unacceptable if:

(*a*) such conduct is unwanted, unreasonable and offensive to the recipient;

(*b*) a person's rejection of or submission to such conduct on the part of employers or workers (including superiors or colleagues) is used explicitly or implicitly as a basis for a decision which affects that person's access to vocational training, access to employment, continued employment, promotion, salary or other employment decisions; and/or

(*c*) such conduct creates an intimidating, hostile or humiliating work environment for the recipient;

and that such conduct may, in certain circumstances, be contrary to the principle of equal treatment within the meaning of Articles 3, 4 and 5 of Directive 76/207/EEC.

Article 2

It is recommended that Member States should take action, in the public sector, to implement the Commission's Code of Practice on the protection of the dignity of women and men at work, annexed hereto. The action of the Member States, in thus initiating and pursuing positive measures designed to create a climate at work in which women and men respect one another's human integrity, should serve as an example to the private sector.

Article 3

It is recommended that Member States encourage employers and employee representatives to develop measures to implement the Commission's Code of Practice on the protection of the dignity of women and men at work.

Article 4

The Member States shall inform the Commission within three years of the date of this Recommendation of the measures taken to give effect to it, in order to allow the Commission to draw up a report on all such measures. The Commission shall, within this period, ensure the widest possible circulation of the Code of Practice. The report

---

[1] *COM (90) 449 final, 6.11.90.*

should examine the degree of awareness of the Code, its perceived effectiveness, its degree of application and the extent of its use in collective bargaining between the social partners.

Article 5
This Recommendation is addressed to the Member States.

PROTECTING THE DIGNITY OF WOMEN AND MEN AT WORK

A Code of Practice on measures to combat sexual harassment

Introduction
This Code of Practice is issued in accordance with the Resolution of the Council of Ministers on the protection of the dignity of women and men at work[1], and to accompany the Commission's Recommendation on this issue.

Its purpose is to give practical guidance to employers, trade unions, and employees on the protection of the dignity of women and men at work. The Code is intended to be applicable in both the public and the private sector and employers are encouraged to follow the recommendations contained in the Code in a way which is appropriate to the size and structure of their organisation. It may be particularly relevant for small and medium-sized enterprises to adapt some of the practical steps to their specific needs.

The aim is to ensure that sexual harassment does not occur and, if it does occur, to ensure that adequate procedures are readily available to deal with the problem and prevent its recurrence. The Code thus seeks to encourage the development and implementation of policies and practices which establish working environments free of sexual harassment and in which women and men respect one another's human integrity.

The expert report carried out on behalf of the Commission found that sexual harassment is a serious problem for many working women in the European Community[2] and research in Member States has proven beyond doubt that sexual harassment at work is not an isolated phenomenon. On the contrary, it is clear that for millions of women in the European Community, sexual harassment is an unpleasant and unavoidable part of their working lives. Men too may suffer sexual harassment and should, of course, have the same rights as women to the protection of their dignity.

Some specific groups are particularly vulnerable to sexual harassment. Research in several Member States, which documents the link between the risk of sexual harassment and the recipient's perceived vulnerability, suggests that divorced and separated women, young women and new entrants to the labour market and those with irregular or precarious employment contracts, women in non-traditional jobs, women with disabilities, lesbians and women from racial minorities are disproportionately at risk. Gay men and young men are also vulnerable to harassment. It is undeniable that harassment on grounds of sexual orientation undermines the dignity at work of those affected and it is impossible to regard such harassment as appropriate workplace behaviour.

---

[1] *90/C 157/02, 27.6.90, s 3.2. See Appendix 1.*
[2] *'The dignity of women at work: a report on the problem of sexual harassment in the Member States of the European Communities', October 1987, by Michael Rubenstein, ISBN 92–825–8–8764–9.*

Sexual harassment pollutes the working environment and can have a devastating effect upon the health, confidence, morale and performance of those affected by it. The anxiety and stress produced by sexual harassment commonly lead to those subjected to it taking time off work due to sickness, being less efficient at work, or leaving their job to seek work elsewhere. Employees often suffer the adverse consequences of the harassment itself and short- and long-term damage to their employment prospects if they are forced to change jobs. Sexual harassment may also have a damaging impact on employees not themselves the object of unwanted behaviour but who are witness to it or have a knowledge of the unwanted behaviour.

There are also adverse consequences arising from sexual harassment for employers. It has a direct impact on the profitability of the enterprise where staff take sick leave or resign their posts because of sexual harassment, and on the economic efficiency of the enterprise where employees' productivity is reduced by having to work in a climate in which individuals' integrity is not respected.

In general terms, sexual harassment is an obstacle to the proper integration of women into the labour market and the Commission is committed to encouraging the development of comprehensive measures to improve such integration[1].

1. Definition
Sexual harassment means 'unwanted conduct of a sexual nature, or other conduct based on sex affecting the dignity of women and men at work'[2]. This can include unwelcome physical, verbal or non-verbal conduct.

Thus, a range of behaviour may be considered to constitute sexual harassment. It is unacceptable if such conduct is unwanted, unreasonable and offensive to the recipient; a person's rejection of or submission to such conduct on the part of employers or workers (including superiors or colleagues) is used explicitly or implicitly as a basis for a decision which affects that person's access to vocational training or to employment, continued employment, promotion, salary or any other employment decisions; and/or such conduct creates an intimidating, hostile or humiliating working environment for the recipient[3].

The essential characteristic of sexual harassment is that it is *unwanted* by the recipient, that it is for each individual to determine what behaviour is acceptable to them and what they regard as offensive. Sexual attention becomes harassment if it is persisted in once it has been made clear that it is regarded by the recipient as offensive, although one incident of harassment may constitute sexual harassment if sufficiently serious. It is the unwanted nature of the conduct which distinguishes sexual harassment from friendly behaviour, which is welcome and mutual.

2. The law and employers' responsibilities
Conduct of a sexual nature or other conduct based on sex affecting the dignity of women and men at work may be contrary to the principle of equal treatment within the meaning of Articles 3, 4 and 5 of Council Directive 76/207/EEC of 9 February 1976 on the implementation of the principle of equal treatment for men and women as regards access to employment, vocational training and promotion and working conditions. This principle means that there shall be no discrimination whatsoever on grounds of sex either directly or indirectly by reference in particular to marital or family status[4].

---

[1] *Third Action Programme on Equal Opportunities for Women and Men, 1991–1995, COM (90) 449, 6.11.90.*
[2] *Council Resolution on the protection of the dignity of women and men at work, 90/C 157/02, 27.6.90, s 1.*
[3] *Council Resolution on the protection of the dignity of women and men at work, 90/C 157/02, 27.6.90, s 1.*
[4] *OJ No. L 39, 14.2.76, p. 40, Article 2 (Appendix II).*

EU Code of Practice

In certain circumstances, and depending upon national law, sexual harassment may also be a criminal offence or may contravene other obligations imposed by the law, such as health and safety duties, or a duty, contractual or otherwise, to be a good employer. Since sexual harassment is a form of employee misconduct, employers have a responsibility to deal with it as they do with any other form of employee misconduct as well as to refrain from harassing employees themselves. Since sexual harassment is a risk to health and safety, employers have a responsibility to take steps to minimise the risk as they do with other hazards. Since sexual harassment often entails an abuse of power, employers may have a responsibility for the misuse of the authority they delegate.

This Code, however, focuses on sexual harassment as a problem of sex discrimination. Sexual harassment is sex discrimination because the gender of the recipient is the determining factor in who is harassed. Conduct of a sexual nature or other conduct based on sex affecting the dignity of women and men at work in some Member States already has been found to contravene national equal treatment laws and employers have a responsibility to seek to ensure that the work environment is free from such conduct[1].

As sexual harassment is often a function of women's status in the employment hierarchy, policies to deal with sexual harassment are likely to be most effective where they are linked to a broader policy to promote equal opportunities and to improve the position of women. Advice on steps which can be taken generally to implement an equal opportunities policy is set out in the Commission's Guide to Positive Action[2].

Similarly, a procedure to deal with complaints of sexual harassment should be regarded as only one component of a strategy to deal with the problem. The prime objective should be to change behaviour and attitudes, to seek to ensure the prevention of sexual harassment.

3. Collective bargaining

The majority of the recommendations contained in this Code are for action by employers, since employers have clear responsibilities to ensure the protection of the dignity of women and men at work.

Trade unions also have responsibilities to their members and they can and should play an important role in the prevention of sexual harassment in the workplace. It is recommended that the question of including appropriate clauses in agreements is examined in the context of the collective bargaining process, with the aim of achieving a work environment free from unwanted conduct of a sexual nature or other conduct based on sex affecting the dignity of women and men at work and free from victimisation of a complainant or of a person wishing to give, or giving, evidence in the event of a complaint.

4. Recommendations to employers

The policies and procedures recommended below should be adopted, where appropriate, after consultation or negotiation with trade unions or employee representatives. Experience suggests that strategies to create and maintain a working environment in which the dignity of employees is respected are more likely to be effective where they are jointly agreed.

It should be emphasised that a distinguishing characteristic of sexual harassment is that

---

[1] *Council Resolution on the protection of the dignity of women and men at work, 90/C, 157/02, 27.6.90, s 2.3(a).*
[2] *'Positive action: equal opportunities for women in employment – a guide', OPCE, 1988.*

employees subjected to it often will be reluctant to complain. An absence of complaints about sexual harassment in a particular organisation, therefore, does not necessarily mean an absence of sexual harassment. It may mean that the recipients of sexual harassment think that there is no point in complaining because nothing will be done about it, or because it will be trivialised or the complainant subjected to ridicule, or because they fear reprisals. Implementing the preventative and procedural recommendations outlined below should facilitate the creation of a climate at work in which such concerns have no place.

A. Prevention
(i) Policy statements
As a first step in showing senior management's concern and their commitment to dealing with the problem of sexual harassment, employers should issue a policy statement which expressly states that all employees have a right to be treated with dignity, that sexual harassment at work will not be permitted or condoned and that employees have a right to complain about it should it occur.

It is recommended that the policy statement makes clear what is considered inappropriate behaviour at work, and explain that such behaviour, in certain circumstances, may be unlawful. It is advisable for the statement to set out a positive duty on managers and supervisors to implement the policy and to take corrective action to ensure compliance with it. It should also place a positive duty on all employees to comply with the policy and to ensure that their colleagues are treated with respect and dignity.

In addition, it is recommended that the statement explains the procedure which should be followed by employees subjected to sexual harassment at work in order to obtain assistance and to whom they should complain; that it contain an undertaking that allegations of sexual harassment will be dealt with seriously, expeditiously and confidentially; and that employees will be protected against victimisation or retaliation for bringing a complaint of sexual harasssment. It should also specify that appropriate disciplinary measures will be taken against employees found guilty of sexual harassment.

(ii) Communicating the policy
Once the policy has been developed, it is important to ensure that it is communicated effectively to all employees, so that they are aware that they have a right to complain and to whom they should complain; that their complaint will be dealt with promptly and fairly; and so that employees are made aware of the likely consequences of engaging in sexual harassment. Such communication will highlight management's commitment to eliminating sexual harassment, thus enhancing a climate in which it will not occur.

(iii) Responsibility
All employees have a responsibility to help to ensure a working environment in which the dignity of employees is respected and managers (including supervisors) have a particular duty to ensure that sexual harassment does not occur in work areas for which they are responsible. It is recommended that managers should explain the organisation's policy to their staff and take steps to positively promote the policy. Managers should also be responsive and supportive to any member of staff who complains about sexual harassment; provide full and clear advice on the procedure to be adopted; maintain confidentiality in any cases of sexual harassment; and ensure that there is no further problem of sexual harassment or any victimisation after a complaint has been resolved.

(iv) Training

An important means of ensuring that sexual harassment does not occur and that, if it does occur, the problem is resolved efficiently is through the provision of training for managers and supervisors. Such training should aim to identify the factors which contribute to a working environment free of sexual harassment and to familiarise participants with the responsibilities under the employer's policy and any problems they are likely to encounter.

In addition, those playing an official role in any formal complaints procedure in respect of sexual harassment should receive specialist training, such as that outlined above.

It is also good practice to include information as to the organisation's policy on sexual harassment and procedures for dealing with it as part of appropriate induction and training programmes.

B. Procedures

The development of clear and precise procedures to deal with sexual harassment once it has occurred is of great importance. The procedures should ensure the resolution of problems in an efficient and effective manner. Practical guidance for employees on how to deal with sexual harassment when it occurs and with its aftermath will make it more likely that it will be dealt with at an early stage. Such guidance should of course draw attention to an employee's legal rights and to any time limits within which they must be exercised.

(i) Resolving problems informally

Most recipients of harassment simply want the harassment to stop. Both informal and formal methods of resolving problems should be available.

Employees should be advised that, if possible, they should attempt to resolve the problem informally in the first instance. In some cases, it may be possible and sufficient for the employee to explain clearly to the person engaging in the unwanted conduct that the behaviour in question is not welcome, that it offends them or makes them uncomfortable, and that it interferes with their work.

In circumstances where it is too difficult or embarassing for an individual to do this on their own behalf, an alternative approach would be to seek support from, or for an initial approach to be made by, a sympathetic friend or confidential counsellor.

If the conduct continues or if it is not appropriate to resolve the problem informally, it should be raised through the formal complaints procedure.

(ii) Advice and assistance

It is recommended that employers should designate someone to provide advice and assistance to employees subjected to sexual harassment, where possible, with responsibilities to assist in the resolution of any problems, whether through informal or formal means. It may be helpful if the officer is designated with the agreement of the trade unions or employees, as this is likely to enhance their acceptability. Such officers could be selected from personnel departments or equal opportunities departments for example. In some organisations they are designated as 'confidential counsellors' or 'sympathetic friends'. Often such a role may be played by someone from the employee's trade union or by women's support groups.

Whatever the location of this responsibility in the organisation, it is recommended that the designated officer receives appropriate training in the best means of resolving problems and in the detail of the organisation's policy and procedures, so that they can perform their role effectively. It is also important that they are given adequate resources to carry out their function, and protection against victimisation for assisting any recipient of sexual harassment.

(iii) Complaints procedure
It is recommended that, where the complainant regards attempts at informal resolution as inappropriate, where informal attempts at resolution have been refused, or where the outcome has been unsatisfactory, a formal procedure for resolving the complaint should be provided. The procedure should give employees confidence that the organisation will take allegations of sexual harassment seriously.

By its nature sexual harassment may make the normal channels of complaint difficult to use because of embarrassment, fears of not being taken seriously, fears of damage to reputation, fears of reprisal or the prospect of damaging the working environment. Therefore, a formal procedure should specify to whom the employee should bring a complaint, and it should also provide an alternative if in the particular circumstances the normal grievance procedure may not be suitable, for example because the alleged harasser is the employee's line manager. It is also advisable to make provision for employees to bring a complaint in the first instance to someone of their own sex, should they so choose.

It is good practice for employers to monitor and review complaints of sexual harassment and how they have been resolved, in order to ensure that their procedures are working effectively.

(iv) Investigations
It is important to ensure that internal investigations of any complaints are handled with sensitivity and with due respect for the rights of both the complainant and the alleged harasser. The investigation should be seen to be independent and objective. Those carrying out the investigation should not be connected with the allegation in any way, and every effort should be made to resolve complaints speedily – grievances should be handled promptly and the procedure should set a time limit within which complaints will be processed, with due regard for any time limits set by national legislation for initiating a complaint through the legal system.

It is recommended as good practice that both the complainant and the alleged harasser have the right to be accompanied and/or represented, perhaps by a representative of their trade union or a friend or colleague, that the alleged harasser be given full details of the nature of the complaint and the opportunity to respond; and that strict confidence be maintained throughout any investigation into an allegation. Where it is necessary to interview witnesses, the importance of confidentiality should be emphasised.

It must be recognised that recounting the experience of sexual harassment is difficult and can damage the employee's dignity. Therefore, a complainant should not be required to repeatedly recount the events complained of where this is unnecessary.

The investigation should focus on the facts of the complaint and it is advisable for the employer to keep a complete record of all meetings and investigations.

(v) Disciplinary offence
It is recommended that violations of the organisation's policy protecting the dignity of employees at work should be treated as a disciplinary offence; and the disciplinary rules should make clear what is regarded as inappropriate behaviour at work. It is also good practice to ensure that the range of penalties to which offenders will be liable for violating the rule is clearly stated and also to make it clear that it will be considered a disciplinary offence to victimise or retaliate against an employee for bringing a complaint of sexual harassment in good faith.

EU Code of Practice

Where a complaint is upheld and it is determined that it is necessary to relocate or transfer one party, consideration should be given, wherever practicable, to allowing the complainant to choose whether he or she wishes to remain in their post or be transferred to another location. No element of penalty should be seen to attach to a complainant whose complaint is upheld and in addition, where a complaint is upheld, the employer should monitor the situation to ensure that the harassment has stopped.

Even where a complaint is not upheld, for example because the evidence is regarded as inconclusive, consideration should be given to transferring or rescheduling the work of one of the employees concerned rather than requiring them to continue to work together against the wishes of either party.

5. Recommendations to trade unions

Sexual harassment is a trade union issue as well as an issue for employers. It is recommended as good practice that trade unions should formulate and issue clear policy statements on sexual harassment and take steps to raise awareness of the problem of sexual harassment in the workplace, in order to help create a climate in which it is neither condoned nor ignored. For example, trade unions could aim to give all officers and representatives training on equality issues, including dealing with sexual harassment and include such information in union-sponsored or approved training courses, as well as information on the union's policy. Trade unions should consider declaring that sexual harassment is inappropriate behaviour and educating members and officials about its consequences is recommended as good practice.

Trade unions should also raise the issue of sexual harassment with employers and encourage the adoption of adequate policies and procedures to protect the dignity of women and men at work in the organisation. It is advisable for trade unions to inform members of their right not to be sexually harassed at work and provide members with clear guidance as to what to do if they are sexually harassed, including guidance on any relevant legal rights.

Where complaints arise, it is important for trade unions to treat them seriously and sympathetically and ensure that the complainant has the opportunity of representation if a complaint is to be pursued. It is important to create an environment in which members feel able to raise such complaints knowing they will receive a sympathetic and supportive response from local union representatives. Trade unions could consider designating specially-trained officials to advise and counsel members with complaints of sexual harassment and act on their behalf if required. This will provide a focal point for support. It is also a good idea to ensure that there are sufficient female representatives to support women subjected to sexual harassment.

It is recommended too, where the trade union is representing both the complainant and the alleged harasser for the purpose of the complaints procedure, that it be made clear that the union is not condoning offensive behaviour by providing representation. In any event, the same official should not represent both parties.

It is good practice to advise members that keeping a record of incidents by the harassed worker will assist it bringing any formal or informal action to a more effective conclusion; and that the union wishes to be informed of any incident of sexual harassment and that such information will be kept confidential. It is also good practice for the union to monitor and review the union's record in responding to complaints and in representing alleged harassers and the harassed, in order to ensure its responses are effective.

6. Employees' responsibilities

Employees have a clear role to play in helping to create a climate at work in which sexual harassment is unacceptable. They can contribute to preventing sexual harassment through an awareness and sensitivity towards the issue and by ensuring that standards of conduct for themselves and for colleagues do not cause offence.

Employees can do much to discourage sexual harassment by making it clear that they find such behaviour unacceptable and by supporting colleagues who suffer such treatment and are considering making a complaint.

Employees who are themselves recipients of harassment should, where practicable, tell the harasser that the behaviour is unwanted and unacceptable. Once the offender understands clearly that the behaviour is unwelcome, this may be enough to put an end to it. If the behaviour is persisted in, employees should inform management and/or their employee representative through the appropriate channels and request assistance in stopping the harassment, whether through informal or formal means.

Appendix 3: Gardner Merchant's equal opportunities policy and code of practice

(Reproduced with the kind permission of Gardner Merchant Limited.)

EQUAL OPPORTUNITIES POLICY

Gardner Merchant is committed to a policy of treating all its employees and job applicants equally. No employee or potential employee shall receive less favourable treatment or consideration on the grounds of race, colour, religion, nationality, ethnic origin, sex, disability or marital status or will be disadvantaged by any conditions of employment or Gardner Merchant's requirements that cannot be justified as necessary on operational grounds.

Every senior executive and member of management and all employees are instructed that:

1. There should be no discrimination on account of race, colour, religion, disability, nationality, ethnic origin, sex, or marital status.

2. Gardner Merchant will appoint, train, develop and promote on the basis of merit and ability.

3. All employees have personal responsibility for the practical application of Gardner Merchant's equal opportunities policy.

4. Special responsibility for the practical application of Gardner Merchant's equal opportunities policy falls upon managers and supervisors involved in the recruitment, selection, promotion and training of employees. These special responsibilities give rise to training needs for which provision should be made.

5. Gardner Merchant's grievance procedure is available to any employee who believes that he or she may have been unfairly discriminated against.

6. Disciplinary action will be taken against any employee who is found to have committed an act of unlawful discrimination. Serious breaches of the policy will be treated as gross misconduct as will sexual or racial harassment.

7. In the case of any doubt or concern about the application of the policy in any particular instance, any member of staff or employee should consult the Personnel Manager.

EQUAL OPPORTUNITIES CODE OF PRACTICE

Objectives

Gardner Merchant has introduced an Equal Opportunities Policy. We regard this as a commitment to make full use of the talents and resources of all our employees, and to provide a healthy environment which will encourage good and productive working relations within the organisation. This Code of Practice describes how the policy is to be applied throughout the Company.

We are particularly concerned to achieve the following objectives:

1. When applying for jobs there is no discrimination against any person on the basis of race, colour, religion, disability, nationality, ethnic origin, sex, or marital status.

Gardner Merchant's equal opportunities policy and code of practice

2. All promotion is strictly on the basis of ability to do the job, irrespective of race, colour, religion, disability, nationality, ethnic origin, sex, or marital status.

Action

As a Company, we are introducing a programme to support our Equal Opportunities Policy.

1. An Equal Opportunities Policy Statement will be displayed on all noticeboards and sent to all staff.

2. The Company will ensure that this Equal Opportunities Code of Practice booklet is available to all staff and in particular it is given to all staff with responsibility for recruitment, selection, and promotion. Up-to-date literature on Equal Opportunities is always available from your Personnel Department.

Recruitment

The recruitment process must result in the selection of the most suitable person for the job in respect of experience and qualifications.

It is against Company policy and against the law to discriminate either directly or indirectly on the grounds of race, colour, religion, disability, nationality, ethnic origin, sex, or marital status at any stage of the recruitment process.

Check that

•   All jobs are made open to all applicants except in the case of a job covered by a Genuine Occupational Qualification (e.g. French waiters in a French style restaurant). All such cases should be referred to the Personnel Manager.

•   No assumptions or pre-judgements are made by managers or recruiters about the suitability of any sex or race for a particular job. (For example, preferences of co-workers, customers, or suppliers must not be pre-supposed. It is not to be assumed that jobs involving heavy physical labour, late hours, travel, or unpleasant surroundings are necessarily unsuitable for women, or that jobs demanding manual dexterity, e.g. the operation of VDUs, are unsuitable for men).

•   No decision is made, or preference stated, in advance, regarding the outcome of the recruitment process. (For example by instructing a Personnel Manager not to recruit a woman.)

•   All applications are given equal consideration.

•   No discrimination is made in the terms on which a job is offered, for example, pay or holidays.

•   All applicants and existing staff are made aware of the Company's policy and practice on recruitment.

•   Managers are advised and trained on the implementation of the Company's recruitment policy.

Recruitment publicity

Recruitment publicity must positively encourage applications from all suitably qualified and experienced people.

Gardner Merchant's equal opportunities policy and code of practice

It must show that the Company offers opportunities at all levels to people of either sex, any colour, of all races and regardless, so far as is practical, of disabilities, and it should avoid any stereotyping of roles. Recruitment solely, or in the first instance, by 'word of mouth' or through recommendations of existing employees can be unlawful and should be avoided.

Check that

- Copies of the Company's written Equal Opportunities Policy are given to all the recruitment and advertising agencies with which we deal.

- In all recruitment and publicity literature and in all internal and external advertisements:

  — job titles and job content are presented without bias either of gender or race.

  — jobs are described in such a way that no qualified person is deterred from applying.

  — there is nothing, in either words or illustrations, to indicate any role stereotyping. Illustrations showing men in managerial positions and women in clerical positions, or white people supervising black people, or workers of minority ethnic origins, are particularly to be avoided.

- Vacancies are advertised in a wide variety of ways to ensure that all groups are informed. (Outlets should include appropriate newspapers and periodicals; competent employment agencies experienced in the recruitment of minority groups, job centres and careers offices; schools, colleges and clubs.)

Selection process

It is vital that the selection process is carried out consistently for all jobs at all levels within our organisation and that it is seen to be fair and non-discriminatory.

Application forms

Application forms are to include only those questions which are necessary at the initial stage of selection.

Check that

- All questions on the application form are relevant and non-discriminatory.

- Application forms include only those questions which are essential at this stage.

- No discrimination is made on the basis of postal code or address.

Interviews

Interviews are to be conducted by trained personnel. All questions will be strictly relevant to the job. In no case will questions be asked or assumptions made about a person's personal and domestic circumstances or plans. Where the requirements of the job will affect the candidate's personal life (e.g. unsocial hours or extensive travel) this should be discussed objectively.

Gardner Merchant's equal opportunities policy and code of practice

Check that

- Staff and managers who conduct recruitment interviews are trained:

    — to take an unbiased approach regardless of the applicant's race, colour, religion, disability, nationality, ethnic origin, sex, or marital status.

    — to ask only questions which relate to the job and which are non-discriminatory (e.g. questions about marriage plans and intention to have a family may be construed as showing discrimination against women).

- Staff and managers who conduct recruitment interviews must ensure that they have read and understood this Code of Practice. If they have any doubts about the legal requirements in respect of Equal Opportunities or Company Policy and practice they should consult the Personnel Department prior to taking any action.

Selection criteria

Only those qualifications and skills which are important for the job are to be established as criteria for selection. They may include educational and professional qualifications, experience, the ability to speak and write 'good English', and physical abilities, subject to being able to demonstrate that they are highly desirable attributes for the position. In the case of any doubt, the Personnel Manager should be consulted, as this is an area where there is a risk of unknowingly infringing discrimination legislation. They must not exclude minority groups or discourage people with minimum qualifications from applying.

Requirements for formal academic or professional qualifications may be waived if candidates can demonstrate their suitability for the job by other means. The candidate's previous experience and willingness to undergo further training will both be taken into account.

Check that

- All selection criteria are strictly job-related.
- The acceptability of equivalents to formal qualifications is stated.
- Positions are not advertised as 'full-time' unless this can be justified. (The Company could be found to be acting unlawfully.)
- Length of residence or experience in the UK, as opposed to overseas, should not be criteria.

Educational and professional qualifications

The Company should not insist on higher educational or professional qualifications than are strictly necessary for the job. In assessing educational qualifications, it should not be assumed that overseas degrees or diplomas are of a lower standard than their UK equivalents.

Check that

- All requirements for educational and professional qualifications are valid and job-related.
- Overseas degrees and diplomas are properly assessed.

Gardner Merchant's equal opportunities policy and code of practice

Experience

We are concerned that wherever possible, experience may count as an equivalent to professional qualifications, and that the value of past experience is accurately assessed.

Check that

- Due recognition is given to experience as a substitute for formal qualifications, wherever possible.

- All previous experience is taken into account, including: paid employment; voluntary and community work; work within the home; family responsibilities and experience.

- Prime consideration is given to the relevance of an applicant's experience, rather than to the length of time spent in a particular job or type of job.

Selection tests

Selection tests are used by some departments in Gardner Merchant to ensure that applicants or job holders have the skills and aptitudes required for the job.

Tests are to be made only of skills which are essential to the job and to a standard no higher than is required for the job.

The tests used by Gardner Merchant will be free of bias and non-discriminatory in content, in administration, and in scoring.

Check that

- All tests used are valid and reliable.

- All tests used are free from gender or race bias and are non-discriminatory.

- All tests are relevant to the position being considered, whether specific to a particular job or general (e.g. to ensure that all employees in a certain grade have a particular essential skill).

- Tests are administered and scored in a consistent and non-discriminatory manner.

Age restrictions

The setting of age limits, as a matter of general recruitment policy or as a criterion of any specific job, must be justifiable and non-discriminatory.

Check that

- Any age restriction which is made is demonstrably valid.

- The setting of age limits is non-discriminatory. (An example of discrimination in this respect is to set a requirement for the age range during which many women have dropped out of the labour market to raise a family.)

Mobility requirements

Mobility requirements can cause problems for all employees. We recognise that the whole family is affected if an employee's job requires her or him to travel extensively or

Gardner Merchant's equal opportunities policy and code of practice

to move. We are therefore concerned to keep such requirements to a minimum, and to devise alternatives for any employee who has difficulty in meeting such requirements.

Check that

- Requirements for travel or removal are demonstrably valid and non-discriminatory.

Shift work/overtime

No discrimination will be made in arranging shifts or overtime by assuming that certain groups, for example women, do not wish or are unable to do such work.

Check that

- Shift work arrangements are made without either direct or indirect discrimination.
- Overtime is offered to all employees, on an equitable basis.

Training

Training is provided for our employees in order to increase their knowledge and skills. This has the advantage to the Company of greater efficiency, while to the employee it opens up new opportunities and prospects.

All training course materials must reflect our policy on Equal Opportunities.

Check that

- Training courses and procedures are continually reviewed and updated.
- Training courses and materials are free from bias and do not discriminate (e.g. by showing women or black people, ethnic minority groups or disabled people in inferior roles).

Career development

We are concerned that career paths within the Company should reflect the situation in the workplace.

As a Company we are committed to ensure that all employees are provided with opportunities to develop their potential.

Check that

- Development policies on promotion and transfer are continually reviewed and updated.
- Qualifications and criteria for promotion and transfer are justifiable.
- Policies make it quite clear that promotion and transfer are open to all suitably qualified and experienced personnel.

Job satisfaction

We must identify all people with potential and encourage appointments to higher grades. We must avoid stereotyped ideas linking certain groups of people with certain jobs and we must enrich the jobs in the lower grades to increase our employees' satisfaction in their jobs.

Check that

- Jobs associated with certain groups of people, e.g. 'a man's job', 'a woman's job', are identified and consideration given as to how these jobs can be filled by members of any group.

- Action is taken to improve both job satisfaction and career progression.

Terms and conditions

All employees doing equal jobs, regardless of race, colour, religion, disability, nationality, ethnic origin, sex, or marital status, are to be treated equally with respect to pay and other conditions of their contracts of employment.

Check that

- All increases are made on an equitable basis and the same rules are followed in all cases.

Benefits, facilities and services

It is against the Company policy and against the law to discriminate with respect to benefits, facilities and services. We will clearly define all the benefits, facilities and services to which our employees are entitled and ensure that they are made available to everyone, irrespective of race, colour, religion, disability, nationality, ethnic origin, sex, or marital status.

Check that

- All benefits, facilities and services to which our employees are entitled are in fact available to them.

- Steps should be taken, if reasonably practical, to ensure that all premises are accessible to disabled people.

Part-time employment

Part-time work is desirable for many people, and can be of advantage to the Company. It is our policy to create opportunities for part-time work or job-sharing where possible, and to ensure that our part-time employees receive fair treatment.

Check that

- Jobs or areas are identified where part-time employees could be introduced.

- Job sharing and similar schemes are considered at all levels.

- Part-time workers are recruited to the jobs so identified.

- A review is made of the position of part-time workers in relation to pay, pension rights, training and promotion.

Gardner Merchant's equal opportunities policy and code of practice

Responsibilities of managers and supervisors

The success of our Equal Opportunities programme depends on the managers and supervisors at all levels in the Company. They must be made aware of what is expected of them by the Company and what is required of them by law, and given continuous training and support.

Check that

- All managers and supervisors are briefed on their responsibilities and supported by regular training.

- All managers who are responsible for selecting employees for training or for allocating work ensure that no discrimination is made, either directly or indirectly. All employees are to be given equal access to training, further education, personal development, and increased job satisfaction, regardless of race, colour, religion, disability, nationality, ethnic origin, sex, or marital status.

- Managers promote Equal Opportunities to their staff and encourage people of both sexes and different races to work together and eliminate discrimination.

Equal opportunities appeals procedure

Equal Opportunities in the workplace will be achieved by the implementation of the policies and programmes outlined in this Code of Practice.

As a safeguard, a grievance procedure is available to individual employees who feel that they have received unfair treatment in any of the following:

- Their right to apply for jobs for which they are qualified or have the experience.

- Selection for interview.

- The interview process itself.

- Training or development opportunities.

- Terms and Conditions of Employment.

The grievance procedure may also be invoked in cases of alleged sexual or racial harassment. (Sexual or racial harassment is defined as unreciprocated and unwelcome comments or actions, which are found objectionable and could threaten an employee's job security or create an intimidating working environment.)

An employee with a grievance under Equal Opportunities should follow the procedure below:

1. Before taking a decision to invoke the Procedure, employees have the right to approach the Personnel Manager for informal, confidential advice.

2. In order to proceed, the employee should make known his or her grievance to the Personnel Manager or Manager involved in the situation. This should be done at the earliest opportunity.

3. If the grievance cannot be resolved at this stage, the grievance procedure should be followed as below. The employee should state that this grievance relates to equal opportunities and the Personnel Director will be informed and may attend the hearing.

4. This procedure will be carried out in the strictest confidence and will not prejudice the employee's current employment or future career prospects.

Gardner Merchant's equal opportunities policy and code of practice

Care should be taken to deal effectively and seriously with all appeals. It should not be assumed that they are made by people who are over-sensitive about discrimination.

Appendix 4: SDA and RRA questionnaire forms

In this Appendix, there are reproduced the standard forms of questionnaire and reply under *SDA s 74* and *RRA s 65*, referred to in QUESTIONNAIRE PROCEDURE (47). Detailed guidance on the procedure is issued with both sets of forms, and the guidance on the *SDA* procedure is reproduced below. (The *RRA* guidance, which is not reproduced, is very similar.)

SEX DISCRIMINATION ACT 1975 – GUIDANCE ON THE QUESTIONS PROCEDURE

PART I – INTRODUCTION

1   The purpose of this guidance is to explain the questions procedure under section 74 of the Sex Discrimination Act 1975*. The procedure is intended to help a person (referred to in this guidance as the **complainant**) who thinks she (or he) has been discriminated against by another (the **respondent**) to obtain information from that person about the treatment in question in order to –

(*a*)   decide whether or not to bring legal proceedings, and

(*b*)   if proceedings are brought, to present her complaint in the most effective way.

A questionnaire has been devised which the complainant can send to the respondent and there is also a matching reply form for use by the respondent (both are included in this booklet). The questionnaire and the reply form have been designed to assist the complainant and respondent to identify information which is relevant to the complaint. It is not, however, obligatory for the questionnaire or the reply form to be used: the exchange of questions and replies may be conducted, for example, by letter.

*The prescribed forms, time limits for serving questions and manner of service of questions and replies under section 74 are specified in The Sex Discrimination (Questions and Replies) Order 1975 (SI 1975 No 2048).

2   This guidance is intended to assist both the complainant and the respondent. Guidance for the complainant on the preparation of the questionnaire is set out in Part II; and guidance for the respondent on the use of the reply form is set out in Part III. The main provisions of the Sex Discrimination Act are referred to in the appendix to this guidance. Further information about the Act will be found in the various leaflets published by the Equal Opportunities Commission and also in the detailed **Guide to the Sex Discrimination Act 1975**. The leaflets and the **Guide** may be obtained, free of charge, from the Equal Opportunities Commission at –

Overseas House
Quay Street
Manchester M3 3HN
Telephone: 0161-833 9244

The **Guide** and the EOC's leaflets on the employment provisions of the Act may also be obtained, free of charge, from any employment office or jobcentre of the Employment Service Agency or from any unemployment benefit office of the Department of Employment. The EOC's leaflets may also be obtained from Citizens Advice Bureaux.

SDA and RRA questionnaire forms

How the questions procedure can benefit both parties

3   The procedure can benefit both the complainant and the respondent in the following ways:–

(1)   If the respondent's answers satisfy the complainant that the treatment was not unlawful discrimination, there will be no need for legal proceedings.

(2)   Even if the respondent's answers do not satisfy the complainant, they should help to identify what is agreed and what is in dispute between the parties. For example, the answers should reveal whether the parties disagree on the facts of the case, or, if they agree on the facts, whether they disagree on how the Act applies. In some cases, this may lead to a settlement of the grievance, again making legal proceedings unnecessary.

(3)   If it turns out that the complainant institutes proceedings against the respondent, the proceedings should be that much simpler because the matters in dispute will have been identified in advance.

What happens if the respondent does not reply or replies evasively

4   The respondent cannot be compelled to reply to the complainant's questions. However, if the respondent deliberately, and without reasonable excuse, does not reply within a reasonable period, or replies in an evasive or **ambiguous** way, his position may be adversely affected should the complainant bring proceedings against him. The respondent's attention is drawn to these possible consequences in the note at the end of the questionnaire.

Period within which questionnaire must be served on the respondent

5   There are different time limits within which a questionnaire must be served in order to be admissible under the questions procedure in any ensuing legal proceedings. Which time limit applies depends on whether the complaint would be under the employment, training and related provisions of the Act (in which case the proceedings would be before an industrial tribunal) or whether it would be under the education, goods, facilities and services or premises provisions (in which case proceedings would be before a county court or, in Scotland, a sheriff court).

Industrial tribunal cases

6   In order to be admissible under the questions procedure in any ensuing industrial tribunal proceedings, the complainant's questionnaire must be served on the respondent either:

(*a*)   before a complaint about the treatment concerned is made to an industrial tribunal, but not more than 3 months after the treatment in question; or

(*b*)   if a complaint has already been made to a tribunal within 21 days beginning when the complaint was received by the tribunal.

However, where the complainant has made a complaint to a tribunal and the period of 21 days has expired, a questionnaire may still be served provided the leave of the tribunal is obtained. This may be done by sending to the Secretary of the Tribunal a written application, which must state the names of the complainant and the respondent and set out the grounds of the application. However, every effort should be made to serve the questionnaire within the period of 21 days as the leave of the tribunal to serve the questionnaire after the expiry of that period will not necessarily be obtained.

Court cases

7   In order to be admissible under the questions procedure in any ensuing county or sheriff court proceedings, the complainant's questionnaire must be served on the respondent before proceedings in respect of the treatment concerned are brought, but not more than 6 months after the treatment*. However, where proceedings have been brought, a questionnaire may still be served provided the leave of the court has been obtained. In the case of county court proceedings, this may be done by obtaining form Ex 23 from the county court office, and completing it and sending it to the Registrar and the respondent, or by applying to the Registrar at the pre-trial review. In the case of sheriff court proceedings, this may be done by making an application to a sheriff.

Where the respondent is a body in charge of a public sector educational establishment, the 6 month period begins when the complaint has been referred to the appropriate Education Minister and 2 months have elapsed or, if this is earlier, the Minister has informed the complainant that he requires no more time to consider the matter.

PART II – GUIDANCE FOR THE COMPLAINANT

NOTES ON PREPARING THE QUESTIONNAIRE

8   Before filling in the questionnaire, you are advised to prepare what you want to say on a separate piece of paper. If you have insufficient room on the questionnaire for what you want to say, you should continue on an additional piece of paper, which should be sent with the questionnaire to the respondent.

Paragraph 2

9   You should give, in the space provided in paragraph 2, as much relevant factual information as you can about the treatment you think may have been unlawful discrimination, and about the circumstances leading up to that treatment. You should also give the date, and if possible and if relevant, the place and approximate time of the treatment. You should bear in mind that in paragraph 4 of the questionnaire you will be asking the respondent whether he agrees with what you say in paragraph 2.

Paragraph 3

10   In paragraph 3 you are telling the respondent that you think the treatment you have described in paragraph 2 may have been unlawful discrimination by him against you. It will help to identify whether there are any legal issues between you and the respondent if you explain in the space provided **why** you think the treatment may have been unlawful discrimination. However, you **do not have** to complete paragraph 3; if you do not wish or are unable to do so, you should delete the word 'because'. If you wish to complete the paragraph, but feel you need more information about the Sex Discrimination Act before doing so, you should look to the appendix to this guidance.

SDA and RRA questionnaire forms

11   If you decide to complete paragraph 3, you may find it useful to indicate –

     (*a*)   what **kind** of discrimination you think the treatment may have been i.e. whether it was

          direct sex discrimination,
          indirect sex discrimination,
          direct discrimination against a married person,
          indirect discrimination against a married person,

          or

          victimisation.

   (For further information about the different kinds of discrimination see paragraph 1 of the appendix**).

     (*b*)   which provision of the Act you think may make unlawful the kind of discrimination you think you may have suffered. (For an indication of the provisions of the Act which make the various kinds of discrimination unlawful, see paragraph 2 of the appendix**).

Paragraph 6

12   You should insert here any other question which you think may help you to obtain relevant information. (For example, if you think you have been discriminated against by having been refused a job, you may want to know what were the qualifications of the person who did get the job and why that person got the job).

13   Paragraph 5 contains questions which are especially important if you think you may have suffered direct sex discrimination, or direct discrimination against a married person, because they ask the respondent whether your sex or marital status had anything to do with your treatment. Paragraph 5 does not, however, ask specific questions relating to indirect sex discrimination, indirect discrimination against a married person or victimisation. If you think you may have suffered indirect sex discrimination (or indirect discrimination against a married person) you may find it helpful to include the following question in the space provided in paragraph 6:

   'Was the reason for my treatment the fact that I could not comply with a condition or requirement which is applied equally to men and women (married and unmarried persons)?

   If so –

     (*a*)   what was the condition or requirement?

     (*b*)   why was it applied?'

14   If you think you may have been victimised you may find it helpful to include the following question in the space provided in paragraph 6:

   'Was the reason for my treatment the fact that I had done, or intended to do, or that you suspected I had done or intended to do, any of the following:

     (*a*)   brought proceedings under the Sex Discrimination Act or the Equal Pay Act; or

     (*b*)   gave evidence or information in connection with proceedings under either Act; or (*c*)   did something else under or by reference to either Act; or

(*d*)   made an allegation that someone acted unlawfully under either Act?'

Signature

15   The questionnaire must be signed and dated. If it is to be signed on behalf of (rather than by) the complainant **the person signing** should –

(*a*)   describe himself (e.g. 'solicitor acting for (*name of complainant*)'), and

(*b*)   give his business (or home, if appropriate) address.

WHAT PAPERS TO SERVE ON THE PERSON TO BE QUESTIONED

16   You should send the person to be questioned the whole of this document (i.e. the guidance, the questionnaire and the reply forms), with the questionnaire completed by you. **You are strongly advised to retain, and keep in a safe place, a copy of the completed questionnaire** (and you might also find it useful to retain a copy of the guidance and the uncompleted reply form).

HOW TO SERVE THE PAPERS

17   You can either deliver the papers in person or send them by post. If you decide to send them by post you are advised to use the recorded delivery service, so that, if necessary, you can produce evidence that they were delivered.

WHERE TO SEND THE PAPERS

18   You can send the papers to the person to be questioned at his usual or last known residence or place of business. If you know he is acting through a solicitor you should send them to him at his solicitor's address. If you wish to question a limited company or other corporate body or a trade union or employers' association, you should send the papers to the secretary or clerk at the registered or principal office of the company, etc. You should be able to find out where its registered or principal office is by enquiring at a public library. If you are unable to do so, however, you will have to send the papers to the place where you think it is most likely they will reach the secretary or clerk (e.g., at, or c/o, the company's local office). It is your responsibility, however, to see that the secretary or clerk receives the papers.

USE OF THE QUESTIONS AND REPLIES IN INDUSTRIAL TRIBUNAL PROCEEDINGS

19   If you decide to make (or already have made) a complaint to an industrial tribunal about the treatment concerned and if you intend to use your questions and the reply (if any) as evidence in the proceedings, you are advised to send copies of your questions and any reply to the Secretary of the Tribunals before the date of the hearing. This should be done as soon as the documents are available; if they are available at the time you submit your complaint to a tribunal, you should send the copies with your complaint to the Secretary of the Tribunals.

SDA and RRA questionnaire forms

PART III – GUIDANCE FOR THE RESPONDENT

NOTES ON COMPLETING THE REPLY FORM

20   Before completing the reply form, you are advised to prepare what you want to say on a separate piece of paper. If you have insufficient room on the reply form for what you want to say, you should continue on an additional piece of paper, which should be attached to the reply form sent to the complainant.

Paragraph 2

21   Here you are answering the question in paragraph 4 of the questionnaire. If you **agree** that the complainant's statement in paragraph 2 of the questionnaire is an accurate **description** of what happened, you should delete the second sentence.

22   If you **disagree** in any way that the statement is an accurate description of what happened, you should explain in the space provided in what respects you disagree, or your version of what happened, or both.

Paragraph 3

23   Here you are answering the question in paragraph 5 of the questionnaire. If, in answer to paragraph 4 of the questionnaire, you have agreed with the complainant's description of her treatment, you will be answering paragraph 5 on the basis of the facts in her description. If, however, you have disagreed with that description, you should answer paragraph 5 on the basis of **your** version of the facts. To answer paragraph 5, you are advised to look at the appendix** to this guidance and also the relevant parts of the **Guide to the Sex Discrimination Act 1975**. You need to know:–

    (*a*)   how the Act defines discrimination – see paragraph 1 of the appendix**;

    (*b*)   in what situations the Act makes discrimination unlawful – see paragraph 2 of the appendix**; and

    (*c*)   what exceptions the Act provides – see paragraph 3 of the appendix**.

24   If you think that an exception (e.g. the exception for employment where a person's sex is a genuine occupational qualification) applies to the treatment described in paragraph 2 of the complainant's questionnaire, you should mention this in paragraph 3a of the reply form and explain why you think the exception applies.

Signature

25   The reply form should be signed and dated. If it is to be signed on behalf of (rather than by) the respondent, the person signing should –

    (*a*)   describe himself (e.g. 'solicitor acting for (*name of respondent*)' or 'personnel manager of (*name of firm*)'), and

    (*b*)   give his business (or home, if appropriate) address.

SERVING THE REPLY FORM ON THE COMPLAINANT

26   If you wish to reply to the questionnaire you are strongly advised to do so without delay. **You should retain, and keep in a safe place, the questionnaire sent to you and a copy of your reply.**

27   You can serve the reply either by delivering it in person to the complainant or by sending it by post. If you decide to send it by post you are advised to use the recorded delivery service, so that, if necessary, you can produce evidence that it was delivered.

28   You should send the reply form to the address indicated in paragraph 7 of the complainant's questionnaire.

(*** Note that the appendix to this guidance is not reproduced.*)

SDA and RRA questionnaire forms

THE SEX DISCRIMINATION ACT 1975 SECTION 74(1)(a)

QUESTIONNAIRE OF PERSON AGGRIEVED (THE COMPLAINANT)

Name of person to be questioned (the respondent)

To ....

Address

of ....

....

....

Name of complainant

1. I ....

Address

of ....

....

consider that you may have discriminated against me contrary to the Sex Discrimination Act 1975.

Give date, approximate time, place and factual description of the treatment received and of the circumstances leading up to the treatment (see paragraph 9 of the guidance)

2. On

Complete if you wish to give reasons, otherwise delete the word "because" (see paragraphs 10 and 11 of the guidance)

3. I consider that this treatment may have been unlawful because

SD 74(a)

340

This is the first of
your questions to the
respondent. You are
advised not to alter it

4. Do you agree that the statement in paragraph 2 is an accurate description of what happened? If not in what respect do you disagree or what is your version of what happened?

This is the second of
your questions to the
respondent. You are
advised not to alter it

5. Do you accept that your treatment of me was unlawful discrimination by you against me?
   If not

   a why not?

   b for what reason did I receive the treatment accorded to me?

   c how far did my sex or marital status affect your treatment of me?

Enter here any other
questions you wish to
ask (see paragraphs
12–14 of the guidance)

6.

*Delete as appropriate
If you delete the first
alternative, insert the
address to which you
want the reply to be
sent

7. My address for any reply you may wish to give to the questions raised above is
   *that set out in paragraph 1 above/the following address

See paragraph 15
of the guidance

Signature of complainant...

Date...

NB *By virtue of section 74 of the Act, this questionnaire and any reply are (subject to the provisions of the section) admissible in proceedings under the Act and a court or tribunal may draw any such inference as is just and equitable from a failure without reasonable excuse to reply within a reasonable period, or from an evasive or equivocal reply, including an inference that the person questioned has discriminated unlawfully.*

SDA and RRA questionnaire forms

THE SEX DISCRIMINATION ACT 1975 SECTION 74(1)(b)

REPLY BY RESPONDENT

Name of complainant	To ....
Address	of ....
	....
Name of respondent	1. I ....
Address	of ....
	....
Complete as appropriate	hereby acknowledge receipt of the questionnaire signed by you and dated
	....which was served on me on (date)...
*Delete as appropriate	2. I *agree/disagree that the statement in paragraph 2 of the questionnaire is an accurate description of what happened.
If you agree that the statement in paragraph 2 of the questionnaire is accurate, delete this sentence. If you disagree complete this sentence (see paragraphs 21 and 22 of the guidance)	I disagree with the statement in paragraph 2 of the questionnaire in that
*Delete as appropriate	3. I *accept/dispute that my treatment of you was unlawful discrimination by me against you.
If you accept the complainant's assertion of unlawful discrimination in paragraph 3 of the questionnaire delete the sentences at a, b, and c. Unless completed a sentence should be deleted (see paragraphs 23 and 24 of the guidance)	a My reasons for so disputing are

SD 74(b)

342

b   The reason why you received the treatment accorded to you is

c   Your sex or marital status affected my treatment of you to the following extent:—

Replies to questions in
paragraph 6 of the
questionnaire should be
entered here

4.

*Delete the whole of
this sentence if you
have answered all the
questions in the
questionnaire. If you
have not answered all
the questions, delete
''unable'' or ''unwilling''
as appropriate and
give your reasons for
not answering.

5.   I have deleted (in whole or in part) the paragraph(s) numbered...
above, since I am **unable/unwilling** to reply to the relevant questions of the
questionnaire for the following reasons:—

See paragraph 25 of
the guidance

Signature of respondent...

Date...

SDA and RRA questionnaire forms

THE RACE RELATIONS ACT 1976 SECTION 65(I)(a)

QUESTIONNAIRE OF PERSON AGGRIEVED (THE COMPLAINANT)

Name of person to be
questioned (the
respondent)

To ....

Address

of ....

....

Name of complainant

1. I ....

Address

of ....

....

consider that you may have discriminated against me contrary to the Race Relations Act 1976.

Give date, approximate
time, place and factual
description of the treat-
ment received and of
the circumstances
leading up to the treat-
ment (see paragraph 9
of the guidance)

2. On

Complete if you wish
to give reasons,
otherwise delete the
word "because" (see
paragraphs 10 and 11
of the guidance)

3. I consider that this treatment may have been unlawful because

RR 65(a)

344

SDA and RRA questionnaire forms

This is the first of your questions to the respondent. You are advised not to alter it

4. Do you agree that the statement in paragraph 2 is an accurate description of what happened? If not in what respect do you disagree or what is your version of what happened?

This is the second of your questions to the respondent. You are advised not to alter it

5. Do you accept that your treatment of me was unlawful discrimination by you against me? If not

    a   why not?

    b   for what reason did I receive the treatment accorded to me, and

    c   how far did considerations of colour, race, nationality (including citizenship) or ethnic or national origins affect your treatment of me?

Enter here any other questions you wish to ask (see paragraphs 12–14 of the guidance)

6.

*Delete as appropriate If you delete the first alternative, insert the address to which you want the reply to be sent

7. My address for any reply you may wish to give to the questions raised above is * that set out in paragraph I above/the following address

See paragraph 15 of the guidance

Signature of complainant ....

Date ....

NB *By virtue of section 65 of the Act, this questionnaire and any reply are (subject to the provisions of the section) admissible in proceedings under the Act and a court or tribunal may draw any such inference as is just and equitable from a failure without reasonable excuse to reply within a reasonable period, or from an evasive or equivocal reply, including an inference that the person questioned has discriminated unlawfully.*

345

SDA and RRA questionnaire forms

THE RACE RELATIONS ACT 1976 SECTION 65(I)(b)

REPLY BY RESPONDENT

Name of complainant	To ....
Address	of ...., ...
	....
Name of respondent	1. I ....
Address	of ....
	....
Complete as appropriate	hereby acknowledge receipt of the questionnaire signed by you and dated ....
	which was served on me on (date) ....
*Delete as appropriate	2. I *agree/disagree that the statement in paragraph 2 of the questionnaire is an accurate description of what happened.
If you agree that the statement in paragraph 2 of the questionnaire is accurate, delete this sentence. If you disagree complete this sentence (see paragraphs 21 and 22 of the guidance)	I disagree with the statement in paragraph 2 of the questionnaire in that
*Delete as appropriate	3. I *accept/dispute that my treatment of you was unlawful discrimination by me against you.
If you accept the complainant's assertion of unlawful discrimination in paragraph 3 of the questionnaire delete the sentences at a, b and c. Unless completed a sentence should be deleted (see paragraphs 23 and 24 of the guidance)	a My reasons for so disputing are

RR 65(b)

346

b   The reason why you received the treatment accorded to you is

c   Consideration of colour, race, nationality (including citizenship) or ethnic or national origins affected my treatment of you to the following extent:—

Replies to questions in paragraph 6 of the questionnaire should be entered here

4.

Delete the whole of this sentence if you have answered all the questions in the questionnaire. If you have not answered all the questions, delete "unable" or "unwilling" as appropriate and give your reasons for not answering.

5.   I have deleted (in whole or in part) the paragraph(s) numbered ....
above, since I am **unable/unwilling** to reply to the relevant questions of the questionnaire for the following reasons:—

See paragraph 25 of the guidance

Signature of respondent ....

Date ....

347

Appendix 5: Addresses of industrial tribunal offices

CENTRAL OFFICE OF THE INDUSTRIAL TRIBUNALS (ENGLAND AND WALES)

Southgate Street
BURY ST EDMUNDS
Suffolk IP33 2AQ

Tel 01284 762300
Fax 01284 706064

REGIONAL OFFICES OF THE INDUSTRIAL TRIBUNALS (ENGLAND AND WALES)

Birmingham

Regional Office
Phoenix House
1–3 Newhall Street
BIRMINGHAM B3 3NH

Tel 0121 236 6051
Fax 0121 236 6026

Bristol

Regional Office
1st Floor
The Crescent Centre
Temple Beck
BRISTOL BS1 6EZ

Tel 0117 9298261
Fax 0117 9253452

Office of the Industrial Tribunals
Renslade House
Bonhay Road
EXETER EX4 3BX

Tel 01392 79665

Bury St Edmunds

Regional Office
Southgate Street
BURY ST EDMUNDS
Suffolk IP33 2AQ

Tel 01284 762171

Office of the Industrial Tribunals
8/10 Howard Street
BEDFORD MK40 3HS

Tel 01234 351306
Fax 01234 352315

Cardiff

Regional Office
Caradog House
1–6 St Andrews Place
CARDIFF CF1 3BE

Tel 01222 372693
Fax 01222 225906

Office of the Industrial Tribunals
Prospect House
Belle Vue Road
SHREWSBURY SY3 7AR

Tel 01743 358341

Leeds

Regional Office
3rd Floor
11 Albion Street
LEEDS LS1 5ES

Tel 0113 2459741
Fax 0113 2428843

Office of the Industrial Tribunals
14 East Parade
SHEFFIELD S1 2ET

Tel 0114 2760348

London North

Regional Office
19–29 Woburn Place
LONDON WC1H 0LU

Tel 0171 273 3000
Fax 0171 278 5068

London South

Regional Office
Montague Court
101 London Road
WEST CROYDON CR0 2RF

Tel 0181 667 9131
Fax 0181 649 9470

Office of the Industrial Tribunals
Tufton House
Tufton Street
ASHFORD
Kent TN23 1RJ

Tel 01233 621346

Manchester

Regional Office
Alexandra House
14–22 The Parsonage
MANCHESTER M3 2JA

Tel 0161 833 0581
Fax 0161 832 0249

Addresses of industrial tribunal offices

Office of the Industrial Tribunals
No 1 Union Court
Cook Street
LIVERPOOL L2 4UJ

Tel 0151 236 9397

Newcastle

Regional Office
Plummer House (3rd Floor)
Market Street East
NEWCASTLE-UPON-TYNE NE1 6NF

Tel 0191 222 8865
Fax 0191 222 1680

Nottingham

Regional Office
7th Floor, Birbeck House
Trinity Square
NOTTINGHAM NG1 4AX

Tel 0115 9475701
Fax 0115 9507612

Office of the Industrial Tribunals
31–33 Millstone Lane
LEICESTER LE1 5JS

Tel 0116 2530119

Southampton

Regional Office
Duke's Keep
(3rd Floor)
Marsh Lane
SOUTHAMPTON SO1 1EX

Tel 01703 639555
Fax 01703 635506

Office of the Industrial Tribunals
St James House
New England Street
BRIGHTON BN1 4GQ

Tel 01273 571488

Office of the Industrial Tribunals
30–31 Friar Street
READING RG1 1DY

Tel 01734 594917/9

CENTRAL OFFICE OF THE INDUSTRIAL TRIBUNALS (SCOTLAND)

Saint Andrew House
141 West Nile Street
GLASGOW G1 2RU

Tel 0141 331 1601

REGIONAL OFFICES OF THE INDUSTRIAL TRIBUNALS (SCOTLAND)

Aberdeen

Regional Office
252 Union Street
ABERDEEN AB1 1PN

Tel 01224 643307

Dundee

Regional Office
13 Albert Square
DUNDEE DD1 1DD

Tel 01382 21578

Edinburgh

Regional Office
124/125 Princes Street
EDINBURGH EH2 4AD

Tel 0131 226 5584

Index

duty to provide explanations, 17.6
effect of, 6.6
employer, instances when on, 6.8
evidence, 6.7
inference, 6.5
innocent explanation, 6.4, 6.6
nature, 6.2
prima facie case, 6.3

C

Checklists for industrial tribunal claims,
employee, 53A
employer or other respondent, 53B
CHILD CARE PROVISION, 7
background, 7.1
nursery or creche on-site, 7.2
taxation, 7.4
temporary provision, 7.5
voucher schemes, 7.3
CODES OF PRACTICE, 8
application to small employers, 8.6
appointment, recommendations, 24.22
content, 8.3
CRE Code, 8.1, 8.4, 9.11
—agencies, 8.11
—employees, 8.11
—employers, 8.11
—standards, 8.12
EOC Code, 8.5, 27.11
legal status, 8.2
power to issue, 8.1
promotion, recommendations, 24.22
sexual harassment, Appendix 2
trade unions, responsibilities of, 52.4
**COMMISSION FOR RACIAL
EQUALITY (CRE), 9**
advertising, proceedings relating to,
2.17
assisting complainants, 9.5, 9.6
Code of Practice, 8.4, 9.11,
Appendix 1
Councils for Racial Equality, 9.16
duties, 9.2
grant aid, 9.12
investigations (*see also* Investigations),
9.7, 9.8, 35.12–35.14
offices, 9.14
organisation, 9.4
other enforcement powers, 9.9
other race relations advisers, 9.17
other race relations bodies, 9.18
powers, 9.3
questionnaire, use by, 47.5

research, 9.13
staffing, 9.15
structure, 9.4
COMPARATOR, 10
comparator in equal pay cases, 10.2–
10.7
comparator in RRA and SDA cases,
10.8–10.10
(*see also* separate entries)
Comparator in equal pay cases,
10.2–10.7, 29.7
associated employer, 10.6, 29.7(e)
comparable man, 10.2
contractors, 10.7, 29.7(e)
different establishment at, 29.8
more than one comparable man
possible, 10.3, 29.7(c)
previous job holder, 10.4, 29.7(d)
real man, must be a, 10.3, 29.7(a)
same employment, must be in, 10.5,
29.7(e)
woman chooses man, 10.3, 29.7(b)
Comparator in RRA and SDA cases,
10.8–10.10
direct discrimination, 10.8
indirect discrimination, 10.10
theoretical comparator, 10.9
Compensation, 49.2–49.8
actual loss, compensation of, 49.4
compensatory award, 49.2–49.3
compromise agreements and, 12.10
contributory fault, no concept of,
49.5
EC law, effect of, 49.5
indirect discrimination cases, in, 36.3,
49.9
injury to feelings, 49.6
interest, 5.14
interest on, 49.8
levels of, 49.19
limits to, 30.3, 49.7
pay, as, 40.4
religious discrimination cases, 49.20
Compromise agreement, 11.12, 12.8
CONCILIATION, 11
ACAS agreements,
—binding nature of, 11.9
—scope of, 11.8
addresses of ACAS offices, 11.10
approaching ACAS, 11.3, 11.4
conciliation – how it works, 11.5
confidentiality of ACAS discussions,
11.6
enforceability of agreements, 11.7

Index

Non-discrimination notice, 37.9–37.14,
37.17
appealing against, 5.3, 37.14
enforcement, 37.17
form, 37.11
issue of, 37.9
procedure prior to issue of, 37.10
register of notices, 37.13
timing in relation to formal
investigation, 37.12
Notice of Appearance, 53.11, 53.12

O
Originating Application, 53.3–53.5

P
PART-TIME EMPLOYEES, 40
benefits, 40.8
exclusion from benefits,
—justification for, 40.9
ex-employees, 40.7
pensions, 40.10
qualifying thresholds, removal of,
21.2, 26.1, 40.1–40.6
two years' service requirements, 40.6
PARTNERSHIPS, 41
discrimination by partnership
unlawful, 41.1
small partnerships exempted from
RRA provisions, 41.2
**PENSIONS AND RETIREMENT AGE,
42**
bridging pensions, 42.4
equal pay legislation and, 29.8
equalisation of, 3.2
equality in, 42.3
part-time employees, 40.10
pensionable age, 3.2, 42.2
single sex schemes, 42.4
types covered by equal pay legislation,
42.2
POSITIVE DISCRIMINATION, 43
advertising and positive action, 43.7
fundamental rule, 43.1
genuine occupational qualification
(GOQ) *(see also* Genuine
Occupational Qualification),
43.4–43.6
—and racial discrimination, 43.6
—and sex discrimination, 43.5
—sex as, 43.5
lawful positive action, 43.4

qualifying body, by, 46.3
quotas, 43.2
RRA: other provisions, 43.10
services, discriminatory provision of,
43.11
targets, 43.3
training and advertising, 43.8
—current staff, and other local
people, 43.7
—national considerations, 43.9
Precedent, use by industrial tribunals of,
16.8
**PREGNANCY AND MATERNITY
RIGHTS, 44**
antenatal rights, 44.2
contractual maternity pay, 44.23
dismissal for pregnancy-related
reason, 44.24
—armed forces dismissals, 44.27
—illness and, 44.26
—redundancy and, 44.25
employment benefits connected with
pregnancy or childbirth, 24.30
extended maternity leave, 44.8, 44.18
fourteen weeks' leave, 44.3, 44.4
maternity checklist for employers,
44A
paternity leave, 44.28–44.31
pay,
—no right to receive, 44.18
remuneration, 44.17
return to work, 44.3, 44.5, 44.9
—employers' postponement, 44.11
—postponement of, 44.7, 44.10
right to return, 44.3, 44.5, 44.10,
44.12
—exclusions, 44.14
—refusal of, 44.13
sex discrimination and, 44.26
statutory maternity pay, 44.19
—effect of dismissal on, 44.22
—eligibility for, 44.20
—maternity pay period, 44.21
suspension from work on maternity
grounds, 44.15
PRESSURE TO DISCRIMINATE, 45
employment agencies, 25.4
enforcement proceedings, 45.2
'instructions to discriminate',
definition, 45.4
'pressure to discriminate', definition,
45.4
sanctions, 45.7
scope, 45.5

Index

TRADE UNIONS AND EMPLOYERS' ORGANISATIONS, 52
advertising by, 2.11
Code of Practice recommendations, 52.4
Commissioner for the Rights of Trade Union Members, 52.8
discrimination by, prohibition on, 52.1
enforcement, 52.7
entry, terms of, 52.2
membership, terms of, 52.3
pressure by trade unions, 52.5
trade union practice, 52.6
Tribunal hearing, 53.20–53.34
adjournment, 53.20
affidavit evidence and unsworn statements, 53.25
appeal (*see* Appeals)
checklists, 53A, 53B
closing the case, 53.27
costs, 53.29
decision, 53.28
documents, bundle of, 53.21
equal value claims, procedure (*see* Equal Value Claims: Procedure)
interest (*see also* Interest), 53.32
presentation, order of, 53.23
procedure, 53.22
review, 53.30
unrepresented parties, 53.26
witnesses, 53.24
TRIBUNALS, 53
addresses of tribunal offices, Appendix 5
breach of contract, jurisdiction, 53.33
burden of proof, 6.6
checklists,
—employee, 53A
—employer or other respondent, 53B
constructive dismissal, approach, 12.3
discovery (*see* Discovery)
equal value claim, procedure in (*see also* Equal Value Claims: Procedure), 53.35–53.42

hearing (*see also* Tribunal Hearing), 53.20–53.34
independent expert procedure, review of, 53.41
interim applications, 53.13–53.18
internal dispute resolution, 53.44
interrogatories, 53.16
introduction, 53.1
Notice of Appearance, 53.11, 53.12
Originating Application, submission of, 53.3, 53.5
pre-hearing review, 53.15, 53A
procedure, outline of, 53.2
time limits, qualification and, 53.6–53.10
—continuing discrimination, 53.7
—enforcement proceedings by CRE and EOC, 53.10
—equal pay, 53.9
—sex and race discrimination, 53.6
—unfair dismissal, 53.9
witness orders, 53.18

U
Unfair Dismissal (*see also* Dismissal)
length of service, 21.1, 26.1

V
VICTIMISATION, 54
comparison for determining, 54.4
definition, 54.1
disability discrimination and, 18.15
employers' correct approach, 54.5
examples of, 54.4
good faith, allegation must be in, 54.8
protected actions, 54.2
scope, 54.6

W
Witness orders, 53.18
Witnesses, 53.24